Out of Paris

Days out and weekend breaks
around the French capital

Vivienne Menkes-Ivry

A & C Black · London

For Charles Sylla, Francilien de la nouvelle génération

Published in 1999
by A&C Black (Publishers) Ltd,
35 Bedford Row, London, WC1R 4JH

Photographs © Joe Cornish
Plan of RER/SNCF network on pp. 24–5 © *RATP*
Other maps and plans drawn by Eugene Fleury

ISBN 0–7136–4195–9

A CIP catalogue record for this book is available from the British Library

The author and the publishers have done their best to ensure the
accuracy of all the information in this guide. They can accept no
responsibility for any loss, injury or inconvenience sustained by any
traveller as a result of information or advice contained in this book

Front cover illustrations from top left: Auvers-sur-Oise, Illiers-Combray,
Chartres Cathedral, Sarzay Chateau, Château de Malmaison, Sancerre,
Argenton-sur-Creuse. Back cover: poppyfields near Sancerre, fountain at
Versailles, Château de Breteuil
Title page illustration: Monet's garden at Giverny

Printed in China through Colorcraft Ltd

Contents

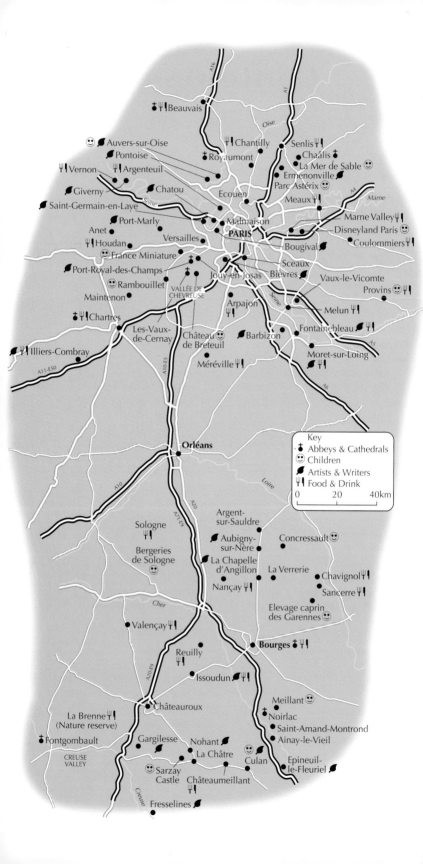

Introduction

The main aim of this guide is to suggest places to visit, sights to see and things to do – sporting, cultural or just plain fun – for anyone staying in Paris, or based there for short or longer periods, and wanting to get out of the city from time to time, or use it as a jumping-off point. However rich in delights the French capital is, it is also a very urban place, with few open spaces within the inner city. Most visitors and longer-term residents feel the need to get out into the countryside after a spate of sightseeing, to explore the leisure opportunities on offer, and to find out about towns and villages, châteaux and cathedrals that can be visited on a day's outing or during a more leisurely trip of several days.

The guide is also designed for those thinking of spending longer in the two areas of France it focuses on. These are the area immediately surrounding Paris, most of which is in the official administrative **Ile de France** region that centres on the capital, and the **Berry**, further south – both surprisingly little known to foreign tourists, or even to the French themselves. Lying as it does due south of Paris, right in the centre of France, the Berry is ignored by the great majority of travellers heading towards the southeast or the southwest of the country. And though it may seem strange to refer to an area that includes such tourist highspots as the royal palaces at Versailles and Fontainebleau, or Chartres Cathedral, as off the beaten track, the Ile de France, with its many forests and charming rural backwaters, its quiet, provincial-seeming towns, attracts relatively few visitors overall. As a result, Provins, its medieval Upper Town virtually unchanged since its glory days as host to important trade fairs and residence of the mighty Counts of Champagne, or Senlis, a little town that seems to be living in a medieval time warp, can be enjoyed without the discomforts engendered by mass tourism. Many of the villages beside the river Seine and the Oise offer peaceful landscapes that are little different from those painted by the Impressionists and their precursors. And you are unlikely to meet crowds even at the wonderfully grand château of Vaux-le-Vicomte, despite its great historical significance. As for Bourges's beautiful Saint-Etienne in the Berry, it must be the least known of the great French Gothic cathedrals.

One of the many delights of such places is precisely their lack of tourists. Another, related, delight is that once you have left behind the capital's suburbs, many restaurants are pleasantly unsophisticated, both in their décor, and in their carefully cooked dishes based on good local produce. And it is often possible to find the sort of small, family-run hotels and inns that are one of the reasons for France's enduring popularity as a holiday or short-break destination. In such places you will find the friendly welcome and helpful service that is often sadly lacking in more tourist-frequented areas.

Both regions are also distinctly 'green': both literally – forests and meadows are ever-present – and in the sense that they appeal to nature lovers and the environmentally conscious. Aware that to compete with better-known areas they must attract modern tourists who want to combine sightseeing with leisure activities, the local authorities have made considerable efforts to offer a wide range of sporting and cultural facilities and events – many of them geared to children as well as to adults – and to make it easy to find out about them. Forests, plains and heathland are crisscrossed by marked footpaths, riding routes and cycle tracks. Sensitively planned recreational facilities enable you to go swimming, sailing or angling, or even rock climbing in the Forêt de Fontainebleau. Bike hire is quite widely available, for instance in the Vallée de Chevreuse southwest of Paris and the Forêt de Fontainebleau, in the pretty rolling countryside in the southern Berry and the nature lovers' paradise of La Brenne – even in the grounds of Versailles's palace. Tourist offices increasingly publish free maps designed for those exploring their area by bike, on horseback or on foot.

How to use this guide

Following the **introduction**, the **practical information** section covers access and local transport, climate, information sources, general tips on hotels and restaurants, fairs and festivals, opening times, museums and historic buildings, sports and leisure activities and themed lists and itineraries. The opening chapters provide background on **cuisine** and **drink**, **shopping ideas** and **history**. The suggested **days out** and **short trips** are grouped into eight regional sections. For each trip, or part of a trip in some cases, a box of **key data** gives postcode; tourist office (T.O.) or other contact address; distance from Paris and other appropriate centres or sights; access by public transport where available; a checklist of main sights with opening periods (which should always be checked locally); suggestions for places to eat or stay; and (indicated by the word 'also'), towns or sights that might be visited before or after.

Full details of suggested hotels, restaurants and private châteaux accommodation, with price banding, appear at the back of the guide, in a single alphabetical listing by town or village for easy reference. Again, closing days/periods should always be double-checked because of frequent changes. The list is preceded by information on selection criteria and prices.

A star (★) in the main text indicates that the hotel or restaurant referred to is included in the list on pp. 237–53.

Themed itineraries

The tourist authorities also offer brochures and maps depicting signposted routes devised to publicize towns or individual buildings linked – sometimes tenuously – by a common theme. One of the best of these is the **Route Jacques-Coeur** in the Berry (see box, p. 12), but there are many more. You can work out your own itineraries by following in the footsteps of painters, by seeking out settings used by novelists like Honoré de Balzac, Alain-Fournier or George Sand, or by visiting the homes of writers, artists and musicians – Turgenev's 'dacha' in Bougival, Claude Monet's magical garden in Giverny, or the composer Claude Debussy's birthplace in Saint-Germain-en-Laye, as well as Marcel Proust's childhood holiday home in Illiers-Combray. I have made suggestions for all of these and described the places in greater detail in the appropriate section.

Catering for kids

Quite apart from outdoor activities, children will find plenty to keep them happy: Disneyland, of course, but various other theme parks, as well as lesser-known places like the collection of miniature historical scenes at the Château de Meillant, the multimedia circuit in the château at Auvers-sur-Oise, or the old schoolroom in Epineuil-le-Fleuriel. For a list of suggestions, see p. 38.

A wealth of sights

As for traditional sightseeing, anyone visiting these areas is spoilt for choice. You will find royal palaces and important art museums, Romanesque churches and Gothic cathedrals, Renaissance mansions

The Ile de France on celluloid

The Ile de France's châteaux, manor houses and medieval streets are often used as a background for films, for both cinema and television. The **Château de Raray★** near Senlis, now a very comfortable hotel (see p. 139) and famous for its strange frieze of sculpted hounds, stags and wild boar running round the main courtyard, was the rather spooky setting for Jean Cocteau's poetic film *La Belle et la Bête* (*Beauty and the Beast*, 1946), with Jean Marais.

Several films have been shot in the picturesque streets of nearby **Senlis** (see pp. 136-9). In 1975, *L'Incorruptible*, directed by Philippe de Broca and starring Jean-Paul Belmondo, was filmed there. Then in 1982, the great Polish director Andrzej Wajda set his dramatic *Danton* in Senlis, with Gérard Depardieu in the lead role. Eight years later, the town was again chosen as a setting for Patrice Lecomte's *Le mari de la coiffeuse*.

Some scenes from Robert Altman's hit *Prêt à porter* were shot at the **Château de Ferrières** (see p. 153), which was also the setting for one of my favourite films, *La Banquière*, with the late, great Romy Schneider. Another château regularly used by film makers is the lovely **Courances**, on the edge of the Forêt de Fontainebleau (see p. 181). In the silent era it was used for filming *The Iron Mask* (1929), with that swashbuckling hero of pre-sound cinema Douglas Fairbanks, who also wrote the screenplay. And among the recent films shot partly there was *Camille Claudel*, with Isabelle Adjani playing the sculptor who was the mistress of Auguste Rodin and the sister of the poet and dramatist Paul Claudel. And Milos Forman chose the **Château de Guermantes**, east of Paris, for scenes from his film about Mozart, *Amadeus*. Not far from here the **Château de Champs** (p. 150-2) boasts of having carried off an Oscar: the one for best décor awarded to Stephen Frears's version of *Les Liaisons Dangereuses* (1989), which was shot at Champs.

Paris's New Towns

In the mid-1960s, the French government embarked on a scheme loosely based on the New Towns that had been built in Britain. Paris's New Towns were designed as a reaction against the vast and often hideous tower blocks that had been hastily put up in the fifties and early sixties to ease the post-war housing crisis, and had created many social problems.

Five sites were chosen for 'Villes nouvelles' (New Towns) in the Ile de France, close to Paris (between 30 and 40 kilometres away) but separate from it, since the idea was to create places that would have their own identity. Key requirements were that the New Towns should have a good mix of high-density housing and open spaces – parks, sports and leisure centres – and that cars and pedestrians should as far as possible be kept apart.

Starting in the west and moving clockwise round Paris, they were **Saint-Quentin-en-Yvelines** and **Cergy-Pontoise** in the north, **Marne-la-Vallée** in the east, and **Evry** and **Melun-Sénart** in the south. Although they have had their problems, and many of their buildings have aged badly, for anyone interested in architecture and town planning they are certainly worth exploring. Here are a few pointers:

● **Saint-Quentin-en-Yvelines**, 30km west of Paris, on the edge of the Vallée de Chevreuse and accessible via RER line C

Highlights are **Les Arcades du Lac** by Spanish architect Ricardo Bofill and the **Theatre** by Stanislas Fiszer

● **Cergy-Pontoise**, 30km northwest of Paris in the Oise Valley, accessible via RER line A or trains from the Gare Saint-Lazare

Highlights are the **Préfecture**, by Henri Bernard, the **Axe majeure** with its belvedere, by Dani Caravan, the **Tour des Célibataires** by Martine and Philippe Deslandes, Stanislas Fiszer's **Joannes**, and his church, **Sainte-Marie-des-Peuples**

● **Marne-la-Vallée**, only 13km east of Paris, accessible via RER line A

Best known nowadays for hosting **Disneyland** (see pp. 155–8), but with some interesting buildings of its own, like Ricardo Bofill's **Palacio d'Abraxas**, a grandiose block of council flats in pink concrete with fluted columns, or **Les Arènes de Picasso** by Manolo Nunez, irreverently known to the locals as 'les camemberts' – they do indeed look rather like the familiar flat round cheeses

● **Melun-Sénart**, 40km southeast of Paris

The last of the five New Towns to be built, and different in its use of individual houses grouped round ponds. Highlights are the **Centre artisanal** (Crafts Centre) by Alain Sarfati, and Fiszer's **Ville du Canal**

● **Evry**, 26km southwest of Paris, trains from Gare de Lyon

Best known now for its dramatic new cathedral (see p. 61), but interesting too for its **Agora** (partly inspired by Le Corbusier), a vast leisure complex, and its cube-based flats-with-gardens in the **Quartier des Pyramides**.

and romantically ruined abbeys – as well as the beautifully restored Noirlac Abbey – and a host of châteaux, some palatial residences, some charming manors or elegant country houses, still lived in and fully furnished. And you can also enjoy strolling around interesting towns, full of good food and other shops as well as historic buildings, like chic Saint-Germain-en-Laye, very close to Paris, or busy little Saint-Amand-Montrond in the Berry, with its excellent market.

Getting about

All of these places can naturally be visited by car, but thanks to France's well-planned public transport system, it is also perfectly feasible to reach the majority of them without driving. Indeed this is often the best solution, as finding your way out of Paris through a maze of ringroads and complex intersections can be exhausting. This guide is arranged as a series of thirty separate outings, some best suited for a day out, or combined with others to cover a longer period, others more appropriate to a weekend away from Paris, or as a short-break destination. As well as giving distances from Paris, and other relevant places, I have indicated how you can reach them by public transport. For further advice, see **Practical Information**.

The Ile de France: a brief portrait

The term 'Ile de France' tends to be used rather loosely. Officially, it covers both Paris and the seven *départements* closest to it. But it is usually seen as simply referring to the part of France near the capital, not including Paris itself, but taking in a number of places in the surrounding administrative regions. Among these are Chartres to the southwest, Beauvais to the north and Senlis to the northeast. I have followed this loose interpretation, focusing on places that are frequently visited from the capital. So as well as Chartres, Beauvais and Senlis, I have described Claude Monet's house at Giverny, technically just in Normandy, and Illiers, the remote village immortalized as 'Combray' by Marcel Proust, which, like Chartres, is on the cereal-growing plain of the Beauce.

An 'island' region?

The term 'Ile de France' or 'Island of France' seems to have originated in the 14th century as the name of one of the country's oldest provinces, covering roughly the feudal domain ruled over by the Frankish king Hugues Capet, the founder of the Capetian royal dynasty. It was the name of one of the twelve *grands gouvernements* or provinces into which the kingdom was divided by the early 17th century, and retained this name after the *département* became the key administrative unit following a decree promulgated by the Constituent Assembly in 1790, the year after the French Revolution.

The name is still widely used today. Yet its origin is unclear. One theory, which seems logical, is that the region was thought to form an island bounded by five rivers – Seine, Oise, Marne, Ourcq and Aisne.

Born in the Ile de France: a personal selection

c 1190   **Vincentius Bellovacensius** (Vincent de Beauvais), enyclopedist, in **Beauvais** (see p. 143)

c 1456   **Jeanne Laisné** ('Jeanne Hachette'), heroine, near **Beauvais** (see p. 146)

c 1515   Jean Bullant, architect of Chantilly's Petit Château, in **Ecouen**

1519   **Gaspard de Coligny**, admiral, Protestant leader, early victim of the St Bartholomew's Day Massacre, in Châtillon-sur-Loing (now **Château-Coligny**)

1560   **Maximilien de Béthune**, **Duc de Sully**, Henri IV's chief minister, in **Rosny-sur-Seine**

1620   **Louis de Buade**, **Comte de Frontenac**, govenor of French possessions in North America, in **Saint-Germain-en-Laye**

1728   **Antoine Baumé**, chemist, in **Senlis** (see p. 137)

1753   **Louis-Alexandre Berthier**, Marshal, Major-General of Napoleon's Grande Armée, in **Versailles**

1768   **Lazare Hoche**, general, war minister, in **Versailles**

1779   **Joseph Bara**, child hero and revolutionary, in **Palaiseau**

1785   **Alexandre Boëly**, composer, in **Versailles**

1788   **Antoine Becquerel**, physicist, in **Châtillon-sur-Loing**

1798   **Eugène Delacroix**, painter, in **Saint-Maurice** (near Créteil)

1810   **Hector Le Fuel**, architect of the new Louvre, in **Versailles**

1862   **Claude Debussy**, composer, in **Saint-Germain-en-Laye** (see p. 115)

1863   **Charles Pathé**, film pioneer, in **Chevry-Cossigny**

1867   **Pierre Bonnard**, painter, in **Fontenay-aux-Roses**

1875   **Jeanne Bourgeois** ('Mistinguett'), music hall artiste, in **Enghien-les-Bains**

1880   **André Derain**, Fauvist painter, in **Chatou**

1882   **Georges Braque**, Cubist painter, in **Argenteuil**

1889   **Jean Cocteau**, poet, novelist, playwright, painter, *cinéaste*, in **Maisons-Laffitte**

1898   **Léonie Barthiat** ('Arletty'), legendary actress, artist's model (for Braque and Matisse), in **Courbevoie**

1908   **Jacques Tatischeff** ('Jacques Tati'), film maker, inventor of Monsieur Hulot, in **Le Pecq**

1910   **Jean-Louis Barrault**, actor, theatre manager, in **Le Vésinet**

1932   **Colette Dacheville** ('Stéphane Audran'), film actress, in **Versailles**

1935   **Alain Delon**, film actor, in Sceaux

One of the many delights of this part of France is its variety. You can cruise along quiet river valleys, relax in forests that were once the hunting ground of kings, and hike across the eastern plateau that has given its name to Brie, perhaps the finest of French cheeses. The immediate outskirts of the city, once famous for their market gardens, are inevitably engulfed in suburban sprawl these days. But even here you will find surprising survivals – relatively unchanged riverscapes on the banks of the Marne, the occasional elegant château or perfectly landscaped garden. And Paris's New Towns are interesting examples of modern town planning (see p. 8). Despite encroaching urbanization, the Vallée de Chevreuse is still an oasis of almost rural peace, with its own large nature park.

Here and elsewhere you can still see old stone village houses, dovecots and wells. And a number of windmills have survived on the Beauce. The Ile de France was the cradle of Gothic architecture and many a modest village church can be admired alongside the great masterpieces of the style like Chartres or Beauvais.

From the tourist point of view, it is in many ways an advantage that the region has always been dominated by Paris. This centralization has enabled quiet backwaters to survive. And yet at the same time they benefit from the good transport facilities designed for com-

Born in the Berry: a personal selection

c 1395	**Jacques Coeur**, merchant, royal treasurer, in **Bourges** (p. 200)
c 1430	**Jean Colombe**, illuminator of *Les Très Riches Heures du Duc de Berry* (p. 134)
c 1480	**Geoffroy Tory**, editor, author of treatises on calligraphy, typography, grammar and spelling, in **Bourges**
1773	**Henri Bertrand**, general, biographer of Napoleon, in Châteauroux (p. 221)
1785	**Hyacinthe Thabaud de la Touche** ('Henri De Latouche'), novelist, translator of Schiller, pamphleteer, in **La Châtre**
1791	**Emile Deschamps**, bureaucrat, Romantic poet, translator of Shakespeare, in **Bourges**
1796	**Zulma Carraud**, bestselling author, in **Nohant-en-Graçay** (p. 223)
1841	**Berthe Morisot**, Impressionist painter, in **Bourges**
1846	**Maurice Rollinat**, poet and musician, in **Châteauroux** (p. 216)
1856	**Maurice McNab**, *chansonnier* (satirical cabaret artiste), in **Vierzon**
1863	**Marguerite Audoux**, shepherdess, seamstress, novelist, in **Sancoins**
1886	**Henri Fournier** ('Alain-Fournier'), novelist, literary critic, in **La Chapelle d'Angillon** (pp. 189, 233–4)
1904	**Maurice Estève**, painter, in **Culan** (p. 234)
1948	**Gérard Depardieu**, actor, in **Châteauroux** (p. 221).

muters working in the capital. Then again, as these transport facilities and the many motorways that nowadays radiate out from Paris encourage more Parisians to move out, once-sleepy places benefit from an influx of energetic newcomers, who restore tumbledown buildings, agitate for more cultural and sports facilities – and are firmly pro-conservationist.

The Berry: a brief portrait

The Berry's capital, attractive Bourges, was once the Gallo-Roman capital of Aquitaine and later flourished as the seat of Charles VII's court. But today the Berry is a quiet rural region bang in the middle of France, south of the Paris basin and north of the Massif Central. In the north are the **Sologne**, a land of game-filled meres and forests popular with both nature lovers and the Paris shooting set, and the vine-clad hills of the **Sancerrois**, where delicious Sancerre wines are produced in villages that are also famous for their goat's cheese. Further south, the **Champagne berrichonne** is a cereal-growing

The Route Jacques-Coeur

The tourist itinerary known as the Route Jacques-Coeur takes its name from one of the Berry's most colourful personalities, the medieval merchant, ambassador and royal financier Jacques Coeur, born in Bourges in about 1395 (see p. 200). He owned two of the châteaux that line the route – the much-altered **Menetou-Salon** and, briefly, just before his downfall, **Ainay-le-Viel**, the feudal fortress-cum-Renaissance-residence in the south of the region. But though the sixteen other high spots on the circuit have no direct association with him, collectively they form an ensemble as interesting and multi-faceted as he was, so to have adopted his name seems fair enough.

The itinerary is one of France's official 'historic routes' and maps and leaflets are available from tourist boards throughout the region, and at all the places along it. The towns and buildings along the itinerary often join forces to stage themed events. These feature in joint programmes, again available from tourist offices. Sometimes candlelit visits are organized – a treat not to be missed – and concerts, plays, exhibitions and happenings of various kinds are held in their courtyards and gardens, grand halls and vaulted cellars.

Most of the châteaux are privately owned, which adds greatly to the enjoyment of a visit. Whereas so many Loire Valley châteaux can seem disappointingly bare inside, however lovely their architecture, the Jacques Coeur châteaux are ofen more like British stately homes, full of furniture and family portraits. And as so many of them are lived in, you will often spot a collection of family photographs in silver frames, or a tray of drinks among the grand furniture – all of this gives a pleasantly personal feel.

Descriptions of the highlights appear in the appropriate sections, along with practical information.

plateau, while the **Brenne**, in the southwest, is a mysterious nature reserve whose reed-fringed meres and marshes create an ideal habitat for hundreds of bird species, some of them very rare, as well as turtles and a wealth of wild flowers. The river Creuse flows east from here through gorges that inspired Claude Monet to launch into one of his painting 'campaigns'. Beyond them, the **Boischaut du Sud**, crisscrossed by pretty river valleys, is made up of rolling meadowland dotted with clumps of trees, where cows peacefully graze.

This is conservative, traditional country, where many local festivals enliven the villages and old beliefs in witchcraft and sorcery linger (see box, p. 16). Lovers of rural architecture will enjoy the sight of Romanesque village churches, mellow stone manor houses and, in the north, half-timbered houses with brick infill arranged in traditional herringbone patterns, and curious church porches of a design seen nowhere else in France.

As well as Bourges, with its wealth of interesting buildings, you can visit Issoudun, where Honoré de Balzac set one of his novels, and dine in the inn he describes, stroll through the old streets in Châteauroux, and enjoy the views down to the Loire from hilly

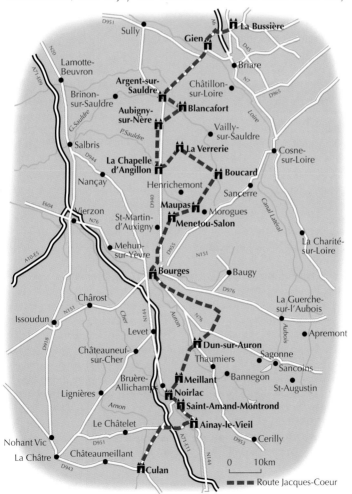

Route Jacques-Coeur

Sancerre. And while you are exploring the châteaux on the Route Jacques-Coeur (pp. 12–13), you will come across many a timeless village or small town with a cosy inn serving regional dishes that will sustain you after a day of sightseeing mixed with walking or biking, riding or birdwatching.

Calling all garden-lovers

Many of the châteaux in the Ile de France and the Berry have well-tended gardens, some formal, some *à l'anglaise*, as the French describe the natural-seeming (though usually carefully planned) parkland surrounding so many English country houses – a style of landscape gardening that evolved as a reaction against the rigid geometry of the *jardin à la française* invented by Louis XIV's master gardener André Le Nôtre, designer of the magnificent formal gardens at Versailles, Vaux-le-Vicomte, Sceaux, Saint-Germain-en-Laye and Dampierre. Both regions also have some less grand gardens that are well worth visiting, including beautiful rose gardens. Here are a few suggestions:

- **Ainay-le-Viel** (p. 231)
- **Apremont-sur-Allier** (50km east of Bourges)

Attractive village on the eastern edge of the Berry, with many medieval houses and beautiful public gardens formed in the 1970s by creating a series of lakes, a waterfall and rock garden, and planting rare species of trees and flowering shrubs, even a 'white garden' inspired by the famous one at Sissinghurst in England. Most unusually for French public gardens, it has rolling lawns on which visitors can walk at will. Parc floral, 18150 Apremont-sur-Allier, ☎ 02-48-80-41-41, open daily June, July, Aug; daily except Tue from Easter to end May and in Sep; restaurant open for lunch only (closed Tue).

Gardening festivals

Two gardening festivals are held annually at **Saint-Jean-de-Beauregard**, a château 28km south of Paris with a restored kitchen garden (see p. 83).

The first, **La Fête des plantes vivaces** (Perennials Festival), takes place over a long weekend (Friday to Sunday inclusive) towards the end of April and is advertised as being the only one of its kind in Europe. As well as stands selling plants, tools, pots, books and CD-Roms (in English as well as French), lectures and talks are given by eminent specialists from all over the world, some of them English speakers.

Then in early November, a fruit and vegetable festival is staged, with the emphasis on old (and sometimes long-forgotten) varieties. This late-autumn **Fête des fruits et légumes d'hier et d'aujourd'hui** also includes a display of wild fungi.

For exact dates and further information, contact Madame de Curel, **Domaine de Saint-Jean-de-Beauregard**, 91940 Saint-Jean-de-Beauregard, ☎ 01-60-12-00-01.

The *vielle* and the *cornemuse*: making music in the Berry

The traditional instrumental ensemble in the Berry, still kept up by folk groups, consists of a *vielle*, a stringed instrument resembling a hurdy-gurdy, and a *cornemuse*, a wind instrument similar to bagpipes. Both these instruments were a common sight in much of medieval Europe, but their continued use is virtually confined to the Berry, where some beautifully made and decorated examples are on display in museums such as the folk art and traditions collection in Argent-sur-Sauldre (see p. 190) or the George Sand museum in La Châtre (p. 208).

The *vielle* was probably invented in the Middle East and imported into Spain by Arab traders. The model used in the Berry has six strings and is roughly almond-shaped. The body is usually made of maple, sycamore or walnut, with the upper part consisting of a thin sheet of pine. Instead of using a bow, the *vielleux*, as the *vielle* players are known, turn a handle that activates a wheel made of some hardwood such as beech or box coated with resin. The end of the instrument, housing the pegs round which the strings are wound, is often carved into the shape of a woman's head, sometimes wearing a traditional headdress.

Vielles are still made in the Berry by local lute builders and would make an interesting souvenir to take home – or you may find a miniature version. To honour this centuries-old production, an international gathering of lute builders takes place annually at Saint-Chartier.

The *cornemuse berrichonne* is another very ancient instrument, originally introduced by the Romans. Three ebony or boxwood pipes are attached to the pouch. One of them is much longer than the other two and lies across the musician's shoulder as he plays. In her novel *Les Maîtres Sonneurs* (1852), George Sand memorably describes the sound produced by these bagpipes as it wafts across the fields and meadows.

- **Arboretum de Chèvreloup** (near Versailles)
'Arboretum' is the term used for an open-air tree museum, displaying in this case over two thousand varieties and species of trees. 30 route de Versailles, 78150 Rocquencourt (bus H from Versailles), ℡ 01-39-55-53-80, ℻ 01-39-55-38-88, open Apr to mid-Nov, weekends and Mon only.
- **Château de Breteuil** (pp. 92–5)
- **Château de Champs-sur-Marne** (p 150)
- **Château de Courances** (p. 181)
- **Château de Culan** (p. 235)
- **Monet's garden at Giverny** (pp. 119–22)
- **Rose garden, L'Haÿ-les-Roses**
The famous rose garden at L'Haÿ, just south of Paris near Sceaux, with its three thousand-plus varieties, including many old roses, is believed to be the earliest in the western world. Roseraie du Val-de-Marne, rue Albert-Watel, 94240 L'Haÿ-les-Roses, ℡ 01-43-99-82-80, ℻ 01-47-40-04-75, open daily mid-May to mid-Sep.
- **Château de Malmaison** (p. 104)

Sorcery and witchcraft in the Berry

The Berry has long had the reputation of being a land of sorcerers and witches, where the local people claim to see mysterious wraiths or will-o'-the-wisps weaving in and out of the mist that so often lingers over the silent meadows and meres. The relative isolation of this rural region until quite recent times could be thought to explain why the villagers cling so firmly to tales of sorcery, ghosts and apparitions, handed down from one generation to the next. Yet the highly educated owners of the local châteaux and manor houses also see it as a topic to be discussed seriously.

The **Musée de la Sorcellerie** (Witchcraft Museum) in Concressault, near Blancafort Château, is particularly geared to children, with its colourful tableaux, scary witches and ghoulish sound effects. But it is also a good place to learn something about the sorcerers, male and female, who have frightened the Berrichons down the ages: the *jeteurs de sorts*, who cast spells, the *birettes* (white apparitions with no visible heads), the *caille-bottiers* whose malign influence dries up the milk in cows' udders. More positively, the *rebouteux* or *guérisseurs* (faith healers) allegedly achieve cures where conventional medicine is impotent, sometimes with the aid of alchemical signs and symbols – which also appear in grand medieval houses like the Hôtel Lallemant (p. 196) or Jacques Coeur's Palace (p. 199), both in Bourges. These healers were often said to be gifted at alleviating a specific ailment, like the *vartraupier* who could get rid of *vartraupes*, a local word for a type of boil.

The museum in nearby **Argent-sur-Sauldre** (p. 190) also has displays on local beliefs connected with witchcraft. And the wine village of Bué near Sancerre, one of several parishes reputed to be disproportionately endowed with witches and sorcerers – and even to be the scene of witches' sabbaths – has sensibly decided to capitalize on this dubious claim to fame by holding an annual **Foire aux Sorciers** (Sorcerers' Fair) in August.

- **Prieuré d'Orsan** (p. 229)
- **Provins's rose gardens** (p. 165)
- **Château de Saint-Jean-de-Beauregard** (p. 83)
- **Château de Vaux-le-Vicomte** (p. 167)
- **Château de Versailles** (p. 68)
- **Potager du Roy, Versailles** (p. 76)
- **Château de Villiers** (40km east of Bourges)

This lovely garden is one of my favourites in the whole of France, seeming more English than French with its lawns and flowering shrubs, its clematis and delphiniums and sundials, and its herbaceous borders crammed with flowers in a very un-French way (French gardeners like to have plenty of earth visible). It has a lake, too, as well as a rose garden, and an orchard, and a beautiful cluster of medlar trees, planted in staggered rows. The mellow stone of the small turreted château, part 15th-century, part 17th-century, makes a gentle backcloth for this romantic place, where a tearoom is open on Sunday afternoons. Château de Villiers, 18800 Chassy, ☏ 02-48-80-21-42, open afternoons in May and June; all day (but with lunch break) Sun and public hols only in July, Aug and most of Sep.

Practical information

Climate and seasons

With their extensive woodlands and forests, both the Ile de France and the Berry are particularly lovely in **autumn**, when the trees blaze with colour, game and locally picked mushrooms feature on restaurant menus, the sun is often still hot in the middle of the day – and the summer tourist rush is over.

But as neither region attracts mass-tourism, **summer** too can be a good time to explore, especially in the cooler countryside (towns can seem sultry). In July and August amenities like swimming pools and boating lakes are bound to be open, châteaux and museums keep fairly long opening hours and stage concerts and exhibitions galore, and the long light evenings lend themselves to refreshing strolls in the woods and by rivers at the end of a day's sightseeing. However, key sights near Paris like Versailles or Fontainebleau are very crowded at the height of the summer season, while pleasant towns such as Bourges or Senlis seem very dead when most of their inhabitants are off on their long summer break and the restaurants and shops they patronize are liable to be closed. June is a better month in this respect, as well as offering gardens looking at their best. The lively summer cultural scene generally gets going round about the Feast of John the Baptist on 24 June.

Spring has a tendency to be wet and chilly, but can also be delightful, with gardens full of birdsong and lilac, and the forests displaying every conceivable shade of green. From Palm Sunday onwards opening hours at tourist sights improve, but Easter week is so popular with French and foreign visitors alike that you must be prepared for crowds if you plan to take in the major tourist sights.

Winter can have considerable charm, especially if you are lucky with the weather. Locals say that you can count on brightish days in the Berry right down to the third week in November, and even early February can be brilliantly sunny. December is a good time to visit towns, their food shops and markets looking festive in the run-up to the Christmas and New Year celebrations. And the winter cultural season, designed for locals rather than for tourists, is often stimulating and less predictable than the standard summer fare of concerts and firework displays. But visiting hours are often drastically curtailed, and some châteaux are not open at all in the winter months.

Telephone numbers

Telephone numbers in France now all consist of ten digits. The country has been divided into five geographical sectors, starting with Paris and the immediately surrounding area, where all numbers start with 01. Otherwise numbers in the northwest quarter of the country start with 02, in the northeast quarter with 03, in the southwest quarter with 05 and in the southeast quarter with 04.

All telephone and fax numbers given in this guide include the appropriate first two digits, which should be used at all times if you are telephoning within France. However, if you are telephoning from outside France, you should omit the 0 in all cases. So after your country's code for making international calls, you should first dial the country code for France, which is 33, then the last nine digits of the French number.

Calls within France are likely to be considerably cheaper if you use a phonecard (*télécarte*) from a public call box, rather than making the call from a hotel or restaurant.

Information sources

Britain
Maison de la France
178 Piccadilly
London W1V OAL
Ⓣ 0891-244-123
Ⓕ 0171-493-6594

The United States
Maison de la France
444 Madison Avenue
16th floor
New York, NY 10022
Ⓣ 900-990-0040
Ⓕ 212 838 7855

Australia
Maison de la France
12th floor
12 Castlereagh St
Sydney, NSW 2000
Ⓣ 2-9231-4244
Ⓕ 2-9221-8682

Canada
Maison de la France
1981 avenue McGill College
Suite 490, Montreal
Quebec H3A 2W9
Ⓣ 514-288-4264
Ⓕ 514-845-4868

Ireland
Maison de la France
35 Lower Abbey St
Dublin 1
Ⓣ 1-703-40-46
Ⓕ 1-874-73-24

South Africa
Maison de la France
196 Oxford Rd
1st floor, Oxford Manor
Illovo 2196
Ⓣ 11-880-80-62

The key bodies for advance information in France are the **departmental tourist boards** (Comités départementaux de tourisme or **CDT**). Most of the places covered in this guide are in one of the five *départements* in the Ile de France administrative region or the two in the Berry. But some are not technically in either region. For instance, Beauvais, Chantilly and Senlis are in the Oise, Chartres in the Eure-et-Loir, Giverny in the Eure and Romorantin in the Loir-et-Cher.

Each *département* has a two-figure identification number, which appears on car number plates and forms the first two digits of the postcode. If you want to contact the CDT for events calendars, brochures listing campsites or b & b accommodation, farms selling local produce and the like, look at the postcode in the relevant **key data** box in this guide, note the first two numbers and use the list below to find the right address for the CDT:

18   CDT du CHER
5 rue de Sérancourt
18000 Bourges
Ⓣ 02-48-67-00-18
Ⓕ 02-48-67-01-44

27   CDT de l'EURE
Hôtel du Département
bld Georges-Chauvin
B.P. 367
27003 Evreux Cedex
Ⓣ 02-32-31-51-51
Ⓕ 02-32-31-05-98

28   CDT de l'EURE-ET-LOIR
19 pl. des Epars
B.P. 67
28002 Chartres
Ⓣ 02-37-84-01-00
Ⓕ 02-37-36-36-39

36   CDT de l'INDRE
1 rue Saint-Martin
B.P. 141
36003 Châteauroux
Ⓣ 02-54-07-36-36
Ⓕ 02-54-22-31-21

41   CDT du LOIR-ET-CHER
5 rue de la Voute-du-
Château
B.P. 149
41005 Blois Cedex
Ⓣ 02-54-78-55-50
Ⓕ 02-54-74-81-79

60   CDT de l'Oise
19 rue Pierre-Jacoby
B.P. 822
60008 Beauvais
Ⓣ 03-44-11-44-11
Ⓕ 03-44-11-45-50

77   CDT de la SEINE-ET-MARNE
Maison du Tourisme
Château Soubiran
170 av. Henri-Barbusse
B.P. 144
77194 Dammarie-les-Lys
Cedex
Ⓣ 01-64-10-10-64
Ⓕ 01-64-10-10-65

78   CDT des YVELINES
Hôtel du Département
2 pl. André-Mignot
78012 Versailles Cedex
Ⓣ 01-39-02-78-78
Ⓕ 01-30-97-78-87

91   CDT de l'ESSONNE
2 cours Monseigneur-
Romero
91025 Evry Cedex
Ⓣ 01-64-97-35-13
Ⓕ 01-64-97-23-70

92   CDT des HAUTS-DE-SEINE
22 rue Pierre-et-Marie-Curie
92140 Clamart
Ⓣ 01-46-42-17-95
Ⓕ 01-46-42-80-52

94   CDT du VAL-DE-MARNE
11 av. de Nogent
94300 Vincennes
Ⓣ 01-48-08-13-00
Ⓕ 01-43-74-81-01

95   CDT du VAL-D'OISE
Château de la Motte
rue François-de-Ganay
95270 Luzarches
Ⓣ 01-34-71-90-00

Local tourist offices

Most towns that have a tourist trade and some villages close to a major sight have their own local tourist office, called the **office de tourisme**, **maison de tourisme** or **syndicat d'initiative**. Addresses are given in the **key data** boxes in this guide, indicated by the letters **T.O.**

Disabled visitors

The Maison de la France in your country (see p. 18) should be able to supply a guide for people with reduced mobility called *Paris-Ile de France for Everyone*.

Espace du Tourisme d'Ile de France

The key place in Paris for anyone intending to explore the Ile de France is this wide-ranging information centre, well sited in the chic new underground shopping mall grandly called **Le Carrousel du Louvre**.

It is packed with leaflets and brochures about themed weekends, ranging from gourmet tours to golf-for-beginners; canal and river cruises; walking tours in nature parks and a wide range of cultural and sporting activities. You can pick up lists of museums and historic buildings with current opening times, and programmes for annual music and other festivals. One-off concerts and happenings of all kinds are advertised too.

But this is more than an information centre. It is a one-stop shop where you can buy metro, RER and rail tickets, museum passes (see p. 36) and maps. With the help of the staff of the RATP (Paris Transport Board) and the SNCF (French Rail), you can work out the best way to travel between sights by public transport, and the most advantageous ticketing possibilities. And you can even hire a car, if this turns out to be the best solution. Sightseeing tours by bus or coach and river cruises can also be booked here.

The centre is closed on Tuesdays, but otherwise open from 10.00 to 19.00. It can also be contacted by telephone, fax or e-mail.

Espace du Tourisme d'Ile de France au Carrousel du Louvre, 99 rue de Rivoli, 75001 Paris, ⓣ 01-44-50-19-90, ⓕ 01-44-50-19-99, e-mail: Tourisme-ile-de-france@wanadoo.fr

Credit card loss

• **American Express**	ⓣ 01-47-77-72-00
• **Diner's Club**	call usual number in your own country, reversing charges
• **Eurocard/Mastercard**	ⓣ 01-45-67-84-84
• **Visa**	ⓣ 0800-902033

Getting there

By rail

Eurostar operates between Waterloo International Terminal and Ashford International Terminal, Kent, and the Gare du Nord in central Paris. Information and bookings can be made direct with Eurostar, ⓣ 0345 30 30 30, and from most mainline stations. Timetable information is available on the faxback information service number ⓣ 0660 600 600 (49p a minute) or from the Web site: www. eurostar.co.uk or www.eurostar.com. To call Eurostar from abroad, ⓣ 1233 617 575; from North America, ⓣ 1212 382 3737.

Le Shuttle drive on, drive off service operates from Cheriton near Folkestone (M20, Junction 11a). The French terminal is near Coquelles, south-west of Calais (A16, Junction 13). For information and reservations, ⓣ 0891 555 566; disabled helpline, ⓣ 01303 273 747. In France, information and reservations, ⓣ 03 21 00 61 00.

Information can be obtained and reservations made at **The Rail Shop** at 179 Piccadilly, London W1V 0BA, ⓣ 0990 300 003.

By sea

Hoverspeed Ferries, Dover–Calais and Folkestone–Boulogne
  ℡ 0990 240 241
Stena Line's catamaran service, Dover–Calais, ℡ 0900 707 070

Ferries, Dover–Calais, P&O ℡ 0990 980 980; Stena Line,
  ℡ 0990 707 070; Sea France, ℡ 0990 711 711
Ramsgate–Dunkerque, Sally Lines, ℡ 01843 595 522
Portsmouth–Le Havre, P&O, ℡ 0990 980 980
Portsmouth–Caen, Brittany Ferries, ℡ 0990 360 360.

By air

From the UK. Information about flights from London Heathrow and Gatwick and other cities in the UK to Paris Charles de Gaulle and Orly can be obtained from **British Airways**, 156 Regent St, London W1R 5TA, ℡ 0171 434 4700, and from **Air France**, 10 Warwick St, London W1, ℡ 0181 742 6600. **British Midland** ℡ 0345 554 554 offers several flights a day from Heathrow and from the East Midlands, as well as from Aberdeen via East Midlands, and Belfast, Edinburgh and Glasgow, via Heathrow or East Midlands. **Air UK** has flights from Stansted and Leeds, ℡ 0141 221 5227.

From the USA

American Airlines, ℡ 800 624 6262. Departures from Boston, Chicago, Dallas, Miami, JFK New York
Continental Airlines, ℡ 800 231 0856. Departures from Houston, Newark New York
Delta Airlines, ℡ 800 241 4141. Departures from Atlanta, Cincinnati, JFK New York
Air France, ℡ 800 AF PARIS. Departures from Chicago, Houston, Los Angeles, Miami, JFK New York, San Francisco, Washington
TWA, ℡ 800 892 4141. Departures from JFK New York, Saint-Louis
United Airlines, ℡ 800 538 2929. Departures from Chicago, Los Angeles, San Francisco, Washington.

Access and local transport

Despite recent decentralization, Paris is still the hub of France's road and public transport networks, so getting out of the city is rarely a problem. A series of motorways (labelled A for *autoroute*) radiate out from it, most of them toll roads, though the portion nearest the city may not require payment. But the old *routes nationales* (labelled N) are still very widely used. Traffic is often heavy, especially on Friday evenings and Saturday mornings, and on Sunday evenings returning to the capital, as a large number of Parisians travel to second homes virtually every weekend. Parisian drivers are not noted for their courtesy and show little patience with those hesitating over which lane or exit to take. A series of complex Spaghetti Junctions can be hair-raising to negotiate.

Speed limits

Speed limits on French roads are strictly enforced and stiff fines are common. Top permitted speeds drop in wet or foggy weather. This change is signalled by overhead electronic signs on motorways, but you will have to use your judgement on other roads.

- **toll motorways**
  - 130km/hr (80mph) in dry weather
  - 110km/hr (68mph) in wet weather
  - 50km/hr (31mph) in foggy weather
- **non-toll motorways**
  - 110km/hr (68mph) in dry weather
  - 100km/hr (62mph) in wet weather
- **dual carriageways**
  - same as non-toll motorways
- **other roads**
  - 90km/hr (56mph) outside built-up areas
  - 50km/hr (31mph) in built-up areas

There is also a **minimum** speed limit of 80km/hr (50mph) in the outside lane on motorways, in daylight hours, on level ground and in normal weather conditions.

Car hire

The major international car hire companies naturally have offices in Paris and at the airports. But remember that driving out of Paris in a hired car means that you will probably be taken for a Parisian and will not benefit from even the occasional tolerance shown to foreign drivers or provincials trying to exit from the capital. It may be advisable to arrange to pick up the car at a station, so that you can have a hassle-free journey out of Paris before starting to drive. Rail-and-drive packages are on offer at a number of stations, and can generally be booked and paid for before you leave for France. Once you are in Paris, the **Espace du Tourisme d'Ile-de-France** (see p. 20 below) offers car hire information and reservation.

Public transport

The Paris transport system is not only admirably efficient, but is also well integrated into the suburban rail network and linked with long-distance trains. Moreover prices are reasonable, with a number of good-value passes on offer. Trains, buses and the express metro, the **Réseau régional express** (or RER), can all be used to travel out of the city.

The whole Ile de France network is divided into eight concentric zones (see map, pp. 24–5). Prices depend on the number of zones you cover. Although single tickets are available, it is generally advantageous to opt for a tourist pass, known as **Paris Visite**, valid for one or more days, or for a **Carte Orange**, the standard season ticket used by Parisians and available for a week (*coupon hebdomadaire*) or a calendar month (*coupon mensuel*), or the single-day **Mobilis** ticket.

Paris Visite

This allows you into first-class carriages in RER and suburban trains, does not require a photograph and entitles you to the occasional reduced-price admission or 'welcome gift'. But it is not as good value as the regular passes. Ask for advice at information offices when you have decided how many trips you will be taking and which zones you will be covering.

Carte Orange

Even if you are only taking a couple of trips out, the weekly pass is generally excellent value, and makes your life a great deal simpler. For instance, you can use it to travel by train to Fontainebleau, then to take a local bus to the château and later on a bus to Barbizon. If you have bought a coupon for zones 1–5, it is also valid for the airports. Passport-sized photographs are required.

Mobilis

This one-day pass does not require a photograph. The price depends on the number of zones.

With all passes, the coupon should be inserted into the turnstile slot at stations, but the whole pass shown to drivers on buses. Do not attempt to slot a transport pass coupon into one of the orange machines at rail stations – they are only to be used for rail tickets.

A word of warning

The various passes apply only to places within the official Ile de France region. So they are not valid for Beauvais, Chantilly, Chartres, Giverny, Senlis and a number of other places in the surrounding administrative regions.

Transport information

RATP telephone operators are supposed to be multilingual. Calls are charged at a higher rate. ℗ 08-36-68-77-14.

For ordinary trains, the **SNCF** (French Rail) number is 01-53-90-20-20. Mainline rail stations have information kiosks with generally helpful staff. Otherwise see **Information sources** below. Network maps are available from metro stations.

Paris mainline rail stations:
Gare Montparnasse for points southwest and west
Gare Saint-Lazare for points west
Gare du Nord for points north
Gare de l'Est for points east
Gare de Lyon for points southeast
Gare d'Austerlitz for points south (including the Berry)

RER lines

The four lines (A, B, C and D) have several branches and new ones are being added all the time. See map on pp. 24–5.

Buses

Suburban bus maps are available from metro stations. In Ile de France towns they usually connect with trains. But many do not run on Sundays.

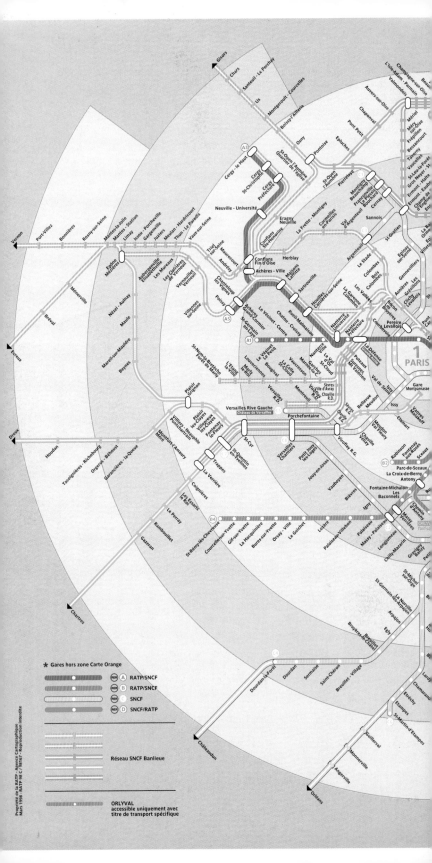

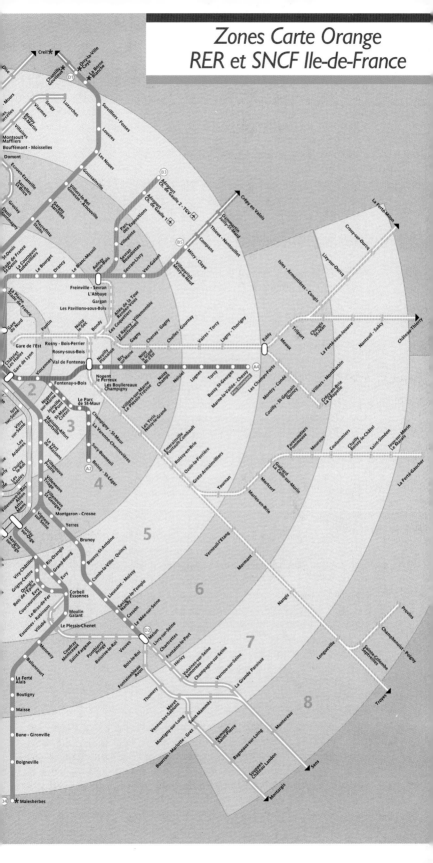

Zones Carte Orange
RER et SNCF Ile-de-France

Travelling in the Berry

The Berry has good bus networks operating out of major centres like Bourges, Châteauroux, La Châtre or Issoudun. However, these are geared to school children and to locals travelling in to these centres to work or shop. So they are likely to be infrequent or non-existent on Sundays, and probably on Saturday afternoons, and may well not operate in the school holidays. Timetables are usually posted up outside bus stations (*gares routières*) and should be available at tourist offices. Drivers and passengers are generally helpful about telling you where to get off, and where the bus stop is – it may not be marked.

The introduction to each section in this guide indicates how easy it is to travel around without a car. The **key data** sections give details of public transport, including trains, which can also be used between some places. **Important**: it is essential (on pain of a fine) to have your rail ticket date-stamped by one of the orange machines in or outside stations.

By bike

Bikes can be taken on virtually all trains within the Ile de France rail network (and on some RER trains) at the weekend and on public holidays. During the week, bikes are not allowed in the rush hours, which are officially deemed to be 16.30 to 19.00 going out of Paris, and 06.30 to 09.00 coming in. Rules and times vary on other trains, so enquire locally. Bike hire at stations can sometimes be arranged as a package when you buy your rail ticket (generally weekends only).

Many roads in the Ile de France near major sights are busy, so biking is best restricted to the ring of forests or river valleys surrounding the capital. In the Berry, roads are quiet and biking is a pleasure.

Maps

The key map for the Ile de France is the Michelin 1/200 000 (1cm = 2km) no. 237, which covers all the places referred to in this guide. This map should be adequate for most purposes, but larger-scale and walking maps can be bought from local bookshops, newsagents or tourist boards.

The same-scale Michelin map for the Berry is no. 238. Again, more localized or larger-scale maps are available locally.

Most tourist offices hand out free street plans, but these only include key streets. Good maps/gazetteers of individual towns are published by Plans Guides Blay.

Hiking

I certainly wouldn't recommend hiking out of Paris, but keen walkers can get much enjoyment from crossing forests or even vineyards from one sight to another, both in the Ile de France and in the Berry. France's major hiking trails bear the letters **GR** (**Grande Randonnée**). But there are other regional tracks called **Grandes Randonnées du Pays** or **GRP** and **Petites Randonnées** or **PR**. These are all well marked, and use conventional symbols, but for safety you might like to buy the relevant ***Topoguide***, which includes a route map and other information (in French only), practical, historical and cultural, as well as a description of the walk, its difficulty and the time it is likely to take.

Less strenuous rambles can be made along marked paths in most of the forests referred to in this guide. Local tourist offices can usually provide a rough map and departmental tourist boards often publish booklets detailing walking routes. (See p. 44.)

Tourist routes

France has an enormous number of signposted tourist routes. Some that cover the areas described in this guide are the **Route Jacques-Coeur** (see box, p. 12), the **Route historique des Parcs et Jardins** (for garden enthusiasts), the **Route des Hauts Dignitaires**, the **Route Historique des Maisons d'Ecrivains** (writers' houses), the **Route George Sand**, the **Routes de Madame de Sévigné**, the **Route historique des Impressionnistes en Val d'Oise** (the Impressionist painters in and around Auvers-sur-Oise), the **Route Thibaud de Champagne**. But there are many more, and departmental tourist boards devise their own localized routes, such as the **Route des Musiciens en Yvelines** (musicians' houses west and southwest of Paris).

Coach excursions

The **RATP** (Paris Tourist Authority) runs tours in comfortable but non-luxury buses to many places of interest in the Ile de France. Guides are usually knowledgeable and particularly good on art and social history; tours are conducted in French. Various other operators such as **Cityrama** or **Paris Vision** run more expensive excursions in luxury coaches to major sights like Fontainebleau, Giverny or Versailles, sometimes combining two such places. These are more geared to mass tourism and English-speaking guides should be available.

Excursions are organized by tourist offices or private operators in some key tourist towns like Bourges, Chartres or Fontainebleau. Enquire locally.

Hotels and other accommodation

If you decide to spend a night or more away from Paris, or to base yourself elsewhere, it is sensible to plan ahead. This applies particularly if your preference is for somewhere quite near the capital.

Over the last couple of decades a vast network of motorways and other express roads leading out of Paris has been built. Taken together with the generally excellent regional express metro lines, they have made it much easier both to spend a day in the country rather than staying overnight, and to travel much further afield for a weekend away. As a result, weekending in a peaceful Ile de France inn or hotel is no longer as common a pastime for Parisians as it once was, though many do still own weekend retreats in places like the leafy Vallée de Chevreuse or the forested area north of the capital.

The inevitable side effect of this sociological change is that many a modest little hotel or inn once catering for a steady clientele of

Les Hôtels Particuliers

The term *hôtel particulier* normally means 'private mansion' and is used for very grand town houses, even palaces. But it is also the name adopted by a group of a dozen hotels under the same ownership, all of which offer attractive weekend and single-night deals and also stage musical weekends. They are all beautifully furnished historic buildings and make a point of offering the sort of cosseting you would hope to find in a grand private house, with blazing fires in winter, cosy lounges and flowers everywhere.

Special deals include '*arrêt d'un soir*' (room + dinner + breakfast), '*weekend particulier*' (room for 2 nights + 2 dinners + 2 breakfasts), '*harmonie d'un soir*' (room + dinner + concert + breakfast + Sunday brunch). Although the basic deal on offer is for two people sharing a room, for once singles can also get good rates for similar packages.

The group includes the **Château d'Ermenonville** near the Abbaye de Chaâlis (see under **Ermenonville** in hotel listing), the **Abbaye des Vaux de Cernay** in the Chevreuse Valley (see under **Les Vaux de Cernay**) and the **Château de Brécourt** near Monet's house at Giverny (see **Douains**).

For a booklet with photos of all the hotels and details of rates, write to: Les Hôtels Particuliers, Groupe Philippe et Gérard Savary, 30 rue des Francs-Bourgeois, 75003 Paris, or fax: 01-48-04-57-97.

Parisian families has had to close, or has been converted into an upmarket restaurant geared largely to the local business community. Others have been drastically modernized, have installed fitness centres and meeting rooms and woo the organizers of seminars, management training sessions and the like. The universal vogue for holding such sessions away from the office has also led to a mushrooming of purpose-built hotels with a mainly business ambience.

But despite these changes you can still find some delightful traditional hotels and inns, or rooms above what is essentially a restaurant. And it is worth bearing in mind that some business-oriented hotels offer special weekend rates. They may be short on atmosphere, but they are comfortable and well-equipped, and often have good restaurants serving a range of fixed-price menus that attract local families for weekend meals or celebrations.

Staying in the Berry

The situation is very different in the Berry. The sociological phenomena I have referred to in relation to the area close to Paris do to a certain extent apply to the rest of the country: younger members of families who have run a hotel for generations are less willing to work the very long hours put in by their parents and grandparents; and when it comes to the regular rites-of-passage gatherings – weddings, christenings, first communions – country people are more likely these days to set off in their cars for a slap-up meal in the nearest town than to patronize the village inn that could once rely on such staple year-round custom.

But the Berry is a traditional rural area, where change comes slowly and people tend to be very attached to their *pays* or village and its immediate surroundings. So it has thankfully preserved a fair number of the family-style hotels that many visitors see as one of the chief delights of holidaying in France.

Room prices are generally moderate in such establishments. They mostly apply to the room, rather than per person. This has long been common practice in France (though it is starting to change in some larger towns). It does of course penalize those travelling alone – single rooms are rare and often disappointingly dingy – but it does mean that couples or families can enjoy prices that are lower than in most other western European countries. An increasing number of hotels are willing to put a third bed into a room for a nominal extra charge.

Hotels in or close to major tourist sights, or to amenities such as boating lakes or golf courses, may have to make a small extra daily charge corresponding to the 'visitor tax' (*taxe de séjour*) levied by the local authority. This will be posted up in the room along with the room rate. So will the price of breakfast, which nowadays is rarely included in the room rate – there is nothing to stop you breakfasting elsewhere if this is practicable. Service is always included in the advertised rates, though it is usual to leave a small tip for the chambermaid. For details of prices see the hotel lists on pp. 238–53.

Keeping an eye on the calendar

Hotels near popular tourist sights are heavily booked during the main tourist season, which essentially means Easter, then July to mid-September. And if you need a hotel during the week, remember that towns such as Chartres or Bourges or Fontainebleau are quite busy commercial centres as well as attracting tourists.

In country districts you may sometimes have to sacrifice a few degrees of comfort, but will be rewarded with picturesque wooden beams, pretty views and cosy dining rooms, with open fires in winter and tables outside in summer. As old-established inns are often beside a road, always ask for a quiet room, preferably overlooking an inner garden or courtyard.

Making the choice

The hotels and inns listed on pp. 238–53 have been chosen because they are well placed for following the suggestions in this guide. I have put the emphasis whenever possible on comfortable but not luxurious places with a French atmosphere, where you can expect a pleasant welcome and – if you want it – help with finding footpaths or local cheesemakers or craft studios or places to swim.

Prices in most of the hotels and inns listed come into the medium range, though I have also included a few more expensive places for special treats, and some more modest ones for days when the budget is tight. For further information on prices see the introduction to the lists.

Bon Week-end en villes

This special offer, generally running only from November to the end of March, but sometimes available year-round, entitles you to two nights in a hotel for the price of one, providing you arrive on either a Friday or a Saturday. It applies both to single rooms (where available) and to doubles, but does not include breakfast. It also includes various extras, like a welcome gift from the town or city's tourist office, reduced-price sightseeing tours, and special offers on tickets for concerts and exhibitions as well as local sports and other amenities. Special rates for car hire may also be on offer.

The towns and cities taking part – around seventy of them – vary from year to year but are likely to include a number of places covered in this guide, such as Beauvais, Bourges, Chartres, Fontainebleau and Saint-Germain-en-Laye. Contact the French Tourist Office or Maison de la France in your country (for addresses see **Information Sources**, p. 18). Or write to **Club Bon Week-end en Villes**, FNOTSI, 280 bld Saint-Germain, 75007 Paris, France.

Closing times

Since most of the hotels are independent establishments and many are family-run, they cannot provide seven-days-a-week, year-round service. Hotels often close for several weeks a year. If they are near sights popular with tourists, their closing periods will probably include January and/or February. Those in towns may close briefly in the summer. The February half-term holidays and early November are common closing times for both types.

Hotel restaurants, like other restaurants big and small, normally close for at least one day a week, and often also for dinner the preceding day or lunch the following day. When the restaurant is shut, the hotel will have only a skeleton staff to greet you and the place may well feel disappointingly dead.

Having checked that the restaurant is open, book your table at the same time as the room if you want to dine there, as it may well be a popular place for non-residents. Some country hotels refuse room bookings from those who do not wish to dine there at least on their first evening.

Hotel chains and associations

The lists do not include chain hotels, unless there is something distinctive about them. France does have a number of hotel chains, ranging from the luxurious to the very modest, no-frills outfits offering budget prices and 'formula' accommodation. On the whole they have no local atmosphere, but they can be convenient for a quick stopover. You will usually find them on the outskirts of towns, or close to the rail station. Names to look out for are **Arcade**, **Climat de France**, **Ibis**, **Novotel**.

Both the Ile de France and the Berry have a good number of hotels belonging to the popular **Logis de France** association. These have to conform to set standards covering such aspects as welcoming atmosphere, regional dishes served in the restaurant – almost all have their own restaurant – and bathrooms, though some hotels are more modest than others and charge correspondingly lower prices.

Another association to look out for is **Relais du Silence**, peaceful hotels that are likely to be in the country, though there are a few in towns.

Alternatives to hotels

Nowadays the famous self-catering *gîtes* can often be rented for only a few days. Ask at tourist offices for addresses of local *gîtes* associations or write to regional or departmental tourist boards (for addresses, see pp. 18–19). The official **Gîtes de France** booklets also give details of

Staying in a private château

Not to be confused with châteaux-hotels (a few of which are included in the hotels listing), private châteaux offering accommodation on a bed-and-breakfast basis can make the perfect setting for a special weekend break or an atmospheric stopover. You will feel like a guest rather than a customer and the owners will go to a great deal of trouble to make you feel that you are staying with the family and being introduced to their and their ancestors' way of life. In some cases you may be able to have dinner with your hosts, by prior arrangement.

Although the room prices may be as high as in an expensive hotel, you are paying for the historic setting, the beautiful furniture and the general atmosphere, not for room service or porterage or round-the-clock communications. Think of it as a different experience from a hotel and enjoy it as such.

Here are two particularly pleasant examples in the Berry:

Château de la Commanderie

Farges-Allichamps   ℡ 02-48-61-04-19
18200 Saint-Amand-Montrond   Ⓕ 02-48-61-01-84

A welcoming creeper-covered manor house dating from the 12th century once belonging to the Knights Templar, plus a much larger and statelier 19th-century château, both offering pleasant rooms. It has been the estate of the Comte de Jouffroy-Gonsans's family for centuries and he and his wife will tell you all about it if you join them for dinner in their pretty candlelit dining room. Well placed for visiting Noirlac Abbey and the châteaux near Saint-Amand-Montrond. Seven rooms.

Château de la Verrerie

18700 Oizon   ℡ 02-48-81-51-60
                              Ⓕ 02-48-58-21-25

This beautiful Renaissance château, built by the Scottish Stuarts and in a lovely lakeside setting surrounded by forest, is a major sight in its own right (see p. 189). The Comte and Comtesse de Vogüé offer eleven very comfortable rooms and one suite, and you will have the run of the grounds, where you can ride, cycle, go boating or fishing, even try a spot of archery. Dinner by arrangement, but the château also has its own cottagey restaurant in the grounds, La Maison d'Hélène.★ Special-interest weekend packages are also offered, involving angling or trekking, winetasting, golfing, even bridge.

farms willing to take campers or paying guests and families offering rooms on a bed-and-breakfast basis. Some local tourist offices keep lists of families with rooms, or sometimes individual flats or houses where you can stay for a night or two; you will usually be offered breakfast, and sometimes an evening meal with the family too. For something special, consider staying in a **private château** (see box, p. 31).

Tourist offices can also provide lists of **campsites** with their official grading.

Restaurants

Although some of the above comments about sociological changes affecting hotels also apply to restaurants, despite rumours to the contrary, France still offers many good-value restaurants serving carefully prepared food based on fresh local produce. Prices will naturally be lower in modest country inns or small-town places frequented by the locals on a daily basis than in gourmet restaurants close to major tourist sights. But even the top-flight restaurants generally have, at least at lunchtime, fixed-price meals on offer (known as *menus* in French) that represent remarkable value.

Some *menus* include wine (or mineral water, if you prefer) and/or coffee. Service is included by law on all prices quoted, and it is also compulsory to post up priced menus outside a restaurant. Many French diners add a few francs extra as a tip, but you must use your

Les Tables gourmandes du Berry

A group of thirty or so Berry chefs known for their excellent cuisine based on traditional regional dishes, but always with inventive and imaginative touches, have clubbed together to promote both themselves and their region. **Les Tables gourmandes du Berry** (Berry's Gourmet Restaurants), as they call themselves, include some of the most attractive restaurants in this part of the world, though not necessarily the most expensive, as they have pledged themselves to offering a good range of fixed-price menus, along with a warm welcome, an attractive setting and information about the Berry in general and local attractions and activities in particular.

Among them are the picturesque **Moulin de Chameron** in Bannegon and **Moulin des Eaux-vives** near Argenton-sur-Creuse, both converted watermills; the Sologne inns **Le Relais de la Poste** in Argent-sur-Sauldre and **La Solognote** in Brinon-sur-Sauldre; Saint-Amand-Montrond's old coaching inn **L'Hôtel de la Poste**; and the delightful **La Cognette** in Issoudun (for details of all of these, see the Hotels and restaurants listing at the back of this guide).

Their eponymous booklet, *Les Tables gourmandes du Berry*, which includes recipes, is widely available in local and regional tourist offices, in hotels and in the restaurants themselves. Or contact **Les Tables gourmandes du Berry**, Chambre du Commerce et de l'Industrie, 24 pl. Gambetta, 36028 Châteauroux Cedex, ⊤ 02-54-53-52-73, ⑤ 02-54-34-17-77.

The romance of mills

Staying or dining in a converted watermill always feels romantic, especially when some of the mill machinery is still in place. Picturesqueness and peace and quiet guaranteed. For full details of these hotels and/or restaurants housed in old mills, consult the hotel and restaurant list at the back of this guide:

- Le Moulin des Eaux-Vives, Tendu (near **Argenton-sur-Creuse**)
- Le Moulin de Chameron, **Bannegon**
- Auberge du Moulin Bureau, **La Châtre**
- Hostellerie du Moulin, **Flagy**
- Le Moulin de Fourges, **Fourges**

own judgement as to whether you would like to reward particularly pleasant service by, say, leaving the small change, or adding a small amount.

The Berry offers many opportunities for trying out regional cuisine (see **Food and drink** for specialities to look out for). *Menus* of regional specialities may be referred to as a *menu berrichon* (Berry meal), or simply a *menu régional* or *menu du terroir*. In the Ile de France, which doesn't have a single regional cuisine, you may find some local dishes, though regional *menus* are less common.

If you feel like a special treat, *menus gastronomiques* (gourmet meals) may be available, though sometimes only if everyone round the same table orders them. Conversely, if you are not hungry, or want to save your appetite for a meal later in the day, you can order a single dish from the *carte*. This practice used to be frowned on by the food-loving French; in these health-conscious times, it has become much more common. But it won't necessarily work out cheaper than a set meal.

Opening times

French mealtimes have loosened up a bit these days, but it is best to assume that restaurant lunches start at about 12 noon and that it may be hard to find anywhere to take you after 13.00 or 13.15, especially in country districts. Evening meals are usually served from about 20.00, though in places attracting many foreign tourists an earlier start is possible. Last orders may be as early as 21.30. Cafés and brasseries generally have a short menu of dishes that can be produced at most times of day, but the good-value *plats du jour* (dishes of the day) and more complicated dishes are more likely to be available between 12.00 and 14.00 or 19.00 and 22.00. Cafés may not serve anything more than snacks in the evening. Tearooms serve light lunches but shut at around 18.00.

Closing periods

Most restaurants (though not cafés or brasseries) have at least one closing day a week. Many are also shut the previous evening or the following lunchtime. Sunday evening closure is almost universal in country districts, where a large Sunday lunch is the norm. As many town dwellers head for the country on Sundays, restaurants in towns without a big tourist trade tend to shut all day.

Many restaurants also observe an annual closing period. In tourist areas this is unlikely to be during the summer season, though September, when the main rush is over, does see closures. In towns with few tourists, a break of up to four weeks in July and/or August is common.

Reserving ahead

It is wise to book in advance for Sunday lunch in the country. Tables should always be reserved in the more expensive restaurants in towns, or near major sights. Smaller restaurants may not take advance reservations by telephone.

Vegetarians

True vegetarians do not fare well in France. In places frequented by foreign tourists, some restaurants do offer a vegetarian dish. But on the whole, and certainly in rural districts in both the Ile de France and the Berry, you will do better in a café, where light egg and cheese dishes are menu staples, and salads are usually available.

Opening times

As so often in France, opening times at museums, **châteaux** and other **tourist sights** change frequently. If you are planning a special trip it is always wise to check before setting out, as sudden closures are common. The good news is that some places do stay open now through the lunch hour or hours, at any rate in the summer months, though this should never be counted on. Even the top sights are generally closed one day a week. It may be possible to visit the grounds when the building itself is closed, which will at least enable you to glimpse the architecture. And the grounds are often open later in the evening, so that you can stroll there after visiting the interior of the building.

Despite its closeness to Paris, the Ile de France is provincial in its **shopping** habits. As in the Berry, food shops generally open early, at about 08.00 or 08.30, close for lunch between about 12.30–13.00 and 15.30–16.00, then stay open till about 19.00 or 19.30. Specialist shops like butchers' and bakers' are often open on Sunday morning, but shut on Monday. Food markets generally operate one day a week in country districts, sometimes more often in towns.

Other shops are also likely to close on Monday morning, or all day on Monday, and few except newsagents are open on Sunday. Closure between roughly 12.00 and 14.00 is the norm, except for the occasional department store.

Most **restaurants** close at least one day a week (see pp. 33–4), and family-run **hotels**, too, have a closing day (see p. 30).

The mushrooming of the cash machine has made **bank** opening times less crucial than they used to be. But don't expect to find a hole in the wall accepting your credit card in every town and village.

Banks outside Paris are generally shut on Monday but open on Saturday. In small towns they may be open only on market day. Travellers' cheques and Eurocheques can often be cashed in **post offices**, whose opening hours vary according to the size of their catchment area. It is safest to assume that they will be open quite early in towns, at 08.00 or 08.30, but may still shut for lunch, between about 12.00 and 14.00, and will shut between 17.00 and 19.00. Village post offices keep shorter hours.

Exchange counters in both banks and post offices often close between about 12.30 and 14.00.

Sightseeing

Opening hours are always a problem in France, as they change frequently, often at short notice. It is always wise to check with the local or regional tourist office, especially outside the key tourist season (Easter, then July and August). If this is not feasible, larger museums and châteaux may be able to answer a basic enquiry in English if your French is not up to it, and so will many private château owners in the Berry. Otherwise ask your hotel to check for you.

Opening hours are often short, with lunchtime closure between 12.00 and 14.00 common, though non-stop opening in July and August is spreading. In country districts opening hours tend to be drastically curtailed after mid-October, or All Saints Day (1 November). Total closure until Palm Sunday (the Sunday before Easter) or Easter is common.

Public holidays are often busy times for museums and historic buildings. This applies especially to Easter and Whit Mondays, and to the Feast of the Ascension, when French families use the long weekends to explore their own heritage. But 1 November (All Saints) and 11 November (Armistice) are solemn days in France, when the dead are commemorated, so closure is likely. Christmas Day and 1 January signal virtually universal closure.

The Paris weekly 'What's On' publications, *Pariscope* and *L'Officiel des spectacles*, give details of public-holiday closures in their sightseeing listings, covering quite a broad geographical area.

The opening periods given in the **key data** sections in this guide were accurate at the time of going to press. But quite apart from potential changes, please bear in mind that 'open year-round' does not necessarily mean that the place is open daily, simply that it does not operate an annual closure.

Public holidays

1 January	14 July
Easter Monday	15 August
1 May	1 November
8 May	11 November
Feast of the Ascension	Christmas Day
Whit Monday	

The great majority of sights make an entrance charge, though this may be waived on Sundays in publicly owned buildings. Bourges is an honourable exception, as all but one of its museums are free at all times. Reductions may be on offer for children (maximum age varies), students (with valid student card) and the over-sixties; sometimes too for teachers and journalists, or for professional artists. Take your passport to prove your age and appropriate documentation. Special rates generally apply to groups of ten or more, but you must give advance warning.

An increasing number of special deals combine rail or bus fare and entrance fee, or restaurant meal and entrance fee. For **museum passes**, see box below.

Museum passes

La carte musées monuments, often abbreviated simply to '**la carte**', is officially translated as the Paris Museum Pass, but in fact is valid for many places in the surrounding area covered in this guide. It offers unlimited access, usually without queuing, to the permanent collections of about eighty top museums and historic buildings, over twenty of them outside Paris. These include the palaces of Versailles and Fontainebleau, the châteaux of Champs, Chantilly, Malmaison and Rambouillet, the Renaissance Museum at Ecouen, the ceramics collections in Sèvres, the museum in Chaâlis Abbey, and the archeology museum in the château at Saint-Germain-en-Laye.

The passes are valid for a single day, or for three or five consecutive days. They are particularly useful if you envisage wanting to leave a large museum or other building for lunch or a walk round the town or in the countryside before returning to see more of the collections, to visit the same place two days running, or to fit several different places into a short space of time.

But before deciding to buy one, bear in mind that a number of museums offer free or reduced-price admission on Sundays and public holidays, and that many do not require under-18s to pay, or charge the full rate to those between 18 and 25 or over 60 (see above). Remember too that the passes do not cover you for special exhibitions or for guided tours.

A brochure listing all the places for which the passes are valid, with current opening times, can be obtained from the French Tourist Office or Maison de la France in your country (see p. 18 for addresses). The passes themselves can be bought at:

- any of the museums or other buildings included in the scheme
- the Paris Tourist Office, 127 av. des Champs-Elysées, 8e
- the Espace Tourisme at the Louvre (see p. 20)
- the tourist information windows or kiosks at Paris's mainline rail stations
- at major metro and RER stations in Paris
- in the Fnac department stores all over France

The museums and châteaux on the **Route Jacques-Coeur** (see pp. 12 and 13) have special offers for those visiting several of them during a limited period.

Star sightseeing weekend

A weekend in mid- or late September is officially designated '**Les Journées du Patrimoine**' (Heritage Days). For these two days, a number of châteaux and other buildings not normally open to the public can be visited. Others extend their opening hours or waive admission charges. Events of all kinds are staged: concerts, talks, exhibitions, demonstrations of how exhibits were used, even wine tastings. Regional, departmental or local tourist offices issue leaflets listing participating sights. The national and local press also list key events and special openings.

If you go on a conducted tour it is normal practice to give a small tip to the guide, especially when the tour is not compulsory. You must use your judgement if the person showing you round is clearly a cut above a paid attendant. But château owners struggling to pay the heating or roofing bills certainly won't spurn an extra donation, and the volunteers manning small museums have out-of-pocket expenses to cover.

Guided tours are often compulsory. However, some sights now hire out walkman-type headsets plus cassettes in French and various other languages, including English, offering commentary when you follow a set itinerary. Others, such as the royal palace at Fontainebleau have **audioguides** that look like mobile telephones and have to be held up to the ear – which can be awkward if you want to carry a guidebook as well. At the château in Auvers-sur-Oise, the multimedia tour called 'A journey into the Impressionists' Era' (p. 127) is based on headsets whose tape is activated when you reach certain points on the tour.

Activity packs for children are increasingly available. These range from fact sheets and colouring booklets to a treasure hunt – at Fontainebleau – or bow and arrows for archery practice at the archeology centre in Argentomagus. The texts can generally be supplied in English as well as French.

Sightseeing checklists

Writers' homes and settings

Marguerite Audoux	Aubigny-sur-Nère (p. 188)
Alain-Fournier	Epineuil-le-Fleuriel, La Chapelle d'Angillon (p. 232)
Honoré de Balzac	Issoudun (p. 222)
Alexandre Dumas *père*	Port-Marly (p. 116)
Victor Hugo	Bièvres (p. 80)
Blaise Pascal	Port-Royal-des-Champs (p. 92)
Marcel Proust	Illiers-Combray (p. 88)
Jean Racine	Port-Royal-des-Champs (p. 92)
Jean-Jacques Rousseau	Ermenonville (p. 139)
George Sand	Nohant, Gargilesse (p. 210)
Ivan Turgenev	Bougival (p. 110)

Keeping children happy

Bergerie nationale, Rambouillet (p. 99)

Bergeries de Sologne (p. 50)

Château d'Auvers (p. 127)

Château de Breteuil (p. 92)

Culan Castle (p. 234)

Disneyland Paris (p. 155)

Elevage caprin des Garennes (p. 50)

Espace Rambouillet (p. 101)

France Miniature, Elancourt (p. 77)

Mer de Sable (p. 141)

Mini'stoire (p. 229)

Musée Rambolitrain, Rambouillet (p. 100)

Parc Astérix (p. 141)

Provins (pp. 159–65)

Sarzay Castle (p. 211)

Thoiry Safari Park (pp. 117–19)

Witchcraft Museum (p. 16)

Fairs, festivals and festivities

Tourist boards publish annual brochures listing events of all kinds on their patch. Here are a few suggestions (for music festivals, see p. 39):

March: Ham and Bric-à-Brac Fair, Chatou.

Palm Sunday weekend: Students' Pilgrimage, Chartres; Wine and Cheese Fair, Coulommiers

Easter weekend: Watercress Fair, Méréville (see box, p. 48)

late April: Perennials Fair, Saint-Jean-de-Beauregard (see box, p. 14)

early June: Photo Fair, Bièvres (first Sat); Wine Fair, Sancerre; Medieval Pageant, Provins; Pardon de la Batellerie, Conflans-Sainte-Honorine; Semaine Hippique, Chantilly

mid-June: Guinguettes Festival, Joinville-le-Pont

late June: Fête de la Musique (21; Fêtes Jeanne Hachette, Beauvais (last weekend, see box, p. 39)

mid-July: Franco-Scots Festival, Aubigny-sur-Nère; Pottery Festival, La Borne

late July/early Aug: Randonnée de la Brenne (Hike), La Brenne

early Aug: Witches'/Sorcerers' Fair, Bué

mid-Aug: Wine Fair, Menetou-Salon; Goat's Cheese Fair, Vailly-sur-Sauldre (near Château de La Verrerie)

late Aug: Wine Fair, Sancerre

mid-Sep: Heritage Days (see box, p. 37); Bean Fair, Arpajon; 'Open days', Senlis (odd-numbered years)

late Sep/early Oct: Ham and Bric-à-Brac Fair, Chatou

late Oct/early Nov: Gourmet Fair, Romorantin-Lanthenay (see box, p. 51)

early Nov: Fruit & Vegetable Fair, Saint-Jean-de-Beauregard (see box, p. 14)

Concerts

Occasional concerts are held in abbeys, churches and châteaux throughout the year. Apart from the Ile de France's busy autumn season (see p. 39), many music festivals are staged in both the Ile de France and the Berry.

Thoiry is one of several châteaux that has a regular concert programme. You can also take advantage of the weekend packages (room + dinner + breakfast + brunch + concert) offered by the **Hôtels particuliers** group (see box, p. 28).

Celebrating a heroine

Beauvais's feisty 'Little Axe Girl' Jeanne Lainé (see box, p. 146) has been fêted during the last weekend in June for over half a millennium with **Les Fêtes Jeanne Hachette**. The whole town is hung with bunting and the dramatic events of 1472, when the town was besieged by the Burgundi-an army, are re-enacted. A costumed pageant features Louis XI, surrounded by his guard, being received by the town's worthies, then processing towards the place Jeanne-Hachette. On Sunday morning, the 'king' attends a mass celebrated as it would have been in the Middle Ages, and in the afternoon, a huge procession winds through the town, with locals dressed as soldiers, knights, guild members and the like. A medieval-style market is held throughout the weekend and brass bands play their hearts out.

Some music festivals

baroque	Château de **Versailles** (early Oct)
chamber	Orangerie de **Sceaux** (mid-July to end Sep)
Chopin	**Nohant** (mid-July)
harp	**Gargilesse** (late Aug)
jazz	Festival Django Reinhardt, **Samois-sur-Seine** (late June)
medieval	**Royaumont Abbey** (early June to end Sep)
organ	Les Riches Heures de l'Orgue en Berry, mainly **Bourges** (Whitsun to end Aug), Grandes Orgues de **Chartres** (July, Aug), Jeux d'Orgues en Yvelines (Oct–Dec)
rock, popular	Printemps de **Bourges** (see p. 40)
romantic	Fêtes Romantiques, **Nohant** (late June/early July)
sacred	Eté de Noirlac, Noirlac Abbey (July, Aug)
vielle	Rencontres internationales des Luthiers et des Maîtres Sonneurs (for players of traditional Berry instruments), **Saint-Chartier** (mid-July)

General classical festivals/seasons

Festival de l'Ile de France (see below)
Festival des églises romanes du Berry (concerts in the Berry's Romanesque churches, July, Aug)
Château de Boucard (see p. 205, July)
Semaine musicale de Rambouillet (Oct)
Festival des Cathédrales de Picardie (includes Beauvais, Senlis, Sep)
Le Château en musique (regular concerts in beautiful music room in **Château de Champs**)

Ile de France Autumn Music Festival

The **Festival d'Ile de France** takes place over a six-week period in September and October. Around thirty concerts are performed in châteaux and other historic buildings throughout the region – a good way of combining sightseeing with listening to top-level musicians. The programme is published in June each year. Call or fax to request a brochure, as advance reservation is advisable.

Festival d'Ile de France, ℗ 01-44-94-28-50, ℗ 01-44-94-28-58.

Bourges's springtime frolics

Le Printemps de Bourges ('Bourges Spring') is the name given to a major two-week international festival of popular song, staged in the city in the second half of April. First held in 1977, it acts as a magnet for a young and lively audience, both French and foreign, who attend officially programmed concerts by professional singers and groups all over town, and throng the cafés in and around the place de Sérancourt listening to impromptu singing and fringe performances by amateur groups. The huge success of the Bourges Spring has led to the opening of a permanent centre, the **Espace Printemps**, where you can listen to contemporary singers, see films, videos and exhibitions about previous festivals and buy tapes and books in various languages on contemporary popular music.

For information about the current festival programme contact the **Maison de la Culture** or the city's **tourist office** (see p. 196 for address). The **Espace Printemps** is at 18 rue des Arènes (closed Sun – except first in month – and Mon).

Sightseeing musts for music lovers

Frédéric Chopin	Nohant (pp. 209–10)
Claude Debussy	Saint-Germain-en-Laye (p. 115)
Pauline Viardot	Bouvigal (pp. 109, 110)

Summer spectaculars

Straight *son-et-lumière* is a thing of the past these days. The original 'sound-and-light' performances, pioneered in the great Loire Valley châteaux in the 1950s, have been superseded by multimedia shows featuring laser beams and fireworks, plus hundreds of costumed actors (usually local amateurs), not to mention horses, creating a colourful pageant re-enacting the history of the town, palace or château. They are very popular, with locals as well as French and foreign tourists, so it is essential to book (contact local tourist offices). These are the main events:

- **Versailles**   Fêtes de Nuit (see p. 75)
- **Provins**   Medieval Pageant (see p. 159)
- **Moret-sur-Loing**   Summer Festival (see p. 183)

Also spectacular are the **fountains** at **Versailles** (see pp. 74–5) and the **candle-lit evenings** at **Vaux-le-Vicomte**. Some of the **Route Jacques-Coeur** châteaux stage candlelit events too.

Sports and leisure activities

As the French become increasingly *sportif* (sporty), the number of sports and leisure activities on offer means that you are spoiled for choice in many places. For instance, the handy **Guide pratique/ A practical guide** in both French and English published by the Indre CDT (see p. 19 for address) lists an amazing number of facilities, ranging from bungee jumping to canoeing. Local and departmental tourist offices are the best source of information on current opening times.

Fête des Loges, Saint-Germain-en-Laye

Although the forest round Saint-Germain-en-Laye, known simply as the Forêt de Saint-Germain, is now much smaller than it used to be, it is still a popular place for weekend walks and for riding, with over 100km of footpaths and another 50km of forest rides. But from late June to the middle of August its popularity increases by leaps and bounds when the annual Fête des Loges is staged there, beneath the ancient oaks and beeches. This lively open-air funfair attracts several million people every year, mostly families from Paris and the Ile de France enjoying a day out. Small children revel in the merry-go-rounds, tuck into candy floss (picturesquely called *barbe à papa* or 'Dad's beard' in French) and join in family meals at one of the many improvised restaurants with benches and trestle tables. The traditional fare is mussels, roast chicken, sucking pig, spicy *merguez* sausages or huge mounds of *choucroute* (sauerkraut) with plump sausages or ham.

The fair began life as a pilgrimage in the 17th century. Louis XIII started a fashion for visiting a hermit who had settled in a spot in the middle of the forest known as Les Loges, which already had a chapel dedicated to St Fiacre, the patron saint of gardeners. It gradually became a place of pilgrimage, especially on 30 August, celebrated in France as the feast day of St Fiacre and all gardeners. In due course a Carmelite monastery was built there. Booths and sideshows would be set up to entertain the pilgrims, and by the 19th century a full-scale fair took place every summer, with dozens of bands to dance to, and stalls selling not only food and drink but toys, haberdashery, cheap jewellery and knick-knacks.

Nowadays a shuttle bus service runs from the RER and bus station in Saint-Germain-en-Laye to the fair, open from midday to 01.30 on weekdays, and midday to 02.30 at the weekend, for about six weeks from late June.

Open-air leisure centres

The Ile de France has a dozen *bases de plein air et de loisirs*, the portmanteau term for sites offering a wide range of open-air activities. For instance, the 135-hectare site at **Bouthiers**, southeast of Fontainebleau (rail from Paris-Lyon to Malesherbes, then 2.5km walk), has rock-climbing, hiking, mountain biking, tennis, nature walks, basketball, handball, volley ball and archery year-round, plus open-air swimming pool, waterslides, mini-golf, table tennis and trampolines in summer. There's a self-service restaurant and a picnic area. And from Whitsun weekend to the first weekend in September you can pay to use the facilities on the 9 hectares of 'relaxation terrain' (the rest is free).

At **Saint-Quentin-en-Yvelines**, on the edge of the Vallée de Chevreuse (RER line C7, or rail from Paris-Montparnasse or La Défense to Saint-Quentin-en-Yvelines, then 10 minutes' walk), you can enjoy a spot of golf (one nine-hole course, plus two eighteen-hole), while your children visit the kids' farm, go windsurfing or canoeing or pony-riding, or, in summer, hire bikes, swim in the pool, ride on a miniature train or in a horse-drawn buggy.

The Berry, too, has its *parcs de loisirs*, another term for the same thing. In the middle of the Brenne nature reserve, the **Etang de Belle-**

Racegoing in the Ile de France

Racecourses in the Ile de France attract a distinctly chic crowd. So people-watching can be fun even if you are not a regular racegoer. The latest fashions are particularly in evidence at **Chantilly** during the 'Semaine hippique' staged in June. This prettiest of all racecourses, set against a backcloth of the twin châteaux, with lake and forest to complete the picture, plays host to the world's grandest racegoers attending the prestigious **Prix du Jockey Club** on the first Sunday in June, followed by the **Prix de Diane** a week later.

You can also go to the races at **Maisons-Laffitte**, near Saint-Germain-en-Laye, where the course is again on the edge of a forest but is also beside the river Seine, and at **Fontainebleau**, whose **Grand Prix** is held in September.

bouche is a good example: a 100-hectare site surrounded by woodland, where you can sail, surfboard, canoe, swim, ride a pedalo, in a large lake; fish in a couple of smaller ones; go jogging or on nature rambles, play mini-golf; eat a snack or a full meal; and even camp or rent a hut if you feel like spending the night. Right in the north of the Berry, the **Etang du Puits** offers every conceivable watersport.

Boating

Departmental tourist boards issue **Tourisme fluvial** brochures covering river cruising and boat hire. For details of river trips on the Marne, just east of Paris, see box on p. 148. Boat trips (and boat hire) are also offered on the Seine, from Saint-Mammès near Moret-sur-Loing, and on the Oise, from Conflans-Saint-Honorine, Pontoise and L'Isle-Adam. In the Berry, there are various possibilities on the Canal latéral à la Loire near Sancerre, canoeing on the Cher and the Creuse, and sailing and canoeing on the Lac d'Eguzon south of Argenton-sur-Creuse.

You can even hire a boat in the grounds of the Grand Canal at Versailles and the Etang aux Carpes at Fontainebleau.

Cycling

The SNCF (French Rail) publishes booklets in conjunction with local tourist offices giving details of trains on which you can travel with your own bike, and where you can hire bikes, as well as suggested itineraries. Most CDTs publish their own booklets on 'Cyclotourisme', or using the words 'à vélo' (as in Les Yvelines à vélo).

Bike hire is widely available, for instance in the Vallée de Chevreuse, at Barbizon (for the Forêt de Fontainebleau), and, in the Berry, at La Châtre and Nohant for exploring the Vallée noire (see p. 208). The tourist office in Mézières-en-Brenne is the best place for hiring a bike in the Brenne nature park. Mountain bikes are also available in the Haute-Touche animal reserve (see p. 217).

Fishing

With their many rivers, the Ile de France and the Berry are popular with anglers. Permits are required. Ask at local tourist offices about day permits, which are often bought from a nearby café or campsite. Some of the open-air leisure centres (see above) include fishing as one of the activities on offer. In the Sologne, the village of Saint-Viâtre, with its Maison des Etangs (see p. 192), naturally attracts enthusiasts. The Indre CDT publishes a brochure called *La Pêche dans l'Indre*, listing not only lakes and meres where day permits are obtainable (including the Etang de Bellebouche in the Brenne, see p. 218), but also *gîtes de pêche*, approved self-catering accommodation close to a lake or a river. The Cher CDT's *Evasion* brochure, covering outdoor activities, has a section on fishing in its rivers, lakes and meres, and in the Loire canal.

Golfing

France is full of golf enthusiasts these days. The official **Ile de France** region has more than sixty courses, including **Golf Disneyland Paris** (see p. 158) and one in the open-air leisure centre at Saint-Quentin-en-Yvelines (see above), and there are more just beyond its borders. A full list can be obtained from:

● **Fédération française de Golf**, 69 av. Victor-Hugo, 75011 Paris, ⓣ 01-44-17-63-00, ⓕ 01-44-17-63-63

Here are some suggestions for courses near major sights, all of which can be used by non-members on payment of a green fee (but not always at the weekend). If you are based in Paris for a while, it may be worth having the **Pass Golf de Seine-et-Marne** (valid for three months).

● **Golf Blue Green Chantilly** (two 18-hole courses) route d'Apremont, ⓣ 03-44-58-47-74 (also hotel packages, including travel)

● **Golf de Fontainebleau** (18-hole), route d'Orléans, 77300 Fontainebleau, ⓣ 01-64-22-22-95 (on edge of town, closed Tue, members only at weekends)

● **Golf de Maintenon** (two 9-hole courses), route de Gallardon, 28130 Maintenon, ⓣ 02-37-27-18-09 (19km from Chartres)

● **Golf de Saint-Germain-en-Laye** (18-hole and 9-hole), route de Poissy, ⓣ 01-39-10-30-30, ⓕ 01-39-10-30-31 (3km from town centre, Tue to Fri only for non-members)

In the **Berry**, you can combine a visit to Sancerre with playing at:

● **Golf du Sancerrois** (18-hole), 18300 Saint-Satur, ⓣ 02-48-54-11-22 (4km from Sancerre)

or play near Bourges at:

● **Golf de Bourges** (9-hole), route de Lazenay, 18000 Bourges, ⓣ 02-48-21-20-01 (5km south of town centre)

or near Châteauroux at:

● **Golf du Val d'Indre** (18-hole), Trégonce, 36320 Villedieu-sur-Indre, ⓣ 02-54-26-59-44, ⓕ 02-54-26-06-37 (10km west, closed Tue; 'golfing break' packages offered by Manoir **du Colombier**★ in Châteauroux and **L'Hermitage**★ in Buzançais)

Then 12km south of La Châtre is an 18-hole course plus hotel, tennis courts and indoor and outdoor swimming pools:

● **Les Dryades**, 36160 Pouligny-Notre-Dame, ⓣ 02-54-06-60-60, ⓕ 02-54-30-10-24

Angling in the Berry

Riding

The CDTs publish **Tourisme equestre** brochures detailing the many opportunities for riding, especially in the forests in both the Ile de France and the Berry. You can also ask for the *Chevauchées en Ile de France* guide published by:

- **Association régionale de Tourisme équestre en Ile de France**, 26 rue Charles-Laffitte, 92200 Neuilly-sur-Seine, ℡ 01-47-22-71-75

Information about riding holidays or weekends on farms designated *fermes équestres* can also be obtained from CDTs, as well as riding schools organizing outings, for instance in the Forêt de Fontainebleau, the Forêt de Compiègne, or the Brenne nature park.

Rock climbing

The **Forêt de Fontainebleau**, with its huge rocky outcrops, is a mecca for Parisians and others wanting to practise rock climbing – some of the rocks are as much as 20m high.

Walking

The opportunties are endless, ranging from full-scale hikes to gentle nature rambles. The forests in and around the Ile de France and the Berry are crisscrossed by hundreds of marked paths, the ones for serious walkers being the **Grande randonnée** or **GR** hiking trails (see pp. 26–7). For example, you can pick up the **GR11** in the east of the Ile de France near Coulommiers, continue southwards to Provins, then west to Moret-sur-Loing and on to Fontainebleau and its forest. The **GR1** also crosses the Forêt de Fontainebleau, visits Barbizon, then moves northwards via Vaux-le-Vicomte. In the Berry, the **GR31** goes through the wine village of Menetou-Salon on the Route Jacques-Coeur, and the pottery village of La Borne, then on to the

Sancerrois vineyards and to the town of Sancerre itself, via the famous goat's cheese centre at Chavignol. A less strenuous series of trails focuses on the Sancerrois. Then the Brenne nature park is the subject of a special *Topo-guide* for walkers. And a **GR du Pays** trail introduces you to the pretty Petit Morin and Grand Morin valleys east of Paris (see p. 154).

Local tourist offices produce maps and leaflets showing recommended marked paths.

Other activities

Steam train enthusiasts can enjoy a trip from the Parc de Saint-Eutrope near Evry, just south of Paris (Easter to mid-Nov, usually weekends only, ℡ 01-45-81-30-28), or from Le Blanc to Argent-sur-Sauldre, and at Grez-sur-Loing, near Moret-sur-Loing (℡ 01-64-28-67-67).

Travelling by **horse-drawn gypsy caravan** is a fun way of exploring the Sologne. And trips in other horse-drawn vehicles called *calèches* can be made in various places, including Senlis, Chartres and inside the grounds at Versailles. Both *calèches* and *charabancs* (horse-drawn wagons with hoods, and benches for seating) can be hired in the Forêt de Fontainebleau, by the hour, or by the day, including a picnic:

- **Attelages de la Forêt de Fontainebleau**, 9 chemin du Vaudoué, 77760 Achères-la-Forêt, ℡ 01-64-69-86-03, Ⓕ 01-64-24-43-08
- **Attelage de Barbizon 'Pégase'**, 6 rue Diaz, 77630 Barbizon, ℡ 01-64-81-92-35

Hot-air ballooning can be enjoyed at the Château de Chantilly (see p. 136), and in the Brie you can even learn how to pilot a balloon yourself, as well as being taken on a flight:

- **Ferme Relais du Couvent**, 77720 Bréau, ℡ 01-64-38-75-15

Houseboats can be rented on the river Marne, east of Paris, for a weekend or longer:

- **Sinope Evasion**, Port de plaisance, 77410 Claye-Souilly, ℡ 01-60-27-05-51
- **Marne Loisirs**, quai Jacques-Prévert prolongé, 77100 Meaux, ℡ 01-64-34-97-97

Food and drink

Ile de France

Mention the Ile de France to a French gourmet and he or she will wax nostalgic about the wonderful fruit and vegetables produced by the region's market gardeners – the little green kidney beans of Arpajon, Argenteuil's asparagus, peas from Clamart or Saint-Germain, the long white turnips grown in and around Meaux, and tender young carrots from nearby Crécy-la-Chapelle (which gave its name to *potage Crécy*, carrot soup). Then will come a panegyric to top-quality fruit, like the succulent strawberries that ensured the livelihood of the people of Bièvres, or the juicy, sharp-tasting cherries from Montmorency, still commemorated in *canard Montmorency*, duck with cherries.

Inevitably, many of the market gardens, which once supplied the great houses in and around Paris, have been swallowed up as the city and its suburbs encroach on the surrounding area. But the excellent vegetables and salad materials piled high in Paris's street markets are still mostly brought in at dawn by an army of Ile de France market gardeners and smallholders, and some places, especially those furthest from the capital, do still have their own specialities. For instance, Méréville, east of Chartres, proudly proclaims its status as France's 'watercress capital' (see box, p. 48) and local restaurateurs produce mouthwatering cress soups and salads, purées and sauces. Not far away, Milly-la-Forêt has continued to grow its famous 'simples' or medicinal plants, especially mint. And Arpajon's centuries-old Bean Fair is still going strong. The best-known variety is the *chevrier*, a flageolet dried by a special process that makes it look and taste like a fresh bean. Then even if asparagus is rarely grown in Argenteuil these days, you may still find *potage Argenteuil*, asparagus soup, on local menus.

But the region's reputation for excellent produce is not confined to fruit and vegetables. Poultry, too, has a high reputation, especially in Houdan, near Anet, which produces black-and-white hens called simply *poules* (or *poulardes*) *de Houdan*, whose meat has a particularly delicate flavour. The hens reared in the Gâtinais, south of Fontainebleau, are also highly prized. But the Gâtinais is best known for its honey, *miel du Gâtinais*, celebrated in a specialist museum (see p. 185). For honey-with-a-difference you must head for Provins, where rose-growing has long been a speciality: honey flavoured with rose petals may sound strange, but is quite delicious, as are the town's rose jams and confectionery (see **Shopping**).

Provins lies on the southern edge of the Brie plateau, known to cheese-lovers the world over as the home of its unctuous eponymous cheese, made in a number of different versions (see box, p. 58). In sophisticated restaurants, brie may be used to make a sauce, as in *filet de boeuf au Brie de Melun*, fillet of beef served with a sauce made from brie and *crème fraîche*. But you will also find it in more modest places as a filling in *bouchée à la reine*, a large vol-au-vent whose inventor, Louis XV's queen Marie Leszczynska, specified brie as the ideal filling, or in *feuilletés au brie*, flaky pastry pasties filled with softened brie flavoured with chervil, chives or tarragon, or sometimes with paprika.

Forest fare

No eulogy of the Ile de France's raw materials could fail to mention the fruits of its forests. Game and wild mushrooms are among the staples of many a popular local restaurant, especially during the autumn shooting season. Barbizon, on the edge of the Forêt de Fontainebleau, has long been known for its wild boar terrines, and you will find casseroled *sanglier* (adult boar) or *marcassin* (young boar) on local menus. Senlis to the north of the capital is again famous for its game terrines.

Hunting for edible fungi is a favourite weekend pastime for Parisians. The region's game dishes are often flavoured with the prized wild mushrooms that grow in the Forêt d'Ermenonville, the Forêt de Fontainebleau, the Forêt de Rambouillet, or the Forêt de Coye near Chantilly: *cèpes* and *girolles* or *chanterelles*, or the ink-black *trompettes de la mort* (horns of plenty) that seem to have such an affinity with rabbit.

Rural feasts

Rabbit often features in Ile de France cuisine, whose basic repertoire is made up of straightforward country dishes. *Gibelotte de lapin* is a rabbit dish frequently found in country inns and small-town restaurants alongside other filling rural staples like *navarin d'agneau*, ragout of lamb with young vegetables, especially carrots, potatoes and turnip, or *matelote d'anguille*, a tasty stew of eels in wine, flavoured with brandy and spices. *Matelote*, also made with a variety of freshwater fish, was traditionally eaten in the lively *guinguettes* that once lined the banks of the river Marne (see pp. 147–50). Another *guinguette* dish is *friture de la Marne*, whitebait. *Matelotes* are also served in L'Isle-Adam and other villages in the Oise valley, where the *Auberge Ravoux* (see pp. 125–7) is a good place for trying out homely dishes like *gigot d'agneau de sept heures* (slow-cooked lamb).

Among first courses you will find terrines and pâtés made with local game: perhaps *terrine de lièvre* (hare terrine) or *terrine de garenne*, the term used for wild rabbit, particularly tasty when flavoured with horns of plenty mushrooms. In the Brie, *soufflé au Brie* (cheese soufflé made with Brie) or *quiche briarde*, again made with Brie cheese, are common.

On this eastern side of the Ile de France, mustard is much used as a flavouring, as the famous grainy Moutarde de Meaux is made in the town of the same name. *Fricassée de lapin à la Moutarde de Meaux*, a variant on *gibelotte de lapin* with a mustardy sauce, is a classic. More unusual is a fish recipe, *brochet à la moutarde de Meaux*, made with pike.

On the fringes

The official Ile de France may be short on typical regional dishes, but the same cannot be said of the areas just outside it. Here restaurants

Méréville watercress

A good 40 per cent of French watercress, or around 7 million bunches a year, comes from the Essonne *département* south of Paris, and most of it from the little market of Méréville, which has been officially labelled the country's 'watercress capital'. It lies not far from Chartres or Milly-la-Forêt, in the pretty Upper Juine Valley, known for its many springs, which produce enough clear running water for Méréville's growers to cultivate 10 hectares of watercress beds.

To celebrate the prosperity brought by its watercress beds, the town stages an annual Watercress Fair (*Foire au cresson*) over the Easter weekend. And the local tourist office has devised two circuits enabling you to do a tour of the beds, one on foot, the other by car.

Wild watercress has been eaten raw in salads for centuries – one chronicler claims that the French king Saint-Louis (Louis IX) was particularly fond of it. Nowadays, local restaurants use the cultivated leaves both for salads and to make delicate sauces and purées. If you have always thought of watercress as no more than an attractive garnish, a meal at Angerville's beautifully converted coaching inn L'Hôtel de France,★ very close to Méréville, will be a revelation. Chef-owner Anne-Marie Tarrene produces dishes like lightly steamed salmon with a watercress purée that are sheer ambrosia.

For maps showing the beds, contact **Office de Tourisme du Canton de Méréville**, 1 pl. des Halles, 91660 Méréville, Ⓣ 01-64-95-11-02, Ⓕ 01-64-95-18-29.

like to reflect the traditional cuisine of their own region. So in the north, in places like Beauvais or Senlis or Chantilly, you may come across *ficelle picarde*, a type of pancake with a mushroom and ham filling that is a Picardy speciality. In the west, the riverside villages in the Seine Valley show the influence of Normandy. Soups are likely to have a generous dose of cream, cider is much used in sauces, and duck is popular.

Then Chartres has been famous for well over a thousand years for its game and meat pies, called simply *pâté de Chartres* (Chartres pie) or *pâté de Pâques* (Easter pie). Once made with game birds like partridge or plover, or even larks and other small songbirds, it is now generally filled with well-seasoned minced pork, flavoured with truffles for special occasions. The wheat-growing Beauce plain surrounding Chartres is known for its *galettes*, flat pastry cakes, as well as its *omelettes beauceronnes*, made with bacon, potatoes and finely chopped sorrel.

Treats for the sweet-toothed

The outlying areas boast a number of traditional cakes and sweet courses too. As well as *galettes*, Chartres's pastry cooks produce *pâvé de Chartres*, a type of gingerbread, while nearby Illiers-Combray had been known for its little *madeleine* buns long before Marcel Proust immortalized them (see p. 89). Senlis has a cake called a *senlisien*, and in Beauvais, crystallized fruit (*fruits confits*) are a speciality, eaten as they are or used in cakes and puddings.

Crème Chantilly

Cream whipped to a froth, sweetened and, in some versions, lightly flavoured with vanilla, is known in French as *crème Chantilly*. The label 'Chantilly' by itself means 'topped with whipped cream'.

Legend relates that the cream was invented, as a sweet course during grand banquets, by the great Vatel when he was steward to Nicolas Fouquet at Vaux-le-Vicomte (see p. 168). It does certainly seem that it was remarked on as a delicious novelty during the famous last banquet given by Fouquet for Louis XIV in the summer of 1661, though some culinary experts claim that it had been popular in the Ile de France for many years by that date.

As Vatel moved on to Chantilly after Fouquet's downfall, he apparently decided to call the fashionable new pudding 'Chantilly cream'.

A good dollop of *crème Chantilly* (see above) may be served with any of these, and with specialities from other towns near Paris, like Provins, whose *niflettes*, small flaky pastry tarts filled with confectioner's custard, are traditionally eaten on All Saints' Day, but in the Middle Ages were reserved as a treat for orphans. Meaux has its version of gingerbread, *pain d'épices de Meaux*, and royal Versailles, naturally enough, its *pavé du roy*. *Sablés briards* are shortbread flavoured with apples and cider.

A favourite pudding in summer, especially with small children, is *fontainebleau*, a fluffy cream cheese that originated in the town, served with thick cream and a sprinkling of sugar, and at its best accompanied by tiny wild strawberries, or the larger cultivated variety.

Berry flavours

The Berry has a distinctive regional cuisine based particularly on game from the Sologne forests and the marshy Brenne, and on fish from the local rivers and meres – including carp, again from the Brenne. Sauces typically include wine from the Sancerrois and the other Berry vine-growing areas, as in the archetypal Berry dish, *poulet en barbouille*, a tasty chicken casserole whose gravy is traditionally thickened with the blood from the bird, though you can use mashed chicken livers or black pudding instead. This technique is also used for the authentic version of *civet de lapin à la berrichonne*, a stew of rabbit pieces marinaded in wine. Another favourite is *rognons à la berrichonne*, a kidney dish where wine is a key ingredient. And in the Brenne you may find carp prepared in the same way, as *carpe de la Brenne à la berrichonne*.

These are essentially filling country dishes, but Berry's finest chefs, who have banded together to form an association, *Les Tables gourmandes du Berry* (see box, p. 32), are adept at producing subtle variants that still have a pronounced local flavour, yet are lighter than the hearty fare favoured by a rural population used to working long hours in the open air. For instance, you may come across a starter of snails, served without their shells, in a delicate wine sauce with walnuts and locally picked mushrooms. In the Sancerrois, *filets de sole au Sancerre rouge* is fillet of sole with a wine sauce, while *magret de*

Visiting farms

The **Bergeries de Sologne**, a sheep farm not far from Romorantin-Lanthenay, welcomes visitors from May to the end of September. Their Solognot sheep (about 500 ewes and 750 lambs) are 'free range', feeding on grass in the meadows plus cereals made on the farm, and the energetic owners (who speak English – they have worked on a farm in Scotland) will tell you all about rearing, demonstrate shearing and spinning wool, and show you sheepdogs in action.

After the interesting tour, you can taste products made on the farm, and buy some (vacuum-packed or in glass preserving jars) to take home. Their speciality is *fumé d'agneau*, smoked leg of lamb, which you can either buy as is, or in delicious made-up dishes for reheating. Tasting takes place in a picturesque beamed barn and the atmosphere is convivial. But you must contact the farm in advance to arrange a time.

● **Bergeries de Sologne**, Ferme de Jaugeny, 41250 Fontaines-en-Sologne, Ⓣ/Ⓕ 12-54-46-45-61.

Then in the Sancerrois, you can visit a farm 3km south of Sancerre, near Vinon, watch the goats being milked (from about 17.00) and learn how goat's cheese is made. The **Elevage caprin des Garennes** also offers tastings and you can buy cheeses to include in a picnic or take home. Again, contact the farm (or ask at the tourist office in Sancerre).

● **Elevage caprin des Garennes**, Ⓣ 02-48-54-03-85.

---

canard réduction de Sancerre is the name given to lightly cooked duck breasts in a subtle sauce that involves reducing the wine by fast boiling after it has been added to the pan. You will find the term *à la sancerroise* attached to sweetbreads (*ris d'agneau*) and brains (*cervelle*) served with a light and creamy wine-based sauce, while *andouillette au sancerre*, tasty chitterling sausage with a similar sauce, is a moderately priced favourite.

Cheesy treats

Chavignol is also the place to try the inelegantly named goat's cheese *crottin de Chavignol* – *crottin* meaning a sheep or goat's turd. The fresh version, still white and soft, is used for a starter or light lunch dish that has become fashionable outside France in recent years: *crottin chaud en salade*. The cheeses are lightly grilled and served on a slice of country bread, sometimes toasted, surrounded by salad with a vinaigrette dressing.

A more sophisticated starter has lightly melted cheese inside *choux* pastry, grandly called *profiteroles au crottin de Chavignol*. And the cheese also makes a good pie, generally called a *tourte*, or sometimes a *pâté*. You may also be offered a *faux-filet* or other cut of beef with a cheesy sauce called *sauce crottin*.

Then when it comes to the cheese course, you might like to try a speciality known by the Berry term *fromagée*: it consists of *fromage blanc* or *fromage frais* whipped up until light and frothy, then mixed in with crottin de Chavignol curd. It may be served with finely chopped herbs.

Les Journées gastronomiques de Sologne

This extraordinary three-day gourmet event, held in Romorantin-Lanthenay in late October or early November, is a real eye-opener. Tens of thousands of local people, plus visitors from far and wide, cram into a huge marquee to admire the work of catering apprentices and professionals and to taste the produce and products on show.

The prizewinning entries are spectacular set pieces made by aspiring pastry cooks, bakers and pork butchers. The most intricate, demanding days or even weeks of work, are whole scenes that display great artistry as well as technical skill. For instance, the young student *charcutiers* create 'Sologne landscapes' where tiny galantines form the body of ducks floating on a lake of aspic, surrounded by rushes and undergrowth concocted from fronds of asparagus or trumpet-shaped mushrooms, while artfully arranged slices of apple and radish make boar piglets.

But here too you will find colourful displays of curious-shaped gourds with even more peculiar names, like 'devil's horns' or 'Turk's head'. And you can taste (and buy) every conceivable local speciality, ranging from pumpkin tart to *poires tapées* (preserved pears), from prune jam to potted rabbit.

● **Journées gastronomiques de Sologne**, pl. de la Paix, 41200 Romorantin-Lanthenay, Ⓣ 02-54-76-43-89, Ⓕ 02-54-76-96-24

Tasty starters and snacks

Another starter that, like the goat's cheese salad, also makes a good light lunch or supper dish is one of my favourites, a leek tart made like a quiche, with a cream and egg mixture that fluffs up beautifully. A small amount of chopped ham may be added to the leek filling. If you eat this on its own, it is good followed by a plain green salad, or perhaps the salad that is served in country districts with a famous Berry speciality, potato pie (*pâté aux pommes de terre*). This is richer than it sounds, as several tablespoons of *crème fraîche* are added as soon as it comes out of the oven, and then the lid is put back on again. The favourite accompaniment is *pissenlits au lard*, tender young dandelions served with a dressing flavoured with chopped garlic and made with wine vinegar and little squares of fat bacon fried gently until the fat runs.

For a soothing quick lunch or supper, *oeufs au vin* (eggs poached in wine) is hard to beat. The wine is added to some gently fried onions, chopped herbs give flavour, and after 10 minutes the eggs are lightly poached in the wine, then served on toast.

But traditional first courses include a wide range of game pâtés and terrines. The Sologne's game produces terrines of pheasant and hare, wild boar and rabbit. For the finest examples you must visit the extraordinary Sologne gourmet fair in Romorantin-Lanthenay (see above), but Berry charcuteries also offer excellent ingredients for a successful picnic. Here and in local restaurants you will find pâtés and terrines studded with ceps and other wild mushrooms, or venison terrine with bilberries (*terrine de biche aux airelles*). Wild boar and rabbit *rillettes* (shredded and potted) are also common, and you may be offered wild boar salami (*saucisson sec de sanglier*).

Then pumpkins and squashes and other gourd-like vegetables are used to make a range of savoury tarts and flans, usually called *tarte à la citrouille*, as well as pies and pasties. Pumpkin soup is a favourite starter. And fishy starters include terrines with carp or pike.

Choosing a main course

Fish from the Berry's meres and rivers feature in a wide range of main courses, again carp and pike, but also *sandre* (pike-perch or zander), as well as *écrevisses* (crayfish or crawfish). If you like frogs, you should be able to find them on menus in and around the Brenne.

Game lovers are in their element in the Berry, which is a good place to try game birds that are not so easy to find elsewhere, like *col-vert* (mallard). Rabbit is also given star treatment here, especially the young creature known as *lapereau*. Look out for *filet de lapereau rôti aux herbes*, roast rabbit flavoured with fragrant local herbs, and for a Berry staple, *lapin farci*. The rabbit is marinated for twenty-four hours in white wine with chopped carrot, onion and various herbs and sea-sonings, then stuffed with pork forcemeat seasoned with nutmeg and more herbs, and stewed slowly in the marinade.

Lentils may accompany rabbit too. Green lentils, called *lentilles vertes du Berry*, are considered a great delicacy and are a good thing to take home, as they are not easily found outside their native soil. And locally picked mushrooms are served with game, meat and even fish dishes, especially in the autumn.

Ending with a flourish

After the cheese board, which will naturally consist mainly of local goat's cheeses, from Valençay as well as the Sancerrois (see p. 155), your appetite will be reawakened by traditional Berry puddings and desserts. The best known are *millas*, a cherry pudding, made with the same batter as the thick pancakes called *sanciaux*. *Poirat* is a pear pie, and the juicy local pears are also poached in wine. Walnut tarts are often served, and so are prune tarts, made with prunes cooked in red wine, then mashed to a purée. In the Sologne, *tarte Tatin* is a favourite – the famous upside-down caramelized apple tart, more apple than tart, invented locally by the Tatin sisters.

An accidental culinary invention

The beginning of the railway era in France came with the opening, on 26 August 1837, of the country's first rail line, running between Paris and Saint-Germain-en-Laye. But culinary lore has it that that first ceremonial run (as far as Le Pecq) represented another landmark in French history.

The train embarrassingly ground to a halt on a steep gradient and it was clear that the celebratory lunch for the top brass present would have to be held up. The panic-stricken chef tossed his *pommes frites* (chips or French fries) into sizzling hot fat for a second time, and *voilà*, they puffed up into the airy little concoctions that, as *pommes soufflées*, are a main-stay of restaurant menus the world over.

Hilly Sancerre, seen beyond the vines

Berry wines

Although excellent *chasselas* grapes are grown for the table at Thomery, near Moret-sur-Loing, from cuttings takes from vines allegedly planted by François Ier at Fontainebleau, the Ile de France is not a wine-producing region. (Cider is made on the fringes, near the Norman border in the northwest and in the Gâtinais in the southeast.)

But the Berry produces some high-quality wines, especially the dry and aromatic **Sancerre** made in and around the little hilltop town of the same name, overlooking the river Loire. Most Sancerres are white, made from the Sauvignon grape. Some experts reckon that the finest of all the many wines produced by the Sauvignon grape come from the Sancerrois, thanks to the specific soil conditions and a good climate – it rarely suffers from the hailstorms that bedevil the Pouilly fumé vineyards round Pouilly-sur-Loire, just the other side of the Loire.

These wines have a pale yellow tinge and an exhilarating, subtle taste that is particularly good with fish and shellfish. But they are also considered to be the perfect accompaniment to the local goat's cheeses, though not for any other cheese. They are also drunk as an apéritif.

A tiny quantity of deliciously refreshing dry **Sancerre rosé** is also made, from the Pinot noir grape. Its light and delicate salmony hue often belies its intensely fruity taste. It is just right with charcuterie and other meat starters, and is also drunk with main courses of white meat. The Pinot noir grape is also the basis of **Sancerre rouge**, again made in minute quantities. According to one authority, this is one red wine that will win over drinkers who maintain a firm preference for whites. It is light, with a fragrance resembling violets, and can be drunk at any time of day, though it is best with red meat, with meat in wine and other sauces, and with game. It is also a good accompaniment to cheese.

Sancerres are generally reasonably priced for their quality, offering better value for money than many French wines, mainly because, although they are popular, they are thought of in France as

53

A Berry way with coffee

Sometimes in private houses in France, and particularly in the Berry, after-lunch or after-dinner coffee will not be served in the usual small cup with matching saucer but in tall, tapering china goblets similar in shape to a heavy-based wine glass, with a short, thick stem. These goblets, which need to be held by the base to avoid burning your fingers, are called *mazagrans*.

The term originally referred to a drink of coffee liberally laced with brandy and served in thick glasses, as drunk by a regiment of 130-odd chasseurs or infantrymen from the Berry who famously withstood a siege of an Algerian village called Mazagran in February 1840. The besieging troops, fighting for the dashing emir Abd el-Kadar, numbered no fewer than 14,000, and the French soldiers later claimed that they could never have survived their three-day ordeal without regular slugs of the drink they now dubbed *un mazagran*.

When they returned home they introduced their fellow Berrichons to the potent potion. Soon an enterprising porcelain factory in Bourges started producing the thick china *mazagrans* that soon became popular in cafés and restaurants all over France.

petits vins, 'minor wines', as indeed are most of the Loire Valley wines. They can be tasted and bought at the **Auberge Joseph Mellot** in the town's main square, and also in several cellars in the surrounding wine villages. It is safest to ask at the Sancerre tourist office for advice, as some only take groups for most of the year, and others change their opening times frequently. If you prefer to take your chance, villages like Bué, Chavignol and Verdigny will usually have at least one place open. One of the best bets is the **Clos de La Perrière** in Verdigny (℡ 02-48-54-16-93, Ⓕ 02-48-54-11-54), whose cellars are in the quarry that produced the stone for Bourges Cathedral. Both wine and goat's cheese can be tasted here. Sancerre holds wine fairs over the Whitsun weekend (local wines only) and in late August (*grands crus* from all over France).

Another *apellation d'origine controlée* wine is made around **Menetou-Salon**, on the western edge of the Sancerrois. Made from the same grapes as Sancerre, it is again dry and fruity. Whites, reds and rosés are all produced, but in small quantities.

The Sauvignon grape is also the basis of two white wines produced in places west of Bourges. The pretty village of **Quincy** beside the river Cher makes very dry, light and fresh-tasting wines, fruity and fragrant, that are particularly good with oysters. They are also drunk with other seafood, and with goat's cheese, which is made locally. **Reuilly**, a small town near Issoudun with some attractive late-Renaissance buildings, has been producing wine since the Middle Ages. Again fruity and aromatic, it has an intense flavour and is often seen on wine lists in chic Paris restaurants. A small amount of red and rosé Reuilly is also made, from Pinot noir and Pinot gris grapes respectively.

The rosé wines have a raspberry note, while the reds are slightly spicy. If you visit Reuilly in July and August, you will also find a small wine museum open.

Châteaumeillant in southern Berry, where wine has been produced since Roman times, is known for its light, very fragrant *vins gris*, though some generally less distinguished red is also made, with a ruby hue.

Lastly, in the northwest of the region, **Valençay**, dominated by its huge château and known for its goat's cheeses, makes wine that does not have the coveted AOC label, but is classed as VDQS (*vin délimité de qualité supérieure*). These are light wines made from a wide variety of grapes. They tend to have a flinty taste and are pleasantly drinkable, especially when young, if not particularly distinguished.

Shopping

Shopping for **food specialities** to take home can be one of the pleasures of your trips out of Paris. **Game terrines** and **pâtés**, in glass preserving jars (*bocaux*) or glazed earthenware pots, are particularly good. Glass **jars of tiny peas or carrots** from the Ile de France's market gardens are another good buy. Or you might like to buy some **made-up dishes**, like the unusual **smoked lamb** from a Sologne sheep farm (see p. 50).

Moutarde de Meaux is probably France's best-known **mustard**, while **heather honey** is a Sologne speciality. Miel du Gâtinais is another highly prized honey – it even has a museum devoted to it (see p. 185). In these major producing areas, honey is treated like wine, so you can buy *miel nouveau* (new season's honey), just as you can enjoy Beaujolais nouveau. Then Provins is the place for an unusual honey flavoured with rose petals. The town also offers virtually anything else made or flavoured with roses: delicious **rose petal jam**, **rose-flavoured sweets**, **essence of roses**, attractive bottles of **rose water** (said to cure insomnia), **rose-flavoured soaps**. Here too you can buy **old rose bushes**.

Confectionery specialities are legion, many of them with long histories. They make good presents, prettily packed in miniature wooden crates, wickerwork boxes or baskets, or simply in sellophane tied with a brightly coloured ribbon. Here are a few suggestions:

- **chasselas de Fontainebleau** (shaped like grapes)
- **chevriers d'Arpajon** (shaped like flageolet beans)
- **demoiselles de Montrond** (from Saint-Amand-Montrond)
- **forestines de Bourges** (see box, p. 57)
- **fûts de Pinard** (from Sancerre, shaped like wine barrels)
- **Malices du Loup** (Sologne, orange-flavoured almond and hazelnut sweets)
- **massepain d'Issoudun** (see box, p. 56)
- **Mentchikoff** (Chartres, see box, p. 87)
- **Petits Berrichons** (Berry, apple-flavoured sweets)
- **praslines**
- **sucre d'orge des religieuses de Moret** (see box, p. 185)

As for **cakes and biscuits**, look out for **sablés de Nançay** (a type of shortbread), **croquets du Berry** (hazelnut biscuits), **macarons de Melun** (macaroons), and **pain d'épices à l'ancienne au miel du Gâtinais** (honey-flavoured gingerbread).

For **cheese**-lovers, the region east of Paris is **Brie** country. You can also find **Coulommiers** here, while the Sancerrois is famous for its little **crottin de Chavignol** goat's cheeses (see p. 204). These are used to flavour other products, like the excellent **croustades du Berry** cocktail biscuits. The same region is also the key place to buy wine, though the Berry has other good wines too (see **Food and drink**).

Other special food products include **poires tapées à l'ancienne**, little jars of pears dried by a secret process, delicious steeped in wine or champagne, then stewed with sugar and cinnamon; **lentilles vertes du Berry** (green lentils); and **cotignac**, quince paste, usually sold in little wooden crates, and eaten cut into squares. For fans of frogs' legs, **mousse de grenouille** (frog mousse) is sometimes found in the Brenne.

Tourist boards are keen to promote local food products and publish helpful booklets (see box, p. 58). These sometimes also give details of where you can buy local **craft work**, and visit artists and craftspeople in their studios, as well as listing the many craft fairs (*foires à l'artisanat*) that take place, especially in the summer months.

Chantilly has long been famous for its **lace**, Provins for its **glazed tiles**, Gien for its **faïence**, La Borne and Fontgombault Abbey for their **pottery**. If **porcelain** appeals to you, the Cher *département* has devised a tourist itinerary called La Route de la Porcelaine that will guide you to specialist shops and workshops, as well as museums. Still in the Berry, look out for miniature copies of the traditional musical instruments still played there (see box, p. 15), or indeed the real thing if you are musically inclined – though they are highly decorative too. In Beauvais, for centuries the home of the royal tapestry

Massepain d'Issoudun

The main confectionery speciality of the Berry town of Issoudun is *massepain* or marzipan cake, a delicious pale gold concoction first made by the local nuns in the 1780s, shortly before the French Revolution. It soon became very popular and legend has it that Napoleon was such a fan of the nuns' secret recipe that he had their marzipan cake sent to him when he was a prisoner on St Helena.

Honoré de Balzac referred to it in rhapsodic terms in his novel *La Rabouilleuse* (1841-2), which is largely set in Issoudun. It was, he wrote, 'one of the finest inventions of French confectionery, and one that no chef, cook, confectioner or jam maker has ever been able to imitate'. Two years later Balzac's passion for *massepain* took concrete form when he opened a confectioner's in the rue Vivienne in Paris, near the Bibliothèque nationale, selling only this one speciality. Thousands of households received his leaflet enthusing about the shop and it became for a while the chic place to be seen, though like so many of Balzac's commercial ventures, its success proved short-lived.

Forestines de Bourges

Berry's capital, the cathedral city of Bourges, boasts what is allegedly the earliest soft-centred hard sweet ever made. **Forestines**, invented in 1878, are filled with chocolate *praliné*, a deliciously smooth mixture of ground roasted almonds and hazelnuts flavoured with chocolate. The outside is shiny and pale, in ice-cream colours like pistachio, vanilla, coffee and chocolate, and the sweets are longish and thin and individually wrapped in sellophane, with the ends twisted in traditional style. They are sold in tall oval tins or boxes with a latticework pattern, which make good presents to take home. And they can be bought, along with flat round yellow and green tins of other 'Berry specialities' with *praliné* fillings, in the attractive shop built by the confectioner who first dreamed them up.

He was one Georges Forest, from Bourbon-l'Archambault a little way south of the Berry. After his journeyman years travelling round France to learn his trade, he settled in Bourges and opened his first confectioner's there in 1825. Over half a century later, on Christmas Eve 1878, he took out a patent for his invention, proudly naming it after himself.

Forestines were soon enjoying great popularity both in France and abroad, and six years later Forest was wealthy enough to commission an impressive 'Maison des Forestines' (Forestines House) in the place Cujas in Bourges. The five-storey building with its wrought-iron balconies is still standing. And the shop at street level is still exactly as he planned it over a century ago, with mirrors and fat glass jars and coffered ceiling and twirly art nouveau decoration.

workshops, modern **tapestries**, or reproductions of traditional and historical designs, can be bought. And Chartres, so famous for the medieval stained glass in its cathedral, has a centre where small **stained-glass** items are sold (see p. 86).

Many châteaux, abbeys and museums these days have attractive small shops selling not only the usual postcards, posters and slides, but also a good range of **books** connected with the history of the building or the area. For instance Royaumont Abbey has a big stock of titles on religious art and architecture, in several languages. Here too you can buy **cassettes and CDs** of the medieval music in which its musical centre specializes, just as Noirlac Abbey sells **Gregorian chant tapes and CDs. Playing cards** and other items featuring the historical figures who lived in châteaux or palaces are often found.

Among specialist museums with particularly interesting shops are the one in Jouy-en-Josas, with a wide range of very attractive items in **toile de Jouy** printed cotton (see p. 81), and the Mini'stoire at the Château de Meillant, selling beautifully made miniature shops and other buildings. At Claude Monet's house in Giverny you can buy copies of his stylish **yellow and blue china**, and at the Absinthe Museum in Auvers-sur-Oise, both antique **absinthe spoons** and modern copies, which are also on sale at the Auberge Ravoux in Auvers. The shop below Van Gogh's bedroom also has some most attractive **jewellery**, as well as books on painting, and **traditional table napkins** used in country bistros.

Buying local produce

Promotion of local produce is a major preoccupation for regional tourist boards these days, now that so many visitors are keen to eat organic, free-range, or at any rate quality-controlled food, and enjoy visiting local producers and buying from them. Ask for brochures listing farmers, smallholders and other producers willing to sell honey, cheese, eggs, poultry, freshly cured ham, fruit and vegetables, sometimes freshwater fish, direct to the public, through farm shops or more informally. In wine regions, winemakers are also included.

Les Produits fermiers du Berry (Berry farm produce) is one such booklet, published by a body called Farming and Tourism in the Indre, and including producers of angora and mohair wool. It is available from **Agriculture et Tourisme dans l'Indre**, Maison de l'Agriculture, 36022 Châteauroux Cedex, and from many local tourist offices. Another focusing specifically on cheese producers in the Sologne entitled to bear the green logo depicting stylized bullrushes and marshland and the word 'Sologne' is available from tourist offices (ask for information on 'Les fromages fermiers de Sologne'). See also box on p. 50 for details of a sheep farm specializing in lamb.

The various Ile de France *départements* use the label 'Produits et Terroir' to denote local producers whose produce is rigorously controlled and who have formed an association under that name to promote their wares and to maintain standards. A series of booklets or leaflets are published, available from departmental tourist boards (see p. 19 for addresses).

Some of the farms listed will make your life easy by selling you baskets full of the ingredients for a splendid picnic, nicely wrapped so that they also make good presents to take home. One example of a farm offering these *paniers gourmands* (gourmet baskets') is **La Ferme du Bon Accueil**, which is convenient for the Loing Valley (77130 Cannes-Ecluses, Ⓣ 01-64-32-05-36, Ⓕ 01-64-32-33-94). Another, in Brie country, roughly equidistant from Rozay-en-Brie and Coulommiers, is **Gaec de Lugin** (12 rue des Fermes, La Fontaine-Pépin, 77970 Jouy-le-Châtel, Ⓣ 01-64-01-59-15, Ⓕ 01-64-01-58-61).

The king of cheeses

Brie de Meaux is acknowledged by true cheese lovers as one of the world's finest cheeses with a soft pâte (the term used for the inside of a cheese), encased by the outer rind. It was also the first French cheese to be granted the official AOC label – an *appellation d'origine contrôlée*, just like that given to wine.

But it had earned a loftier title during the Congress of Vienna held at the end of the Napoleonic Wars, starting in November 1814. Two of the delegates, the towering European statesman Prince Metternich, Austria's foreign minister, and the French politician and diplomat Talleyrand, decided to organize a cheese competition. Brie de Meaux won hands down, whereupon it was pronounced 'Le roi des fromages', ('The king of cheeses').

A little history

The Ile de France: some historical pointers

Just as the Ile de France has never had clearly defined geographical boundaries, so it has no true historical unity. Indeed, the term was not used at all until as late as the 13th century. Excavations have revealed that the central part of what is now called the Paris Basin was certainly inhabited in the prehistoric era. The region is dotted with prehistoric sites, ranging from Guerville (near Mantes) in the west to Coulommiers in the east; from modern Beauvais in the north to Ecoulles or Genevraye (near Moret-sur-Loing) in the south.

The region was probably first settled in the 6th century BC, by various **Celtic tribes**. Alongisde the Parisi, who gave their name to Paris, they included the **Meldi**, who are commemorated in the name of **Meaux**, once their stronghold. A couple of hundred years later, in the **4th century**, another Celtic tribe, the **Belgae**, settled in the north, along the valley of today's River Oise.

The **Roman Conquest** came in 52 BC, after Caesar had soundly defeated the Gallic chieftain Vercingetorix in battle. The Romans, in their usual businesslike way, turned the Parisii's island stronghold into a city they called Lutetia, and gradually set about colonizing the surrounding region. They built roads and villas, and towns like what is now Beauvais, on the site of a fortress called Bratuspontium. But the period of prosperity under the Romans was soon shattered by the **Barbarian invasions** that eventually led to the collapse of the Roman Empire and put an end to the Gallo-Roman period in the **5th century**. The Salian **Franks** came out on top in the fierce struggles against and among the various invading hordes, especially after Attila and his Huns had been defeated at a major battle east of Paris, in **451**.

In **486** the Franks' king Clovis, founder of the **Merovingian** dynasty, beat a Roman army at Soissons, east of Compiègne. Ten years later he became a Christian and in **497** entered Paris. The whole of the region surrounding Paris was now part of the Frankish kingdom that gave its name to France – and in due course to the Ile de France.

The chronological table on the following pages spotlights some of the key moments in the history of the Ile de France. To find out more, look up the place names given in bold type in the index and turn to the sections where they are described in greater detail.

Some key dates

c 500	Clovis makes **Senlis** a royal residence
843	Treaty of Verdun makes Charlemagne's grandson Charles II ('Charles the Bald') king of what is now the Ile de France
878	Charles the Bald donates Virgin Mary's chemise to **Chartres**
c 950	**Provins** becomes a major commercial centre
987	Hugues Capet, founder of the Capetian dynasty, elected

	king at **Senlis**; his wife Adelaide founds a royal chapel there, dedicated to St Fraimbault
1128	**Vaux-de-Cernay** Abbey built
c 1130	Royal hunting lodge built at **Fontainebleau**
1136	**Chaâlis** Abbey founded
1153	Work starts on **Senlis** Cathedral
1194	**Chartres**'s Romanesque cathedral burns down
1222	Philippe-Auguste builds castle at **Dourdan**
1227	Work starts on **Beauvais** Cathedral
1228	**Royaumont** Abbey founded by 'Saint Louis' (Louis IX)
1275	Edmund of Lancaster marries widow of Count of Champagne and becomes lord of **Provins**, adding the town's red rose to his family's coat of arms (see box, p. 159)
1260	New Gothic cathedral consecrated at **Chartres**
1337	Beginning of Hundred Years' War; Ile de France theatre of much fighting
1472	Citizens of **Beauvais** withstand siege by Charles the Bold, led by 'Jeanne Hachette' (see box, p. 39)
1527	François 1er commissions group of Italian artists, including Primaticcio, to rebuild **Fontainebleau**
1528	Work starts on palace at **Chantilly**
1547	François 1er dies at **Rambouillet**
1559	On Henri II's death, his favourite Diane de Poitiers retires to **Anet**
1573	Tower and spire of **Beauvais** Cathedral collapse
1602	Angélique Arnaud becomes abbess of **Port-Royal**, at age of 11
1624	Work starts on modest hunting lodge for Louis XIII at **Versailles**
1638	Louis XIV born at **Saint-Germain-en-Laye**
1661	Nicolas Fouquet, royal finance superintendent, precipitates his downfall by throwing a lavish party at **Vaux-le-Vicomte**; Louis XIV promptly decides to outdo him by building a magnificent palace of his own at **Versailles**
1664	Louis's chief minister, Jean-Baptiste Colbert, founds tapestry factory at **Beauvais**
1674	Françoise d'Aubigny, widow of poet Paul Scarron and royal favourite, buys **Maintenon**
1685	Louis XIV signs revocation of Edict of Nantes at **Fontainebleau**
1682	Palace of **Versailles** becomes seat of court and government
1689	Spire of Saint-Quiriace church in **Provins** collapses; exiled James II of England takes refuge in **Saint-Germain-en-Laye** and sets up court there
1725	Marie Leszcznyska, daughter of King Stanislas of Poland, is ceremonially greeted by future husband Louis XV at **Moret-sur-Loing**
1756	Royal porcelain factory opened at **Sèvres**
1757	Royal mistress Madame de Pompadour rents Château de **Champs**
1760	Christophe-Philippe Oberkampf opens fabric workshop at **Jouy-en-Josas**

1774	Marie-Antoinette's 'hamlet' is built at **Versailles**
1778	Jean-Jacques Rousseau stays at **Ermenonville**, raves about its natural beauty, then dies there
1789	Estates-General meet at **Versailles**, as prelude to French Revolution; five months later royal family are forced by Paris mob to leave the palace for the capital
1799	Josephine Bonaparte buys **La Malmaison**
1814	Napoleon abdicates, bidding emotional farewell to his Old Guard at **Fontainebleau**
1815	Maison Fournaise opens on Ile de **Chatou**
1837	France's first rail line opens, between Paris and **Saint-Germain-en-Laye**; Louis-Philippe turns Palace of **Versailles** into Museum of French History
1846	Work starts on Alexandre Dumas *père*'s Château de Monte-Cristo at **Port-Marly**
1847	Théodore Rousseau rents cottage in **Barbizon**, which soon becomes artists' centre
1871	Wilhelm I proclaimed German Kaiser in Galerie des Glaces in **Versailles**, following French defeat in Franco-Prussian War
1882	Marcel Proust's asthma puts a stop to his summer holidays at Illiers, now renamed **Illiers-Combray** in his honour
1883	Ivan Turgenev dies in his '*dacha*' at **Bougival**; Claude Monet and family move to **Giverny**
1890	Vincent van Gogh shoots himself in **Auvers-sur-Oise** after two frenzied months of painting and dies two days later

A cathedral for the new millennium

If you thought that French cathedrals were all Gothic, or just possibly late 19th-century, you would be proved wrong at **Evry**, a New Town of mainly high-rise buildings just south of Paris (see p. 8). Its **Notre Dame de la Résurrection**, consecrated in May 1997, is the first new cathedral to be built in France for over a century and a half.

The local parishioners attended their first mass there two years earlier, at Easter 1995. Their new place of worship is an uncompromisingly modern cylinder with sloping walls of red brick, more reminiscent of a castle than a cathedral with its arrow-slit windows, though the interior turns out to be much lighter than you would expect, as light streams in through the roof and through a circular window that presumably gives a nod to the rose windows of old. The sloping top of the cylinder bristles not with machicolations, but with a couple of dozen lime trees. And a metal belfry bears the only external concession to tradition – a cross.

The cathedral's interior, an impressive space with no aisles or transept, seats 1440 – symbolically, exactly the same number as the nearby mosque. It has modern stained glass and a 19th-century figure of Christ carved in Tanzania. And a **Museum of Religious Art** has been cleverly concealed between the inner and outer walls.

Open daily (except over lunchtime on Sun); guided tours Sat mornings and in the afternoon on Sun and public hols. For times, check with local tourist offices or ☏ 01-64-97-93-55.

1897	Duc d'Aumale's Will leaves **Chantilly** and his fabulous collections to the Institut de France
1899	Alfred Sisley, Franco-British painter, dies at **Moret-sur-Loing**
1907	Edward VII of England visits **Breteuil** Château
1912	Maurice Denis buys Le Prieuré at **Saint-Germain-en-Laye**
1914	First Battle of the Marne ends in French defeat
1919	Treaty of **Versailles**, after Allied victory in First World War
1940	**Beauvais**'s tapestry factory destroyed by bombing1965
1965	Government takes decision to build five New Towns round Paris (see box, p. 8)
1967	'Machine de **Marly**' stops functioning
1981	First-ever cross between lions and tigers succeeds at **Thoiry**
1985	**Chevreuse Valley** designated as nature park
1989	**Parc Astérix** opens
1992	Eurodisney, now **Disneyland Paris**, opens at **Marne-la-Vallée**
1994	Jean Tinguely's *Cyclops* unveiled near **Milly-la-Forêt**
1997	First new cathedral for over 150 years consecrated at Evry (see box, p. 61)

The Berry: a shared history

Unlike the inhabitants of the Ile de France, true *Berrichons* do share a historic destiny that has enabled the region to retain its identity over the centuries. The Berry was certainly inhabited in the **pre-historic era**, particularly the valley carved out by the river Creuse in the southwest. The collections of the **Musée du Berry**, in Bourges, and the **Argentomagus Archeological Museum** outside Argenton-sur-Creuse provide ample evidence of this. But the first settlers of whom much is known were a bronze-working Celtic tribe called the **Bituriges**, one of several rival peoples who migrated westwards to occupy most of what is now France. Their name, probably taken from a distant founder called Biturix, meaning 'master of the universe', is the origin of the term 'Berry'. They appear to have reached this part of the world in about the **7th century BC**, and according to the Roman historian Livy were already exercising considerable sway over large stretches of ancient Gaul by the **6th century** – a quotation from Livy about them features on Bourges's coat of arms: *Penes Bituriges summa imperii*, meaning roughly 'The Bituriges hold supreme power'. Among their fortified settlements were **Argento-magus** (now Saint-Marcel, see p. 214), **Avaricum** (the forerunner of Bourges) and **Mediolanum** (modern Châteaumeillant).

Some key dates

c AD 300	Avaricum is capital of Aquitania Prima (Gallo-Roman province)
468	Visigoths conquer Romans at **Déols**
507	Franks drive out Visigoths; Berry subsequently becomes seat of counts and viscounts

917	Abbey founded at **Déols**
1101	Philip I, King of France, buys county of Bourges
1130	Abbey founded at **Noirlac**
1195	Work starts on **Bourges** cathedral
1200	King John of England forced to hand over Berry possessions to Blanche of Castille, future wife of Louis VIII
1230	Count of Champagne hands over **Sancerre** to French crown
1356	Black Prince's army destroys parts of **Châteauroux** and **Issoudun**
1360	Dukedom of Berry set up
c 1411	Jean, Duc de Berry, commissions famous Book of Hours (p. 134); **Bourges** is now brilliant centre of art and commerce
1422	Charles VII ('King of Bourges') proclaimed king at Mehun-sur-Yèvre; Sir John Stewart of Darnley becomes lord of **Aubigny**
1429/30	Joan of Art spends winter in Bourges and visits **Culan**
1451	Jacques Coeur arrested (p. 200)
1487	**Bourges** largely destroyed by fire
1540s	**Sancerre** becomes first of several Protestant centres in Berry
1573	**Sancerre** besieged by militant Catholic aristocrats
1605	Duc de Sully, Henri IV's chief minister, founds **Henrichemont**
1621	Prince de Condé captures **Sancerre** and tears down its walls
1652	**Saint-Amand-Montrond** besieged
1835	Honoré de Balzac stays with Zulma Carraud (p. 223) near **Issoudun** and collects material for *La Rabouilleuse*, partly set in the town
1839	Frédéric Chopin and George Sand spend first summer together at **Nohant**
1891	Future Alain-Fournier's family moves to **Epineuil-le-Fleuriel**
1974	President Giscard d'Estaing's government ends tax breaks for entertaining business clients at shooting parties: **Sologne** badly affected, with many job losses
1977	First 'Bourges Spring' popular music festival (p. 40)
1989	**Brenne** becomes official nature park

Pinpointing the centre of France

Berry is right in the middle of France, but working out the exact centre of the country is another matter. The village of **Bruère-Allichamps** in the south of the region, near Noirlac Abbey, seems to have won the battle. A 3rd-century Gallo-Roman milestone which was excavated locally has been set up as a marker for the geographic centre. However, **Saulzais-le-Potier**, 16km south of Saint-Amand-Montrond, also has a 'centre of France' marker stone, and its claim is supported by local experts. In recent years the National Geographic Institute has supported a third claimant, **Vesdun**, just east of the Château de Culan. Here a mosaic depicting France has been erected at the spot plumped for by the researchers in the *commune* called Le Coussier.

The Berry's Scots connection

The French dauphin, soon to be Charles VII, was so grateful for the support of Sir John Stewart of Darnley, a member of the powerful (and royal) Scots House of Stewart, in fighting the English army under Thomas, Duke of Clarence at the Battle of Baugé in March 1421 that he rewarded him with the lordship of Concressault in the Berry. Then the following year, when Charles ascended the throne on the death of his insane father, known as Charles the Foolish, he presented his Scots ally with another Berry lordship, Aubigny. Seven years later the new lord of Aubigny was killed during the siege of Orléans, but the town remained a possession of the Stuarts (as the French invariably spell them) for the next two and half centuries, right down to 1672.

Sir John was succeeded by his son, another John, also known as Bérault, who started building the nearby château of La Verrerie (p. 189) – its lovely setting between lake and forest still has a distinctly Scots flavour. Next in line was Robert Stewart, Maréchal d'Aubigny, who fought for François I in Italy. On his return he built Aubigny's château and also completed La Verrerie, which is still lived in by indirect descendants.

But the Stewarts were not the only Scots in the Berry. Local records show that eleven of their countrymen owned substantial houses in Bourges and that the king's bodyguard was made up entirely of Scots. Many of these noblemen married local girls and some Gallicized their names almost beyond recognition – Quenede for Kennedy, for instance. They were followed by a whole colony of Scots weavers, glass blowers and other craftsmen and tradespeople, who settled in and around Aubigny. The town's Scots connection is still cherished. The Musée de la Vieille Alliance celebrates the Auld Alliance between Scotland and France that had led to the Scots troops' presence at Baugé. And every year on 14 July many Scots still travel to Aubigny for a whole series of revelries.

Sancerre, too, had a Scots colony in the mid-18th century, started by Jacobite exiles after the Battle of Culloden. The distinguished soldier Marshal MacDonald (1765–1840) was a descendant of the dozen Scots families who settled there. He was brought up in Sancerre (his house is still standing, in the rue MacDonald) and rose to the rank of Marshal of France after playing a key part in Napoleon's victory at the Battle of Wagram (1809).

A checklist of architectural styles

Dates are approximate, as there was much overlapping, but this will give you a rough idea of what style was prevalent when:

Romanesque	late 10th to early 12th century
Early Gothic	early 12th to early 13th century
Gothic	13th and 14th centuries
Late (or Flamboyant) Gothic	late 14th to early 16th centuries
Renaissance	16th century
Classical	17th and 18th centuries
Directoire	1790s
Empire	1810s
Second Empire	1850s and 1860s

Ile de France ~ southwest of Paris

The forested region immediately southwest of Paris boasts the Ile de France's most popular sight, the majestic royal palace at **Versailles**, just north of the **Vallée de Chevreuse**, an oasis of greenery ringed by urban development, where you can combine walking, biking or riding with visiting two châteaux – **Breteuil** and **Dampierre** – as well as the ruins of two abbeys – **Port-Royal-des-Champs** and **Les Vaux-de-Cernay**. Further south, the **Forêt de Rambouillet** is another mecca for Parisians in need of fresh air and exercise, as is the **Parc de Sceaux**, to the east.

In this area you can ponder the role of royal favourites by studying Diane de Poitiers's **Château d'Anet**, and Madame de Maintenon's pretty château of the same name beside the river Eure, which also flows through the old town of **Chartres**, dominated by its great Gothic cathedral, visible for miles across the cereal-growing plain of the **Beauce**. Anyone interested in French literature should continue on to **Illiers-Combray**, with its Proustian associations, as well as visiting the Victor Hugo museum in **Bièvres**. Bièvres also has an old-established photography museum, while nearby **Jouy-en-Josas** has a good display of the fabrics to which it has given its name, and **Sèvres** a famous porcelain collection.

This area is on the whole well served by public transport, with

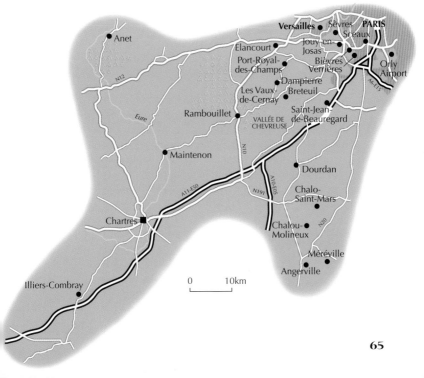

RER and rail lines reaching most places, though you sometimes have to change from one to the other. Versailles is particularly well served, and also makes a good base for reaching other places and sights. Bike hire is available in the Vallée de Chevreuse and in the Forêt de Rambouillet, where riding can also be arranged. You can even cycle round the lovely grounds at Versailles, or go rowing on the canal near the palace. Walkers have many opportunities, including the GR11 hiking trail, which sets out from the Château de Sceaux.

1 Versailles

The historian John Julius Norwich has described Versailles as the most palatial of palaces, 'just as its creator, Louis XIV, was the most magnificent of monarchs'. Few of the four million plus visitors who admire its splendours every year would disagree with this. But the **Château de Versailles** lying only 23 kilometres west of the capital, is far more than a showcase for past French glories. Its symbolic and historical significance make it the most interesting of places for anyone interested in France's history and in the character of her people, despite what can sometimes be the rigours of a visit. These rigours are thankfully liable to diminish over the period down to 2010, as a scheme is set in motion to create 'le Grand Versailles', inspired by the great success of 'le Grand Louvre' in Paris.

The long queues in the courtyard, exposed to the elements on this notoriously windy hill, will be channelled via a stylish new entrance in the **Grand Commun du Roi**, a huge building originally designed to house the kitchens and administrative offices for a palace peopled by as many as ten thousand courtiers, government ministers and officials, as well as the extended royal family. This has recently been vacated by the army and reacquired by the palace to form a large reception area, an exhibition gallery, a museum shop, a bank, a café, maybe even a post office, plus library and documentation centre, and – again an idea inspired by the born-again Louvre – a glassed-over courtyard filled with some of the sculptures carved for the vast gardens but now languishing unseen in storerooms. The woefully inadequate lavatories will be replaced by proper modern facilities, in more generous numbers, and the gloomy basement cafeteria should be superseded by a restaurant-cum-tearoom.

Other plans include the reopening of the **Museum of French History**, initially set up by France's last king, Louis-Philippe, then restored and reorganized in the 1960s, but never fully reopened. The **Grandes Ecuries**, one of two elegant stable blocks, will also be open to the public, and it is hoped to lay on frequent equestrian displays. Then more restoration is planned in the beautiful grounds, now covering only 800 odd hectares compared to the original 3000 hectares, but still vast enough to afford many hours of happy strolling, or peaceful meditation on the fate of kings.

Perhaps most exciting of all, a plan is afoot to bring the palace back to life by staging a full programme of plays, concerts and ballets, some of them, if all goes well, in the enchanting little theatre built in the grounds by Marie-Antoinette. Together with the famous '*Fêtes de Nuit*' spectaculars (see p. 75), this should help to give a real sense of what life was like for courtiers in the days of Versailles's presiding genius, the Sun King. The king regularly spent a couple of hours a day dancing, listened to music even when he was dying, and staged a series of extravaganzas in the gardens, featuring the work of the finest dramatists, poets and musicians of the *Grand Siècle,* France's golden age in the arts, even while the palace itself was still a building site.

Golden Age

A little history

In fact much of Versailles must have been a building site for most of the brief period – only about 175 years – from when a spartan hunting lodge in a woodcutters' village on inhospitably marshy terrain started being transformed into first a pleasure palace, then the seat of government and court of a country ruled over by a monarchy at the height of its glory, before finally witnessing the downfall of that monarchy as the French Revolution of 1789 changed France for ever.

At the beginning of the 17th century, Versailles was an insignificant village that had the advantage – in the eyes of the passionate huntsman then ruling France – of being on the edge of a forest conveniently near both the capital and the royal court at Saint Germain-en-Laye (see p. 114). Louis XIII therefore bought a small piece of land there, and commissioned a little known architect called Philibert Le Roy to build a plain stone and brick hunting lodge with a slate roof. That was in 1624. Eight years later the king had managed to buy the lordship of Versailles, and Le Roy set about enlarging the lodge to create a small château, adding two short wings perpendicular to the main building, plus four corner pavilions. This 'house of cards', as the Duc de Saint-Simon cattily referred to it in his gossipy memoirs of life at Louis XIV's court, is still standing, right at the heart of the palace that grew up around it.

Hunting Lodge

It had been virtually abandoned after Louis's death in 1643, used only occasionally during hunting sorties, until another death, that of chief minister Cardinal Mazarin in 1661, emboldened the young Louis XIV into becoming his own man. He was now twenty-two and as keen on hunting as his father. He also saw Versailles as a chance to escape – often with his first mistress, Louise de La Vallière – from the nearby court. As he distrusted Paris, whose rebellious citizens he had seen at close quarters when he was a boy, during the Fronde uprisings, Versailles came to seem the perfect site for the splendid new palace he was determined to build, his imagination fired by his intense irritation at seeing the opulent residence of his finance supremo Nicolas Fouquet (see **Vaux-le-Vicomte**).

Fouquet's team

Taking over Fouquet's brilliant three-man team of Louis Le Vau (architect), André Le Nôtre (landscape gardener) and Charles Le Brun (painter and interior designer), but closely involved himself in all the planning and design details, he set to work. As the scheme developed, he began to nurture the idea of proving to the world that

France was a supreme power, with artists and craftsmen as fine as the Italian specialists who had built previous royal palaces (see **Fontainebleau**) – an aim in which he was fully supported by his chief minister Jean-Baptiste Colbert. At the same time, he felt the need to demonstrate to his nobles that his was the supreme authority, to prevent another Fronde-style rebellion.

Work proceeded throughout the half century and more that remained of his reign. The vast project involved draining marshes, moving tonnes of earth to enlarge the narrow hill from which Louis XIII's little château had surveyed the surrounding forest, and creating a series of terraces supporting Le Nôtre's magnificent gardens, channelling water from the Seine. Hundreds of thousands of labourers, horses, craftsmen and artists were employed over the years, and on average, the building swallowed up over 2 per cent of France's budget annually (as much as 5 per cent during the most intensive phases).

Le Nôtre

But to begin with Le Vau merely built on to the existing château and redesigned it to create a comfortable royal residence intended for occasional use. Leaving the basic structure untouched, he made the place altogether grander by adorning it with busts, urns and wrought-iron balconies, then adding two free-standing wings to house servants' quarters and ancillary services, on either side of a much larger outer courtyard. Inside, he created a new layout upstairs in which the king's rooms were sited on the north side and the queen's on the south, as they still are today. Meanwhile, Le Nôtre's grandiose garden design was taking shape, so much so that as early as 1664, he was working with the great dramatist Molière to stage an elaborate open-air pageant in which Louis himself played a dashing equestrian role.

Le Vau

Molière

The success of this and later festivities encouraged the king to turn his congenial pleasure palace into not just a royal residence, but the seat of court and government. Le Vau wanted to knock down the enlarged château and start from scratch. But Louis would not hear of it. So instead he ingeniously wrapped a new and very different building round it, in stone this time, creating what architectural historians call 'The Envelope'. This explains why the courtyard façade is still in Louis XIII style, while the taller garden façades are pure Louis XIV. In the centre was a wide terrace from which the king could survey the geometrically arranged gardens, the 'Green Carpet' of lawn and the 'Grand Canal' sweeping away from the palace. Flanking this terrace, two new sets of state rooms, the **Grands Appartements**, backed on to the king's and queen's original rooms, which now became private suites or **Petits Appartements**.

'The Envelope'

Le Brun's decorative schemes for these grand state rooms featured a great deal of richly coloured marble and imposing allegorical paintings. There was more marble in the entrance courtyard, still known as the **Cour de Marbre** (Marble Courtyard).

Le Brun

The later building stages

Versailles was still not a permanent residence when this stage of work was completed in the early 1670s. The next stage was not embarked on until 1678, when the Peace of Nijmegen brought a

Apollo's Chariot: one of Versailles' many fountains

temporary halt in the expenditure on foreign wars that was an even greater drain on the nation's coffers. Le Vau was now dead and Jules Hardouin-Mansart was commissioned to enlarge the palace once again, to create a fitting permanent residence for a monarch who was by now held in awe throughout Europe.

Hardouin-Mansart

The most celebrated feature of Mansart's vast campaign, which was to continue right down to his death in 1708, was the conversion of the terrace on the garden front into the dazzling **Galerie des Glaces** or **Hall of Mirrors**, again decorated by Le Brun's team of artists and craftsmen. But he also added two huge three-storey wings, called simply **L'Aile du Nord** (North Wing) and **L'Aile du Midi** (South Wing), extending the main structure on either side to a total length of 580 metres. Two more free-standing buildings were added to the outer courtyard, known as the **Ailes des Ministres** (Ministers' Wings) because they housed government ministers and their officials. And behind one of them rose up the large service block – the **Grand Commun du Roi**.

With their thousands of bedrooms for courtiers and officials, their kitchens and administrative offices, these new buildings increased the palace to five times its size. It was now ready to receive the huge population who moved in only four years after Mansart had been given the go-ahead, in 1682 – albeit in notoriously cramped and unhygienic conditions, with virtually no sanitation. Their horses appear to have been lodged in considerably more comfort in the **Grandes Ecuries** and **Petites Ecuries** (Large and Small Stables) facing the palace, again designed by the prolific Mansart, and flanked and separated by three wide avenues radiating out from the palace gates.

The Stables

Inside, Mansart underscored the Sun King's central role in the kingdom by creating a new **Chambre du Roi** (King's Bedchamber) right in the centre of the palace, overlooking the Marble Courtyard and appropriately lit by the rays of the rising sun. It was here that the ceremonial 'Rising' and 'Setting' (or 'Retiring') took place every day, though as he grew older Louis sensibly slept in his cosier private bedroom, a practice copied by his successors. Next to the official bedchamber was the **Cabinet du Conseil** (Council Chamber), where great affairs of state would be transacted.

Mansart's final contribution was his masterpiece, the appropriately regal **Chapel**, completed after his death by his brother-in-law Robert de Cotte.

This third building stage, ending seven years before the death of their royal master, essentially resulted in the palace as you see it today from the outside. The only major later addition was the lovely *Ange-Jacques Gabriel* **Opéra Royal** (Theatre/Opera House) built by Louis XV's architect Ange-Jacques Gabriel, at the far end of the North Wing. This ingeniously multi-purpose building could be converted into a ballroom or banqueting hall – as it was when it was first thrown open, to stage the celebrations following the wedding of the young Marie-Antoinette to the future Louis XVI in 1770.

An ill-considered withdrawal

Both Louis XV and Louis XVI did make some alterations to the interior. These illustrate the difference between their attitude to kingship and that of their predecessor, and in making them they can be said to have sown the seeds for the monarchy's destruction.

Louis XIV was every inch a tactician. One strand of his strategy in building Versailles was to create a symbol of the divine right of kings. The elaborately orchestrated ritual of his *Levers* and *Couchers*, his *The Sun King's ritual* dinners in public and his 'Entrances', along with the rigid court etiquette, was partly designed to dazzle ordinary citizens with the lustre of their monarchy. The king himself seemed to be constantly on display, the living embodiment of that majesty. His successors failed to understand the importance of this and withdrew increasingly behind the great state rooms into the 'inner royal cabinets', where only a few favoured courtiers were allowed to follow them. They spent considerable sums on reorganizing these rooms, and having them decorated and furnished by the finest artists and cabinetmakers of the day, who also worked on the warren of new private suites they carved out for themselves, mostly on the top floor. In these small and *Royal mistresses* intimate rooms they could live completely out of sight, conducting behind-the-scenes diplomacy in quiet studies, turning their hands to various crafts in specially designed workshops, meditating in roof gardens, even breeding birds in an aviary. Up here too were the rooms set aside for Louis XV's mistresses, first Madame de Pompadour, then Madame du Barry.

Another strand of Louis XIV's strategy was to keep his nobles away from their power bases in the provinces, or even in Paris, by setting up a complex system of favours and privileges. However uncomfortable their quarters, aristocrats knew that anyone who counted must be ensconced at Versailles, angling for the right to play some minor role in the king's ritual. Bewigged and resplendent in silk, the greatest in the land dwelt in what has been described as 'gilded idleness', too involved in petty intrigue and court gossip to plan a new uprising.

In placing so much less importance on public show, Louis XV, and still more Louis XVI, a shy man who valued his privacy, unknowingly encouraged the growing tide of republicanism. Louis XVI's queen Marie Antoinette hastened the process by making it clear that she loathed the rigidities of court etiquette and slipping off for days or even weeks at a time to the miniature palaces in the grounds, where she happily spent large sums on exquisite furniture and decoration that was seen only by a few intimates, acted in plays for a tiny audience, and played at being a milkmaid.

Marie Antoinette

The final stages
It was here that she learnt that the revolutionary mob was converging on Versailles. That was on 5 October 1789. The following day she and her family were hustled off to Paris, imprisonment and, eventually, the guillotine. Versailles's day as a royal palace was over.

Four years later the revolutionaries started to auction off the paintings, tapestries and furniture, the priceless *objets d'art* and the silk hangings. The whole process took over a year. Some items have since been bought back by the French State, or donated by generous collectors. But much of what you see today is beautiful pieces from the same period, reflecting the known tastes of avid collectors like Madame de Pompadour.

Madame de Pompadour

Parts of the palace were briefly turned into a natural history museum, plus a museum of French painting and sculpture.

Then after the revolutionary period was over, Napoleon ordered some restoration. There was later some talk of pulling the whole place down. But in the 1830s, France's last monarch, the sensible 'citizen-king' Louis-Philippe, stepped in to save his ancestors' palace. Using his own money, he built up a collection of thousands of historical paintings, portraits and sculptures and created a series of huge 'Historical Galleries', now known as the Museum of French History. This sadly involved demolishing whole floors of beautiful 17th- and 18th-century rooms. But the great state rooms and private royal suites were untouched. Since the 1950s they have gradually been restored, along with the opera house and the chapel, thanks to the work of the finest artists and craftsmen of our own day.

History Museum

Visiting the palace
To describe all the rooms, even in outline, would require a book in itself. I can merely offer some practical advice and guidance, and refer to a few highlights.

First of all, until the planned new reception area is ready, you must be prepared for long queues. A complicated system of guided tours means that it is advisable to decide in advance what you want to see – to visit everything would require several days. If you are allergic to guided tours, you can visit the **Grands Appartements**, the **Galerie des Glaces** and the **Appartement de la Reine** (Queen's Rooms) on your own. You can also hire a headset and tape to fill you in on the **Chambre du Roi**, the sumptuous State Bedchamber. A few rooms in the **Museum of French History** can be visited without a guide.

Practical tips

For everything else you must join one of the many tours on offer, some of which also include the Galerie des Glaces. For instance, it features in the frequent 'Splendours of Versailles' tour. Other tours focus on a single set of private rooms, such as Marie Antoinette's pretty suite.

Guided tours

If you plan to do at least one of the tours, check times carefully. Most are available in English as well as French, but they usually stop considerably earlier than the overall closing time. Book your place as soon as you arrive. If you want to fit in the grounds and their various sights, you must make some firm decisions about what to leave out in the palace.

The Grands Appartements

State rooms

Clearly not to be left out on a first visit are the key sights. These include the magnificent set of state rooms leading one into the other and bringing you to the second 'must', the **Galerie des Glaces**. With their names taken from classical mythology – the Hercules Salon, the Venus Salon and so on – and their rich decoration of marble, gilding, portraits and painted ceilings, they clearly splendidly fulfilled their function of demonstrating the skills of French artists and craftsmen and the apparently unlimited resources of the French State. But since these resources were in fact finite, especially in time of war, you must, in your mind's eye, replace the beautiful inlaid furniture with the original glittering pieces in solid silver that subsequently had to be melted down to pay for yet more wars.

The ceiling paintings are worth studying carefully. The **Salon de Diane** naturally enough depicts the goddess Diana brandishing a curving crossbow, the **Salon de Mars**, Mars's chariot drawn by fierce-looking wolves, the **Salon de Vénus**, a swan in the central oval. Among the portraits are a rather stout Marie Leszczynska looking pleased with herself and with a little dog at her feet, while a snooty-looking bust of her husband Louis XV sits on the table in front of her, in the Salon de Mars. The original paintings in the **Salle du Trône** (Throne Room) are now back in place, including the famous portrait of Louis XIV with a nicely turned calf by Hyacinthe Rigaud. The king reappears in a white bas-relief in the **Salon de la Guerre** (War Salon), which offers a splendid view down the length of the Galerie des Glaces, dazzling even on a grey day with its tall mirrors reflecting the gardens.

Royal births

At the far end the **Salon de la Paix** (Peace Salon) leads into the **Appartement de la Reine** (Queen's Rooms). In the very grand but also very pretty **Queen's Bedroom**, no fewer than nineteen royal infants were born, most of them in full view of the public, before Louis XVI insisted on privacy for Marie Antoinette. The flowery silk hangings have been beautifully woven in exact imitation of the originals, as a tiny piece of fabric had survived.

Beyond here the **Salle du Sacre** displays a copy by David of his famous painting of Napoleon crowning himself at his coronation, and a large canvas depicting the Battle of Aboukir in 1799. This is a prelude to the **Galerie des Batailles**, part of Louis-Philippe's French History Museum, with its even huger battle scenes. If you prefer boudoirs to battles, behind the Queen's Rooms are the private rooms used by successive queens, the **Cabinets intérieurs de la Reine**, but they can only be visited with a guide. This also applies to the **Appartement du Roi**, whose finest room is the **Chambre du Roi** (Royal Bedchamber), now splendidly restored. But the various antechambers are almost as richly decorated: the **Salon de l'Oeil-de-Boeuf** is decorated with a frieze of children playing, by special request from Louis XIV, who at the end of his reign was always urging Mansart to 'put children everywhere'. In the **Salon du Conseil** (Council Chamber) is the desk on which the Treaty of Versailles was signed in June 1919, the peace treaty concluding the First World War – though the actual signing took place in the Galerie des Glaces. But for the finest furniture you must linger in the **Cabinet de Travail**, Louis XV's study, whose beautiful inlaid desk by the brilliant cabinetmaker Jean-Paul Riesener has been returned. The tour also takes you into the king's secret study, the **Arrière Cabinet**, and, next to it, the pretty little room used as a music room by one of his daughters.

Treaty of Versailles

The opera/theatre and chapel
The pretty **Opéra Royal** with its three tiers of boxes and its half-chandeliers reflected in mirrors is all sky-blue and gold. What looks like marble is in fact painted wood, which makes for much better acoustics. Concerts and plays are staged here. There is much gilding, too, in the lofty **Chapel**, with its painted ceiling and tiers of white pillars, and its curving balustrade.

The private suites
If you have found the state rooms, and even the inner rooms behind them, overwhelming, change perspective by joining one of the tours of the **Petits Appartements**. Their decoration is on a human scale, though they are often full of priceless furniture and furnishings. Here you can see intricately carved panelling and many charming details, especially in the tiny rooms designed for Madame de Pompadour and Madame du Barry, high up on the top floor. The private rooms on the ground floor, the **Appartements du Dauphin et de la Dauphine**, are not as lavish as the suites inhabited by the royal mistresses, but they have some beautiful furniture and decoration, and many 18th-century paintings, including portraits of the eight daughters of Louis XV, who lived here at one point.

Priceless furniture

The museum
Apart from the **Galerie des Batailles** (see above), you may be able to get into the **Salles du Dix-Septième Siècle** (17th-century Rooms) on the ground and first floors, full of portraits of key figures of the age: look out for Jean de La Fontaine, the author of the *Fables*, and for that greatest of gardeners, André Le Nôtre.

The grounds
To appreciate Le Nôtre's genius, you must allow plenty of time to enjoy his gardens, in which Louis XIV was passionately interested – so much so that he even wrote a little guidebook to them. La Fontaine once commented that Le Nôtre 'had the power to make nature obey him'. This 'power' was aquired by heroic efforts in two

A gardener of genius

A Victorian 'adventure'

In 1911, two British academics, Charlotte Anne Elizabeth Moberly and Eleanor Frances Jourdain, published a pseudonymous book that was to become a bestseller and a *cause célèbre*.

An Adventure, by 'Elizabeth Morison' and 'Frances Lamont', was an account of how the two women, on holiday in Paris, travelled to Versailles one hot August afternoon in 1901. As they strolled near the Petit Trianon, they were overwhelmed by a feeling of oppression, then experienced some sort of vision in which they were transported back to the pre-Revolutionary period, seeing the landscape and buildings exactly as they had looked over a century earlier. They also saw and even spoke to various historical figures, including, in Miss Moberly's case, Marie Antoinette, wearing 'a shady white hat perched low on a good deal of fair hair that fluffed round her forehead', and a low-cut dress with a green fichu over her shoulders.

Miss Moberly was the god-daughter of the popular novelist Charlotte M. Yonge, and the seventh child of the Bishop of Salisbury. She was sixty-five in 1901, and principal of St Hugh's College, Oxford. Miss Jourdain, eighteen years younger, was prettier and more at ease in society than the brusque and severe-looking Miss Moberly. A gifted amateur artist, she had been one of Oxford's earliest women graduates, and was running a private school near London with a friend (she was later to be vice-principal at St Hugh's). Miss Jourdain was interested in mysticism, but neither woman had been involved in research into psychical phenomena.

With the reticence of Victorian ladies, neither at first mentioned the incident. The book was based on descriptions written separately a week later, and again in November, when it emerged that they had not seen exactly the same scenes.

Miss Jourdain now realized that they had visited Versailles on 10 August, the key date in 1792 when the revolutionary mob had attacked the Tuileries Palace and the Legislative Assembly had suspended Louis XVI from his functions as king. A French friend then reported that 'on a certain day in August, Marie-Antoinette is regularly seen sitting outside the garden front at the Petit Trianon'. The women came to believe that they had relived a 'reverie' indulged in by the queen on that fateful day 109 years earlier, transporting her 'in a trance-like state' from her grim Paris cell to her adored Petit Trianon.

contradictory directions: draining the marshy land and at the same time providing enough water to feed the hundreds of ornamental pools and over a thousand fountains that featured in his designs, which soon became the talk of Europe. He even experimented with deviating the course of the river Eure and channelling its waters via a vast aqueduct, though this ambitious project was eventually abandoned (see **Maintenon**).

The fountains Over 600 of the original 1400 **water jets** have been restored to working order. They are a riot of gilded nymphs and bearded gods, frogs and lions, stags and satyrs, rearing horses and sea monsters. Beautiful when lying quietly in their pools, they seem to spring to life when the water gushes out of gaping mouths, spews up in giant plumes of spray, rains down on writhing monsters or frolicking cupids. Some were designed by Le Brun, others by Le Nôtre himself, some later ones by Gabriel. The sculpture includes work by major artists like Antoine Coysevox.

Among the best-known are the **Bassin de Latone**, featuring Apollo and Diana/Artemis with their mother Latona or Leto, plus assorted frogs and toads, the **Bassin d'Apollon**, where the Sun God drives his chariot up out of the water drawn by prancing steeds, their manes flying, and the **Bassin d'Automne**, with Bacchus sprawling casually on a mound of grapes, surrounded by youthful and visibly tipsy satyrs.

You can enjoy the sight of a selection of fountains playing on summer Sundays (May to mid-September, usually afternoons only), with musical accompaniment. Four or five times a year (generally at weekends) the largest pool of all, the **Bassin de Neptune**, is the setting for the 'Fêtes de Nuit', evening spectaculars featuring dramatic lighting and fireworks to highlight the effect of the elaborate fountain (advance reservation essential).

Fêtes de Nuit

Another much-admired feature of Le Nôtre's overall scheme was his *bosquets* or groves. Some were designed as open-air theatres, others as settings for al fresco supper parties. Their sculptures and fountains are gradually being restored and the trees and shrubs replanted.

Plans of the grounds showing the main features are available. Do ask for one, or buy a booklet, as it is very easy to get lost, and the signposting is generally poor, even for such well-known sights as the Trianon palaces. For Le Nôtre's prodigious labours were complemented during the palace's third building phase by the work of the royal architect. Mansart designed first an **Orangerie** (Orangery) and an elegant **Colonnade**, then a sumptuous miniature palace, at the far end of the Grand Canal, on the site of the hamlet of Trianon, where Louis XIV and his then mistress Madame de Montespan had enjoyed some privacy in a delicate little château designed by Le Vau, its façades decorated with Delft tiles. Mansart replaced this with a sturdier structure, clad in pinkish marble and featuring a peristyle linking two separate single-storey buildings.

The lovely formal gardens are, oddly enough, popular with Japanese wedding parties, but otherwise the **Grand Trianon** is rarely crowded. This Italianate palace was a favourite retreat of Napoleon and Josephine, and much of the furniture and furnishings you see today dates from their Empire period. The elegant **Gallery** is lined with interesting paintings of the gardens at Versailles, as they were in Louis XIV's day.

Grand Trianon

From here you can walk on to Marie Antoinette's beloved **Petit Trianon**, in fact designed for Madame de Pompadour, but not completed by Louis XV's architect Gabriel, in elegant Classical style, until 1768, four years after her death. On the way you can admire the **Pavillon français**, again designed by Gabriel, which Madame de Pompadour was able to enjoy, and behind it, the **Théâtre de la Reine**, Marie Antoinette's private theatre, the **Glacières**, where the huge quantities of ice needed by the royal kitchens were stored, and the romantic octagonal **Belvedere**.

Petit Trianon

The rooms in the Petit Trianon have recently been restored and offer a good illustration of the elegant style chosen by Marie Antoinette for her bolthole away from the suffocating rigidity of court life. She took this escapist policy a stage further in the **Hameau**, the charming little fake 'village' where she assuaged her yearning for 'rustic simplicity'. The thatched cottages, the little garden with its *Royal milkmaid* nasturtiums and cabbages, the windmill, dovecot and dairy – it was here that the queen and her ladies-in-wating dressed up as milk-maids – are certainly a far cry from the almost oppressive splendour of the state rooms.

You can reach the Trianons via a little train that trundles through the grounds from the Grand Canal, or even in a horse-drawn carriage. Both options are worth considering, especially on hot and dusty summer days, as the distances are quite great. Another alternative is to hire a bike. And if the water looks tempting, why not do some gentle rowing on the Grand Canal? When you start feeling peckish, *La Flotille*, facing the canal, with tables beneath the spreading chest-nuts in fine weather, is handy for lunch or a snack.

To walk off your lunch, consider exploring the wilder parts of the grounds, beyond the formal gardens, though still intersected by geo-metrically planned rides. Here you will find some real woodland, with lords-and-ladies lurking shyly in the undergrowth.

Visiting the town

Although there is so much to see in the palace and grounds, it would be a pity not to enjoy a stroll round the town. Built virtually as an adjunct to the palace, it has many sober, elegant, classical buildings, mostly 18th-century, lining wide avenues. But the **Quartier Saint-Louis**, south of the palace and near Versailles-Rive Gauche station, is rather different. Beyond the **Cathédrale Saint-Louis**, built for Louis *Quartier Saint-Louis* XV, and fronted by a square with a fountain charmingly decorated with a relief of swans, the **Carrés Saint-Louis** form a villagey enclave of little squares surrounded by low 18th-century houses, some now housing antique shops, as well as a few pleasant restaurants well away from the tourist hordes. This was once virtually a covered mar-ket made up of rows of small shops, built for Louis XIV.

Royal kitchen gardens On the other side of the cathedral, the **Potager du Roy** (Royal Kitchen Garden) was also planted for Louis XIV, to provide the finest of produce for his table. It is now the home of the National Horti-cultural Academy and can be visited – you can even buy your own fruit and veg here on Friday.

Just north of the palace, near Versailles-Rive Droite station, the **Musée Lambinet**, housed in an attractive 18th-century mansion with gilded balconies and a charming garden, is undeservedly neglected. With its discreetly carved panelling, its black and white tiled floors, painted overdoors and marble fireplaces, its soft powder blues and dove greys, it well conveys the elegance of the decorative style of the period. A good porcelain collection, engraved copper plates for print-ing the **toile de Jouy** fabrics so popular at this time (see **Jouy-en-Josas**), snuff boxes and miniatures add to the pleasure of your visit. So do the beautiful furniture and the paintings, including a lovely view of the house in autumn. The **Salle Charlotte Corday** displays mementoes of the murderess of Marat, while other rooms are devoted to the history of the town and palace.

Close to the museum in the rue Hoche, the **Eglise Notre-Dame** was built for the fledgling town by Mansart in the 1680s. This Quartier Notre-Dame is much busier than the **Quartier Saint-Louis**, but also has its cluster of antique shops, some of them in the **passage des Antiquaires** leading off the rue Rameau.

Quartier Notre-Dame

Beyond Versailles

If you are driving to Versailles, or travelling by bus from the Pont de Sèvres, you can stop off to see the **Manufacture nationale de Porcelaine** (Porcelain Workshops), set up by Madame de Pompadour and Louis XV in 1756. The original buildings can still be seen, but those used today – Sèvres is still a working factory – date from the 19th century. They house an interesting museum, the **Musée national de Céramique**.

Sèvres porcelain

The large, light rooms display some of the finest pieces of Sèvres ware over the centuries, along with work from Italy and the Far East, and from the various French regions. Here you can admire the attractive faïence from Moustiers in Provençe, the sunny Mediterranean yellows of the flower-bedecked services made in Marseilles, china stoves from Strasbourg, and some curious pieces referred to as *trompe-l'oeil* – though it is hard to envisage anyone being deceived by the tureens in the shape of cabbages (the artichokes and olives are more lifelike).

You can watch video (and sometimes real-life) presentations of the techniques of porcelain-making, see the type of pieces being made today, and buy modern designs from the showroom.

A short drive or taxi ride west of Versailles brings you to **France Miniature** at Elancourt, which can also be reached by bus from the station at La Verrière. This is a theme park with a difference: a gigantic

Sèvres's Russian connection

The dramatic bronze equestrian monument to Peter the Great beside the Neva in St Petersburg, famous for its breathtakingly bold design, with the rearing horse's forelegs pawing the air quite unsupported, was carved by the Director of Sculpture at the Sèvres Porcelain Manufactory. Etienne-Marcel Falconet (1716–91) also worked from time to time for Madame de Pompadour after being appointed to the post at Sèvres in 1757. But in 1766 the Russian empress Catherine II commissioned him to make the huge monument. She was acting on the advice of the French philosopher Denis Diderot, whose vast library of books (collected when he was working on his Encyclopaedia) she had bought, appointing him librarian of his own collection. Diderot told the empress that Falconet was willing to spend eight years working on it, though in the end it took him over a decade.

By the time it was finally hoisted into place, Falconet had fallen out with Catherine and was back in France. But his masterpiece is still St Petersburg's finest statue, immortalized in Pushkin's ballad *The Bronze Horseman*.

three-dimensional map of France dotted with a couple of thousand scale models of the country's best-known sites. They feature in the appropriate place on the map, surrounded as in real life by mountains, rivers or whatever. Whole villages and farms can be seen too, as well as the odd modern building, such as a nuclear power station.

Fun and a painless way of learning some geography, this is a good place to bring children, who can rush about along the paths, watch planes taking off or trains hurtling over viaducts. And once they have pronounced on their favourite region, they can order a dish from there in the park's restaurant, Les Provinces (fast-food kiosks and picnic area also available).

Key data

VERSAILLES **78000**

T.O.   7 rue des Réservoirs, ⊤ 01-39-50-36-22; also 6 av. du Général-de-Gaulle (almost opposite Rive Gauche station); in summer, information tents just outside palace gates

Access   Paris 23km; **RER** line C4 to Versailles-Rive Gauche; **rail** from Paris-Montparnasse to Versailles Chantiers, or from Paris-Saint-Lazare to Versailles-Rive Droite; **bus** no. 171 from Ⓜ Pont de Sèvres (stops right by palace)

Sights   **Carrés Saint-Louis** (former 18th-century market); **Cathédrale Saint-Louis** (Classical Cathedral); **Château et Domaine de Versailles** (royal palace and grounds), ⊤ 01-30-84-74-00, closed Mon (but grounds open daily): includes **Grand Trianon** (17th-century palace in grounds), **Petit Trianon** (18th-century palace in grounds), **Musée de l'Histoire de France** (Museum of French History); **Eglise Notre-Dame** (court and parish church); **Musée Lambinet** (local history, paintings, china, 18th-century furniture, in 18th-century mansion), 54 blvd de la Reine, ⊤ 01-39-50-30-32, closed Mon; **Potager du Roy** (Royal Kitchen Gardens), 6 rue Hardy, ⊤ 01-39-24-62-62, open Apr to mid-Nov, Wed–Sun

Lunch   Versailles
Staying Versailles
Also   Jouy-en-Josas, Vallée de Chevreuse

Musée national de Céramique
92310 Sèvres, ⊤ 01-41-14-04-20, closed Tue; Ⓜ Pont-de-Sèvres, then short walk or **bus** no. 171

France Miniature
78990 Elancourt, ⊤ 01-30-51-51-51, open mid-Mar to mid-Nov; **rail** from Paris-Montparnasse or La Défense to La Verrière, then **bus** no. 421

2 Sceaux, Bièvres, and Jouy-en-Josas

Sceaux

Louis XIV's great garden designer André Le Nôtre lived to the age of eighty-seven. But it sometimes seems as if even that long life was not long enough to encompass all he achieved. For despite the many years he spent wresting the magnificent gardens at Versailles from the unfavourable terrain the king had saddled him with, he created a host of other gardens in and around Paris (and even contributed to St James's Park in London).

One of these is the **Parc de Sceaux**, laid out for Louis's chief minister Jean-Baptiste Colbert in the 1670s, when the work at Versailles was still at its height. As at the royal palace, though on a much smaller scale, it features a Grand Canal, a Green Carpet, a series of *bosquets* or groves, ornamental pools and fountains, as well as the geometrically precise flowerbeds that complete the *jardin à la française*, the formal garden that was his creation. But as Sceaux's grounds are on hilly land, he could include a splendid stepped waterfall, 'Les Grandes Cascades', which do indeed cascade down towards a mirror-like octagonal pool.

Le Nôtre's gardens

Colbert's château, too, was the work of some of those top-flight artists who created Versailles. One was the architect Jules Hardouin-Mansart, though here working with Claude Perrault, responsible for one of the masterpieces of French classical architecture, the Colonnade fronting the Louvre in Paris. Another was Charles Le Brun, who was in charge of the interior decoration, and yet another was the sculptor Antoine Coysevox.

Hardouin-Mansart

Alas, the château was demolished during the French Revolution, except for the elegant **Pavillon de l'Aurore**, its dome, painted by Le Brun, now beautifully restored, and the **Orangerie**, built by Mansart for Colbert's son, France's Navy Minister, who enjoyed spending money as much as his father enjoyed penny-pinching. When his mounting debts forced him to sell, the new owner was the Duc du Maine, Louis XIV's elder son by Madame de Montespan. Here his duchess held her famous literary and political *salon*. One of its leading lights was Voltaire, who returned to live at Sceaux decades later, and wrote some of his best-known work there, including the philosophical tale *Zadig* (1748).

Voltaire

A new château was built in the 19th century by the Duc de Trévise, who also restored the gardens. For a while Sceaux was once again the scene of festivities rivalling the Duchesse du Maine's glamorous evening parties known as 'Les Nuits de Sceaux'. But then it was abandoned and the grounds became a romantic wilderness that was one of the inspirations behind the 'lost domain' in *Le Grand Meaulnes*, the elegaic novel by Alain-Fournier, a pupil at the **Lycée Lakanal** next to the château (see **Epineuil-le-Fleuriel**).

Alain-Fournier

Now restored, the château houses the **Musée de l'Ile de France**, a most interesting collection of paintings and other exhibits connected with the wealth of historic towns and buildings scattered through the region, its forests and gardens, and its people.

Concerts

Good special exhibitions are staged, and chamber music concerts take place in the Orangerie on Fridays, Saturdays and Sundays in July, August and September (**Festival de l'Orangerie de Sceaux** programme, Ⓣ 01-46-60-07-79, Ⓕ 01-69-46-26-04, or write to: BP 52, 92333 Sceaux Cedex).

Bièvres

The little town of Bièvres on the edge of the Forêt de Verrières, southwest of Sceaux, is known for its focus on photography. A museum devoted to the subject, the **Musée français de la Photographie**, has a good collection of early equipment, and stages a 'Foire à la Photo' (Photo Fair) every June. The main pretext for this specialization is the fact that the great photographer Nadar took the first-ever aerial photograph nearby in 1858.

Nadar

But there are other attractions, too, these days. The pink-washed **Château des Roches** was the country house of Louis-François Bertin, a generous patron of writers and musicians and proprietor-cum-editor of the outspoken daily newspaper *Le Journal des Débats*, founded in 1789, the year of the outbreak of the French Revolution. And among the authors who regularly visited him was the great Victor Hugo. For several years in the 1830s Hugo would spent part of the summer here with his (estranged) wife and children, interspersing his writing with contemplative walks beside the river Bièvre. In 1834 and 1835 he also rented a house a couple of miles away, on the edge of Jouy-en-Josas, for his devoted mistress, the actress Juliette Drouet.

Victor Hugo

In Hugo's honour, the richly furnished château has become the **Maison littéraire de Victor Hugo**, with rooms displaying manuscripts, photographs, first editions, and much other material illustrating his life and work, with particular emphasis on his social and political thinking, and his work in the field of human rights and other humanitarian causes.

The grounds are most attractive, part formal garden, part romantic park with many mature trees, leading to the river with its fringe of weeping willows. A little open-air tearoom serves drinks and snacks.

Picasso, Braque

Not far from Les Roches, in the hamlet of Vauboyen (one stop on the train from Bièvres), a 16th- and 17th-century windmill has been converted into a gallery of modern art. The **Moulin Vauboyen** has decorations by major artists like Pablo Picasso and Georges Braque in its exhibition rooms and chapel, tapestries designed by Jean Cocteau and Raoul Dufy, and temporary shows by contemporary painters, and also sculptors, whose work peoples the garden.

Jouy-en-Josas

The waters of the Bièvre have long been known for their exceptional purity, making them well suited to fabric dyeing. Upstream in Paris, they were used by the celebrated Gobelins workshops. Just west of Bièvres at Jouy-en-Josas, they encouraged Christophe-Philippe Oberkampf to launch into the printed cottons that have immortalized

Toile de Jouy

The walls of many a French manor house or château are covered in the elegant printed fabric known as *toile de Jouy*. The best-known patterns have red, blue or green motifs on a white background, but other colours such as golden yellow or a reddish brown are also found.

The first printed cottons and calicoes used in France were imported from India in the 17th century – hence the term *indienne*, still used today for printed fabrics. They were soon so popular that the livelihood of indigenous producers was threatened and eventually anyone wanting to import them, or even produce them locally, was refused a permit. The ban lasted for over seventy years, but was lifted in 1759.

The following year, Christophe-Philippe Oberkampf, the grandson of a German immigrant specializing in dyeing, opened his own workshop in Jouy at the early age of twenty-two. His earliest designs were as multi-coloured as the Indian cottons that had inspired them, mainly with floral patterns. But soon the single-colour motifs that make the Jouy style instantly recognizable were introduced. Typical examples have detailed vignettes of country life, historical and mythological scenes, or graceful oriental cameos full of pagodas and latticework bridges.

Oberkampf's fabrics soon became all the rage and by 1783 his workshop was awarded the official title of 'Royal Manufactory', which put it on the same footing as Sèvres for porcelain (p. 77) or Beauvais for tapestries (see p. 145). In its heyday it had over 1200 employees.

Oberkampf amassed a considerable fortune. When he died in 1815, the business was run by his son Emile for the next seven years. By the time he sold it in 1822, competition from abroad and at home, along with the recession brought about by the Napoleonic Wars, had seriously undermined its profitablity. It closed down in 1843.

the name of Jouy for anyone interested in interior decoration and social history (see above).

You can admire *toile de Jouy* in the very pleasant **Musée Municipal de la Toile de Jouy**, housed in a late 19th-century château with a garden cleverly designed to illustrate the way in which Oberkampf's lengths of cloth would be spread out in the surrounding meadows to dry in the sun. Long, thin beds are planted with flowers in strong colours – bright purples and oranges, hot pinks and golden yellows – that really do resemble strips of printed fabric.

Toile de Jouy

The rooms inside (rather hot in high summer because of the central glass-roofed section) have well-displayed collections of fabric samples and copper printing plates that trace the development of the designs from the first, mainly floral and pastoral, period in the mid-18th century, to the geometric patterns and scenes from classical antiquity that characterize the middle period, in the late 18th and early 19th centuries, and finally the years 1810 to 1821, when tiny repetitive patterns were in vogue. You can see typical hunting scenes and Chinese motifs, many of them designed by the painter and decorator Jean-Baptiste Huet, and note how contemporary events could inspire motifs, like the first flight in a hot-air balloon. Some of the

Jean-Baptiste Huet

patterns, especially from the earliest period, look surprisingly modern. You can learn about printing techniques, about other fabric-printing centres in France and elsewhere, and about the life of Oberkampf and his family.

The museum shop has many attractive, if rather expensive, items in Jouy fabrics, ranging from tablecloths to desk sets and umbrellas. The mats, tea cosies, napkins used in the elegant tearoom are naturally all *toile de Jouy* too. Light lunches, or tea and coffee and cakes, are served, with tables outside overlooking the garden in fine weather.

Museum shop

Key data

SCEAUX   92330
Access   **RER** line B2
Sights   **Musée de l'Ile de France**, in 19th-century Château, ℡ 01-46-61-06-71, closed Tue; **Parc de Sceaux** (17th-century château grounds designed by Le Nôtre), open daily; fountains play year-round (up to 21.00 June, July);

BIEVRES   91570
Access   **RER** line B4 to Massy-Palaiseau, then **rail** to Bièvres (line to Versailles-Chantiers); or **rail** from Versailles-Chantiers
Sights   **Maison littéraire de Victor Hugo**, 45 rue de Vauboyen, ℡ 01-69-41-82-84 (15/20-min walk from station), open Mar to end Nov, weekend pm only; **Moulin de Vauboyen** (modern art gallery), ℡ 01-69-41-01-21 (5-min walk from Vauboyen station), pm only, closed Aug; **Musée français de la Photographie**, 78 rue de Paris, ℡ 01-69-35-16-50 (15/20-min walk from station), open daily year-round

JOUY-EN-JOSAS   78350
Access   **RER** line B4 to Massy-Palaiseau, then **rail** to Petit Jouy-Les Loges, plus 5-min walk; or **rail** to Versailles-Chantiers from Paris-Montparnasse, then change to Juvisy line for Petit-Jouy-les-Loges
Sights   **church** with Romanesque Virgin and Child; **Musée Léon-Blum**, 4 rue Léon-Blum, ℡ 01-30-70-68-46, open Sun pm only; **Musée municipal de la Toile de Jouy**, Château de l'Eglantine, 54 rue Charles-de-Gaulle, ℡ 01-39-56-48-64, open Tue–Sun, but pm only weekends and public hols
Lunch   Light meals at museum
Also   Versailles

CHÂTEAU DE SAINT-JEAN-DE-BEAUREGARD
91940   Saint-Jean-de-Beauregard, ℡ 01-60-12-00-01
Access   Paris 28km; **RER** line B4 to Orsay-Ville, then **bus** to Les Ulis and 15-min walk
Open   mid-Mar to mid-Nov, pm Sun and public hols only
Lunch   Saint-Jean-de-Beauregard; meals on site during garden festivals

Jouy was the home, for the last five years of his life, of the statesman Léon Blum, prime minister in the 1930s and again briefly in 1946. His house is now the **Musée Léon-Blum**, displaying much interesting material connected with his life, and his career as a leading socialist. The church in Jouy has a well-preserved 12th-century Virgin and Child statue, the feet of the rather large Infant Jesus – more young lad than infant – supported by a pair of kneeling angels.

Léon Blum

Saint-Jean-de-Beauregard
South of Bièvres, the **Château de Saint-Jean-de-Beauregard** is of the greatest interest to garden lovers, but also offers a good example of a 17th-century *domaine* (estate) that still looks much as it did in the days when its most important feature – its large kitchen garden – fed a household of forty, including servants. The impressive dovecot, another major source of sustenance, is still there too, large enough to house 4500 pigeons – whose droppings also provided sustenance for the kitchen garden.

17th-century kitchen garden

The château, built from 1612 in typical Louis XIII style with tall slate roofs and even taller brick chimneys, is still lived in. The garden façade overlooks a pretty rose garden, but most visitors come to see the walled *potager* or kitchen garden, replanted virtually as it would have been in the 17th century. Covering 2 hectares, it follows the traditional layout of sixteen large square beds of vegetables, many of them ancient varieties rarely seen today, surrounded by a flower border: narcissi and irises in spring, old roses and peonies in summer. A single colour predominates in each square – pink or blue, yellow or white – creating a most pleasing effect. A wide variety of herbs and aromatic plants is grown, and in the outhouses you can see grapes being preserved by the traditional 'Thomery' method.

Two popular garden festivals are held annually (see box, p. 14). Botanical tours of the gardens are also arranged.

3 Chartres, Illiers-Combray

Chartres
For centuries the almost mystical sight of the twin spires of Chartres's great Gothic cathedral apparently rising up out of the wheatfields on the flat plain of the Beauce was viewed with awe by the crowds of pilgrims flocking to the town. It still causes an intake of breath today, when more tourists than pilgrims travel to the cathedral – though it is still a pilgrimage centre.

This awe is a prelude to the impression most visitors, believers or non-believers, experience as they enter through the great carved portals and are overwhelmed by the soaring height of the nave and the glowing colours of the medieval stained glass. It is extraordinary to think that **Notre-Dame de Chartres**, often referred to as the finest building in western Christendom, was built in a mere twenty-five years, largely by the townspeople in a communal act of faith. Hence the unity of style that sets it apart from France's other Gothic cathedrals.

It was only to be expected that it should be dedicated to Our Lady, since pilgrims were coming to venerate the most precious of relics – the chemise or tunic allegedly worn by the Virgin Mary at the Annunciation, presented in the late 9th century by Charlemagne's grandson Charles le Chauve. And it was the unexpected survival of that relic that inspired the building you see today.

History of the cathedral

It is the sixth Christian place of worship on the same site, which had previously been occupied by a Druidic cult centred on a Gallo-Roman well that can still be seen in the vast crypt. The Romanesque basilica immediately preceding today's structure was started in about 1020. In the following century, freestanding towers were added, and in due course a whole new west front was built to link them, dominated by the richly carved, tripartite **Portail Royal** (Royal Portal). Its curiously elongated figures of saints and prophets, Old Testament kings and queens, its solemn Christ in Majesty and its wealth of vivid scenes on the capitals and curving round the portals – once all painted and gilded – can still be admired today. But in 1194 fire swept through the town and destroyed the top half of this façade and most of the rest of the great edifice – otherwise only the towers survived, together with the crypt. It seemed that the sacred relic must have been swallowed up by the flames. Then days later, as the fire died down, an iron trap door was flung up and a little procession of clerics emerged triumphantly from the crypt, brandishing the reliquary with its precious contents.

The seemingly miraculous survival of their relic inspired an outburst of religious fervour among the Chartrains. (Cynics point out that their livelihood, and the town's prosperity, depended on the pilgrim trade.) The rich gave money. The poor offered their labour, both on the site and off it – some dragged handcarts laden with huge blocks of stone over huge distances, others prepared sacks of flour or barrels of wine to sustain the army of labourers and stonemasons. Sacred relics – though not the precious tunic – were sent off on tour round the country, to encourage donations from the citizens of distant towns. And the local guilds and corporations paid for over forty stained-glass windows.

The work proceeded rapidly, in the new Gothic style that had been pioneered by Abbot Suger in the choir at Saint-Denis. The lofty vault, supported by buttresses, was the tallest ever built. The walls of the choir and the nave had virtually vanished, to be replaced by acres of stained glass in jewel-like colours whose secret formula – especially that of the famous 'Chartres blue' – has never been fully identified. These windows magnificently fulfil Abbot Suger's precepts about 'flooding the interior with a new light'. But taken together with the stone sculpture that seems to cover every available surface, they form what can only be called a vast visual encyclopaedia, depicting a wealth of biblical stories and parables, a host of symbols and metaphysical concepts, and at the same time providing a detailed record of everyday life in the Middle Ages: everywhere you can spot figures drawing wine from barrels, weighing out goods, shoeing horses, tapping hammers on

Stained glass

anvils, tending sheep, counting out eggs.

Except on brilliantly sunny days, it is liable to be too dark to make out everything (binoculars help). But booklets detailing all the windows are available, or you can take one of the generally excellent guided tours (many in English) that will point you towards some of the key scenes. They include the few survivals from the Romanesque basilica, like the famous **Notre-Dame de la Belle Verrière**, the Virgin and Child in the top left-hand side of the first window in the south aisle of the choir, or the Tree of Jesse in one of the windows on the west front. Particularly interesting are the little scenes depicting members of the donor corporations at work, at the bottom of the windows in the aisles or the ambulatory, where they could

Chartres Cathedral: Royal Portal

easily be seen by potential customers in the congregation – a form of medieval advertising. One of them gruesomely depicts a butcher in the slaughterhouse, with a carcase strung up behind him.

The Gothic high altar was replaced in the 18th century – one of thousands of such acts of well-intentioned vandalism. Some fragments of the old rood screen have been discovered and can be seen in the **Trésor** (closed Mon) in the **Chapelle Saint-Piat** at the far end of the apse, which also houses the reliquary with the Virgin's tunic. Among the fragments is a delightful Nativity, in which Mary is tenderly pulling down the swaddling clothes at the Infant Jesus's neck to peep at his face, while an ass seems to be licking his feet. The Late Gothic screen enclosing the choir is also beautifully carved, with scenes from the life of the Virgin and of Jesus. On the floor of the nave you can still see the medieval **labyrinth** (often barely visible beneath the chairs) – a circular maze carefully marked out and originally ending in a central paving stone inscribed with the names and portraits of the men behind the building of the cathedral, the bishop and the architects. The maze symbolized the path to the Holy Land and pilgrims rich and poor would laboriously make their way through it on their knees.

Pilgrims' maze

The exterior

The entrance to the impressive **crypt** is outside the cathedral, just beyond the **south portal**, whose rich carved decoration features scenes from the New Testament. Leaflets are available detailing all these scenes, and the iconography of the rose window above, which includes the twenty-four elders of the Apocalypse, as well as the Old Testament scenes on the **north portal** and its own rose window. The crypt, with its many radiating chapels, has some interesting 12th-century mural paintings (guided tours are on offer).

The crypt

The asymmetrical **towers** are both Romanesque. The **north tower** is the earlier, but is confusingly called the 'Clocher neuf' (New Belfry) because a lacy new stone spire replaced the original wooden one in the 16th century. This Flamboyant Gothic spire contrasts interestingly with the more sober, and lower, spire on the **south tower** or Clocher vieux (Old Belfry). It is sometimes possible to make the stiff climb up to the north tower. There are wonderful views to be seen, of the gargoyles and flying buttresses but also over the old roofs of the medieval district round the cathedral.

The towers

Visiting the town

Quite apart from the cathedral, Chartres has many attractive medieval buildings and a number of picturesque streets, those by the river offering interesting views of the cathedral. Before exploring them, you have two more places to visit close to the cathedral, both on the north side. The first is the **Musée des Beaux-Arts**, housed in the 18th-century bishop's palace. Its painting collections include a landscape by Hubert Robert, the designer of the famous garden at nearby Méréville (see pp. 90–1), depicting the huge aqueduct at Maintenon (see p. 98), and work by other major 18th-century artists such as Honoré Fragonard or Jean-Baptiste Chardin. Also here is a fine portrait of Erasmus by Hans Holbein, as well as collections of tapestries, Renaissance enamels, arms and armour, and a section devoted to the history of the town and the cathedral. The second is the **Cellier de Loëns** (also referred to as the **Enclos de Loëns**), once the storehouse for the cathedral chapter, now the home of the **Musée/Centre du Vitrail**, a collection of stained glass displayed in the old grain store with its splendid wooden rafters, and in the vaulted medieval wine cellars. If you feel inspired to buy a piece of stained glass, head for the Galerie du Vitrail, opposite the north porch.

Art Museum

To explore the **Vieux Quartiers** (Old Districts), walk round to the south porch and across the **Cloître Notre-Dame**, with several medieval houses and a couple of cafés for a drink or a light meal, to the **rue aux Herbes**. There are some steep streets and steps to negotiate beyond this little enclave of streets right by the cathedral, but the distances are not great. However, if you're feeling tired, you can take a ride in a little train, or even in a horse-drawn vehicle. Ask at the tourist office, which will also hire you a *cassettophone* (walkman and tape).

Medieval streets

The rue aux Herbes itself, its continuation in the **rue de la Petite Cordonnerie** and the **rue au Lait** at right angles to it all have picturesque half-timbered houses, some of them converted into atmospheric restaurants. So does the **place de la Poissonnerie**, beside the good indoor food market. Here you will find two of the best-known houses, the **Maison au Saumon** and the **Maison de la Truie-qui-file**. From the place de la Poissonnerie a set of steps leads down (look for the sign 'Quartiers historiques') to the **Chapelle Saint-Eman**, once part

Le Mentchikoff: a local delicacy

After visiting Chartres Cathedral, do head for a confectioner's and try out the town's other major claim to fame, a special sweet or candy called the Mentchikoff. It comes in various different shapes, but the commonest recipe produces an oval fondant praline with an almond green outer covering.

The name is something of a puzzle. It is one of the French versions of the surname of Prince Aleksandr Danilovich Menshikov (*c* 1665–1729), the Russian field marshal and statesman who rose from humble beginnings to become a close friend and companion of Peter the Great. He introduced the czar to his mistress Martha Skavronska, the daughter of a Lithuanian peasant, who went on to become first Peter's mistress and then, after being baptised into the Greek Orthodox Church and taking the name of Catherine Alexievna, his wife. When Peter died she was proclaimed Empress of Russia as Catherine I.

Prince Menshikov had fallen out of favour before Peter's death, but he now returned to play a key role as virtual governor of Russia under Catherine and her successor Peter II, though he spent his final years in exile in Siberia. Inspired by his colourful history, a local confectioner called Dausmenil decided to use his name for a recipe he invented in 1893, at the height of the fashion for things Russian that was sweeping through France in the wake of the new Franco-Russian alliance.

of a priory. To the left of it, the Tertre Saint-Eman brings you to the rue de la Corroierie, then the Impasse des Oiseaux, offering a glimpse of a surprisingly rural Chartres. The Impasse du Tripot on the left leads to a quiet, rather unkempt garden with handy picnic benches, shaded by part of the old ramparts. The rue des Trois Moulins on the other side of the rue de la Corroierie takes you down to the river Eure.

A detour to the right before you reach the river will bring you via the **rue aux Juifs**, or slightly higher up the **rue des Ecuyers**, through a district of recently restored old houses (note the staircase tower of the house known as 'à la Reine Berthe' in the rue des Ecuyers), to the **rue Saint Pierre** and the church of the same name. The Gothic **Eglise Saint-Pierre** shows that not all Chartres's best stained glass was made for the cathedral. A pleasant stroll through more old streets takes you back to the bridge. *Saint-Pierre*

The **rue de la Tannerie** on the other side of the river, once inhabited, as the name suggests, by tanners, is lined by villagey houses with shutters and little vegetable gardens. You can see the odd wash house too, but sadly the Moulin du Ponceau, an old watermill converted into a delightful restaurant/bar, has burnt down. Continue along the **rue du Massacre**, offering good views up to the bishop's palace, then cross back over the iron bridge to see the **Eglise Saint-André**. This Romanesque collegiate church, built right over the river, was deconsecrated during the French Revolution and is now in a poor state, though it is used as an occasional concert and exhibition venue. To see the interior, walk through the attractive 'apothecary's garden', its little box-bordered squares planted with herbs and medicinal plants. Turn right out of the garden to see the Romanesque *Tanners' district* *Saint-André*

A road sweeper's visionary palace

La Maison Picassiette has often been called one of the most extraordinary places in France. It was created by a road sweeper called Raymond Isidore, who was born in 1900 and plied his trade in the local cemetery. But every evening after work he would wander about the countryside picking up bits of coloured glass and fragments of broken china. Over a period of thirty-three years – he died in 1964 – he collected some 15 tonnes of material and used it to cover the walls of his house, and the floors and ceilings, even the furniture, as well as much of the garden, with brightly coloured mosaic patterns and scenes, some religious, some purely imaginary.

The result is an extraordinary example of naïve art. Isidore claimed that he was inspired by views on postcards and calendars, by illustrations in books and magazines, but also insisted that there was some mystical guiding spirit behind his 'dream made concrete'. Feeling that in giving him work in the cemetery, the local council had 'relegated him to the realm of the dead', he fashioned his own fantastic realm instead, bringing the whole wide world to his door.

Everywhere you look you can see giraffes and palm trees, camels and huge butterflies. In the chapel attached to the back of the house, the walls and ceiling are again completely covered in a mosaic pattern of flowers and a large cross and a rather sinister figure of Christ, dressed all in black, pointing to the three crosses on Mount Calvary. And beyond the chapel is the Cour noire (Black Courtyard) with its black mosaic tomb topped by a scaled-down version of Chartres Cathedral and decorated with an image of the Virgin Mary and a whole series of symbols, while a huge mosaic of Jerusalem, the Holy City, dominates the garden.

portal, which still has some interesting carving – look out for the figure at the top sticking out his tongue.

Almost opposite here several flights of steps lead back up, via a formal garden or an atmospheric cobbled street between high walls, to the **rue du Cardinal-Pie** with its 18th-century seminary. On the way, beautiful views of the east end of the cathedral give you a real sense of the rhythm of the architecture. The rue des Lisses brings you through an archway and along the little rue Saint-Yorre to the north portal of the cathedral.

Chartres has one more sight, accessible on foot via the place Saint-Pierre (about half an hour's walk from the cathedral), the **Maison Picassiette**, an extraordinary example of naïve art (see box).

Illiers-Combray

Marcel Proust

Admirers of Marcel Proust make their own pilgrimage beyond Chartres, travelling the 25 kilometres southwest (local trains from Chartres) across the plain to Illiers-Combray, the village where his father's family came from and where he spent happy holidays up to the age of nine, when his severe asthma put an end to stays in the country. It was just Illiers in those days. The 'Combray' has been added in deference to the village's reincarnation under that name in the pages of Proust's great novel *A la recherche du temps perdu*

The Pré Catalan at Illiers-Combray

(*Remembrance of Times Past*, 1913–27). But in other respects, the empty countryside, peopled only by the odd bereted figure cycling slowly along, and the village itself are curiously untouched by tourism – this sleepy, remote spot seems to take little notice of the homage paid to Proust at the **Maison de Tante Léonie**, the house where his father's sister lived.

The house can only be visited on the dot of 14.30 and 16.00 six days a week, so you must time yourself carefully, though there are many other sites from the novel to keep you busy while you are waiting for the magic hour.

'The past never dies in us,' wrote Proust. At Illiers-Combray it has been faithfully preserved in aspic, which means that even for those unfamiliar with his novel, the house offers a fascinating glimpse into a bourgeois way of life in provincial, rural France in the late 19th century, complete with antimacassars and artificial flower arrangements beneath glass domes. The dark, neat little rooms re-create the setting for episodes in *Du Côté de chez Swann* (*Swann's Way*), the first volume of *A la recherche du temps perdu*: the nervy narrator's childhood bedroom, complete with magic lantern, where he waited in agony for his mother's goodnight kiss; 'Tante Léonie''s bedroom, with *tisane* and madeleine at the ready on the bedside table; and the kitchen with its gleaming copper pans.

The tiny garden is unchanged, too. You can almost hear Swann's double ring at the traditional metal garden gate. The contrast between the quiet provincial background of Proust's father's family and the fashionable life in Paris high society led by Proust as he gathered material for his novel is well illustrated by the permanent exhibition in the outhouse (grandly called 'The Orangery') of photographs by Paul Nadar of some of his closest friends. The house next door has been turned into a small museum.

Swann's Gate

Elsewhere in the village you can visit the **Pré Catalan**, his uncle's flower garden ('Tansonville' in the novel); the **church of Saint-Jacques** ('Saint-Hilaire'), with painted ceiling beams, enclosed pews and some interesting modern stained glass; the famous hawthorn hedge and much more. Leaflets with a map pinpointing these places are available from the tourist office (5 rue Henri-Germond, ⓣ 02-37-24-21-79). But as it keeps short hours, and is shut altogether from November to the end of March, I recommend that you ask for one at the Chartres tourist office, or write to the departmental tourist board (see p. 19).

East of Chartres

The flat countryside dotted with windmills and sleepy villages seems much further away from Paris than the map suggests. Beyond **Angerville** (46km southeast), a small town with a pleasant hotel★ converted from an old coaching inn, **Méréville** is famous for its watercress (see p. 48) and also has a splendid 16th-century market building. The gardens of the local château were redesigned in the 18th century for a wealthy banker by the landscape painter Hubert Robert and François Belanger, the architect of the little Bagatelle Château in Paris's Bois de Boulogne. The result was a supremely romantic garden dotted with what were known as

Méréville

Key data

CHARTRES 28000

T.O.   pl. de la Cathédrale, ⓣ 02-37-21-50-00

Access Paris 88km, Maintenon 19km, Rambouillet 41km, Versailles 70km; **rail** from Paris-Montparnasse

Sights **Cathédrale Notre-Dame** (Gothic cathedral); **Eglise Saint-André** (ruined Romanesque church); **Eglise Saint-Pierre** (Romanesque and Gothic church); **Maison Picassiette** (see box, p. 88), 22 rue du Repos, ⓣ 02-37-34-10-78, closed Tue and Nov–end Mar (but visits arranged by prior appointment; inquire at T.O.); **Musée des Beaux-Arts** (painting, sculpture, history of cathedral) in former Bishop's Palace, 29 cloître Notre-Dame, ⓣ 02-37-36-41-39, closed Tue; **Musée/Centre du Vitrail** (exhibition on stained glass techniques), in **Cellier de Loëns** (cathedral storehouse), 5 rue du Cardinal-Pie, ⓣ 02-37-21-65-72, closed am weekends; **Vieux quartiers** (medieval streets)

Lunch Chartres

Staying Chartres, Angerville, Saint-Symphorien-le-Château

Also   Maintenon

Château de Dourdan (medieval castle), 91416 Dourdan, ⓣ 01-64-59-86-97, open Wed–Sun; **Maison de Tante Léonie** (Marcel Proust memorial/museum), 4 rue du Docteur-Proust, 28120 Illiers-Combray, ⓣ 02-37-24-30-97, closed Mon; visits only at 14.30 and 16.00.

fabriques: miniature buildings, grottoes and a variety of architectural features adding interest to the landscape. Two of these can still be seen, the **Tour Trajan**, modelled on Trajan's Column in Rome, and the **Lavoir** (wash house) on the banks of the river Juigne.

Northwest of Méréville, **Chalou-Moulineux** marks the beginning of the pretty, winding Chalouette Valley. The stretch from there to **Chalo-Saint-Mars** allows you to see some attractive stone buildings. Then further north, surrounded by forests, the ancient town of **Dourdan** (accessible from Paris on the RER C4 line), once a stronghold of Hugues Capet, has a ruined feudal **castle** built in the early 13th century by King Philippe-Auguste. The tall keep has survived, along with the bottom portion of the curtain wall, several towers, and the gatehouse. A local history museum can be visited inside the castle, which is one of the buildings featured in the famous Book of Hours, *Les Très Riches Heures du Duc de Berry* (see p. 134).

Dourdan

4 Vallée de Chevreuse

The Bois de Boulogne on the western edge of Paris is often referred to as the city's 'lung'. But it always seems something of a misnomer for an area crossed by busy roads. It would be more appropriate to use the term for the Vallée de Chevreuse, a stretch of countryside that has long been popular with ramblers and riders, and also with wealthy Parisians seeking boltholes easily reached from the capital.

The area officially known as the **Haute Vallée de Chevreuse** (Upper Chevreuse Valley) starts only about 20 kilometres southwest of Paris, and is close to the New Town of Saint-Quentin-en-Yvelines (see p. 8), yet has remained surprisingly rural, with its woods and meadows, its old stone village houses, dovecots and working farms.

When property developers began to take too close an interest in the area, the regional council took action to ensure the right balance between environmental protection and economic development, and the valley was officially designated a nature park in 1985.

The **Parc naturel régional de la Haute Vallée de Chevreuse** covers about 25,000 hectares, with woodland or forest making up 40 per cent of it. It includes some important tourist sights like the **Château de Breteuil**, the **Château de Dampierre**, the ruins of **Les Vaux-de-Cernay Abbey**, and the **Port-Royal-des-Champs** abbey buildings, with their literary associations, plus many attractive private châteaux or manor houses. Several of the villages still have relatively rustic inns where you can spend a peaceful night or two, though some are also popular for weddings and business lunches. Ramblers can also stay in modest accommodation known as *gîtes d'étape* near the village of La-Celle-les-Bordes or near Dampierre, where there is also a campsite.

Nature park

Over 200 kilometres of marked paths and hiking trails have been plotted and the **GR1(C)** and **GR11** hiking trails also go through the nature park. On the southern edge is the Espace Rambouillet (see p. 101).

The park has an information centre in Chevreuse, the **Maison du Parc**, where exhibitions are sometimes staged. During the weekend and on Wednesdays, leaflets and maps showing footpaths and hiking trails are available from the tourist office opposite the RER station in Saint-Rémy-les-Chevreuse. Bikes can be rented from various places. Check locally or ☎ 01-34-86-84-51. You may be able to arrange to have bikes delivered to a hotel, station or other convenient place by this firm, called **Loca Cycles**, which specializes in mountain bikes. Another firm in Dampierre (☎ 01-30-02-56-40) provides the same service.

● **Maison du Parc natural régional**, Château de la Madeleine, BP 73, 78460 Chevreuse, ☎ 01-30-52-09-09 (Mon–Sat), ℻ 01-30-52-12-43
● **T.O. de Saint-Rémy**, 1 rue Ditte, 78470 Saint-Rémy-les-Chevreuse, ☎ 01-30-52-22-49

Chevreuse

The village that gives the valley its name lies on the river Yvette, over-looked by its ruined medieval castle, the **Château de la Madeleine**, once owned by the powerful (and princely) Guise family. It was knocked down in the 17th century on the orders of Louis XIII's min-ister Cardinal Richelieu, who made a habit of demolishing aristo-cratic residences that might put his own in the shade. But it still looks impressive with its keep and its old walls and machicolated towers. It houses the nature park's information office, but is often otherwise closed for restoration.

Before climbing up there, do head for the river, running parallel to the village high street, and enjoy a delightful walk past wash houses and little bridges linking the path with a row of back gardens.

Port-Royal-des-Champs

Jean Racine

Chevreuse's castle is the starting-point for the **Chemin de Jean Racine**, a marked footpath that will take you, in the footsteps of the great classical dramatist, through a wooded valley to what is left of the Abbaye de Port-Royal-des-Champs, where Racine was educated between the ages of fifteen and eighteen, acquiring the detailed knowledge of Greek and Roman history and literature that underpins his tragedies.

Strange as it seems, this quiet setting was the scene, three cen-turies ago, of bitter religious disputes between the Jesuits and the pro-ponents of the austere doctrine of Jansenism.

There is very little left of the abbey, but the site is peaceful and beautiful, a good place for some contemplation of your own. To find out more about Jansenism, and the prolonged (and somewhat obscure to the non-specialist) disputes with the Jesuits, follow the signs to the **Musée national des Granges de Port-Royal**.

Château de Breteuil

South of Chevreuse, in a rural setting close to the GR11 hiking trail, lies one of the pleasantest places to visit close to Paris. The unstuffy atmosphere at the **Château de Breteuil**, the energetic efforts of the owners to make sure that everyone, young and old, enjoys the visit, make it seem rather like an English stately home. To add to this impression, the Marquis de Breteuil and his wife, who have restored and embellished the château mainly by their own labours, and live in one of the lodges, often greet you in person, especially at weekends. This is a good place to bring children, as there is plenty to keep them amused.

The château was virtually abandoned when M. de Breteuil, then only twenty-three, was given it by his father as a wedding present in 1967. It had been built in the early 17th century, and lived in by his family since 1712.

The Château de Breteuil

The central brick and stone structure facing you as you walk through the entrance gates is part of the original building, typical of the Henri IV style with its tall slate roofs. But the flanking portions were added in the 19th century, and the side wings at the beginning of the 20th, in the same overall style so that the general impression is of a harmonious whole.

Visiting the château

The château may not be particularly special architecturally speaking, but the Breteuils have produced some strong personalities who have played important parts in France's – and Europe's – history. So as well as being well furnished, mainly in 18th-century style, the interior has been enlivened by a series of waxwork tableaux illustrating some key incidents. One shows the second Baron de Breteuil, a top ambassador and later minister, handing over to Louis XVI, under the close scrutiny of Marie-Antoinette (a great fan of the baron), the document setting out his greatest diplomatic coup: the Peace of Teschen of May 1779, which ended the War of the Bavarian Succession between Prussia and Austria. He was rewarded by the Austrian empress Maria Theresia, Marie-Antoinette's mother, with the gift of a fabulous gilt-bronze table whose top is inlaid with 128 gems and semi-precious stones, each carefully numbered, and surrounded by garlands and oval medallions in Meissen porcelain. This 'Teschen Table' is the château's greatest treasure, beautifully displayed (the idea for presenting it came from the couturier Karl Lagerfeld).

The Teschen Table

93

The baron eventually became prime minister, but the timing of the appointment was decidedly unfortunate: 11 July 1789, just three days before the storming of the Bastille spelled the outbreak of the French Revolution. Almost a century later, in March 1881, a meeting at the château involving another head of government sowed the seeds for another document that was to have a far-reaching effect on Europe – the Entente Cordiale between France and Britain. A tableau in the smoking room features Léon Gambetta, leaning casually back on the sofa, and enjoying brandy and cigars with the eighth Marquis de Breteuil and his friend the Prince of Wales, the future Edward VII.

The eighth marquis was famous for his lavish entertaining of the *crème de la crème* of Europe. Not just his fellow-aristocrats, but politicians, artists and writers, and scientists. Marcel Proust, a frequent visitor, used him as the model for the Marquis de Bréauté-Consalvi in his *A la recherche du temps perdu* (where he turns out to have been one of Odette's lovers). So a languidly reclining Proust, wrapped cosily in a cashmere dressing gown and with a hot-water bottle, can be seen in the splendid chinoiserie bed in the Chambre de Laque (Lacquered Bedroom).

Marcel Proust

A third prime minister, the Duc Decazes – an ancestor of the present marquise – appears in the tableau in the library along with her husband's ancestor Charles de Breteuil, and Louis XVIII, who met them here in 1820. The king, suffering from gout, is sitting in a leather-upholstered armchair by the great cabinet-maker Georges Jacob that is in fact a cleverly disguised wheelchair.

The tableaux are very well done, as are the waxwork scenes in the kitchens, commemorating the 'downstairs' element of a lunch party given in May 1905 for Edward VII. Upstairs you have seen the table laid with the finest Sèvres china in the panelled dining room. Below stairs, the butler and chambermaid entertain the king's chauffeur at their own lunch party, while Madame la Marquise congratulates the chefs next door. Also down here is a reconstruction of *The Sleeping Beauty*, whose author Charles Perrault worked for a Breteuil.

Visiting the grounds

More characters from Perrault's fairytales dot the grounds: Puss in Boots in the stables, Red Riding Hood in the Dolls' House, Tom Thumb in the orchard, and a scene from *Peau d'Ane* in the wash house.

Flower lovers should head for the **Jardin des Princes** (Princes' Garden, commemorating the visits of two Princes of Wales). It has been replanted and designed in 18th-century style, with many roses and peonies. The **formal gardens**, with their ornamental pools, their velvety sweep of lawn, their statues and terracotta urns, have been restored, and an interesting box maze planted. Beyond them you can walk in an ancient chestnut grove, and inspect dozens of species of ducks and geese on the ponds. Nearer the château are the medieval **dovecot**, the **orangery**, and the **ice store**. You are positively encouraged to picnic at wooden tables and benches, some roofed over for use in rainy or very hot weather, though on summer Sundays and public holidays you can have a snack and a drink at the **crêperie**. There is even a children's playground.

Formal gardens

Beauty and brains

Perhaps the most attractive portrait in the Château de Breteuil is that of Gabrielle-Emilie Le Tonnelier de Breteuil, Marquise du Châtelet Lomont, elegantly attired – and holding a pair of compasses.

She was clever as well as beautiful, becoming famous in scientific circles both in her own right, and as the translator into French of Isaac Newton's *Principia*, and texts by the German philosopher and mathematician Gottfried Leibniz. She was born in 1706, the daughter of the first Baron de Breteuil, who taught her Latin and Italian. She then moved on to study maths and science. She became a distinguished physicist and chemist, and also wrote on philosophy, attempting to use advanced mathematics to explain the nature of matter. She was one of the leading lights of the court at the Château de Lunéville, near Nancy, presided over by ex-king Stanislas of Poland.

At one time she lived in the lovely Hôtel Lambert on the Ile Saint-Louis in Paris, where she gave shelter to Voltaire, her lover for sixteen years. During their sometimes stormy relationship, he spent ten years living with her at her husband's ancestral château at Cirey-sur Blaise in Champagne, writing many of his philosophical texts (including one on Newton's work), and so much enjoying the meals she served him that he once wrote to a friend that he fully expected that they would both live to a hundred.

But it was not to be, as she died at Lunéville in her early forties. In his memoirs, Voltaire paid her what his contemporaries no doubt felt to be the highest of compliments: "This woman who has translated Newton and explained his work is, in short, a very great man."

Les Vaux-de-Cernay

West of Breteuil, the wooded valley called Les Vaux-de-Cernay is popular with weekending Parisians. With its boulders picturesquely scattered among the trees, its waterfalls and its lake, it offers many delightful walks (and a few modest places to eat beside the lake). The lake was used as a fishtank by the monks from the **Abbaye des Vaux-de-Cernay**, a medieval abbey that was partly rebuilt during the Renaissance. Much of it was demolished during the French Revolution, but part of the nave of the abbey church has survived, the stone tracery that once enclosed the rose window making a wonderful sight against the sky. The ruins are in the grounds of a most attractive hotel★, now occupying the baronial hall-style buildings converted from what was left of the abbey by the Rothschilds in the 19th century. The grounds are open to the public (small charge at weekends), and various restored parts of the abbey are used for occasional concerts (see p. 28).

Château de Dampierre

Dampierre is north of the abbey, near the pretty little village of Senlisse, which has a pleasant auberge★ and, on the way to Dampierre, the Château de la Cour-Senlisse, not open to the public but a fine sight with its large pepperpot towers, set amid peaceful meadows.

Dampierre is busier, as it is frequented by groups of cyclists (bike hire available). It has several restaurants, one of them in the stables of the moated 17th-century **château**.

Ruins of medieval Vaux-de-Cernay Abbey

You can enjoy a bird's eye view of the classical façades in pinkish brick and yellowish stone, beautifully set against the dark green backcloth of the forest, by climbing up to the top of the grassy mound opposite. This gives you a chance to appreciate, in a way that is rarely possible, the overall layout of this distinguished and very French château, designed by Jules Hardouin-Mansart and surrounded by grounds landscaped by André Le Nôtre, Mansart's colleague at Versailles. The interior seems rather lifeless after Breteuil. But the white and gold salons, their walls lined with portraits, are fine examples of the Louis XV style. The **Chambre de la Reine** (Queen's Bedroom) was decorated for Louis XV's queen Marie Leszczynska. She often stayed here as she was a close friend of the Duc de Luynes, whose descendants still own the château today.

Bird's-eye view of Château de Dampierre

Key data

Cᴴᴇᴠʀᴇᴜsᴇ 78460
T.O. pl. du Général-de-Gaulle, ☏ 01-30-52-02-27
Access Paris 32km, Versailles 16km, Rambouillet 18km; **RER** line B4 to
Saint-Rémy-les-Chevreuse, then **bus** or 2km walk or taxi ride
Sights **Château de la Madeleine** (ruined medieval château), housing
nature park information office
Lunch Chevreuse, Dampierre, Senlisse, Les Vaux-de-Cernay
Staying Dampierre, Senlisse, Les Vaux-de-Cernay
Also Rambouillet, Versailles

Abbaye des Vaux-de-Cernay (ruined medieval abbey)
78720 Cernay-la-Ville, ☏ 01-34-85-23-00 (**buses** from Saint-Rémy-les
Chevreuse via Chevreuse, Dampierre to Cernay, then 2km walk),
open year-round
Château de Breteuil
78460 Choisel, ☏ 01-30-52-05-11 (occasional **buses** on summer
Suns from Saint-Rémy via Chevreuse, Dampierre, Senlisse, or from
Rambouillet; 7km marked path from Chevreuse), open year-round:
château pm only (but from 11.00 Sun, public hols and throughout
French school holidays); grounds open all day
Château de Dampierre
78720 Dampierre-en-Yvelines, ☏ 01-30-52-53-24, open Apr to mid-
Oct, pm only, closed Tue (**buses** from Saint-Rémy via Chevreuse, from
Rambouillet via Senlisse)
Musée national des Granges de Port-Royal (Jansenism)
78470 Magny-les-Hameaux, ☏ 01-30-43-73-05 (**buses** from Saint-
Rémy via Chevreuse, then 10-min walk, or 5km walk or taxi ride),
closed Tue

5 Maintenon, Rambouillet

Château de Maintenon

The attractive turreted and moated **Château de Maintenon**, whose
name was adopted by its best-known owner, Louis XIV's morganatic
second wife Madame de Maintenon, is one of those places that has
been much altered and added to over the centuries and yet forms a
pleasingly harmonious whole. Built chiefly in warm pinkish brick
with slate roofs, it still has its square medieval tower, but the main
structure, with cylindrical towers, dates from the early 16th century,
when it was acquired by the royal treasurer in settlement of a debt.
He added a Renaissance wing, decorating it with the lizards and
crescents on his coat of arms.

It was one of his descendants who sold it in 1674 to Françoise
d'Aubigné, granddaughter of the Huguenot diplomat, soldier and
poet Agrippa d'Aubigné and widow of the crippled satirical poet Paul

Madame de Maintenon

Scarron. After her husband's death she became friendly with Louis XIV's mistress, the beautiful and haughty Marquise de Montespan, who asked her in 1669 to become governess to her growing number of children by the king. She accepted, but had to remain well out of sight until 1671, when her illegitimate charges were officially legitimized. From then on she was frequently to be seen at court with them, and the king gave her the money to buy a château where both their parents could visit them openly – some of the later offspring were even born at their governess's home.

Louis now started calling her 'Madame de Maintenon', and in due course switched his affections from La Montespan to the somewhat severe governess, who was busy adding a new wing to her château, as well as starting up schools, workshops and a hospital in and around the village. A few months after the death in 1683 of his Spanish queen Maria Theresa, the king married Madame de Maintenon in a secret ceremony. She now lived chiefly at Versailles, though she still spent some time in her own much loved château, and Louis and his court also stayed there at intervals during the building of the famous Maintenon Aqueduct. But in 1698 she presented the château to her niece, on her marriage to a member of the aristocratic Noailles family, which still owns it today. After the king's death she withdrew to the convent school she had founded near Versailles at Saint-Cyr, where she died four years later, in 1719.

Maintenon still had one brief role to play in the history of France's monarchy: it was here, in 1830, that Louis's grandson Charles X spent the night on his way from Rambouillet into exile. Twenty years later the Duc de Noailles converted a corridor into a splendid gallery lined by portraits of his ancestors. Although the château was badly damaged during the Franco-Prussian War in 1870–1, and again in both world wars, it has now been carefully restored and displays many portraits and mementoes of its eponymous chatelaine (invariably looking distinctly severe – in one, depicting Peter the Great visiting her, she looks a positive harridan).

The prettiest of the reception rooms still have their 18th-century wallpaper, hand painted in China and featuring bamboos and flocks of birds. Madame de Maintenon's bedroom, small yet rather grand, has pale blue silk hangings and gilded panelling, while the walls of her anteroom are covered in patterned leather. The chapel can also be visited, with its mausoleum to the great lady.

Jean Racine

The romantic gardens, laid out by André Le Nôtre, were a favourite strolling place for the great playwright Jean Racine (see **Port-Royal**), who wrote two religious tragedies at the château for Madame de Maintenon, *Esther* (1689) and *Athalie* (1691), to be performed by the aristocratic young ladies at Saint-Cyr. The views of the aqueduct in the distance, and then back towards the château, are delightful, especially on hazy autumn days.

Rambouillet

Of all the many forests near Paris where France's monarchs could indulge their passion for hunting, the **Forêt de Rambouillet** is reputed, even today, to have the most plentiful stocks of game. Hence the frequent visits of those same kings to the **Château de Rambouillet**, and hence its small size in relation to the huge outbuildings, where horses could be stabled and groomed, hounds and servants quartered, saddles stored and the household run round the daily hunting sorties.

The forest

The forest is still the main attraction at Rambouillet (for walking, riding, biking and nature rambles rather than hunting), since the château is not particularly distinguished architecturally, looking more like a rather grand country house hotel set in well-kept grounds than a royal residence, though the interior does have some exceptionally fine panelling. This is just as well, as since the 1890s it has been an official residence for France's presidents. At such times it is naturally closed to the public, so always check before setting out.

It was built in the late 14th century, then bought a few years later by the d'Angennes family, one of whose descendants was captain of François Ier's bodyguard. In February 1547 the king, always a restless man, constantly on the move, but already seriously ill, had a sudden yen for a spot of hunting, claiming it would revive him. So he stopped off at Rambouillet on his way back to Paris from visiting his mistress, the Duchesse d'Etampes. But the fresh air and exercise failed to work their usual magic. His health deteriorated rapidly, and on 30 March

Key data

MAINTENON 28130

Access   Paris 69km, Chartres 19km, Rambouillet 25km; **rail** from Paris-Montparnasse (via Versailles-Chantiers and Rambouillet) and Chartres

Sights   Château de Maintenon (mainly 17th-century, residence of Madame de Maintenon), ☏ 02-37-23-00-09, open pm only, closed Tue and Jan; weekends only Nov to end Mar

Lunch   Maintenon

Staying   Maintenon

Also   Chartres, Anet

RAMBOUILLET 78120

T.O.   Hôtel de Ville (opposite château), ☏ 01-34-83-21-21

Access   Paris 49km, Maintenon 25km, Versailles 32km, Chartres 41km; **rail** from Paris-Montparnasse (via Versailles-Chantiers) or Chartres

Sights   **Château**, ☏ 01-34-83-00-25, closed Tue*; **Laiterie de la Reine** (Marie-Antoinette's Diary), closed Tue and some weekends*; **Bergerie Nationale** (National Sheep Farm), ☏ 01-34-83-68-00, open Wed to Sun; **Musée Rambolitrain**, (model trains and toys), pl. Jeanne-d'Arc, ☏ 01-34-83-15-93, open Wed to Sun

Lunch   Rambouillet

Also   Chartres, Vallée de Chevreuse, Versailles

*As the château is used by the French president as an occasional residence, always check on day whether it is open to the public.

he died in the keep, known ever since as the Tour François 1er.

Shortly afterwards the rest of the medieval castle was turned into a residence more in keeping with the times. One of its chatelaines in the next century was the celebrated Marquise de Rambouillet whose Paris *salon* was frequented by the leading literary lights of the day. By the early 18th century the château had its first royal owner: the Comte de Toulouse, the youngest of Louis XIV's sons by Madame de Montespan.

One of the king's first additions was a modern sheep farm, where he bred Merino sheep from a flock specially shepherded all the way from Spain. Virtually all of them made it to Rambouillet, where their distant descendants can still be admired in what is now the **Bergerie nationale** (National Sheep Farm), doubling as a training school for today's shepherds. To keep his queen Marie-Antoinette happy – she did not care for Rambouillet – he also built a dairy for her, the **Laiterie de la Reine**, similar in spirit to the one in her 'hamlet' at Versailles (p. 76), but in the style of a classical temple. This, too, can be visited, complete with its little grotto for cooling the milk churns.

Sheep farm

The last king to stay at Rambouillet was Charles X, in 1830. But he was not there for the hunting: the Parisians were manning the barricades during the '*Trois Glorieuses*', the 'Three Glorious Days' of street-fighting at the end of July that spelt the end of the Restoration and eventually put Louis-Philippe on the throne. A couple of days after his arrival he was forced to abdicate and set off for exile in England via Maintenon. Oddly enough, fifteen years earlier, Napoleon, an occasional resident during the hunting season, had spent his last night at Rambouillet before setting off on his own exile, to St Helena.

Visiting the château

The most interesting rooms are the pleasantly intimate state suite designed for the Comte de Toulouse, with delicately carved panelling, some painted and gilded, some stripped to the bare wood, and Gobelins and Beauvais tapestries – don't miss the chairs covered with scenes from La Fontaine's *Fables*. The guided tour also includes the marble-clad **Salle de Marbre**, dating from the Renaissance, originally the summer dining room, now a presidential meeting room, and **Napoleon's Bathroom**, decorated with landscapes and buildings familiar to him, and featuring his bee emblem.

The gardens

The formal garden, with its Grand Canal and twin islands, watched over by recumbent bronze stags, and its Cypress Walk (planted by Napoleon), leads into the informal **Jardin anglais**. Here you can visit the curious **Chaumière des Coquillages** (Shell Cottage). The walls of one room in this little architectural folly are covered in thousands of seashells and bits of mother of pearl.

Beyond the château

Model trains

Near the château in the place Jeanne-d'Arc, the **Musée Rambolitrain** is popular with small (and grown-up) boys for its large collection of model trains. Over four thousand exhibits are on show, including some 19th-century models.

But the biggest draw is the forest, much frequented by ramblers, bikers – there are around 100km of marked cycle paths – anglers and swimmers (at the **Etangs de Hollande**, where pedalos and windsurfing gear can be hired). The **Espace Rambouillet**, 8km southeast of the château in the Massif des Yvelines, is a nature reserve where you can observe deer and wild boar roaming freely, and watch, weather permitting, demonstrations involving birds of prey. (℡ 01-34-83-05-00, open year-round, but closed Mon from Nov to end Mar.)

Nature reserve

6 Anet

Royal mistresses often wielded extraordinary influence in France. A visit to what remains of the Renaissance **Château d'Anet**, in pretty countryside on the edge of the Forêt de Dreux, shows how one of them, Diane de Poitiers, the coldly calculating favourite of Henri II, was able to enlarge and embellish the château she had inherited from her husband until it rivalled many a royal palace.

Diane de Poitiers

Handsome, with broad shoulders, long legs and a high domed forehead, intelligent and cultured, she first attracted Henri, the second son of François Ier, when he was a boy of eleven. And though she was twenty years older, he loved her till the day he died. Once lady in-waiting to his mother, Claude de France, she was the widow of Louis de Brézé, Grand Seneschal of Normandy, a grandson of Charles VII and his own beautiful mistress Agnès Sorel – and said to be the ugliest man in France. She had been a faithful wife to him, despite his own infidelities, and never wore any colour other than black or white after his death in 1531. (As she was well aware, this colour scheme only served to emphasize her proud, dignified bearing.)

The architect she and Henri chose for Anet was Philibert Delorme. His Italianate design featured three wings round a central courtyard, whose fourth side was a much longer entrance front, mainly in stone, but with much brick patterning too, centring on a monumental gatehouse. The rear façade overlooked large formal gardens. For the interior decoration, Diane commissioned work from the leading artists of the day, including Benvenuto Cellini, who had been summoned to France by François Ier (see **Fontainebleau**). It was he who cast

Château d'Anet: monumental gateway

the bronze bas-relief of a recumbent Diane adorning the gatehouse (though the version you see today is a copy, as the original is in the Louvre). The sculptor Germain Pilon, later to carve Henri's tomb at Saint-Denis, worked at Anet, and so did Jean Goujon, whose medallion of Diane with her arms entwined round a stag can still be seen there.

After Diane's death, a number of additions and alterations were made by the new owner, a great-grandson of Henri IV and yet another royal mistress, Gabrielle d'Estrées. In the 18th century the château was owned by the Duchesse du Maine, who held splendid receptions there, as she did at Sceaux (see p. 79). Much was demolished during the French Revolution, though some portions were sold off and have survived. For instance the elegant portico on the main courtyard façade can now be seen in Paris, at the Ecole des Beaux-Arts.

Visiting the château

The long entrance front is intact and makes an impressive sight as you approach the château, with its sculpture group of a stag and a pair of hounds surmounting the gateway, silhouetted against the sky. You can visit Delorme's domed chapel in the shape of a Greek cross, its marble paving echoing the complex design of the cupola. The west wing has survived, too. The guided tour includes Diane's bedroom, with its large fireplace and a portrait of her by Primaticcio, and the splendid staircase added after her death, offering lovely views over the canal and lawns from the landing. The Salon Rouge has a pretty painted ceiling and some good Renaissance furniture, the dining room some fine tapestries and work by Jean Goujon.

A few minutes' walk away, the **Chapelle funéraire**, a mausoleum built to house Diane's tomb, is covered by the same admission charge. It was presumably planned by Diane – who was reputed to have become rather pious in retirement – since work started on it before her death. The tomb was smashed open during the Revolution and her remains were flung into a hastily dug ditch. They were subsequently rescued and reburied beside the parish church. But the rather creepy interior of the mausoleum, now restored, is the place to ponder on the kneeling statue of the ever-youthful royal mistress, with bare-breasted sphinxes below her.

Key data

ANET 28260

T.O.	8 rue Delacroix, ☏ 02-37-41-49-09
Access	Paris 78km, Dreux 16km, Thoiry 30km, Giverny 40km; **rail** from Paris-Montparnasse to Dreux or Paris-Saint-Lazare to Bueil, then connecting **bus**
Sights	**Château d'Anet** (Renaissance château), ☏ 02-37-41-90-07, open Feb to end Nov, pm only: May to end Oct, daily except Tue; Feb, Mar and Nov, weekends and public hols only; **Chapelle funéraire** (Diane de Poitiers's mausoleum), same opening times as château
Lunch	Anet

Ile de France ~ west of Paris

The upmarket residential area just west of Paris is crossed by the busy N13 road, a major artery leading out of the city. Yet as soon as you head away from it, the 20th century impinges surprisingly little. The **Château de Malmaison** and its annex the **Château de Bois-Préau**, both housing Napoleonic collections, are set in peaceful gardens that are delightful for strolling. And a little further west, Ivan Turgenev's 'dacha', a little bit of Russia hidden in the trees, is a world away from the traffic pounding past at the foot of the hill.

The **river Seine**, once thronged with boating merrymakers, meanders quietly beside you as you trace the route taken by many an Impressionist painter, though the frenzy of those sunny outings, captured on so many canvases, can once again be sensed when you visit the **Maison Fournaise**, on an island in the river at **Chatou**.

The Seine flows on past **Marly-le-Roi**, whose royal château is no more, and the fabulous residence built by Alexandre Dumas *père* at **Port Marly**, towards elegant **Saint-Germain-en-Laye**, long the seat of the royal court, now a pleasant and quite lively town. Several meanders later, on the edge of Normandy, it reaches the riverside villages so often painted by Claude Monet, whose house and garden at **Giverny** are one of the tourist highspots of the area round Paris. Southeast of here, the safari park at the **Château de Thoiry** is another highspot, especially for anyone with children.

Buses from La Défense and the RER make visiting the area as far as Saint-Germain-en-Laye easy without a car. Giverny requires a train journey and a walk or taxi ride. Biking is a good way of exploring the nearby villages. For Thoiry, a car is preferable, though train-plus-taxi is also possible.

7 Malmaison, Chatou, Bougival, Marly

Malmaison

One of those familiar watercolours of roses by Pierre-Joseph Redouté is a good image to have in your mind's eye as you make your way westwards through a dull residential area interspersed with the French headquarters of multinational companies. For you are heading towards the **Château de Malmaison**, close to a big loop of the

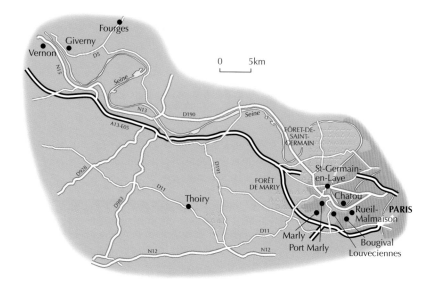

Josephine

river Seine at **Rueil-Malmaison**, and it was in this relatively modest house that Napoleon's first wife Josephine created a famous rose garden, commissioning her employee Redouté to paint the two hundred and more varieties and species she grew there. He never quite finished the assignment, but his beautiful watercolours, first published a few years after Josephine's death, have been used to re-create the smaller rose garden that is one of the main attractions of a summer visit today.

La Malmaison, as it was known then, was the setting for the happiest periods in her marriage, when Napoleon was First Consul and they spent a great deal of time there. But she always loved the house, and it was here that she withdrew, after she had been repudiated in December 1809 so that Napoleon could further his dynastic ambitions with a new young bride. And it was here that she died less than five years later, after catching a chill as, in doing the honours of the garden to Czar Nicholas I, she lingered too long out of doors on a chilly moonlit night, wearing a flimsy low-cut gown in the fashionable Empire style she had helped to create.

Napoleon Bonaparte

A chastened Napoleon visited the house less than a year later, following his escape from Elba, to pay his last respects to the beautiful, exotic creature who had played an important part in helping him to consolidate his authority during the Consulate. And he returned briefly after his defeat at the Battle of Waterloo, for a few days of solitary contemplation, before being forced into a second and final exile on St Helena.

The house seemed to lend itself to quiet reflection, for it was at La Malmaison, as he sat in his study or paced up and down the gardens, that he had thought through the major reforms that are the lasting legacy of his fifteen years as ruler of France. The detailed Civil Code that is still the basis of French law was planned here. So was the final shape of the administrative reorganization of the country that had started soon after the French Revolution. Here he devised the unified structure of secondary and higher education that is the basis of today's educational system, and set up the coveted Légion d'Honneur awards. And here too he came to the conclusion that religion was a necessary part of national life and reversed the Revolution's abolition of the Catholic Church in France.

The background

It is as well to remember all this as you visit what is usually thought of as Josephine's home. It is true that she bought it – though Napoleon later paid for it – as she had taken a liking to the area when staying with friends nearby.

Josephine's house

That was in 1799, three years after their wedding. It had been built in the 1620s, as a country house for a wealthy lawyer, then enlarged in the 18th century, when it was used as a summer residence by a group of liberal-minded men and women of letters that included the early Romantic poet André Chénier.

It was also Josephine who commissioned a pair of young architects, Charles Percier and Pierre-François Fontaine, to create an elegant residence, with reception rooms suitable for entertaining the brilliant society who were soon being invited to La Malmaison. Percier and Fontaine were to become the leading exponents of the 'Empire' decorative style, and here they added pillars and friezes to produce what was then known as a 'Roman' or 'Pompeian' effect. But although they would have preferred to pull the house down and start again, they also decided to bring out the house's original role as a country seat intended only for the summer months. So the rooms have a summery feel, with their long french windows opening into the gardens, and the marquee-like canopies both in the decor and on the façade.

Napoleon was soon decreeing that a ground-floor room must be converted into a Council Chamber, and having a library built on. But by 1802, when he was proclaimed First Consul for life and thus was to all intents and purposes sole head of state, he was

La Malmaison: Empress Josephine's home

spending most of his time in the palaces lived in by his royal predecessors. He still enjoyed brief stays at La Malmaison for the remaining two years of the Consulate. And during his prolonged absences on the battlefields of Europe, the newly crowned Empress Josephine made it her main residence, lavishing a great deal of money on enlarging the estate, redesigning the gardens, and embellishing the house.

So it is appropriate that a reorganization of the State's Napoleonic collections has turned the château into a museum focusing on Napoleon as general and consul, as well as on Josephine herself, while Emperor Napoleon is commemorated in Fontainebleau Palace (see pp. 169–77); and his final period of exile on St Helena, plus his enduring posthumous fame, is the subject addressed in the **Château de Bois-Préau**, on the adjoining estate to La Malmaison, bought by Josephine in 1810.

A last-minute reprieve

It would not be a museum at all, or even still standing, had it not been for a part-Egyptian banker poetically known as 'Osiris'. In 1896, after many vicissitudes, it was about to be auctioned off and demolition seemed certain. But 'Osiris' happened to hear about the auction, bought it himself, spent vast sums on restoring it, and handed it over to the State a few years later on condition that it would become a Napoleonic Museum. This benefactor's own art collection can now be seen in the **Pavillon Osiris** in the grounds.

Visiting the château

The interior offers an interesting mix of the grand and the elegantly pretty, of private portraits and military set pieces. The **council chamber** has the feel of an army field tent, with its striped canopy and solid mahogany furniture – a reminder that Napoleon's strategic genius was first displayed on the battlefield. In the **library**, his desk is equipped with long flat drawers for storing military plans. But this is a light room with a pretty painted ceiling. The **salon**, too, is light, and the **dining room** most elegant, with its 'Pompeian' dancing figures. Also on the ground floor is the romantic **music room**, where Josephine played the harp and her daughter Hortense, the piano, surrounded by beautiful Jacob furniture.

Upstairs, **Napoleon's bedroom** is all understated elegance: pale gold upholstery, écru silk hangings. In his **sitting room** hang portraits of himself in coronation robes, of his formidable mother, and of Josephine at Malmaison, all by Baron Gérard, whose wonderfully romantic canvas of Napoleon crossing the Alps is one of the highlights of the **Salle Marengo**. The flowing lines of his cloak, echoed in the rearing horse's mane and tail, give an impression of invincible energy and vitality well suited to this allegory of Napoleon as Hannibal.

Napoleonic allegory

Beyond this room dedicated to Napoleon as general and First Consul is one focusing on Josephine. Here you can study many of her personal possessions, as well as some of the plates from Redouté's book on her beloved roses. But the most breathtaking of her possessions is in her bedroom: this *nécessaire de toilette* (toilet case) is quite beautiful, encrusted with mother of pearl and tortoiseshell, every implement made with the greatest artistry. Her bed – the very one in which she died – continues the canopy motif, which is repeated in the oval 'tent' draping the ceiling. On the floor above you can admire some of the delicate embroidered muslin dresses she loved wearing, alongside her state robes.

Château de Bois-Préau

Josephine's second and smaller château was built in the late 17th century, and once owned by Marie Antoinette's steward, who had risen from lowly beginnings as a very junior chef's assistant. By the time Josephine had her eye on it, it was an elegant dwelling with an elaborate garden – and an owner determined not to sell. She eventually managed to buy it in 1809, a couple of months before she and Napoleon were divorced. It became an annex of the main château, a home for various members of her entourage, and for her large collection of curios.

Curio collection

Bois-Préau was bought and sold many times during the century after her death, rebuilt in the Second Empire style prevailing in the mid-19th century, and eventually saved for the nation by the generosity of a former American consul in Paris, Edward Tuck, and his wife Julia. They bought it in 1920, restored it, lived there themselves, then gave it to the French State a few years later.

Visiting the museum

Whereas Malmaison is full of reminders of Napoleon's glory days, here you are invited to reflect on his downfall, and on his lonely death from stomach cancer (or just possibly arsenic poisoning) on St Helena. But also on his subsequent glorification. There are paintings and sketches of him on his deathbed, and many moving mementoes of those last years: the chess sets with which he whiled away the days, his flimsy-looking camp bed with the inevitable canopy, even a few pieces of liquorice, which he was fond of chewing during his last illness. You can see his slippers and riding boots, a dressing gown cut like his famous fitted greatcoat, his familiar triangular hat. Here too are the pictures of his baby son, the King of Rome, that he so often gazed at. A piece of wall fabric with arsenic in hints at the rumours surrounding his death. Perhaps the most poignant exhibit is the clock that was stopped at the exact time he died, and has never been restarted.

Napoleon's last years

After the pathos of this collection, displays illustrating the adulation that greeted his remains when they were returned to France a couple of decades later show how the Napoleonic legend, born in the early days of his brilliant army career, had rapidly grown. And a whole range of 'Napoleon souvenirs', from snuff boxes to inkwells, from fans to handkerchiefs, even a tobacco box in the shape of his coffin, make it clear why that legend will never entirely be vanquished in the hearts and minds of his compatriots.

Napoleonic legend

The church in Rueil-Malmaison, **Saint-Pierre-Saint-Paul**, not far from Bois-Préau, houses Josephine's tomb, topped by an effigy of her wearing just the sort of low-cut gown in which she caught her death. Here too lies her daughter Hortense, who became Napoleon's sister-in law as well as his step-daughter when she married his brother Louis. She also became Queen of Holland, and the mother of the future emperor Napoleon III.

Josephine's tomb

The Machine de Marly

Beside the busy road running along the banks of the Seine between Bougival and Louveciennes you can still see the strange sight of the 'Marly Machine', commissioned by Louis XIV's chief minister Colbert. This impressive contraption, designed to pump water from the Seine to feed both the fountains at Versailles and the ornamental pools at Marly, was invented in 1681 by Arnold de Ville (or Deville), a Belgian engineer from Liége and his compatriot and assistant Rennequin Sualem.

The Machine de Marly consisted of fourteen enormous water wheels activating over two hundred pumps, which carried water from the Seine to a height of over 150 metres above the level of the river, producing some 5000 cubic metres of water per 24 hours. It was rebuilt in 1812, but was still in operation right down to the end of the 1960s.

If you stand in the little garden on the other side of the road, which is adorned with a reproduction of Alfred Sisley's 1876 painting *Barrage de la Machine de Marly*, you get a good view of the 18th-century pump buildings – still apparently used by the Service des Eaux et Fontaines and emitting an eerie humming sound – and the huge pipes snaking up the hillside.

Exploring the river

Beyond La Malmaison the Seine widens and loops, presenting a placid picture, with nothing but the odd houseboat or barge sauntering slowly past. But if you had been here on a summer Sunday during most of the 19th century, those placid waters would have been heaving with crowds of oarsmen, practising what was then France's favourite sport. Some had rowed all the way from Paris. Others had travelled by river steamer. And after the arrival of the railway to Saint-Germain in the 1830s, the trains would disgorge merrymakers in their thousands: office workers relaxing on their day off, good-time girls determined to have a good time, bohemian artists and writers, and families with huge picnic baskets.

The canotiers

This was the age of the *canotiers*, those dashing creatures immortalized on the canvases of painters from Pierre-Auguste Renoir to Gustave Caillebotte, and best translated, according to a recent reviewer of a Caillebotte exhibition, as 'men in a boat', in the Jerome K. Jerome tradition.

All these pleasure-seekers naturally needed somewhere to eat and drink, and maybe enjoy a spot of dancing. So dozens of lively riverside restaurants and cafés sprang up. There was *La Grenouillère* at **Croissy-sur-Seine**, famous for its 'floating café' made up of moored boats roped together, which became a floating dancehall at night.

Then **Bougival** boasted *Le Bal des Canotiers*, again painted by Renoir. But according to Renoir, 'the loveliest spot in the whole area round Paris' was **La Maison Fournaise**, a lively restaurant at **Chatou**

Chatou

that is the sole survivor of all these *guinguettes* (see pp. 147–50), now restored and once again housing a restaurant,★ more decorous than in its heyday, but still cheerful and friendly, and also a small museum.

The Fournaise family had been boat-builders and innkeepers beside the Seine since the mid-18th century. In 1857 Alphonse

Fournaise started renting out boats to Sunday revellers, and shortly afterwards opened a restaurant, with his wife as cook. A small hotel followed. Renoir's *Déjeuner des Canotiers* (1880), the best known of the thirty-odd canvases he painted here, depicts the Fournaises' pretty daughter Alphonsine leaning on the new wrought-iron balustrade, surrounded by happy diners.

Auguste Renoir

By the early 20th century the golden age of the *canotiers* was over. Alphonsine closed the family restaurant down in 1906. By then La Grenouillère's floating café had burnt down, though it was partly rebuilt and lingered on until 1914. But the restoration of the Maison Fournaise gives you a chance to glimpse something of the atmosphere captured in Renoir's sunny paintings.

The short walk from Rueil-Malmaison RER station to the **Ile des Impressionnistes**, as the Ile de Chatou is now called, offers an interesting contrast. (Irritatingly, the museum is not signposted, as it is in another *département*: get out at the front of the train, go down the escalator, turn right, cross over the road, then follow the traffic signs to Chatou.) Beyond a dreary group of high-rise modern buildings, the busy road offers glimpses of the river, and when you turn off to the right down a sloping road, you suddenly find yourself in an oasis of peace.

The museum is in what was once the hotel. It has much interesting material illustrating the history of the Maison Fournaise and its fellow restaurants, the riotous time had by all, and the work of the artists who painted there (temporary exhibitions focus on individual artists). You can see reproductions of key canvases, and watch a good video presentation, in both French and English.

If you enjoy junk shops, come here during the spring and autumn *Foires au jambon et à la brocante*, held on the island: among dozens

Junk fair

The singing Garciá sisters

Maria de la Felicidád Garciá (1808–36) and her younger sister Pauline (1821–1910) were both born in Paris, the daughters of the Spanish tenor and composer Manuel Garciá. Both girls were to become world-famous sopranos under their married names, Maria Malibran and Pauline Viardot, while their older brother Manuel, born before the family moved to France, taught singing in both London and Paris.

'La Malibran', a dramatic-looking, dark-haired beauty with a high forehead, won a huge following as a mezzo-soprano in roles such as Desdemona in Rossini's *Otello*. She died in Manchester after a riding accident when she was only twenty-eight and was mourned by the whole of Europe.

Pauline was again a mezzo-soprano but also composed operettas and songs, as well as being a fine pianist. Unlike her sister, she was no beauty. But her high intelligence, her vivacity, her nobility of carriage, her dedication to her art, combined with an extraordinary singing voice won her the friendship and admiration of a distinguished circle and the utter devotion of the great Russian novelist Ivan Turgenev, who saw her on stage in St Petersburg when he was twenty-five, fell wildly in love and loved her till his dying day. The house he built near hers in Bougival is now open to the public.

of stands selling bric-à-brac large and small are booths and open-air restaurants.

Visiting Turgenev

Ivan Turgenev

One of the writers who occasionally enjoyed a meal at the Maison Fournaise was the Russian novelist Ivan Turgenev, who spent his summers from 1875 in Bougival, in a house that has also become a museum. He lived here in a form of *ménage à trois* with the famous soprano Pauline Viardot and her husband and manager Louis (see box, p. 109). The Viardots started spending the summer in the existing porticoed neo-classical mansion, while Turgenev had a two-storey wooden 'chalet' built among the trees. This can be visited today as the **Musée Tourgueniev**.

This atmospheric place feels more like a private house than a museum. It is full of paintings, photographs and sketches of Turgenev himself, and of the Viardots and Garciás. Extracts from letters are everywhere, some written by the main protagonists, others by a host of celebrated writers, artists and musicians. As is only appropriate, concerts are sometimes held here too.

The Impressionist trail

The riverside restaurants were not the only subjects favoured by the Impressionists and other painters who frequented the broad loop of the Seine between Chatou and Port-Marly. The local tourist office has had the excellent idea of posting up reproductions of over twenty canvases of bridges and riverscapes, village lanes and orchards, on the very spot where they were painted, not only by Renoir and Monet, but also by Alfred Sisley, Camille Pissarro and Maurice de Vlaminck. A leaflet called *Le Chemin des Impressionnistes* (obtainable from the Marly tourist office, 2 av. des Combattants, 78160 Marly-le-Roi, ℡ 01-30-61-61-35, or the departmental and regional tourist boards has a useful map showing where they can be found. For instance, the reproduction of Sisley's *Barrage de la Machine de Marly* (1876), near the lock between two islands, the Ile de la Loge and the Ile de Bougival, brings you close to the famous **Machine de Marly** (see box, p. 108), as well as to one of my favourite riverside restaurants, the *Auberge des Tilleuls*.★ The trail also climbs up to the **Parc de Marly**, once the grounds of a now-vanished royal palace.

Parc de Marly

The Château de Marly was built by Louis XIV in 1679 as a place where he could escape from the formalities of court life at Versailles. The royal architect, painter and gardener, Jules Hardouin-Mansart, Charles Le Brun and André Le Nôtre, were summoned to his chosen site among Marly's woods to create a secluded country retreat, but one that had all the splendour of a royal palace. The result was two rows of six *pavillons*, linked by a portico or pergola, on either side of a long lake, plus, at the far end of the lake and built on a raised platform, a larger building for the king's private use. The conceit behind Mansart's scheme was the twelve signs of the zodiac revolving round the sun. So the king's miniature palace was called the 'Pavillon du Soleil' (Sun Pavilion) and presented a suitably glittering impression with its lavish external gilding, though the marble cladding was not marble at all, but *trompe-l'oeil* painting. Beyond it was more glitter, in the shape of the sparkling waterfall tumbling down the hillside over pink marble steps.

An invitation to join the king and his close family at Marly soon became the most coveted of royal favours, accorded to a privileged few. Alas, nothing is left now of this thirteen-part pleasure palace. It was dismantled during the Revolution, after suffering the indignity of being used as a barracks. All you can see is a group of paving stones marking out the spot where the Sun Pavilion stood. Even the **Abreuvoir**, the ornamental 'drinking trough' at the entrance to the grounds, has lost its giant horses sculpted by Guillaume Coustou, the famous 'Chevaux de Marly' that were resited at the bottom of the avenue des Champs-Elysées in Paris, but are now in the Louvre.

Royal favour

But walking in the park or sitting beside the lake is very pleasant. And you can see how the palace looked by visiting the **Musée-Promenade** near the **Grille Royale**, the original entrance gates. It has an interesting collection of paintings, engravings and documents, plus exhibits connected with the painters who lived and worked in

Key data

RUEIL-MALMAISON 92500
T.O.   160 av. Paul-Doumer, ☎ 01-47-32-35-75
Access   Paris 14km, Versailles 12km; **bus** no. 258 from La Défense (stops by Château de Bois-Préau and Château de Malmaison)
Sights   **Château de Bois-Préau** (Napoleonic Museum), av. de l'Impératrice-Joséphine, ☎ 01-41-29-05-55, open Thur–Sun, pm only; **Château de Malmaison** (Empress Josephine's home, Napoleonic Museum), av. du Château-de-Malmaison, ☎ 01-41-29-05-55, closed Tue; **Eglise Saint-Pierre-Saint-Paul** (church housing tombs of Josephine and daughter Hortense)
Lunch   Bougival, Chatou, Louveciennes, Marly-le-Roi
Staying   Bougival
Also   Saint-Germain-en-Laye

Maison Fournaise (riverside restaurant frequented by painters, now also museum); Ile des Impressionnistes, 78400 Chatou, ☎ 01-34-80-36-22; **RER** line A1 to Rueil-Malmaison, then 10-min walk), open Thur–Sun

Musée-Promenade Marly-le-Roi-Louveciennes
Grille Royale, Parc de Marly, 78430 Louveciennes, ☎ 01-30-61-61-35 (**rail** Paris-Saint-Lazare to Marly-le-Roi, then 20-min walk, or **RER** line A1 to Saint-Germain-en-Laye, then **bus** no. 1), pm only, closed Mon, Tue, public hols

Musée Tourgueniev (Ivan Turgenev's 'dacha')
16 rue Ivan-Tourgueniev, ☎ 01-39-18-22-30 (**bus** 258 from La Défense), Sun only, or by appointment, closed mid-Dec to mid-Mar

the villages of **Marly-le-Roi** and **Louveciennes**, which are worth exploring. Both have interesting churches and some attractive houses, and on the hill above the Machine de Marly you can see the neo-classical château given by Louis XV to his mistress Madame du Barry.

8 Saint-Germain-en-Laye

The attractive town of Saint-Germain-en-Laye, just west of Paris and easily reached by the express metro, was long the seat of the royal court, before Versailles took over this role. Thanks to its beautiful site, on a plateau high up above one of the broad meanders of the river Seine, and on the edge of an ancient forest where Charlemagne once hunted, it is today a fashionable residential area, with a network of lively pedestrian streets lined with stylish fashion boutiques and excellent food shops.

A stylish town

As you stroll round the town you will come across many fine 17th century stone mansions built for princes and aristocrats. Though often partly rebuilt in the 18th century, some still have their original elegant wrought-iron balconies and double 'carriage doors', and most have been sensitively restored in recent years. But Saint-Germain is best known for the sweeping views over the Seine Valley from the **Grande Terrasse**, which attracted so many weekending Parisians in the 19th century that France's first-ever railway line was built to cater for them (see box, p. 52). The terrace was designed for Louis XIV by the royal gardener André Le Nôtre (see **Versailles**), when he was laying out the gardens of the royal palace, dating from a century earlier, that once stood on the edge of the plateau. That palace, known as the **Château Neuf**, was demolished in the 18th century and plans to rebuild it never materialized. So all you can see of it now is the **Pavillon Henri IV** (see box). But the much earlier palace a short distance away, the **Château Vieux**, is still standing, now housing an important archeological museum.

The palace and its history

The palace

The first building on this site was a monastery dedicated to St Germain, built in the early 11th century for Robert le Pieux, son of the first King of the French, Hugues Capet. A century later Louis le Gros put up a royal castle at the heart of the cluster of buildings that had grown up round the monastery. This was then rebuilt in the 13th century by Saint Louis, who added the beautiful Gothic **Sainte Chapelle** with its delicate tracery (though sadly now lacking its stained glass). The chapel was designed by Pierre de Montreuil, later the architect of Paris's famous chapel of the same name.

This fortress was badly damaged during the Hundred Years War, then rebuilt by Charles V. But it owes its present appearance to François Ier. As at Fontainebleau (p. 171), he kept the medieval keep and built on the foundations of the castle, retaining the same asymmetrical configuration of five sides round a central courtyard.

The Pavillon Henri IV

The Château Neuf or New Château at Saint-Germain, built by Philibert Delorme for Henri II, then continued by Jacques Androuet du Cerceau and Jean de Fourcy for Henri IV, had a small central building extended by long galleries ending in domed brick *pavillons* (the French term used for such separate structures). One of these, originally at the eastern end right on the edge of the Petite Terrasse, is still standing and now houses a rather grand hotel and restaurant called Le Pavillon Henri IV. Part of this building was initially used as a chapel and it was here that Louis XIV was brought to be christened on the very day of his birth in the Château Neuf, 5 September 1638.

The Pavillon also holds an important place in culinary history. In the 1830s the hotelier Collinet allegedly invented *sauce béarnaise* here. This chervil- and tarragon-flavoured sauce, soon to become one of the most famous in French classical cuisine, was probably so called because Henri IV came from the Béarn region in southwest France.

But the building features on the literary map of France too. Alexandre Dumas *père* moved in a decade after Collinet's invention, staying in the annex known as the Villa Médicis with his twenty-year old son, also Alexandre, the future author of *The Lady of the Camellias*. Dumas *père* wrote most of *The Three Musketeers* during this stay, as well as his *Monte-Cristo*, which was to give its name to the château he was soon building nearby (see pp. 116–17).

He also happily spared the chapel, where he had married Claude de France in 1514, the year before he succeeded his father-in-law Louis XII. His architect Pierre de Chambiges (who later worked at Fontainebleau) created a Renaissance palace that still had elements of a medieval castle, but took advantage of the site by designing a flat roof where the king and his guests could walk and lean on decorative balustrades to admire the view.

This new palace was not new for long. François's son Henri II, who was born there, thought it too forbidding and commissioned Philibert Delorme (see **Anet**) to design a 'pleasure palace' right on the edge of the plateau, so that its inhabitants could enjoy the views from their bedrooms and reception rooms, without having to climb up to the roof. This became the **Château Neuf** (New Château), while the earlier palace was relegated to the position of **Château Vieux** (Old Château).

Among the inhabitants of the new single-storey palace was Mary, Queen of Scots, who was brought up at the French court from the age of six, as the future bride of the Dauphin François. He worshipped her, but his health was poor, and he died of an ear infection a couple of years after the wedding, and just a year after becoming king in 1559, whereupon his young widow was packed off to rule over her Scots kingdom.

Mary, Queen of Scots

Henri had not lived to see the new palace in its final glory. The finishing touches were the work of Henri IV, who excited the admiration of his contemporaries by creating what they referred to as the 'hanging gardens of Babylon': a series of broad terraces descending in stages towards the Seine, apparently modelled on the famous Villa

Ingenious gardens

113

d'Este gardens at Tivoli in Italy. Especially admired were the 'grottoes' hollowed out of the hillside below the terraces. These were clad in marble or mosaics, *rocaille* (artificial cladding imitating rocks), shells or mother-of-pearl, and adorned with nymphs and urns, pilasters and pediments. Their fanciful names – the Orpheus Grotto, the Neptune Grotto, the Dragon Grotto and so on – were related to the 'automatons' who lurked in their depths. As visitors stepped into the grotto, they would spring eerily to life, activated by water pressure, thanks to a complex system of pipes and reservoirs. Mercury would blow a trumpet, Bacchus would raise a glass to his lips, Orpheus would play his lyre while the beasts of the fields and even the trees crept towards him, and the dragon would flap its wings in sinister fashion.

Grottoes

Alas, all these ingenious tableaux have vanished, along with the palace. But the Château Neuf remained a favourite residence for king and court for most of the next two reigns. Louis XIII spent most of his time at Saint-Germain, dying there in 1643 five years after the future Louis XIV – a longed-for heir after twenty-three years of marriage – was born in the royal bedroom and christened in the Pavillon Henri IV. After the traumatic experience of the Fronde rebellions, the young prince and his mother Anne of Austria escaped from Paris to Saint-Germain (see **Versailles**). Following Anne's death in 1666, Louis decided to settle there, and it was to become his favourite residence for well over half his reign, until he took the court off to Versailles.

Royal birth

His court was predominantly young, and dazzling parties and festivities were held here, as Louis was increasingly determined to demonstrate the strength of the crown with lavish displays.

As by this time he was exercising absolute power, Saint-Germain was also the seat of the government, for nearly twenty years, from 1666 to 1682. Not surprisingly, the growing influx of courtiers and officials necessitated some alterations. Jules Hardouin-Mansart was commissioned to enlarge the Châteaux Vieux by demolishing the corner turrets and replacing them with five new pavilions – which were in turn demolished in the 19th century. And Le Nôtre laid out gardens with shady paths where the court could take the air, then the Grande Terrasse for longer walks.

But by 1682 the splendid new palace at Versailles was ready and Saint-Germain was deserted by king and court. After that, its only royal inhabitant was the exiled James II of England, who was offered refuge there by Louis in 1689. His queen Mary of Modena and their son had already received a warm welcome a few years earlier – Louis greeted her with flowers in her room, a layette for the Prince of Wales, and a little chest full of silver to tide her over.

James II of England

James died in the palace in 1701 and his heart remained there – buried in the church opposite. Curiously enough, this fact was the cause of the palace's being converted into a museum. It had survived the demolition of the ruined Château Neuf, but had lost the sumptuous decoration and furniture commissioned by Louis XIV. After the Revolution it housed first a cavalry school, then a prison. It was still a prison in 1855, when Queen Victoria, on a visit to Paris, announced her intention of paying her respects to the remains of James II. Napoleon III took her off to Saint-Germain, but was so embarrassed at finding this place 'full of great and glorious memories' serving such an inglorious purpose that he promptly decided that it should become a museum of Celtic and Gallo-Roman 'antiquities' – a subject in which he was himself greatly interested. Major restoration work was embarked on, and the five later pavilions were pulled down so that it would look as it had when it was built for François Ier. The emperor opened the new museum with due pomp in 1867. It was reorganized a century later and renamed the **Musée des Antiquités nationales**.

Visiting the palace

The museum's prehistoric collections have been acclaimed as the most important in Europe. Recent modernization has made this a well-planned and instructive place to visit for anyone interested in archeology and prehistory, and in the history of France from the Gallo-Roman period down to the onset of the Middle Ages. On the ground floor is a reconstruction of the country's best-known prehistoric site, the Lascaux Caves.

Archeology collection

You can also admire the interior of the Sainte-Chapelle, and pay your own respects to its builder Saint-Louis, whose likeness can be glimpsed among the carved heads, along with that of his mother Blanche of Castile and assorted relations. If you also want to follow Queen Victoria's example, you will find that James II's heart now rests in the nearby church beneath a mausoleum donated by her.

Visiting the town

A short walk from the church is the lively **rue au Pain**. At no. 38, now housing the tourist office (good range of brochures and maps of hiking trails and cycle paths in the forest), is the small **Musée Claude Debussy**, devoted to the composer, who was born in this house in 1862.

Claude Debussy

This is one of Saint-Germain's earliest surviving buildings, dating from the 1640s, though the attractive wooden staircase leading from the courtyard is probably an 18th-century addition. The museum does not attempt to re-create the upper rooms as they were when the Debussys moved there, but aims to give a picture of his life and work, as critic and conductor as well as composer, of the context in which he was working, and of his influence on French music. There is a great deal of interest here, with intelligently arranged displays on topics such as Debussy's first masterpiece, his setting for Mallarmé's *L'Après-midi d'un faune*. The influence on him of Edgar Allan Poe is well brought out. One room is arranged as a study, and is full of personal objects donated by Debussy's step-daughter, including his unexpected frog and toad mascots.

One of the first people to agitate for a Debussy museum was the painter Maurice Denis, who had worked briefly with him, and had illustrated the score for his *La Damoiselle élue*. Denis, the theorist of the 'Nabis' group of painters, lived in Saint-Germain from 1914 until his death in 1943. His house, which he called Le Prieuré (The Priory), has also been turned into a museum. The **Musée du Prieuré**, devoted to the Nabis and Symbolists, is housed in an elegant classical building a short walk from the centre.

Nabis & Symbolist art

The museum's collections range wider than the Nabis and the Symbolists, as they also include work by Henri de Toulouse-Lautrec, James Ensor, Piet Mondrian, Alphonse Mucha, and the designer of Paris's art nouveau Metro station entrances, Hector Guimard, as well as glass by Daum. There is a pleasant feeling of visiting a private house as you go down the old stone steps into the pretty garden, adorned with sculptures – I like the patient figure of Penelope waiting for Odysseus, by Antoine Bourdelle – and visit the chapel decorated by Denis, then his studio, and continue into the main building.

Around Saint-Germain

The **Fôret de Saint-Germain** is popular with walkers and nature lovers (bike hire available – ask at the tourist office). But there is also a building of great interest to be seen only about 2km from the town (no. 10 bus takes you most of the way) at **Port-Marly**.

Alexandre Dumas

The **Château de Monte-Cristo** was the highly extravagant residence – 'folly' might be a better word – built by playwright and novelist Alexandre Dumas *père*, whose talents as a storyteller, ear for dialogue and prodigiously hard work had brought him fame and fortune. One of the three hundred-odd novels and plays he turned out at great speed (sometimes with the help of collaborators) was the famous thriller *The Count of Monte-Cristo*, published in 1844–5 with enormous success.

Dumas, the son of a mulatto general in the Revolutionary army and grandson of a marquis and a Black Haitian, was a larger-than-life character himself, and his house was equally exuberant. The original plan had been to build a small country cottage. The enterprise rapidly escalated, costing at least ten times as much as the original estimate.

Key data

SAINT-GERMAIN-EN-LAYE 78100

T.O.   38 rue au Pain, ℡ 01-34-51-05-12

Access   Paris 22km, Versailles 12km; **RER** line A1; **buses** 258 from La Défense (via Malmaison, Bougival, Port-Marly)

Sights   **Musée des Antiquités nationales** (archeological museum) housed in **Vieux Château** (former royal palace), ℡ 01-34-51-53-65, open year-round, closed Tue; **Musée Claude Debussy**, 38 rue au Pain, ℡ 01-34-51-05-12, open Tue to Sat, pm only; **Musée du Prieuré** (Nabis, Symbolists, life, work and times of Maurice Denis), 2bis rue Maurice-Denis, ℡ 01-39-73-77-87, open year-round, Weds to Sun

Lunch   Saint-Germain-en-Laye, Bougival, Louveciennes, Marly-le-Roi, Port-Marly

Staying   Saint-Germain-en-Laye

Also   Bougival, Chatou, Malmaison, Versailles

Château de Monte-Cristo (Alexandre Dumas *père*'s house) 78560 Le Port-Marly, ℡ 01-30-61-61-35, open Apr to end Oct, Tue–Sun; Nov to end Mar, Sun pm only

One commentator called the result a 'weird confusion of Bohemia and the Arabian Nights'. It was a mock-Renaissance château complete with turrets, bell towers – and minarets. The façades were carved with portrait medallions of Dumas's favourite authors. The rooms included a picture gallery and a 'Moorish salon'. And the interior decoration ranged from Gothic to Louis XIV. The place was crammed with pictures and furniture, and a jumble of objects, some precious, some mere curios. In the grounds was a tiny neo-Gothic house on an island, reached by a drawbridge: a private study for the master of the house.

The house is great fun to visit. The pictures include portraits of Dumas, engravings of actors in his plays, family trees, and sketch plans for the Monte-Cristo gardens. There are exhibits connected with his most famous books and plays, early copies of which are also on display. And the Moorish room, restored at the expense of King Hassan of Morocco, and by experts sent to France by him, is amazingly opulent.

9 Thoiry

Thoiry Château and its safari park have all the ingredients for a successful family day out, though this is one of the few places in the Ile de France that is not easy to reach by public transport. The château can if necessary suggest a taxi firm that will meet a train.

The **château** is Renaissance and, most unusually, has been lived in by the same family for over four centuries. It was designed in 1564 by Philibert Delorme, the architect of Anet, the Château Neuf at Saint

Two of the inmates in Thoiry's Safari Park

Ligrons: a zoological breakthrough

In 1981, Thoiry Château and its popular safari park became the focus of enormous excitement in natural history circles. An 'accident' had resulted in a male lion called Bichon and a female tiger, Jeannette, mating and producing the first-ever lion/tiger cross, which was soon labelled a 'ligron'. They had two offspring. One was a female, who was given the name Julie, and the other a male, later dubbed La Force Tranquille.

Not to be outdone, Jeannette's sister promptly succumbed to Bichon's advances and was soon the proud mother of two more ligrons, a female, Sarah, and a male, Patchwork.

The following year, Thoiry's owners, the Viscomte and Viscomtesse de La Panouse, were invited by the Chinese government to travel to China so that M. de La Panouse could give lectures to the country's scientific establishment, and to heads of wild animal reserves, on his breeding techniques. They decided to take Sarah and La Force Tranquille (the name was chosen by the Chinese) as a gift to Beijing Zoo.

Then in 1984 Julie confounded the world's zoological experts by giving birth to a second-generation male ligron, who was called Pascal. This new birth disproved the received wisdom that hybrids were invariably sterile, and raised some important questions about the degree of genetic difference between lions and tigers. Sadly Pascal died a few months later of cat fever, but his arrival had written a whole new chapter in zoological genetic research.

Julie went on to die of old age at Thoiry, and Patchwork, too, died in 1996. But Sarah and La Force Tranquille are still flourishing in China. They have been lent to all the major Chinese zoos over the years, becoming household names in their adopted country.

Germain-en-Laye and parts of Fontainebleau. He followed the Knights Templar tradition in designing it to face due south, so that at the summer and winter solstices the sun seems to rise and set in the Great Hall, creating an eerie effect of total transparency. The garden designer was equally distinguished – the great Andre Le Nôtre. The formal parterres and embroidery-like patterns have been beautifully restored and the gardens now include a maze made up of over five thousand yews.

The current chatelain is the Viscomte Paul de La Panouse, the descendant of an ancient line whose history – starting in the 11th century – can be traced in the various salons and dining rooms open to the public. There is some good furniture, and an impressive Gobelins tapestry depicting Don Quixote. One room is devoted to an **Archives Museum**, full of documents, letters to family members from the famous, including Napoleon and Benjamin Franklin, papal bulls, even the only known copy of the document officially annexing Alsace and Lorraine. In pride of place are two previously unknown manuscript Chopin waltzes, unearthed by the American pianist Byron Janis in the attics, hidden in a trunk crammed with long-discarded clothes.

In the old pantries, a **Gourmet Museum** (Musée de la Gastronomie) displays some extraordinary *pièces montées*, copies by modern confectioners of those elaborate spun-sugar concoctions, some over 4.5 metres high, that traditionally formed the centrepiece of French banquets.

The safari park
The viscount and his energetic American wife have restored the family's fortunes by turning Thoiry into a successful business. Many visitors come chiefly for the '**African Reserve**', with its bears and antelopes, lions and tigers, rhinoceroses, zebras and rare snow leopards, roaming freely in the open. An ingenious system of walkways enables you to see the animals at close quarters but in complete safety, and there are carefully monitored circuits for those with cars or on foot.

African reserve

But the safari park and its zoo also represent an important zoological research centre. Thoiry is involved in the European Breeding Programme of Endangered Species and hit the world's headlines in the 1980s when it successfully crossed lions and tigers (see box).

Key data

CHATEAU DE THOIRY 78770 Thoiry, ☎ 01-34-87-52-25
Access Paris 51km, Rambouillet 31km, Versailles 30km; **train** from Paris-Montparnasse to Montfort-L'Amaury-Méré, then **taxi** (12km)
Open Both château and **Réserve africaine** (safari park) are open year-round
Lunch Self-service restaurant in grounds; Thoiry
Staying Thoiry

10 Giverny

The little village of Giverny in the Seine Valley, right on the edge of Normandy, has been a highspot on the map of art-lovers since the house of its most famous inhabitant was opened to the public in 1980. Claude Monet, the greatest of the Impressionist painters, lived in Giverny for exactly half his long life, in a long, low pink house with bright green shutters and doors. And in front of it he created a glorious garden, crammed with flowers, vibrant with colour, that was a constant source of inspiration.

Claude Monet

This garden, known as the **Clos normand**, is not landscaped, but is more like a huge and wonderful cottage garden, complete with apple trees. On the far side of what was then a dirt track and a railway line (now reached via a specially constructed tunnel), he later added the very different **Jardin d'eau** (Water Garden), Japanese in

Key data

GIVERNY 27620

Access Paris 75km; **rail** from Paris Saint-Lazare to Vernon, then taxi or 4km walk; **excursions** from Paris

Sights **Maison de Monet** (Claude Monet's house and garden), ☏ 02-32-51-28-21; **Musée américain,** 92 rue Claude-Monet, ☏ 02-32-51-94-65; **Ancien Hôtel Baudy** (house where American painters lived), 81 rue Claude-Monet, ☏ 02-32-21-10-03; all these are open Apr to end Oct but closed Mon

Lunch Giverny, Fourges, La Roche-Guyon, Vernon

Staying Chérence, Douais, La Roche-Guyon, Vernon

Also Anet, Thoiry

Château de la Roche-Guyon
95780 La Roche-Guyon, ☏ 01-34-79-74-42, open daily late Mar to mid-Nov **Musée Alphonse-Georges Poulain** (local history, painting, sculpture) 12 rue du Pont, 27200 Vernon, ☏ 02-32-21-28-09, open year-round, Tue–Sun, pm only

Water garden spirit, whose lily pond he captured in so many changing lights, most famously in his extraordinary late series of *Waterlily Decorations* that are almost abstract in their splashes of shimmering colour.

Giverny's first curator, the energetic Gerald van der Kemp, has described the resuscitation of Giverny as a miracle. It is hard to see this as an exaggeration as you visit the gardens, replanted exactly as they were in Monet's day, and the modest family house, restored and redecorated in the strong, bright, clear colours he chose as a background for his favourite Japanese prints, and for his personal collection of his own paintings and those of his friends and fellow artists, including Cézanne and Renoir, Pissarro and Degas.

The miracle has involved a great deal of money, most of it given by generous American art-lovers, and the result is superb, despite the inevitable crowds. The magic is perhaps at its height in the spring, when the apple blossom is out and the lawns are a sea of daffodils and narcissi, tulips and irises. But the profusion of summer flowers is wonderful too, especially the brilliant nasturtiums tumbling over the paths. The water garden, its 'Japanese bridge' draped with a curtain of wistaria, mauve in spring, white in summer, is beautiful at any time of day or year (see opposite).

A house and its history

Monet started renting the house in 1883, when he was forty-three and virtually penniless. He moved in with his two small sons and Alice Hoschedé, plus her four children.

Despite his precarious financial situation, he immediately set about designing the garden and reorganizing the house, turning a barn into a studio-cum-drawing room. And all the time he painted, in the garden and in the surrounding countryside, starting at first

The wistaria-hung 'Japanese bridge' spanning Giverny's water garden

light, embarking on series of paintings on a single theme – haystacks or poplars, wistaria or waterlilies.

By the end of the decade his reputation was made and he was earning enough from his painting to buy the house. He lived there for the rest of his life, constantly embellishing both garden and house, to which he added a second studio, then, fifteen years later, a large new studio specially designed to take the large *Nénuphars* (Waterlily Decorations) that he presented to the state in 1922. *Waterlily decorations*

He died in 1926, at the age of eighty-six. The house and garden were looked after for the next twenty years by Alice's daughter Blanche, who had married one of Monet's sons. After her death, his other son Michel neglected them, living elsewhere, gradually selling off the paintings. When he died in a car crash near Giverny in 1966, aged eighty-eight, his will bequeathed them to the Académie des Beaux-Arts in Paris.

A decade later the full restoration began, with an attention to detail that has ensured that you really can see the place as Monet and his friends and admirers knew it.

Visiting the house

There are no paintings in the house: the forty-six remaining canvases were hastily moved from the decaying rooms to the Musée Marmottan in Paris. But thanks to modern technology, the reproductions on the walls of the **salon-atelier** (studio-drawing room) are remarkably faithful. And Monet's magnificent collection of prints by the greatest of Japanese artists – Utamaro, Hiroshige and Hokusai – hang once again in **Alice's bedroom**, in **Monet's and Alice's dressing rooms**, and in the beautiful **dining room**. This extraordinary room, with its buttercup yellow walls and furniture, and its bright blue and yellow china (copies *Japanese prints* are on sale in the **waterlily studio**, now a sales and reception area), shows how far Monet's decorative scheme was from the dark, heavy, fussy interiors favoured in his day.

All the rooms are painted in strong, plain colours, with wainscoting and picture rails, dadoes and details of mirror frames picked out in a different shade of the same colour: blues, naturally enough, in the **Salon Bleu** (Blue Drawing Room), blue and turquoise in the **kitchen**, with its blue-and-white tiles and gleaming copper pans, blue and green in the little **hall**, blue, green and lilac in the **épicerie** (Storeroom), creams in **Monet's bedroom**, cobalt blue and sea green in **Alice's bedroom**.

Visiting the village

US connections

As Monet's fame grew, painters began to flock to Giverny to visit him, or to try to emulate him. Some even settled in the village. The American contingent was particularly large – and it led to an American connection when one of these painters, Theodore Butler, married Alice's daughter Suzanne, Monet's favourite model. The link continued after Suzanne's early death, as Butler subsequently married her sister Marthe.

The American painters scattered when the First World War broke out. But their erstwhile presence has recently been commemorated in the **Musée américain**, a stylish modern building in white stone close to Monet's house. Its aim is twofold: to illustrate the links between French and American artists during the Impressionist era; and to display to European audiences, who tend to be familiar only with contemporary American art, the type of work produced by American painters in earlier periods. The museum has a pleasant restaurant with a terrace overlooking the garden, and a bookshop.

Many of Giverny's Americans lived in an inn in the village, later upgraded to a hotel. The **Hôtel Baudy** has now been restored and can also be visited, along with the little studio in the garden.

Beyond Giverny

Vernon

The small town of **Vernon**, extensively rebuilt after Second World War bombing, with some attractive half-timbered houses, has a museum with a collection of work by Giverny's artists, including a *Waterlilies* canvas donated by Monet himself, the **Musée Alphonse-Georges Poulain**.

Seine villages

Bike hire is available at Vernon station for anyone wanting to explore the pretty villages in the winding Seine Valley, or on the banks of the Epte, a narrow tributary that Monet was granted permission to divert to feed his water garden. Several have pleasant restaurants, too, like the converted watermill★ in **Fourges**, once frequented by the Impressionists. The landscapes and riverscapes are still as harmonious today, as they are in and around **La Roche-Guyon**, on the other side of the Seine. Its ruined keep at the top of a tall chalk cliff, surrounded by a double row of walls, is an impressive sight. At the foot of the cliff, linked to it via a tunnel-cum-staircase cut into the chalk, the **château** was popular with both François Ier and Henri II, as a place to bring their courts for an extended stay during the hunting season.

La Roche-Guyon

A series of itineraries have been mapped out, one covering the remains of the medieval castle, another the panelled reception rooms, another the chapel built into the cliff, and the last the old orangery, also built into the cliff, leading to the vaulted chambers dug out on the orders of Field-Marshal Rommel, who made the château his headquarters in 1944. The large and elegant 18th-century stable block houses temporary art exhibitions and summer concerts take place in the orangery. The château's *boves* – the name given to cellars and the like hollowed out of the cliff all along the valley – are the setting for a 35-minute audiovisual presentation called *Impressions*, focusing on the light and the misty landscapes that have so inspired both painters and photographers.

River walks

Walking beside the river is very pleasant here, and boat trips can also be made on summer afternoons. But for the best views you must climb or drive up to the **Route des Crêtes** ('**Mountain Road**'). The riverscapes embracing the broad meanders, romantically hazy much of the time, will make you feel like taking to paints and brushes yourself. High up here, the ancient village of **Chérence**, with a cosy inn★ and a part-Romanesque church, is on the edge of a chalky plateau where naturalists search for rare orchids.

Chérence

Painters' homes and inspirations

Camille Corot	Forêt de Fontainebleau (p. 179)
Charles-François Daubigny	Auvers-sur-Oise (p. 127)
Maurice Denis	Saint-Germain-en-Laye (p. 115)
Maurice Estève	Culan (p. 234)
Jean-François Millet	Barbizon (p. 178)
Claude Monet	Giverny, Fresselines (pp. 119, 215)
Camille Pissarro	Pontoise (p. 129)
Auguste Renoir	Chatou (p. 109)
Théodore Rousseau	Barbizon (p. 178)
Alfred Sisley	Moret-sur-Loing (p. 182)
Vincent van Gogh	Auvers-sur-Oise (p. 125)

Ile de France ~ north of Paris

Paris's unlovely 'red belt' suburbs seem distinctly unpromising as you head northwards out of the city. But the dreary rows of houses and the high-rise blocks, the tangle of busy commuter roads soon give way to woodland, and the valley of the river Oise has changed surprisingly little since painters like Cézanne and Daubigny, Vlaminck, Monet and, most famously, Van Gogh stayed in or near the charming village of **Auvers-sur-Oise**, attracted especially by the quality of the light.

Several more riverside villages offer pleasant restaurants, swimming and boating, while further east **Royaumont Abbey** is one of the most pleasant places to visit in the Ile de France. Beyond here, **Chantilly** and its racecourse, on the edge of the forest of the same name, is surrounded by interesting places to explore: medieval **Senlis**, **Chaâlis Abbey**, **Ermenonville** where Jean-Jacques Rousseau so happily stayed, and where he died. Then there are two fun theme-

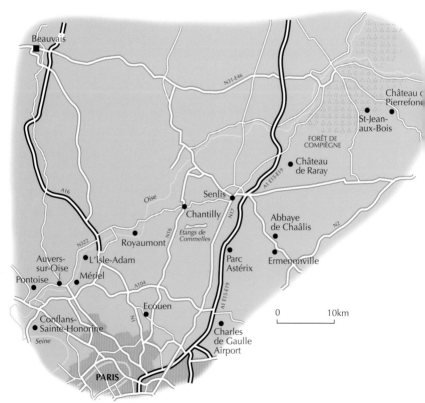

cum-amusement parks to keep children happy – the **Parc Astérix** and the strange **Mer de Sable**.

Northwest of Paris, the town of **Beauvais** and its amazing, never-finished cathedral, are surrounded by arable farmland.

The area is well served by public transport and bike hire is available in the forests. The GR1 hiking trail crosses the Forêt de L'Isle-Adam, while all the forests have a good choice of marked footpaths. Mini-cruises along the river Oise take place on summer weekends, and you can even hire a houseboat.

11 Auvers-sur-Oise

The peaceful village of Auvers-sur-Oise seems much further from Paris than the 30-odd kilometres that separate it from the capital. If you came across it by chance and were strolling towards the archetypal squarish town hall with a little belfry on top, proudly fronted by the traditional *place de la Mairie* (Town Hall Square), you might be in any one of thousands of small towns and villages whose inhabitants lead mostly uneventful lives in their little corner of provincial France.

But then you would become aware of something vaguely familiar about this particular *mairie*, especially if it was a public holiday and it was bedecked with tricolour flags fluttering in the breeze. And that modest little inn on the other side of the square would remind you of something too. By the time you had climbed up to the church with its bulbous east end, it would suddenly dawn on you that this charming place is for ever associated with Vincent van Gogh, who spent his last tragic weeks frantically painting in and around Auvers and eventually shot himself in a nearby cornfield, dying a couple of days later in that very inn on the square.

The **Auberge Ravoux** (see p. 126) was his home for the last two months of his life. And when he died in his tiny top-floor room in the early hours of 29 July

Van Gogh's room in the Auberge Ravoux

The Auberge Ravoux

In 1985 a Belgian marketing executive called Dominique-Charles Janssens was seriously injured in a car crash in Auvers. According to the police report, the accident had happened outside a café called *La Maison de Van Gogh* (Van Gogh's House). He idly decided to find out what was behind the name, and as he slowly recovered started reading the painter's letters to his brother Theo. Once he realized that Van Gogh had indeed lived, briefly, in this café-inn, before dying there nearly a century earlier, he felt sure that fate had had a hand in his accident and vowed that he would one day ensure that it became a permanent memorial.

He discovered that the house dated from 1855, when it was built by a local mason as a home for himself and his new bride. Twenty-one years later their daughter and son-in-law opened a wine shop there. By the mid-1880s it was doing well enough for them to build on a café in the traditional French style with a glass frontage overlooking the town hall square.

In 1889 a manager was brought in, one Arthur-Gustave Ravoux. On 20 May the following year Ravoux let one of his tiny attic rooms to Vincent van Gogh on full-board terms, charging him a modest 3 francs 50 centimes a night.

Van Gogh had come to Auvers at the suggestion of his brother, to be near Dr Paul Gachet, an art lover and specialist in nervous disorders. He seemed to settle in well, wrote to Theo that Auvers was very attractive, and was popular with the Ravoux and their teenage daughter Adeline, whom he painted several times. His letters show that he was hoping that Theo, with his wife and new baby, would spend the summer with him at the inn.

But it was not to be. His painting became more and more obsessive. On 27 July he dragged himself back to the inn after shooting himself in the chest. Hearing him crying out in pain, Ravoux sent for Dr Gachet and the local doctor. Theo was contacted by Dr Gachet and hurried to Auvers the following day, spending hours talking to Vincent. He was with him when he died during the night.

In 1985, still much frequented by a group of local artists, the inn was officially listed as a 'historic monument'. The widowed owner was ready to retire, and a group of local politicians tried to persuade the State and the regional council to buy it and turn it into an Impressionist Museum. The idea was turned down at the end of June and an auction sale loomed. Enter M. Janssens, who eventually persuaded the owner that he would not merely restore it, but preserve it as a shrine to the painter.

Frenzied creativity

1890, his devoted brother Theo found, crammed beneath the iron bedstead and stacked behind it, recently painted canvases that are now among the most famous paintings in the world. During his seventy days in Auvers, Van Gogh launched into a frenzied bout of creativity, producing over eighty canvases ← more than one a day. Many depict Auvers itself: the *mairie*, the church, the inn, the innkeeper and his daughter, boats by the river, the cornfields, the old cottages. As you walk round Auvers you can see the same scenes, and compare them with Van Gogh's vision of them thanks to a series of panels with reproductions of his work posted strategically round the village.

In coming to Auvers, Van Gogh was following in the footsteps of many a painter who had been attracted by its peaceful riverscapes, its picturesque thatched cottages and the light that they all described as special. Jean-Baptiste Corot painted here, so did Paul Cézanne and Auguste Renoir. Camille Pissarro travelled here from his home in nearby Pontoise, Charles-François Daubigny had a house-cum-studio built in the village.

Yet although their presence is attested by dozens of paintings in museums all over the world, it is not exploited in the village, which is remarkably free of overt commercialism. When you walk past the gaunt sculpture of Van Gogh by Ossip Zadkine in the public gardens and reach the Auberge Ravoux, you might expect to see Vincent T-shirts and the sort of tasteless souvenirs that are sold even in respectable museums. Happily you will find nothing of the kind. The owner of the 'Maison Van Gogh' describes it as a place of pilgrimage rather than a tourist highspot, and so it feels as you climb the narrow stairs to see the empty room where the painter died and the one next to it, furnished as in his day. Only five people are allowed up at a time, so you will not be crowded as you experience what most people find an intensely moving moment.

The video presentation in the attic is very well done, too. On the first floor you can buy books about Van Gogh, painting and Auvers, plus a few stylish pieces of jewellery, or a table napkin identical to those used in the café-restaurant downstairs, which serves excellent, good-value cuisine. A series of panels in the side passage and courtyard tell you more about Van Gogh and Auvers before you make your way towards the **Musée Daubigny**, in an attractive house that also houses the tourist office. The museum has a small collection of 19th- and 20th-century paintings and engravings, including canvases by Daubigny himself, and by the minor Impressionist Armand Guillaumin.

A walk through the garden brings you to the rue Daubigny, where the house built by the painter in 1860 is open to the public as **L'Atelier Daubigny**. This is again full of atmosphere. In the garden you can see a 'floating studio' of the type used by Daubigny to paint his riverscapes. And inside, the house and studio (still owned by his family) are decorated with delightful paintings by himself, his children, Corot and Daumier: scenes from *Little Red Riding Hood* and other fairytales in his daughter's bedroom, along with garlands of wild flowers and children's games; rabbits and a rooster in the dining room; huge landscapes and herons in the studio.

Charles Daubigny

A short walk from here, the **Château d'Auvers** presents a very effective 90-minute multimedia 'tour' designed to take you on a journey back to the Impressionist period. Armed with a headset supplying commentary in French or English, you walk from room to room, plunging into the heart of 1860s Paris, watching a noisy auction of Impressionist paintings, sitting in a nightclub to enjoy a cabaret, rattling along in a train for a day in the country, even peeping into a brothel. The whole thing is instructive yet great fun, and a good place to take older children. The château has three restaurants, too, plus a shop.

Impressionist tour

To learn more about a specific aspect of 19th-century social history, walk on to the **Musée de l'Absinthe** (Absinthe Museum). This

The green muse

small museum focuses on the 'green muse' (or 'green fairy', as the French call it) that was such a part of café life in France from soon after it was invented in Switzerland at the end of the 18th century to when it was banned in 1915. Here you can see posters and labels, menus and sketches, glasses and special absinthe spoons (originals and copies are on sale).

Van Gogh's grave

Before leaving Auvers you must make two more pilgrimages. Go first to the **church**, to see how accurate Van Gogh's famous painting is, despite its apparent distortions, then on to the **cemetery**, where two plain tombstones intertwined with ivy mark the graves of the Van Gogh brothers. Paying homage to them in this peaceful spot, the crows wheeling overhead as they do in Vincent's paintings, makes a fitting end to a day in this very special place.

Beyond Auvers

On the other side of the river from Auvers, **Mériel** honours its most famous son, the archetypal French film actor Jean Gabin (see box). A little further on (pleasant walk along the towpath from Auvers,

Key data

AUVERS-SUR-OISE 95430

T.O. Manoir de Colombières, rue de la Sansonne,
Ⓣ 01-30-36-10-06

Access Paris 30km, L'Isle-Adam 6km, Pontoise 7km; **rail** from Paris-Nord or Paris-Saint-Lazare to Pontoise, then connecting train; **RER** line A3 to Cergy-Prefecture, then bus

Sights **Auberge Ravoux** (inn where Van Gogh died), pl. de la Mairie, Ⓣ 01-34-48-05-47, open year-round; **Atelier de Daubigny** (house where Charles-François Daubigny lived and painted), 61 rue Daubigny, Ⓣ 01-30-36-79-42, open year-round; **Château d'Auvers** (Impressionism themed tour), rue de Léry, Ⓣ 01-34-48-48-48, open year-round; **Musée de l'Absinthe** (Absinthe Museum), 44 rue Callé, Ⓣ 01-30-36-83-26, open year-round (weekends only Oct to end May); **Musée Daubigny**, Manoir des Colombières, rue de la Sansonne, Ⓣ 01-30-36-80-20; **Van Gogh's grave** in the village cemetery

Lunch Auvers-sur-Oise; also in château

Staying L'Isle-Adam

Musée de la Batellerie
(river transport) pl. Jules-Gévelot, 78700 Conflans-Sainte-Honorine, Ⓣ 01-39-72-58-05, open year-round

Musée Jean Gabin
1 pl. Jean-Gabin, 95630 Mériel, Ⓣ 01-34-64-87-92, open year-round (pm weekends and Mon only)

Musée Pissarro
17 rue du Château, 95300 Pontoise, Ⓣ 01-30-38-02-40, open year-round, pm only

A screen hero

Jean Gabin, whose real name was the considerably less punchy Alexis Mon-courgé, starred in hundreds of French movies over a forty-year period. He was born in Mériel, on the other side of the river from Auvers-sur-Oise, in 1904, started making films in the early 1930s and continued until a few years before his death in 1976. He is unforgettable in two pictures directed by Marcel Carné that are generally reckoned to be among the greatest films of all time – *Quai des Brumes* (1938) and *Le Jour se lève* (1939), both scripted by the poet Jacques Prévert. And in between he was the dashing coal-streaked engine driver hero of Jean Renoir's *La Bête humaine* (1938), based on Emile Zola's passionate novel of the same name.

Once he had lost his youthful good looks, his versatility as an actor and, in the words of the film buff *par excellence* Leslie Halliwell, his 'stocky viril-ity and world-weary features' ensured that he was never off the screen. He was a highly convincing Inspector Maigret, excellent alongside Alain Delon in one of my favourites, *The Sicilian Clan* (1970), and just right as Jean Val-jean in a 1957 version of *Les Misérables*. The bust of him in front of the eponymous museum in his birthplace is a remarkable likeness, and the museum itself a must for anyone interested in French cinema.

cruises on summer Sundays), **L'Isle-Adam** was a favoured weekend-ing resort for Parisians in the 19th and early 20th century, when it acquired an organized beach on the river bank. Now it has two open-air swimming pools, one surrounded by a sandy area for sun-bathing, the other a full-scale Olympic pool. Also here are tennis courts, a miniature golf course, and boats and pedalos for hire.

On the way back to Paris you can visit another small museum devoted to a painter who never lost his delight in the riverscapes of the Oise: Camille Pissarro, the only artist to take part in all eight of the Impressionist exhibitions. He worked in **Pontoise** in the 1860s and lived there for over a decade from 1872, painting some three hundred canvases. Among the work on display are woodcuts and drawings by his son Lucien, who lived in England, working mainly as a printer and book illustrator. Then where the Oise meets the Seine, **Conflans-Sainte-Honorine** is a good place to appreciate the impor-tance of river transport in this part of the world, even today. The **Musée de la Batellerie** in the town's château (lovely views from the adjoining public garden of the river with its hundreds of moored barges) has models and many other exhibits illustrating the history and technology of French inland waterways in general and of this cen-turies-old river port in particular. And there are pleasant walks to be had beside the Seine, as well as cruises on some summer afternoons.

During one June weekend, the town stages the **Pardon national de la Batterie**, a traditional ceremony including a mass said on a boat.

Camille Pissarro

Barges on the Seine

12 Ecouen, Royaumont

Château d'Ecouen

Renaissance Museum

The **Château d'Ecouen** is now on the edge of a dull suburban area, but for anyone interested in art and architecture it is worth making a special journey to see the major museum it has been converted into, the **Musée national de la Renaissance** (Renaissance Museum). Appropriately enough, the château is itself a superb, sober Renaissance building with an elegant formal garden, rather reminiscent of the great Loire Valley châteaux. It was built between 1538 and 1555 for Anne, Duc de Montmorency, Connétable (Constable) of France, a distinguished, if arrogant, army commander from one of France's oldest families, and a patron of the arts whose château at Chantilly was being built at about the same time (see pp. 132–5).

The south wing, with its slightly later portico or 'frontispiece' decorated with columns and niches, was where the Connétable had his own rooms. It was designed by his architect Jean Bullant, who was born in Ecouen and lived there, to display the famous statues of captured slaves sculpted by Michelangelo for Pope Julius II's tomb (now in the Louvre in Paris).

The interior is sadly lacking in atmosphere – it has the unloved feeling of so many state-owned museums – but is full of truly beautiful things. So you must try to imagine the pleasingly proportioned rooms when richly clothed guests gathered round the tall painted fireplaces and the tables were set with lavish banquets. The star exhibit is a set of lively tapestries depicting the biblical story of David and Bathsheba, woven in Brussels between 1510 and 1520 and glittering with gold and silver threads. The individual scenes are crammed with figures with strong, expressive faces, caparisoned horses, and lances pointing skywards.

Among so many lovely objects on the **ground floor** – sculpture and ironwork, enamels and ivories – I particularly like an ivory scene of Orpheus playing his lyre to an enthralled audience of cow, sheep, horse, lion and stag. The **second floor** has a roomful of stained glass. It is a treat to see it close up, instead of craning your neck in churches and cathedrals. It includes a striking Flight into Egypt of about

Stained glass

1540, all sepia and white except for the Virgin Mary's bright gold hair, and a window from the Sainte-Chapelle in Vincennes Castle depicting François Ier, easily recongizable from his sardonic expression. Here too is a collection of ceramics, some from Iznik in Turkey, some French, and a room of wedding chests painted with battle and other scenes (note the Trojan horse, and the knights weighed down by their armour). Among the jewellery, don't miss the little ship with strings of pearls for sails.

You then go down to the **first floor** and the suites of rooms used by the Connétable and his wife Madeleine de Savoie, which feel more lived in than the rest of the museum. The painted fireplaces are beautiful, and as well as the David and Bathsheba tapestries, I like those illustrating the Labours of Hercules, with their many-headed

Hydra and a lion whose curly mane is just like Hercules's own hair and beard. You can also visit the chapel, adorned with a copy, by a contemporary, of a Leonardo da Vinci *Last Supper*.

Royaumont Abbey

The ruined Cistercian **Abbaye de Royaumont** is close to a network of busy roads, but seems a haven of peace as you cross a lazy stream where ducks potter contentedly, then walk down an avenue of trees towards the abbey. The views of the main building are beautiful, the atmosphere serene, and as you skirt a lilypond ringed by trees, its surface occasionally disturbed by leaping fish, you almost feel as if you were pacing contemplatively round a cloister.

It is a good start to a visit to this harmonious place, founded by the pious Louis IX in 1228 and presided over by his mother, the equally pious Spanish princess Blanche of Castile, who had acted as regent when he set off on a crusade. Louis XIII's chief minister Cardinal Richelieu regularly went into retreat at Royaumont, and his successor Cardinal Mazarin even became abbot. 'St Louis' himself had often stayed here, joining in the life of the monks and performing humble tasks like serving meals. *St Louis*

You are free to wander about, visiting the main building, the **Bâtiment des Pères**, and contemplating the turret and base of a column that is all that the depredations of the Revolution left standing of the abbey church – a strange and romantic sight with its garland of roses. To the right a circle of sawn-off columns indicates the chancel. You can then walk into the **cloisters**, with a formal garden in the middle, and into the **sacristy** leading off them, with a display of statuary. The Gothic **refectory** is devoted to medieval musical instruments – monochord and rebec, *vielle* (see box, p. 15) and organistrum are all here, and you can even hear a tape of how they sounded if you press the appropriate knob. Beyond here the **kitchens** display the 'Virgin of Royaumont', a beautiful medieval statue.

On the way out you pass a building that seems eminently practical: built over a narrow canal, it housed the latrines, but the flowing water did not merely flush them, it also set in motion a waterwheel that in turn activated various bits of machinery in the monks' workshops.

Throughout its history Royaumont has been an artistic and intellectual centre as well as a religious one. The Royaumont Foundation, set up in 1964, continues this role today by staging a four-month summer 'music season', with concerts every weekend from June to the end of September in various parts of the building. In particular it is a centre for research into medieval music and its performance – hence the instrument display. If you attend a concert (℡ 01-34-68-05-50 for information and booking), you can visit the abbey at no extra charge earlier in the day. *Summer concerts*

The foundation is also known for its work in the field of poetry in translation. A selection of titles are on sale in the pleasant bookshop near the entrance, where you can also buy tapes of Gregorian chant and medieval instruments, and a good range of books on art and architecture, and on the Middle Ages in general.

Royaumont Abbey

Key data

Château d'Ecouen housing **Musée national de la Renaissance**
95400 Ecouen, ☎ 01-34-38-38-50, open year-round
Access   Paris 20km, **RER** line D to Sarcelles, then **bus** 269

Abbaye de Royaumont
95270 Asnières-sur-Oise, ☎ 01-30-35-59-00, open year-round
Access   Paris 35km, Chantilly 10km, L'Isle-Adam 12km; **rail** from
Paris-Nord (suburban line) to Viarmes (2.5km)
Lunch   light meals in abbey at weekend
Staying   Chantilly, Luzarches
Also   Chantilly, Oise Valley

13 In and around Chantilly and Senlis

Chantilly

Chantilly could be said, in appropriately racegoing jargon, to have pulled off a *tiercé gagnant*, a winning triple bet. Firstly, it has an attractive forest setting. Secondly, its twin châteaux, romantically built on a lake, house one of France's top art collections. And thirdly, it boasts what must surely be the world's loveliest racecourse, framed by a backdrop of both châteaux and forest, attracting the world's most elegant racegoers. The only drawback is that it also attracts large crowds of tourists, especially at the weekend. Another problem is that although it

Chantilly: the Petit Château seeming to float on the lake

offers a good range of restaurants, it has few hotels in town.

The town (which is naturally enough twinned with Epsom, that great British racing centre) has a prosperous feel with its comfortable mansions lining the roads near the racecourse. But there is nothing special to see apart from the châteaux, which are easily reached from the station by a pleasant and clearly signposted walk of about 2km (there are buses, too, for part of the way). It was not developed until the mid-17th century, but the land and its good hunting terrain was long the fief of some of France's most powerful families. One was the Montmorency clan, the grandest of whom, known as 'Le Grand Connétable', was Anne, Duc de Montmorency (see p. 130). He it was who had a palatial residence built here in the early 16th century. Alas, it was demolished during the French Revolution, after serving as a prison. But the more intimate **Petit Château** (Little Château), linked to the palace by a bridge, is still standing.

Little Château

The Connétable's great-grandson bore the name of another influential family, the Princes de Condé. He was a 'Great', too, 'Le Grand Condé'. He brought in that great gardener André Le Nôtre (see **Versailles**) to landscape the grounds and turned Chantilly into a mecca for literary and artistic lions as well as the most fashionable aristocrats of the day. After the Revolution and the Empire it recovered its pre-eminence under his descendants, who had the palace rebuilt. But the Condé line died out and the estate was inherited by a royal prince, the Duc d'Aumale. He built yet another **Grand Château**, the one you see today, in a monumental late 19th-century version of the Renaissance style, designed to house his outstanding collection of paintings and his equally outstanding library of rare books and illuminated manuscripts, including the celebrated Book of Hours commissioned by the Duc de Berry (see p. 134).

So what you visit is not so much a residence, or even a museum (though it is known as the **Musée Condé**), as a setting chosen by this great collector to show his fabulous treasures to best advantage. He

Musée de Condé

Les Très Riches Heures du Duc de Berry

The illuminated Book of Hours commissioned by the first Duke of Berry is one of the masterpieces of the style known as 'International Gothic'. It was also the undoubted star of the duke's legendary manuscript collection – and today is perhaps the major draw among the many priceless treasures in the Musée Condé in Chantilly.

In the late Middle Ages, rich patrons liked to commission illuminated copies of the *Horae* or 'Hours of the Virgin', a widely used volume of private devotions intended not for priests or monks, but for lay people, and including a calendar of feast days. In the versions produced for the wealthy, the calendar would be illustrated with original miniatures depicting the traditional occupations of the twelve months, identified by the signs of the zodiac.

For his Book of Hours, Jean, Duc de Berry, turned to three of his court painters, the Limbourg brothers, Pol, the eldest, Hennequin and Herman. Their names suggest that they were Flemish, though they are often referred to as French. At any rate, the younger two are known to have been apprenticed to a Flemish goldsmith with a workshop in Paris, no doubt learning there the precision and attention to minute detail that is so evident in their exquisite miniatures. In 1400, during this apprenticeship, Paris was beset by an outbreak of the plague, and the two boys – they were still only children – were apparently on their way home to escape it when they somehow got mixed up in a battle and finished up as prisoners in Brussels. We know of this dramatic, if somewhat mysterious incident because they were released thanks to the Duke of Burgundy.

The Limbourgs were related to Jehan Malouel, one of the painters working at the duke's court in Dijon, which explains how he heard about their plight. After he had paid a ransom to have them freed, he took both of them on, along with their elder brother, as court painters. They appear to have been kept on the payroll of his son Jean sans Peur ('John the Fearless'), but in 1411 moved on to Jean's uncle's court in Bourges.

Five years later all of them were dead, though there is no record of how they died. But in that short time they had produced 39 superb illuminations for their patron's Book of Hours, revered not only for their outstanding technical mastery, but because they offer many charming insights into life in medieval France. Their detailed depictions of costumes and everyday objects, landscape and architecture are clearly based on direct observation, not on standard motifs. For instance, in one of them the Château of Saumur in the Loire Valley is easily recognizable.

Presumably they had not finished their task at their death, as further, less perfect illuminations were added about seventy years later by another painter. This time he was a Berry man born and bred, Jean Colombe, the son of a painter and brother of Michel Colombe, one of France's finest pre-Renaissance sculptors.

bequeathed the whole estate to the Institut de France, with the proviso that it must stay as he left it. This explains why you really do feel, despite the crowds, that you are privileged to view a private collection, not least because the way each room is crammed with pictures – which I personally like – goes against modern museum practice.

I have no space to describe the many rooms in detail, so can only suggest you collect a plan from the entrance and point you towards some of the highlights. You are free to wander at will in the Grand Château, whereas the suites of residential rooms in the Petit Château (also called the **Capitainerie** and also full of treasures) can only be seen without a guide on Sunday afternoons.

The Duc de Berry's Book of Hours is in the **library** (though the original is not on display), along with other rare manuscripts and literally thousands of superbly bound volumes. The **Chambre de Monsieur le Prince** is very pretty, with its white and gold panelling and animal and bird scenes set into the wall, and the early 18th-century **Salon des Singes** (monkey drawing room) charming. Among the paintings, the **Rotonde** has a lovely Piero di Cosimo portrait of a Florentine lady with pearls wound through her hair. In the **Cabinet des Clouet** is a group of portraits by Jean and François Clouet, many of which once belonged to Catherine de Médicis. Here you can see François Ier, Henri II as a child clutching a small dog, or possibly a monkey, Henris II and IV astride caparisoned horses, a severe-looking Catherine de Médicis herself, her husband Henri II in an elegant cream-and-black-striped outfit, as well as Mary, Queen of Scots and Anne Boleyn. The **Santuario** houses forty superb miniatures by Jean Fouquet, painted in strong colours like orange and bright blue, and a buxom, rosy-cheeked Virgin plus bonny Child by Raphael, as well as his surprisingly small *Three Graces*. *The Clouets* *Raphael*

More beautiful miniatures await you in the **Cabinet des Gemmes**, including tiny 18th-century views of Chantilly, a portrait of Le Grand Condé with flowing curls and a thoughtful-looking, rather plump Madame de Sévigné. But the highlight here is the famous 'pink diamond' – a copy, for safety. Among a wealth of paintings in the **Tribune**, don't miss Botticelli's firmly striding *Autumn*, a portrait of the great French dramatist Molière by Pierre Mignard and Hyacinthe Rigaud's portrait of Louis XIV, shapely legs well in evidence.

Beyond the châteaux

There is so much to see that you must be careful to leave enough time to enjoy the huge **grounds**, with various beautiful stretches of water, a small **Hameau** that predates Marie Antoinette's (see **Versailles**) and several attractive buildings. Then there are the **stables**. It would be a mistake to miss them, as Chantilly life is so much bound up with horses. If you are a racing fan, the dates to remember are the first and second Sundays in June, when the Prix du Jockey Club (known as the 'French Derby') and the Prix de Diane (the 'French Oaks') turn Chantilly into *the* place for the smart set to be seen. The first of these top races started in 1836, only two years after the racecourse opened for business, and the second seven years later. Nowadays, according to the tourist office, over 800 racehorse owners stable some 3000 thoroughbreds in and around Chantilly, and over 1000 stable boys (or 'lads', as the Anglophile French racing fraternity calls them) exercise and groom them year-round. *The races*

But you don't need to be a racegoer, or even a horse lover, to

The stables enjoy visiting the elegant stable buildings, **Les Grandes Ecuries**, proudly topped by a dome and built by a great-grandson of Le Grand Condé. Legend famously has it that he was such a passionate horseman that he fully expected to be a horse in some future life. This explains why he built such sumptuous lodgings for his future equine companions. They were designed in the early 18th century by Jean Aubert, who worked with Jacques Gabriel on the Hôtel Biron in Paris (now the Rodin Museum), and were originally to be even larger. As you come closer the horses' heads carved everywhere seem almost to be alive, especially those over the door, clearly highly strung thoroughbreds, nervy, sinewy, trembling. And since 1982 the stables themselves have been brought to life again by another passionate horseman, a one-time riding instructor called Yves Bienaimé, who has turned them into the **Musée vivant du Cheval** (Living Horse Museum). The principle behind this privately owned museum is to show horses in action, though to begin with you walk past stabled beasts and then through a series of rooms on themes connected with horses.

Dressage displays Dressage displays and demonstrations (with commentary only in French) are staged two or three times a day depending on the time of year. In fine weather you can even watch them while enjoying a meal in the *Carrousel Gourmand*, overlooking the open air **Cour des Chenils** and serving regional cuisine. Otherwise they take place in a ring (more like a splendid ballroom) below the dome. Equestrian pageants are performed during the first weekend of most months, with occasional evening shows.

The best way of viewing the lovely setting of both châteaux and stables is from the air. So why not try taking a balloon trip? It will *Balloon trips* be completely safe because the balloon is attached to the ground by a cable. (Easter to end Oct, ☏ 03-44-57-35-35, combined ticket with châteaux and/or grounds.)

Senlis

The attractive old town of Senlis, full of cobbled streets lined with medieval houses, some still with their staircase turrets, is one of those places that seems rather charmingly to exist in a time warp. It has had an interesting history: among many other royal events, its castle saw the election of Hugues Capet, founder of the Capetian dynasty, in 987, and, in 1420, the wedding of Henry V of England to Catherine de Valois, the youngest daughter of the French king whom his troops had defeated five years earlier at the Battle of Agincourt.

But it now seems a quiet provincial backwater, rather staid and proper, its streets clean and neat, with something of the atmosphere of a small town in the 1950s. Some of the shops still have a delightfully old-fashioned look and I have spotted little girls wearing dresses and cardigans and white ankle socks at weekends, rather than the universal jeans or dungarees. All this adds greatly to the pleasure of strolling round the old streets – or you might consider a ride in a *calèche*, an open horse-drawn carriage.

It is only a few minutes' walk from the stop for buses from Chantilly (beside the now-disused rail station) into the old heart of the

An 18th-century inventor

In February 1728 the once-royal town of Senlis witnessed the birth of an innkeeper's son who was destined to become a major figure in the scientific establishment of the day.

When he was fifteen, **Antoine Baumé** was apprenticed to a pharmacist in nearby Compiègne. Two years later he was taken on by a dispensary in Paris and became engrossed in theoretical chemistry. By 1752 he had qualified as a master apothecary and was able to open his own dispensary in the busy, if somewhat dispreputable rue Saint-Denis near Les Halles, the huge central food market. Over the next fifteen years, as well as running the business, he designed apparatus for use in laboratories and in industry, and supplied pieces designed by himself and others to clients all over France. In 1767 he added another string to his bow, becoming the country's first large-scale producer of ammonium chloride.

But 1768 was the key date in his career: he invented the 'aerometer', an instrument used for measuring the weight and the density of air and gases, now named after him. He was now seen as an authority on chemistry and pharmacy and in 1757 published an outline textbook on these two subjects, which he taught from then until the early 1770s. His many other publications included contributions to the two-volume encyclopedia whose lengthy title started *Dictionnaire portatif des arts et métiers*, one of the many weighty tomes produced by the Age of Englightenment.

After writing a thesis on ether, he was elected to the French Academy of Sciences, though his election was opposed by some of his fellow-scientists, with whom he had apparently engaged in long-running feuds. By then he was in his mid-forties and had started to amass a considerable fortune. The outbreak of the French Revolution seventeen years later put paid to that fortune, and his pension as a member of one of France's prestigious academies also dried up. But he managed to persuade one of the revolutionary committees to allow him to open another dispensary in 1796, when he was not far off seventy. Eight years later his full life ended in Paris, his place in the history of science secure.

town, enclosed within the oval ring dictated by its walls – parts of the Gallo-Roman fortifications are still standing. You come first to the **Eglise Saint-Pierre**, with a host of beasts crouching in rows on the gables and piers of its Late Gothic façade, and a huge Renaissance belfry. From here you can already glimpse the **Cathédrale Notre-Dame**. As you walk round the curving, cobbled **rue aux Flageards**, with ivy-covered walls and a pleasing brick and half-timbered house (once the chapter's library) on your right, you can enjoy a splendid view of its flying buttresses, lacy spire, cylindrical towers, carved balustrades and grotesque gargoyles. In front is a well-kept garden with a lawn, and roses climbing up the railings, creating the impression that you are in an English cathedral close rather than a small French town.

The cathedral

You can enter the cathedral from here, via the **north portal**, adorned with François Ier's salamander. The interior is light and on a slightly irregular plan, because it was built partly on to the Roman

Frambaldus/Frambourg = Lancelot?

St Frambaldus of Laceo, also known as Frambald, Frambaud, Framburg and, in France, Frambourg, was probably born into a wealthy family in the Auvergne in about 500. He is said to have been a companion of King Arthur and in due course one of his Knights of the Round Table. An intriguing theory suggests that he served as a model for Lancelot of the Lake when the 12th-century poet Chrétien de Troyes wrote his great Arthurian romances.

For a start, they both had the same emblems: a clover leaf or trefoil, a sword and a chalice. Then etymologists point out that the name Frambaldus was derived from Latin *framea* (and a similar Old High German word) that has survived in modern French as *framée*, meaning a long lance or javelin used by the Franks, plus the Old High German (and Old English) *Bald*, from which English 'bold' is derived. And 'Laceo' is related to 'lac' or lake.

So his name can be read as 'bold lancer of the lake', whence Chrétien de Troyes's 'Lancelot du Lac', and Sir Thomas Malory's 'Lancelot of the Lake' in the *Morte d'Arthur*.

walls. Work started on the cathedral in the mid-12th century and continued over a long period, followed by major rebuilding after a fire in 1504. So you can follow the development of the Gothic style down to the 'Flamboyant' (Late Gothic) tracery that decorates the work done after the fire. You can also peer down into the much earlier crypt, dating from about 1000 and dedicated to Sts Gervase and Protase.

You can leave via the south portal, then walk round to view the richly carved **Grand Portail** or west portal, teeming with saints and biblical figures. I particularly like Abraham clutching the elect to his bosom like so many babies in swaddling clothes, and the lively Dormition of the Virgin, with angels with huge wings hovering over her bed.

Beside this west portal, the 12th-century **Hôtel de Vermandois** shows a helpful video focusing on details of the sculpture, and another on the history of Senlis. This small museum (gradually being enlarged) also has some medieval sculpture and work by the local 19th-century history painter Thomas Couture.

Also overlooking the **place du Parvis** (the cathedral square) is the ruined **Château Royal**, in a flower-filled courtyard. Just inside the entrance, the **Musée des Spahis** is for anyone interested in military history: it relates the story of the North African cavalrymen in the French army, whose name comes from the same Persian root as 'sepoys', and who were garrisoned in Senlis at one time. Also within this complex of buildings is a museum on hunting, the **Musée de la Vénerie**, full of hunting horns and paintings by artists specializing in animal scenes, like the 18th-century artist Jean-Baptiste Oudry.

Military & hunting museums

Opposite the cathedral's south portal, the former archbishop's residence houses Senlis's fourth and most interesting museum. The **Musée d'Art** has a collection of Gallo-Roman artefacts excavated locally, including some very realistic bronze crayfish, fibulae, jewellery and toilet instruments, and a beautifully lit crypt peopled with a slightly sinister army of ex-voto figurines found in the 1960s in the nearby Forêt d'Halatte. A video presentation dramatically shows the heads in close up. The eclectic painting collection has more canvases by Thomas Couture, a pretty little beach scene by Eugène Boudin, and some naïve art by another local artist known as 'Séraphine of Senlis'.

The **place Saint-Frambourg** leads to the **Chapelle Saint-Frambourg**, restored by the Hungarian pianist Georges Cziffra to house a foundation that organizes concerts here. The chapel was founded in 993 by Hugues Capet's queen Adelaide, a descendant of Charlemagne, to house the relics of St Frambault or Frambourg (see box). A well-preserved skeleton inside a tomb unearthed in 1988 in what is now the crypt of the Early Gothic church you see today is thought to be that of this tall, dark-haired, highly educated woman, as the chroniclers describe her. If you are able to get into the church – it is open only weekend afternoons or during performances in the May–September concert season – you can admire stained glass commissioned from the Spanish painter Joan Miró, believed to be the only work he ever did in this field.

Summer concerts

Do allow time to explore other picturesque streets like the **rue de la Chancellerie** and the **rue de la Treille**, as well as the garden behind the Château Royal, where you can see part of the Roman walls. Best of all, time your visit for the last weekend in September in years whose date ends with an odd number. During this '**Rendez-vous de Septembre**', cars are banned, owners of historic houses open them to the public, open-air concerts take place, and in the evening the whole of the Old Town is illuminated. Then you will soon see why Senlis has so often been used by film-makers (see p. 7).

September event

Beyond Senlis

To see another spectacular film location, travel 12km northeast to the 17th-century **Château de Raray** (see p. 7), whose extraordinary frieze of hounds, stags and wild boar memorably featured in Jean Cocteau's *Beauty and the Beast* (1946). But the main points of interest in the area lie south of the town, in or on the edge of the lovely **Forêt d'Ermenonville**.

It is a pretty bus ride or drive to the village of **Ermenonville**, whose château, now an upmarket hotel,★ was owned in the 18th century by the Marquis de Girardin, a friend and patron of Jean-Jacques Rousseau, and an admirer of his 'natural' philosophy and educational theories. Following principles gleaned from Rousseau's romantic novel *La Nouvelle Héloïse*, the marquis converted his large estate into a romantic (and Romantic) landscape, adorned with grottoes and waterfalls, groves and temples. In 1778 Rousseau accepted his offer of a virtual sinecure as tutor and music teacher to his children, plus board and lodging in the grounds. Here he died suddenly, apparently of a stroke, on 2 July, after many weeks of happy wandering in the gardens, now appropriately called the **Parc Jean-Jacques Rousseau**, still well worth visiting, though now separated from the château.

Ermenonville

Jean-Jacques Rousseau

In them you can see the mausoleum that the marquis commissioned for his hero from the artist Hubert Robert, a specialist in landscapes featuring romantic ruins.

You can still see the tomb, as well as a suitably romantic statue of Rousseau in the village. And 3km away you can see a collection of

Chaâlis   Rousseau memorabilia in the grounds of another highly romantic place, the ruined **Abbaye de Chaâlis**. This Cistercian abbey was founded in the early 12th century. As so often, it was demolished by the revolutionary mob, who left only parts of the chancel of the abbey church and the early Gothic chapel standing. The ruins are a picturesque sight in their forest setting, with roses climbing over crum-

---

Key data

CHANTILLY 60500

T.O.   23 av. du Maréchal-Joffre, ☏ 03-44-57-08-58

Access   Paris 40km, Senlis 10km, Compiègne 42km, Beauvais 52km; **rail** from Paris-Nord; **RER** line D1; **buses** from Senlis

Sights   **Grand Château** and **Petit Château**, housing **Musée Condé** (famous art collections), ☏ 03-44-57-08-00, open year-round; **Musée vivant du Cheval** (Horse Museum, with dressage demonstrations and equestrian displays), in **Grandes Ecuries** (18th-century stables), ☏ 03-44-57-13-13, open Apr to end Oct

Lunch   Chantilly

Staying   Chantilly, Creil, Ermenonville, Fontaine-Chaâlis, Senlis

Also   Royaumont Abbey

SENLIS 60300

T.O.   pl. du Parvis Notre-Dame, ☏ 03-44-53-06-40

Access   Paris 51km, Chantilly 10km, Compiègne 32km, Beauvais 52km; **rail** from Paris-Nord, then connecting bus; **buses** from Compiègne

Sights   **Cathédrale Notre-Dame** (Gothic cathedral); **Chapelle Saint-Frambourg** (Early Gothic church with remains of 10th-century church in crypt); **Château Royal** (ruined medieval castle), housing **Musée des Spahis** (North African cavalry) and **Musée de la Vénerie** (hunting), both ☏ 03-44-53-00-80, open year-round; **Eglise Saint-Pierre** (Late Gothic church); **Musée d'Art** (art and archeology, in former archbishop's palace), pl. Notre-Dame, ☏ 03-44-53-00-80, open year-round; **Musée de l'Hôtel de Vermandois** (local history, architecture, in medieval house), pl. Notre-Dame, ☏ 03-44-53-00-80, open year-round; **Roman walls**

Lunch   Senlis, Fleurines, Fontaine-Chaâlis

Staying   Senlis, Ermenonville, Fontaine-Chaâlis, Raray

Abbaye de Chaâlis (ruined Cistercian abbey) and **Musée Jacque-mart-André** (fine and applied art)
60305 Fontaine-Chaâlis, ☏ 03-44-54-04-02 (Ermenonville 3km, Senlis 10km), open year-round (Sun only Nov to end Feb)
Mer de Sable (amusement park)
60950 Ermenonville, ☏ 03-44-54-00-96 (Ermenonville 3km, Senlis 10km), open Easter to end Sep; from Paris: **RER** line B3 to Roissy-Charles-de-Gaulle, then **bus**

bling arches and gargoyles silhouetted against the sky. One is no grotesque beast, but a swooping angel pouring water from a pitcher.

The 18th-century abbot's residence, designed by Jean Aubert, the architect of Chantilly's magnificent stables (see p. 136), was not destroyed during the Revolution and was restored in the 19th century. The estate was bought in 1902 by Nélie Jacquemart-André, the wealthy widow of a banker. She had spent her childhood there and wanted to fill the rooms with her huge and eclectic collections of paintings (including two Giottos, a Van Loo and a portrait by Nicolas Largillière), tapestries, marble busts, sculpture, plus furniture, china, silks, oriental *objets d'art*.

Art collections

She bequeathed the estate and her collections to the Institut de France. The whole place, neglected for years, is gradually being catalogued and restored, and Madame André's richly furnished private rooms are now open to the public too.

Walking through the gardens to the miniature lake beyond the museum building is pleasant – don't miss the curiously stocky little sphinx on her stone pedestal.

The odd fairground sound drifting across the quiet lawns comes from the **Mer de Sable**, an amusement park opposite the abbey. The name means 'Sea of Sand' – a natural curiosity brought about when the monks deforested land that had been under the sea in the Tertiary geological era and set off an ecological reaction that brought a large stretch of white sand to the surface. Despite the rival attractions and greater glamour of Disneyland Paris (see pp. 155–8), this amusement park, started up in the 1960s, is still very popular. It makes full use of the desert-like setting with cowboys and Indians chasing across the sand, dromedaries and bisons, ranches and corrals. A wide range of rides includes shooting the rapids on the river Cheyenne, and there are frequent Western and equestrian shows. The all-in price is modest, and the many themed restaurants are good value too.

But as well as Disneyland, the Sea of Sand has another rival nearer at hand, the Asterix park (see next section).

14   Parc Astérix

Three years before Disneyland opened to the east of Paris, Albert Uderzo's and René Goscinny's ever-popular hero Asterix the Gaul started welcoming wide-eyed children to his very own theme park. It was then three decades since Asterix, his mountainous sidekick Obelix and a handful of Gallic chums had first outwitted the Roman legionaries in a magazine comic strip. By then the cartoon books were big business, selling over six million copies worldwide, and translated into 57 languages and dialects.

Asterix the Gaul

Asterix Park was a success from the outset, as it makes a great fun day out for kids and is popular with adults too: it is well run, will keep

Key data

PARC ASTERIX 60128 Plailly
B.P. 8, ⓣ 03-44-62-34-04
Access   Paris 35km, Roissy-Charles-de-Gaulle airport 12km, Senlis
17km; **RER** line B3 to Roissy-CDG, then **shuttle bus** (approx
30-min intervals until 13.30; return bus from 16.30); ask for
all-in RER/bus/admission ticket
Open   early Apr to mid-Oct
Lunch   wide range inside park
Staying Ermenonville, Senlis
Also   Chaâlis, Chantilly, Ermenonville, Mer de Sable, Royaumont,
Senlis

their offspring amused for hours, and may even teach them a bit of
history. (For the record, Asterix's exploits are supposed to be loosely
based on the gallant Vercingetorix and his Gallic tribe – see p. 59.)
And naturally enough, the French did not view it with the same 'cultural imperialism' reservations as beset Disneyland in the early days.

There are getting on for thirty rides on offer, including a couple of
giant roller-coasters, plus ten theatres, twenty-odd themed shops and
craft stalls, and over forty places to eat, six of them proper restaurants,
where you can feast on wild boar paté and the like (wild boar ham-
burgers feature on the fast-food menus). And every day twenty or so
shows are put on. You can watch a 'dolphin ballet' in Poseidon's
Theatre, or be entertained by an action-packed spectacular,
crammed with special effects, improbably called 'The Mona Lisa
Caper' (*Main basse sur la Joconde* in French), all about a gang trying
to relieve the Louvre of its best-known painting.

The whole complex covers 50 hectares and is approached along
the **Via Antiqua**, leading to the **Roman City** or **Ancient Greece** or the
Lake-Dwellings, as well as **Asterix's Village**, complete with thatched
huts. At the far side is **La Rue de Paris**, for a whirlwind tour through
post-Gallo-Roman French history, reached through crazily leaning
gate towers and peopled with medieval craftsmen.

The latest in hi-tech wizardry creates some pretty impressive effects,
but meeting Asterix and Obelix, Getafix and Vitalstatistix is what many
kids enjoy. The atmosphere is definitely French and few concessions
are made to non-French speakers. But it never seems to matter, as the
emphasis is on joining in and role-playing, with kids dressing up as
Gauls and Roman centurions or 19th-century tourists in Paris. Even
the shyest soon mingle happily with their French counterparts as they
whitewater raft down the River Styx in giant buoys, cheer on the
Three Musketeers or struggle to steer chariot dodgems.

A few highlights:
- **Le Grand Splatch** (The Big Splash) river trip with drop down 15m
waterfall
- **Goudurix** Europe's biggest roller-coaster turns you upside-down
seven times

- **Tonnerre de Zeus** (Zeus's Thunder) another spectacular roller-coaster with speeds over 80kph
- **Camp Petitbonum** Roman fortress with slides (for smaller children to explore)
- **Les Stars de l'Empire** (Imperial Stars) show with gladiators and circus acts
- **Menhir Express** (Standing Stone Express) Big-dipper ride on a floating standing stone, ending in lake
- **Le Vol d'Icare** (Icarus's Flight) labyrinth leading to the sun and Minos's Palace

15 Beauvais

Beauvais, built on a hill at the heart of a region of large farms, suffered terribly from Second World War bombing, which destroyed a good 80 per cent of the town, including many medieval houses. But its greatest treasure, the extraordinary cathedral of Saint-Pierre, somehow survived almost unscathed and is essential viewing for anyone interested in Gothic architecture. The bombing put an end to centuries of Beauvais's pre-eminence in tapestry-making, dating back to 1664, when Louis XIV's chief minister, Jean-Baptiste Colbert, a great patron of French industry and commerce, chose it as the site of one of the new 'royal factories', the Manufacture royale de la Tapisserie. But in 1989 a large new tapestry works opened that can be visited, while some fine examples of traditional Beauvais tapestries are displayed beside the cathedral.

The **Cathédrale Saint-Pierre** was one of the last in a great wave of cathedral-building in medieval France and certainly the most daring in its upwards striving design. The transept reaches the dizzying

Building high

A medieval compiler

Vincent de Beauvais (c. 1190–1264), often known by the Latinized version of his name, Vincentius Bellovacensius, was a Dominican monk and scholar. Thanks to the patronage of Saint Louis, the French king Louis IX, he was able to embark on the ambitious project of compiling an encyclopedia embracing the whole of human knowledge acquired by the 13th century.

His magisterial *Speculum Majus* was divided into three parts: *Speculum Naturale*, *Speculum Doctrinale* and *Speculum Historiale*. A fourth part, *Speculum Morale*, was added later by an unknown author, and the whole vast enterprise was first published in its entirety over two centuries after his death, in 1473. But the *Speculum Historiale* had been translated into French as early as 1330, as *Miroir historial*, by a Hospitaller called Jean de Vignal.

Vincent de Beauvais's work was certainly known in England by the 14th century, as he is mentioned by Geoffrey Chaucer in the prologue to his *The Legend of Good Women*.

height of over 48 metres – which makes it the tallest in the world. Work started on the east end in 1247, on foundations from several earlier attempts that had succumbed to fire. But the unknown architect had been over-ambitious. The piers were too far apart and the flying buttresses did not give a big enough thrust to hold the whole structure up. In 1284 they collapsed, bringing down part of the vaulting. Rebuilding was eventually completed, with more buttressing, including another six piers. But in the turmoil of the Hundred Years War no further work was undertaken.

The transept was at last built in the 16th century. But then disaster struck again when it was rashly decided to add a stone belfry over the crossing, with a spire soaring 153 metres into the air. Such a height had never been reached before, and the gamble failed when in 1573, only four years after it had been completed, the piers supporting the crossing collapsed. A prisoner who had been condemned to death was granted a free pardon in return for risking his life by climbing up and sending what was left of the vault crashing down before it could do further damage.

Perhaps not suprisingly, after such a chequered history, no one came forward with the funding to build the nave, so what you admire today is only half a cathedral – a truncated masterpiece that is breathtakingly beautiful in its seemingly endless height, with its tall, slender windows and soaring columns.

A light meal or a coffee in one of several cafés opposite the cathedral will give you a chance to admire the wonderfully lacy sculpture and the arching flying buttresses silhouetted against the sky. Once inside, bring your gaze down eventually from the lofty vaulting to look at the stained glass, especially the earliest, in the Lady Chapel, including a Tree of Jesse, and the rose windows. But the modern window in swirling patterns in the Chapelle des Fonts Baptismaux to the right of the main entrance is beautiful too. The pretty clock dating

Key data

BEAUVAIS 60000

T.O.	1 rue Beauregard, ℡ 03-44-45-08-18
Access	Paris 76km, Chantilly 51km, Senlis 52km, Compiègne 57km; **rail** from Paris-Nord
Sights	**Cathédrale Saint-Pierre** (Gothic cathedral); **Eglise Saint-Etienne** (Transitional church); **Galerie nationale de la Tapisserie** (Tapestry Museum), 1 rue Saint-Pierre, ℡ 03-44-05-14-28, open year-round; **Manufacture nationale de la Tapisserie** (tapestry workshops), 24 rue Henri-Brispot, ℡ 03-44-05-14-28, open year-round, Tue, Wed, Thur pm only; **Musée départemental de l'Oise** (archeology, sculpture, furniture, ceramics, paintings)
Lunch	Beauvais, Savignies
Staying	Beauvais
Also	Chantilly, Senlis

Beauvais, the world's tallest cathedral

from 1302 is believed to be the earliest in the world still chiming, but it is outshone in complexity by the huge **astronomical clock**, dating from over half a millennium later and recently restored by a team of *meilleurs ouvriers de France* (see **Bourges**, p. 197). A host of brightly coloured automata enact scenes from the Last Judgement, while a series of over fifty dials enable you to tell the time in the world's major cities, or even work out tide tables. A type of *son-et-lumière* explains its workings.

Beyond the wall that abruptly closes off the interior you can visit the **Basse-Oeuvre**, the name given to what is left of the 10th-century church – which would have been knocked down to make room for the nave. You can also walk through into the peaceful cloisters, with a patterned brick gallery surmounting the elegant stone arcade.

The cathedral once had some fine tapestries, but these are no longer in Beauvais, so you must visit the **Galerie nationale de la Tapisserie**, a faceless modern building beside the cathedral, to see a permanent display of some of the finest Beauvais work, traditionally made on a low warp.

A visit to the new **Manufacture nationale de la Tapisserie**, converted from the vast old slaughterhouses, enables you to see the work of today's master weavers, employing the same techniques, but often to surprisingly contemporary designs. An international tapestry festival is held in the town every two years.

Beauvais tapestries

On the other side of the cathedral from the Tapestry Museum is the richly decorated medieval building that was once the bishop's palace, a fine sight with its shiny, pointed, slate-roofed turrets glittering like steel when the sun catches them. It now houses the **Musée départemental de l'Oise**, whose well-displayed collections include an archaeology section in the old cellars, ceramics on the first floor, along with paintings, many by local artists, and on the second floor a series of mock house interiors displaying furniture, including some

The little axe girl

In 1472, Charles the Bold, Duke of Burgundy, the richest and most powerful man in the kingdom, laid siege to Beauvais. This 'frontier town' on the edge of the Ile de France, with its thick walls, massive postern gates and wide moats, was proud of its reputation as an impregnable bastion. And sure enough, Charles's troops failed to capture the town, largely thanks to the inspiration of Jeanne Laisné, a local girl who earned a meagre living braking wool. She was allegedly only about sixteen, but her defiant spirit encouraged the townswomen to defend their citadel under her leadership as she charged forth wielding a small axe (*hachette* in French) – and earned herself a place among France's heroines under the nickname 'Jeanne Hachette'.

A festival to celebrate her exploits is held every year, during the last weekend in June.

good art nouveau pieces. Don't miss the impressive timber framework supporting the roof.

A few medieval houses have survived behind the cathedral, and Beauvais also has an interesting example of the transition from Romanesque to Gothic architecture in the **Eglise Saint-Etienne**, which you can reach by walking through lively pedestrian streets, then the modern place Jeanne-Hachette, with a statute of the eponymous local heroine (see box), and on past the town hall. Saint-Etienne has some lovely 16th-century stained glass, including another Tree of Jesse in the chancel, which, with its double row of flying buttresses, is Late Gothic. The nave and transept are essentially Romanesque, but their interior clearly shows the influence of the Early Gothic style.

Abbeys to visit

- **Chaâlis**: ruins of Cistercian abbey near Ermenonville and Senlis (p. 140)
- **Fontgombault**: Benedictine abbey on the edge of the Brenne nature reserve, rebuilt by Trappists in the 19th century, now again Benedictine (p. 220)
- **Noirlac**: well-restored Cistercian abbey in southern Berry, famous for its summer concerts of sacred music (p. 227)
- **Port-Royal-des-Champs**: ruins of Cistercian abbey in Vallée de Chevreuse, southwest of Paris, once major Jansenist centre (p. 92)
- **Royaumont**: ruins of large Cistercian abbey near Chantilly, now an arts foundation (p. 131)
- **Les Vaux-de-Cernay**: ruined Cistercian abbey in Vallée de Chevreuse, in the grounds of a very comfortable hotel (p. 95)

and Gothic cathedrals
- Beauvais (p. 143)
- Bourges (p. 197)
- Chartres (p. 83)

Ile de France ~ east of Paris

As with so many large cities, Paris's development seems to have favoured the western rather than the eastern outskirts. The **Marne river valley**, not so long ago the haunt of dapper oarsmen sporting boaters and a favourite outing for weekending Parisians, is engulfed in dormitory towns and dull suburban sprawl. The Val de Beauté, where Charles VII's lovely mistress, Agnès Sorel, 'la Dame de Beauté', once had her residence, seems distinctly unromantic today. Yet the popular dancing places beside the river known as *guinguettes* are enjoying a modest revival, and on summer Sundays you can still sense something of the jolly ambience that used to prevail here.

Then this heavily built up area rather surprisingly boasts three elegant châteaux: **Champs**, **Ferrières** and **Guermantes**. And a little further east, a new tourist mecca has sprouted where beetroots once grew – **Disneyland Paris**, a full-scale resort, American-style.

Further east still is the **Brie**, a rural plateau where the eponymous cheese is made, plus some pretty, unspoilt countryside through which twin rivers gently meander, the Grand Morin and Petit Morin. And on the southeastern edge of the plateau, the medieval Upper Town of **Provins** is sheer delight.

Virtually all these places can be reached by public transport, and there are many pleasant walks to be had in the more rural areas. If you are driving, you might like to follow the tourist itinerary called the **Route Thibaud de Champagne**, which includes the three châteaux, parts of the Brie and Provins.

16 Guinguette and cheese country

For the romantically inclined, and for anyone prepared to make a little effort of the imagination, a visit to **Nogent-sur-Marne**, just east of Paris, is much more interesting than your first sight of the densely built eastern suburbs would lead you to expect. It allows you to think yourself back into the time when Nogent, nicknamed the 'Sunday Eldorado' – Marcel Carné made a film there in 1929 called just that – was the most popular of places for weekend entertainment.

Nogent

Marne river cruises

Short trips from Nogent-sur-Marne, lasting about 45 minutes, are run at the weekend from April to the end of September by:

- **Vedettes du Pont-Neuf** (℡ 01-53-00-98-98)

But you can also start out from Paris and enjoy a whole-day cruise, including a lunch stop (meal extra, or take a picnic)

- **Canauxrama** (℡ 01-42-39-15-00)

Cruises, called '*Au pays des guinguettes*', start from the Port de l'Arsenal (check locally for dates and times)

- **Paris Canal** (℡ 01-42-40-96-97)

Cruises start from in front of the Musée d'Orsay and include a lunch stop at the Ile Brise-Pain in Créteil, with lunch at the delightful Domaine Sainte-Catherine (see p. 149) as an optional extra (weekends in July and Aug)

That golden age lasted from about the middle of the 19th century right down to the 1950s.

With the arrival of the railway line running from the Bastille in Paris to Nogent itself, to **Joinville-le-Pont** and **Champigny-sur-Marne**, the banks of the river Marne became a magnet for ordinary working families who had previously ventured no further than the villages that are now part of Paris – Montmartre, Belleville, Charonne, Bercy. Moreover, once these villages had been offically annexed to the capital in 1860, they no longer enjoyed the 'tax-exempt' status that had previously enabled their bars and restaurants to charge much less for wine than those within the city – a status that was still enjoyed by the villages on the banks of the Marne.

Cheap wine

To cater for these flocks of people eager to enjoy a day out for all the family, dozens of popular bars and restaurants with open-air terraces overlooking the river opened up, offering dancing and, in many cases, swings and slides, even archery, to keep the children amused, as well as boules for the grown-ups. These convivial places were known as **guinguettes** (see box, p. 150).

Guingettes

Most *guinguettes* attracted a mainly working-class clientele, who danced to accordion music and, in the words of Henry James (in *Parisian Sketches*, 1876), were 'indulging in a cheap idyll'. But some had a more upmarket image and were frequented by the bourgeoisie who owned weekend cottages beside the Marne, dancing to full-scale bands. The dances in both types of establishment were the same: waltzes and mazurkas, quadrilles and schottisches and polkas. And so was the food served in some of the *guinguettes*, and in the many riverside restaurants that soon sprung up alongside them: *friture de goujons* (whitebait lightly fried in butter), *matelote* (fish stew flavoured with red wine, brandy, garlic and spices, and made with carp, eels, pike and barbel from the river), washed down by generous quantities of white wine, and preceded by *anisette*, the fashionable aniseed-flavoured aperitif similar to modern *pastis*.

Before, after or during a spell at one of the *guinguettes* weekending Parisians might well go boating, or take a ferry ride from Nogent to Joinville. Rowing races, river jousts, competition for the best-

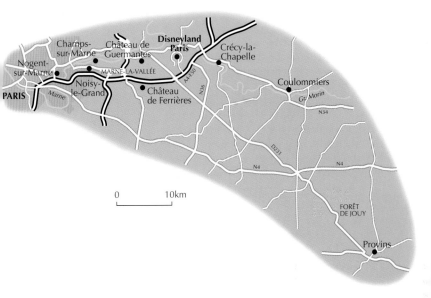

decorated boat, all these were organized throughout the summer, especially during Nogent's mid-August 'Viaduct Festival', started up in 1875.

The spread of car ownership in the 1950s spelled the end of most of the *guinguettes*, as families drove further afield for their weekend outings. But in recent years there has been a determined attempt to revive them. So you can now go dancing again at **Chez Gégène** in Joinville, which features in a famous photograph by the great Robert Doisneau, or at **Le Petit Robinson**, also in Joinville, spend the day at the **Ile du Martin Pêcheur** at Champigny-sur-Marne or enjoy the typical riverside setting at the **Domaine Sainte-Catherine** in Créteil.

- **Chez Gégène**, 162 quai de Polangis, Joinville-le-Pont,
  ℡ 01-48-83-29-43 (mostly frequented for dancing)
- **Domaine Sainte-Catherine**, Allée centrale, Pont de Créteil, Créteil, ℡ 01-42-07-19-18
- **La Goulue**, 17 quai Gabriel-Péri, Joinville-le-Pont,
  ℡ 01-48-83-21-77
- **Ile du Martin-Pêcheur**, 41 quai Victor-Hugo, Champigny-sur-Marne, ℡ 01-49-83-03-02 (on island reached by raft; family atmosphere, children's playground, *boules*)
- **La Grenouillière**, 68 av. du 11-novembre, La Varenne-Saint-Hilaire, ℡ 01-48-89-23-32 (small *guinguette* with dancing to a single accordion)
- **Le Petit Robinson**, 164 quai de Polangis, Joinville-le-Pont,
  ℡ 01-48-89-04-39 (mostly for dancing, ambience more 'bourgeois' than 'popular')

As a rule, *guinguettes* operate only at the weekend, especially Saturday evening and Sunday afternoon, though they may serve meals, without dancing, during the week. And you must go in summer to

A little etymology

The noun *guinguette* is believed to be derived from *guinguet*, an Old French adjective meaning 'narrow'. So according to this theory, a guinguette was short for a *maison guinguette*, 'a narrow house'. But then *guinguet* is related to another Old French word, this time a verb, ginguer, also spelled *guinguer*, meaning 'to jump' – so related to the English use of 'a hop' in the sense of an informal dance.

Then again, *guinguet* is an obsolete term for an acid, poor-quality wine, so that too seems a plausible explanation, since the wine drunk in *guinguettes* was never of the finest vintage. To confuse the situation further, *guincher* is a slang verb meaning 'to dance', and may well come from the same distant root as *guinguette*.

At any rate, guinguettes were usually narrow little houses where patrons drank run-of-the-mill wine and enjoyed a dance or hop, so all these various derivations seem logical.

appreciate the full *guinguette* experience. 'Miss Guinguette' is elected at the Ile du Martin-Pêcheur on 14 July and festivals are staged at various places along the river in high summer. For further information contact the **Association Culture Guinguette**, 13 rue Jean-Guy-Labarbe, 94130 Nogent-sur-Marne, ℡ 01-48-73-44-11, Ⓕ 01-48-73-39-11.

Château de Champs-sur-Marne

Early 18th-century Champs is the closest to Paris of all the Ile de France's châteaux. So it is perhaps not surprising that it is often described as looking more like an urban residence than a country seat, closer in style to the palatial Paris town houses of the same period. But the big difference is that its lovely rooms overlook a long sweep of gardens descending in stages to the banks of the river Marne, dotted with statues and sphinxes, flower-filled urns and orange trees in wooden tubs, and including a beautiful example of the intricately patterned *jardin à la française* that seems to owe more to the art of embroidery than to gardening.

Madame de Pompadour

The grounds were probably designed initially by the royal gardener Claude Desgots, a great-nephew of France's most famous landscape gardener André Le Nôtre, and completed by Desgots's son-in-law, Garnier d'Isle, who was frequently employed by Louis XV's all-powerful mistress Madame de Pompadour, Champs's best-known inhabitant. She was never the owner, but rented it furnished for a few years from 1757 from the Duc de La Vallière, himself a relation of an earlier royal mistress, the 'shy violet' Louise de La Vallière (see p. 67), whose daughter by Louis XIV, the Princesse de Conti, was given the château for a song by her royal father's successor in 1718.

Madame de Pompadour lavished a great deal of money on Champs, imprinting her impeccable taste on its decoration and furnishings. But this elegant château, with its sober classical façade, is really the creation of bankers and tax farmers rather than royal mistresses or aristocrats.

The land had been in aristocratic hands for centuries when a banker and royal treasurer called Charles Renouard de la Touane bought it towards the end of Louis XIV's reign. But he was declared bankrupt in 1701, and Champs was bought by another banker, Paul Poisson de Bourvallais, the son of a Breton farmer. (La Pompadour's real name was Jeanne-Antoinette Poisson, so it is tempting to think there might be some connection, or to see the hand of fate at work.) Bourvallais was an influential figure in France for a couple of decades, holding a key post as secretary to the royal council and famous for his skill at thinking up new taxes and his unscrupulous business methods. After Louis XIV's death in 1715, the overweening financiers of the end of his reign fell out of favour and Bourvallais, like Jacques Coeur and Nicolas Fouquet before him (see p. 200 and pp. 166–9), was arrested and imprisoned. Luckier, or more cunning, than them, he managed to hang on to much of his fortune and avoid a trial by striking a deal whereby Champs went to the crown and thence to the Princesse de Conti.

After the princess's descendants had moved to the more fashionable western outskirts of Paris, the château passed through several hands, was badly damaged during the Revolution, and finished up in the late 19th century as the possession of yet another money man, the banker Comte Louis Cahen d'Anvers. He spent colossal sums restoring it and furnishing it with beautiful pieces, then having the gardens replanted according to the original plans. His son gave it to the state in the 1930s, on condition that the furniture must never be moved.

Visiting Champs

The château bought by Bourvallais had probably been designed by Pierre Bullet, the architect of the Porte Saint-Martin in Paris. The new design, completed in 1707, was in the spirit of Louis Le Vau's plans for Vaux-le-Vicomte, with a wonderfully light **Salon oval** (Oval Drawing Rroom) in the centre of the garden façade, flanked by other reception rooms, all of them offering lovely garden views agains a forest backcloth. More vistas can be viewed from another oval room on the floor above, the **Salon de Musique** or Music Room.

But in other respects the arrangement of the rooms was highly innovative, so much so that it has required little alteration since. For instance, the rooms were grouped into suites made up of bedroom, small sitting room and dressing room (which had become a bathroom by Madame de Pompadour's day), with individual access, thus affording privacy to guests and hosts alike. And Champs boasted what is thought to be France's first-ever dining room, modelled on the dedicated eating rooms already in use in England. The normal practice in grand French houses was to set up boards on trestles wherever the owner felt like eating, and cover them with a heavy rug-like fabric and then with a tablecloth. To furnish the dining room, new pieces of furniture were devised, like the marble console tables against the walls, and the elaborate water fountains with marble basins that you can admire today.

Like most of the rooms, this room has its original panelling. Much of the panelling is painted. Particularly lovely is the **Salon**

chinois (Chinese drawing room), with its little scenes of Chinese figures busy gardening – don't miss the little boy digging with his pigtail sticking up – or fishing, playing cards or hunting, its birds and monkeys and ostrich hunt, painted in about 1740 by Christophe Huet, who also designed the pretty **Boudoir** in shades of blue. There is wonderful painted panelling too in **Madame de Pompadour's Bedroom**, and in the **Salon d'Angle** (corner drawing room), a painting of her by Hubert Drouais in elaborate 'gardening dress', looking rather thin and peaky (she died of tuberculosis a few years after leaving Champs).

Painted panelling

You can either take a guided tour or explore the house on your own with the help of a little booklet in French or English, which gives you more time to enjoy the details of the decoration, like the little carved figures playing musical instruments on the cornice in the music room. Either way, do leave enough time for a leisurely walk in the gardens. Concerts take place in the music room on some weekend afternoons.

Around Champs

Modern architecture

South of the château, **Noisy-le-Grand**, part of the 'New Town' of **Marne la-Vallée**, has some spectacular modern buildings (see p. 8).

Then northeast of here, as the suburban sprawl thins slightly, is another elegant château, this time with a more elegant name than pedestrian 'Champs'. In fact Marcel Proust thought the name 'Guermantes' so magical that he wrote to the owners asking if they would object to his borrowing it for a key group of aristocratic characters in the novel he was slowly constructing. The answer was presumably favourable, since 'these powerful Guermantes', as one member of the clan, the Duc de Guermantes's brother Baron de Charlus, refers to them, duly appeared in *A la recherche du temps perdu* (*Remembrance of Things Past*).

A magical name

Guermantes

The real **Château de Guermantes** has the harmonious, sober lines and blend of warm brick and pale stone, with tall chimneys, that characterize the style known as Louis XIII. It was built in the early 17th century for royal counsellor Claude Viole and his son Pierre, the president of the hereditary judicial assembly or *Parlement* in Paris. It still has some of the original decoration, especially in the **Chambre Viole**, with its painted ceiling beams and panelling, and beautiful inlaid wooden floor. Louis XIV really did sleep in the **Chambre du Roi** (King's Bedroom) in 1652, at the height of the Fronde rebellions, when he was just fourteen and his mother Anne of Austria had to flee from Paris. At the end of the century a new owner, another legal bigwig, made substantial alterations, building on the wonderful light-filled **Gallery**. Its decoration was designed by Robert de Cotte, the architect of the palace chapel at Versailles, and also of Guermantes's own chapel. The gallery's ceiling was painted in the mid-19th century by a pupil of Eugène Delacroix.

The château is still privately owned and lived in, and you are free to wander round the lovely rooms, admiring the fine furniture, panelling and paintings, including portraits of Louis XV and his queen Marie Leszczynska by the royal painter Carle Van Loo. The grounds are beautiful too, with their lofty trees and large free-standing 17th-century dovecot.

Château de Ferrières

South of Guermantes, Ferrières, like Champs, is a banker's residence. But this time the banker's name has a familiar ring: Baron James de Rothschild, the founder of the French branch of the dynasty. From the late 1820s onwards the baron gradually bought up parcels of land that had once belonged to Joseph Fouché, Duc d'Otrante, Napoleon's ruthlessly efficient police minister. By 1855 he had acquired enough land to fulfil his plans for a luxurious residence that would set off his superb art collections, surrounded by grounds and forest where he could organize exclusive shooting parties. As architect and landscape gardener he appointed a man whose name again has a familiar ring to British visitors, Joseph Paxton, designer of London's late-lamented Crystal Palace.

A Rothschild residence

Paxton opted for a large squarish building on the model of an Italian Renaissance *palazzo*, with corner towers. It was fitted out with all the modern accoutrements insisted on by the baron: central heating, hot and cold running water in all main bedrooms – some even had baths in solid silver. And the lavish interior decoration was entrusted to the French painter Eugène Lami. He mixed reproductions of grand French decorative styles, from Louis XIII to Louis XVI, with Italian features to create an impression of opulence. The grandest of many grand reception rooms is the lofty **Salon d'honneur**, with its 'minstrels' gallery supported on caryatids and its glass roof.

Joseph Paxton

The château was the setting for dozens of balls and parties attended by the cream of French society. Emperor Napoleon III was a guest in 1862. But only eight years later, it was the scene of a historic meeting between the German statesman Prince Bismarck and the French foreign minister during the Franco-Prussian War. Known to historians as 'the Interview at Ferrières', it failed to prevent the Siege of Paris, which started that very day. During the Second World War, Hermann Goering followed Bismarck and the Kaiser's example by setting up his headquarters in the château. And he requisitioned the fabulous Rothschild collections, which were sent off to Germany.

After the Second World War Ferrières was uninhabited until 1959, when Baron Guy de Rothschild and his wife Marie-Hélène restored it to something like its earlier splendour and staged another series of lavish balls and receptions. In 1976 they donated it to the Universities of Paris as a Rothschild Foundation organizing academic gatherings and conferences. But many of the rooms can still be visited, along with the **Musée de l'Imaginaire**, a series of rooms devoted to contemporary art.

The grounds are also open to the public. They were landscaped by Paxton in what the French know as the 'English style', as opposed to the formal geometry of the 'French style'. The apparent informality is in fact carefully planned, with clumps of trees, many of them rare species, artfully arranged. A map pinpointing the main trees with their names in Latin or French is available, including the giant sequoia planted by Napoleon III in 1862.

Brie country

The whole of this area, the site of many First World War battles, was historically in the Brie, in itself part of Champagne. But to reach the fertile plateau nowadays referred to as 'la Brie' you must go further east, beyond the new **Disneyland** resort (see next section). The most attractive stretch is the meandering valley of the **Grand Morin** river, with its pretty villages, apple orchards and peaceful riverside walks.

Crécy   Highlights here include **Crécy-la-Chapelle**, known locally as 'Brie's Venice' because it is picturesquely crisscrossed by canals once used by tanners. It has several medieval buildings, the remains of fortifications, and just outside to the east, at **La Chapelle-sur-Crécy**, a beautiful 13th-century church beside the river, the **Collégiale Notre-Dame**. One of the ninety-nine towers that once bristled along the medieval walls was used by the painter Camille Corot as a studio.

Coulommiers   Further east, **Coulommiers**, an attractive market town worth exploring (temporary exhibitions are held in the 12th-century **Commanderie des Templiers** in the Ville Haute or Upper Town), has given its name to a well-known cheese of the Brie family, smaller and less flat than the familiar Brie cheeses that are still made throughout the region (see box, p. 155).

Hiking trail   One way of getting to know this area is to follow the GRP regional hiking trail (see **Practical Information**) called Vallée de la Marne – Pays des Morins. This includes the valleys of the Grand Morin and the Petit Morin, and Coulommiers, which, like Crécy-la-Chapelle, can

Key data

NOGENT-SUR-MARNE 94130
T.O.   5 av. de Joinville, ℡ 01-48-73-73-97
Access Paris 14km, **RER** line A2
Sights **Musée de Nogent** (local history), 36 blvd Galliéni,
            ℡ 01-48-75-51-25, open year-round, closed Mon, Fri;
            Pavillon Baltard (market pavilion), 12 av. Victor-Hugo,
            ℡ 01-43-94-08-00
Lunch   see **guinguettes** (p. 149)

Château de Champs-sur-Marne
31 rue de Paris, 77420 Champs-sur-Marne, ℡ 01-60-05-24-43, open year-round, closed Tue; **RER** line A4 to Noisiel, then 10–15 mins' walk (clearly signposted)
Château de Ferrières
77164 Ferrières, ℡ 01-64-66-31-25, open year-round, pm only (Wed–Sun May to end Sep, weekends Oct to end Apr); **RER** line A4 to Bussy-Saint-Georges, then 2.5km walk
Château de Guermantes
77600 Bussy-Saint-Georges, ℡ 01-64-30-00-94, open mid-Mar to mid-Nov, pm weekends and public hols only; **RER** line A4 to Bussy-Saint-Georges, then 3km walk, or **rail** from Paris-Est to Lagny-Thorigny, then 3km walk

Some local cheeses

- **Brie**
  Cheese aficionados claim that the finest version of the 'king of cheeses', a cow's milk cheese made in the Brie region east of Paris, comes from Meaux, but as well as **Brie de Meaux** you will also find **Brie de Melun** (smaller, saltier and stonger-tasting); **Brie de Montereau** (similar to the Melun version, but still smaller); and **Brie de Provins** (made only on a small scale)
- **Coulommiers**
  A member of the Brie family of cheeses, made near the town of the same name east of Paris; smaller and less shallow than the standard Brie shape; when it is well ripened some people can detect a taste of almonds
- **Crottin de Chavignol**
  Small round goat's milk cheese made near Sancerre (see p. 204)
- **Fontainebleau**
  Fluffy fresh cow's milk cheese, traditionally sold wrapped in muslin; sweet and very creamy, quite delicious served as a dessert or pudding with raspberries, strawberries, bilberries, or – best of all – tiny wild strawberries
- **Fougerou** (also spelled **Fougerus**)
  Cow's milk cheese similar to coulommiers and ripened with a large sprig of fern (*fougère* in French) laid on the top, to give an unusual flavour
- **Valençay**
  Goat's cheese with ash coating made in the northwest of the Berry, immediately recognizable by its shape – it forms a truncated pyramid

be reached by rail from Paris-Est. Crécy and the nearby **Forêt de Crécy** are also on the GR1 hiking trail, which continues southwest to **Vaux-le-Vicomte** (pp. 166–7) and the **Forêt de Fontainebleau** (pp. 177–8), while the GR11 crosses the Grand Morin east of Coulommiers and continues south to **Provins** (pp. 159–65).

17 Disneyland Paris

Initially known as Euro Disney, Europe's only Disneyland is much more than a theme park. Opened (on schedule) in 1992 on a flat stretch of land 32km east of Paris that used to be unromantically covered with beetroot fields, it is the largest leisure complex in Europe, a full-scale holiday resort with six large hotels and a nearby 'ranch', dozens of eating places both inside and outside the park itself, a Disney Village leading to an artifical lake where you can go boating in wooden swans, cinemas, even its own golf course. And it can be reached by two of France's sleekest means of transport: the regional express metro (RER) from Paris, and high-speed train (TGV) from many places in France, including Roissy-CDG airport and Lille (with connections from London Waterloo by Eurostar, as well as direct Eurostars at peak times).

A full-scale resort

Forget the negative media coverage in the early days. It's true that the Disney empire made some errors of judgement, like banning alcohol and then expecting French families to traipse there for a day out without so much as a glass of wine for the grown-ups over lunch. Prices, too, proved prohibitively expensive at first. And it certainly didn't take off with a bang financially, as visitor numbers were well below the 11 million first-year target. But now things have settled down. Prices are more realistic, you can have a glass of wine inside the park as well as outside, and it is both a financial and a popular success: in profit since 1994/5, and attracting visitors from all over Europe, including a large British contingent.

It is of course all-American in ambience, with English spoken everywhere. So don't expect a Gallic Mickey and Minnie Mouse. But 50–60 per cent of the visitors are French, French is spoken too, and part of the fun is seeing how French children (and their parents) react as their American dream – heavily coloured by Hollywood – comes true.

A warning   A word of warning: the distances to be covered are quite great, especially if you're staying in one of the hotels, all of which are outside the park, though linked by individual shuttle buses. So it is worth planning carefully to make sure that children don't turn grizzly through exhaustion. The whole 'resort' covers about 600 hectares, or about 10 times the size of the actual theme park.

Visiting the Disney park

There was no way even the giant Disney machine could make the weather in the Paris basin begin to feel like Florida or California year-round (though apparently the only other Disneyland outside the United States, the very successful Tokyo version, has much bigger weather problems). But they were determined to keep the place open 365 days a year, and enough of the rides and other attractions are indoors, or partly so, for foul weather visits to be feasible. Bright-yellow poncho-style macs with hoods and a Mickey Mouse face help to take your mind off rain. And when the sun shines, as it often does for much of the year, Sleeping Beauty's Castle and all the other beautifully finished highspots look pretty spectacular against a brilliant blue sky.

'Beautifully finished' is the watchword throughout. Everything has been produced with impressive attention to detail, and with the professionalism that characterizes the way the whole vast operation is run. This first strikes you as you make your way through landscaped gardens and into the park, then cross **Town Square** to reach **Main Street**, leading to **Sleeping Beauty's Castle**, the park's centrepiece, fronted by **Central Plaza**. This area, with its low wooden houses and shops, is designed to look like small-town America when the great Walt (born in 1901) was a boy. Here you can buy Disney character souvenirs in every imaginable shape and form, but also glassware and children's clothes, ribbons and bows and books and stationery, in turn-of-the-century-style stores full of period details, or eat a meal or a snack in a host of cafés and 'bake shops', ice cream parlours and delis. **City Hall** on Town Square is an information point where you can get a detailed plan of the park and a timetable for the day's parades and other events. And at right angles to it is **Main Street**

Station, one of four on the Disney Railroad that circles the park.

Although the queues can be off-putting at peak times, a rail trip is a good way of getting your bearings, as you distinguish between the separate 'lands' that make the Magic Kingdom, as Disney likes to call it, a four-theme park, or five if you include Main Street, USA.

Disney Railroad

Travelling clockwise, you come first to **Frontierland**, depicting the life of the pioneers when the West was won; then to **Adventureland**, a kind of outward-bound course for adventure-minded kids; then **Fantasyland**, featuring traditional fairytale characters; and lastly **Discoveryland**, a futuristic enclave particularly popular with budding space travellers. The train stops at all but Adventureland, so you can start your exploration wherever the fancy takes you. Each 'land' has its own shops and eating places, plus plenty of trolleys and stalls selling snacks if the kids prefer to keep on the move. All rides are covered by the daily admission charge.

● **Frontierland** is reached via Fort Comstock and a Cheyenne Indian village, then ahead of you as you walk through into the Wild West Frontier is **Big Thunder Mountain**, a jagged mass of reddish peaks set in a lake. The crazy helter-skelter ride round the mountain in a runaway mining train is fun to watch, and even more fun to ride on, providing you're over 1.02m tall – and have strong nerves.

Frontierland

Small children can admire the farm animals in **Critter Corral** or play in the **Pocahontas Indian Village**, while older ones enjoy a frisson in the heart-stopping **Phantom Manor**, with its eerie ballroom full of ghosts, its doors silently opening and shutting, and its creepy ride on gondola-like vessels. Then the whole family can relax by climbing aboard a paddle steamer for a cruise from **Thunder Mesa Riverboat Landing**. The *Lucky Nugget Saloon* puts on a lunchtime Western show and the restaurants serve cowboy fare, majoring on spare ribs and charcoal grills.

● In **Adventureland**, entered via a North African fortress and bazaar, the star attraction is **Pirates of the Caribbean**, with a splendid pirate ship and a host of special effects as the pirates raid a Spanish port. But **Indiana Jones**, described as a 'high-speed thrill adventure through an archeological excavation' has its aficionados (in the over 1.4m bracket) and so do **La Cabane des Robinson** (the Swiss Family Robinson's treetop hut) and, for smaller kids, **Aladdin's Magic Tunnel**.

Adventureland

● **Fantasyland** may seem all-American, but it is in part a homage to a Frenchman: Charles Perrault, the 17th-century creator of Cinderella and the Sleeping Beauty, the key fairy story figures celebrated here. This is the place to bring little children, especially girls. The area behind **Sleeping Beauty's Castle**, with its tapestries and stained glass and its dragon in the dungeons, is generally less frenetic than elsewhere, and they will love Cinderella's glass coach in the *Auberge de Cendrillon*★, offering a rare opportunity to enjoy French cuisine. But this is also the land of Snow White and the Seven Dwarfs, Peter Pan (a ride simulating a flight over London to Never-Never Land), the Mad Hatter (giant teacups whirling round the Tea Party table), Alice in Wonderland (in a maze leered over by the Cheshire Cat), Toad of Toad

Fantasyland

Key data

DISNEYLAND PARIS *77777*

Marne-la-Vallée ℡ 01-60-30-60-30

Access	Paris 32km; **RER** line A4 to Marne-la-Vallée-Chessy; **buses** from Roissy-CDG and Orly airports, Provins; **rail** from Roissy-CDG airport (also from Lille and, at certain times, direct from London Waterloo); also **bus** from both Paris airports
Open	Daily year-round; longer opening hours weekends and public hols, longer still (to 23.00) in July and Aug, Christmas period and some other weekends and French school holidays; **Disney Village** open year-round
Lunch	Disneyland
Staying	Disneyland, Gressy-en-France, Provins
Also	Provins

Hall and Pinocchio. Be warned that the pretty *Confiserie des Trois Fées* (Three Fairies' Confectioner's) smells so delicious that you'll soon find yourself parting with your money. But there's still a boat ride and a circus train through **Storybook Land**, not to mention **Dumbo the Flying Elephant**, an aerial merry-go-round. **It's a Small World**, with its all-singing, all-dancing dolls, is strictly for kitsch enthusiasts.

Discovery-land

● **Discoveryland** is another world. Here the top ride is **Space Mountain**, where a rocket catapults you into interstellar space – definitely not for the faint-hearted. But you can also go on a dizzying **Star Tours** spaceship journey, time-travel with Jules Verne in the Visionarium or plunge 20,000 leagues under the sea with Verne's Captain Nemo and his submarine Nautilus. Michael Jackson appears (on celluloid) in a 3D musical space extravaganza, **CinéMagique**, while **Videopolis**, popular with smaller children, has live shows and Disney animated cartoons.

Disney Village

Just outside the park, this is a Californian architect's vision of downtown America, open till the early hours and attracting fun-seekers from greater Paris for a night out. This Disneyland for (mainly) grown-ups seems slightly tawdry by day, but has its own magic when darkness falls and you stroll beneath a canopy of twinkling stars as if you were on the edge of the desert. **Buffalo Bill's Wild West Show**, a cowboys-and-Indians, horses-and-bisons all-in evening, including a meal of chilli con carne, spare ribs and the like, is very popular (book through your hotel or ℡ 01-60-45-71-00). But there are half a dozen other restaurants, another half-dozen bars, a discothèque, shops, a video games arcade, and a multi-screen cinema that houses France's largest movie screen. Dancing to country-and-western music, listening to jazz and rock take place all over, indoors and out.

Wild West show

Final hints

If the non-stop fun begins to pall, you can always escape for a spot of serious golf a short way away at **Golf Disneyland Paris**. Clubs can be hired and the club house has bar, restaurant and shops. (Open year-round, ☏ 01-60-45-69-14.)

Disney golf

One final suggestion: once the kids have seen Disney's medieval architecture, why not take them to see the real thing at **Provins** (see next section)? It's only an hour's bus ride away – buses from beside the rail station.

18 Provins

Writing in 1840, the novelist Honoré de Balzac described Provins as 'one of the most delightful towns in France'. It is still delightful, not least because its many historic buildings were spared the wholesale reconstruction undertaken in so many places in France in the 19th century. The **Ville Haute** or Upper Town, with its ramparts, half-timbered houses and huge castle keep, seems hardly to have changed since the early Middle Ages when, strange as it seems today, the town was one of the most important economic centres in the country, the seat of the powerful Counts of Champagne and Brie, who also made it a centre of the arts, and the site of major trade fairs that attracted tens of thousands of merchants and traders from all over Europe and even the Middle East.

'A delight-ful town'

To experience something of the atmosphere of those prosperous days, you must visit the town during the June weekend when it stages its **Fête Médiévale** (Medieval Celebration). Getting on for two thousand people take part in this splendid pageant, dressed as jesters and courtiers, crusaders and knights on horseback, nuns and

Medieval pageant

Provins and the Wars of the Roses

Every British schoolchild is familiar with the term 'The Wars of the Roses', first used by the 19th-century novelist Sir Walter Scott as a name for the civil wars that shook England in the second half of the 15th century. And most pupils know that one side, the House of Lancaster, had a red rose as its emblem, while their enemies, the House of York, were distinguished by a white rose. But it is safe to assume that very few of them are aware that the Lancastrian red rose was borrowed from Provins.

One of the members of the House of Lancaster, a branch of the Plantagenets, was Edmund of Lancaster (1245–96), who in 1275 married the widow of one of the Counts of Champagne, Henri le Gros. Ironically enough, she was called Blanche ('White'). During his few years as Lord of Provins, Edmund presumably became fond of the famous crimson roses allegedly brought to the town by an earlier count (see p. 161) and decided to introduce them into his family's coat of arms.

priests. But at any time of year, as you explore the quiet streets, you can easily imagine that you have stepped back some seven and a half centuries, to the time when Count Thibaud le Chansonnier, back from the Crusades flourishing a five petalled red rose with a golden heart, wooed the lovely Blanche of Castile with songs of his own composition (see box, p. 161). The local tourist office and various private companies help to maintain the illusion by organizing performances that bring the town's colourful past to life: a falconry display, a demonstration of siege warfare, and a joust, all in medieval dress.

With so much to see and do, Provins definitely merits at least an overnight stay, though it is perfectly possible to enjoy a day trip if your time is limited.

A brief prosperity

Originally a Roman settlement, then a Frankish citadel, it acquired a cult importance in the 10th century when pilgrims flocked to the church and monastery built to house the relics of St Ayoul, hidden by Benedictine monks in marshy territory at the foot of the hill a century earlier. The Lower Town grew up round this religious centre, and by the middle of the 11th century both Upper and Lower Town, surrounded by massive fortifications, formed a secure capital for the Counts of Champagne and Brie. This flourished for almost two and a half centuries, but the marriage of the daughter of Count Henri le Gros to the King of France, Philippe le Bel, in 1285 brought the fiefs of Champagne and Brie into the royal orbit, and, together with the repercussions of the plague and the Hundred Years War, gradually relegated Provins to the position of a sleepy provincial backwater – as it has remained ever since.

Counts of Champagne & Brie

Exploring the town

The most interesting journey to this remote corner of the Ile de France by car or bus takes you through the **Forêt de Crécy**, then the Brie plateau, followed by another small patch of woodland, the **Forêt de Jouy**, offering glimpses of peaceful villages and the occasional turreted manor house, then large fields with grain silos, slender trees weighed down with mistletoe, and harmonious groups of farm buildings. As you approach the town, with its huge domed church perched high up above you, you become aware of the strategic importance of the site, dominating the plateau.

Forests & villages

If you are driving, the easy solution is to park in the large free car park beside the tourist office, just outside the Upper Town. And a local bus from the rail station (where buses from Marne-la-Vallée-Chessy also stop) will take you up to the tourist office too. But I prefer the approach on foot through the Lower Town, which heightens the sense of time travel when you climb up to the medieval streets in the Upper Town.

The rue Moreau opposite the station takes you across two bridges spanning the river Voulzie, attractively wept over by willows. Branch left into the rue du Four-des-Raines, then slightly left again into the **rue des Marais**, following the river and giving you good views of the Upper Town, as well as charming glimpses to the left of little water-

A royal song writer

Thibaud IV, Count of Champagne, is often nicknamed *Thibaud le Chansonnier*, or 'Thibaud the Song Writer'. A poet and the patron of many writers, he wrote and set to music poems of courtly love, sometimes having them painted on to the walls of his palace. He took part in the crusade against the Albigenses, which perhaps explains how he came to be influenced by the work of the Troubadours, who had flourished in the sect's heartland in southwest France. He is particularly known for his *jeux partis*, a category of medieval lyric in the form of a debate between poets, invented by the Troubadours, but he also wrote *pastourelles*, poems with a complex metrical pattern, again designed to be sung.

He was born in Troyes in 1201, the son of Thibaud III and of Blanche de Navarre, and after coming into his inheritance when he reached his majority, set up a court that was even more brilliant than that of Marie de Champagne, wife of his ancestor Henri le Libéral and daughter of Eleanor of Aquitaine, who was another patron of poets. He is said to have been in love with Blanche of Castile, wife of Louis VIII, and to have written many of his songs for her.

In 1234 he became a king as well as a count, inheriting the kingdom of Navarre from his uncle and bearing the title Thibaud I de Navarre. He joined the sixth crusade to the Holy Land, earning a permanent place in the hearts of the Provinois by bringing back the 'rose of Damascus', the *rosa damascena*. When crossed with the wild rose or eglantine growing in France, this produced the crimson *rose de Provins*, the ancestor of all the roses grown throughout Europe today, and an important source of income for modern Provins (see p. 55).

courses with overhanging trees and wash houses. Turn right into the busy place Honoré-de-Balzac and continue along the rue des Cordeliers to the traffic-free **rue du Val**, with some interesting shops, leading up to the Upper Town.

The Lower Town

Before heading along it, you can visit two of the Lower Town's churches. **Sainte-Croix**, just beyond here in the street of the same name, has suffered badly over the centuries from fire and flooding but still has its Romanesque crossing and tower, as well as an elaborately carved portal on the west front, part Late Gothic, part Renaissance. The church was named to honour the little piece of the True Cross brought back, according to local tradition, by Thibaud IV from the Crusades.

Beyond the place du Général-Leclerc, the **rue de la Cordonnerie** leads to **Saint-Ayoul**, the successor to the pilgrimage church that spawned the Lower Town. It has been rebuilt so often that it offers a curious mixture of architectural styles, but the west portal, its statuary now sadly mutilated, is definitely Gothic. The interior has some fine 17th-century panelling and an early Renaissance *Pietà*. The tall gatehouse or belfry in the nearby rue Vieille-Notre-Dame is all that has survived of a now-vanished church, **Notre-Dame du Val**.

Entering the Old Town

Now walk along the rue du Val, past narrow streets with picturesque medieval names like Garlic Street (rue des Aulx) or Piglet Street (rue des Porcelets) until you reach the **Hôtel-Dieu**, once the palace of the Countesses of Champagne. It now houses the entrance to the mysterious **Souterrains**, the warren of underground passages tunnelling beneath the town. For as well as its Upper and Lower Towns, Provins has a third Subterrranean Town, and one that is well worth visiting (bring a torch).

Underground town

It is reckoned that there are some 100 kilometres of intersecting passages altogether, on several different levels. Parts of this network, with its crypt-like vaulted chambers, were used by weavers, since the ambient humidity created ideal conditions – the town had over 3500 looms in the Middle Ages, for a population of around 10,000. It was also a place used for storing merchandise sold during the weeks-long trade fairs, and as a gigantic wine cellar. Many of the wooden houses in the Upper Town have large vaulted stone cellars linked to the underground passages providing both a means of moving goods about and an escape route in times of danger.

But this underground labyrinth may have had another function: it seems that some of Provins's trade visitors were involved in secret initiation rites held under cover of the fairs. Signs and symbols have been carved into the walls of the lowest level of passages, probably dug before the Middle Ages: wild boar and hanged men, human skulls, fish and concentric circles, whose meaning is unclear, but which may have led to one of the medieval popes attempting to have the passages filled in. Provins certainly continued to be a freemasonry centre in later centuries.

Not a wild boar but a porcupine gives its name to one of the alleyways and sets of steps leading off the **rue Saint-Thibault** to the left: climb up the **Grimpon du Porc-Epic** towards the church of **Saint-Quiriace**, whose huge bulk looms above you. But first turn round for fine views over the town and the countryside. On the hill opposite, the **Abbaye des Dames Cordelières**, a convent founded in 1248 by Thibaud IV, allegedly as the result of a vision experienced close to where you are standing, was converted into a hospital by Louis XV half a century later and is now an outpost of France's National Library.

Continue past the **Lycée Thibault-de-Champagne**, on the site of the Counts of Champagne's castle. The peaceful **Jardin des Brébans** is a good place for a rest as you contemplate the **Collégiale Saint-Quiriace**, which you can reach by turning left into the little **rue Pierre-Ythier**, then right into the **place Saint-Quiriace**, where a plaque tells you that Joan of Arc and Charles VII attended mass here on 3 August 1429, on their way back from the king's coronation in Rheims.

Saint-Quiriace

Although Saint-Quiriace looks impressively large, it was originally intended to be at least a third as long again. Work started in 1160, and this initial phase, covering the building of the chancel and the apsé, continued down to 1185, so the style is Transitional (between Romanesque and Gothic). The nave, begun in the 1230s, progressed

Provins: falconry demonstration in medieval dress

no further than a double bay, a victim of Provins's waning prosperity. A free-standing belfry collapsed in the 17th century, shortly before the addition of the slate dome.

The interior is beautiful: a lofty, light-filled space surrounded by pale honey-coloured stone, with much blind arcading. The eight-part chancel vaulting, added when work started on the nave, is unusual and impressive. Don't miss the stained-glass window and chapel dedicated to a man known to the French as St Edme, but to his fellow-Englishmen as St Edmund Rich, Archbishop of Canterbury, who died near Provins in 1240.

At the other end of the square looms another huge building, the medieval keep called the **Tour César**, with an octagonal upper storey rising above four pepperpot turrets. It was captured by the English army in 1432, almost three hundred years after it was built, and still has the masonry platform built by the English at that date, though the watchtower that once surmounted the whole structure has disappeared. You can visit the vaulted guardroom and peer into the cells in the turrets (the keep was turned into a prison at one point), then explore the sentry walks. The staircases are steep, narrow and awkward and a good head for heights is essential, but the views over the town and the Brie are breathtaking.

Tour César

The little rue des Beaux-Arts leading off the place Saint-Quiriace (delicious rose petal-flavoured honey on sale in *La Route des Abeilles*) brings you to the **rue du Palais**. Turn left into it to find the **Musée de Provins et du Provinois**, an attractive local history museum housed in one of the town's earliest secular buildings, though it may later have been a rabbinical school, or even a synagogue. Like so many houses of the period, it has large vaulted cellars,

Local history museum

where an interesting archeological collection is now displayed.

The rooms on the other floors include examples of the glazed pottery traditionally made in the region, especially the little square or hexagonal medieval floor tiles with decorative motifs (copies are on sale in the town) and ornamental chimney cowls. Also here, among complicated medieval locks, painted wooden sculptures, paintings and elaborately decorated poles used in guild processions and ceremonies, is a collection of objects connected with Provins's Freemasons' Lodge.

Beyond the museum the rue du Palais continues to the long **place du Châtelet**, where the great medieval fairs were held. Among the picturesque houses surrounding it are several restaurants, and shops selling confectionery and jams flavoured with rose petals. The rue Couverte in the far left-hand corner leads into the atmospheric **rue de Jouy**, but brings you first to the **Grange aux Dîmes** (Tithe Barn) on the corner of the **rue Saint-Jean**. This splendid half-timbered building was originally used both for storing goods sold during the fairs and as temporary lodgings for fair visitors, but also acted as an indoor market. A well designed exhibition inside recreates the ambience of the time, with tableaux illustrating the importance of traditional industries like weaving or leather working.

Exploring the ramparts

Walk the ramparts

From here you can continue along the rue Saint-Jean to the **Porte Saint-Jean**, a gateway flanked by twin towers, admire the view along the ramparts, then head for the **Maison du Visiteur** (tourist office) to see a scale model of the medieval town and watch a video presentation before exploring the ramparts and seeing one or more of the afternoon events. This is also the starting-point for a circuit in a minitrain, if your legs are feeling tired by now.

Alternatively, after leaving the tithe barn you can first walk along the **rue de Jouy**, peer down into the **Caveau du Saint-Esprit**, then walk round the ramparts via the **Porte de Jouy** until you come to the Porte Saint-Jean. Either way, don't miss the tower called the **Tour des Engins**, close to the **Brèche des Anglais**, where the invading English are thought to have breached the town's fortifications.

Falconers' art

The tower serves as a backdrop to the rightly popular show called **Les Aigles de Provins**, where 'falconers' in medieval dress make their entrance on caparisoned horses and orchestrate an aerial ballet performed by eagles and falcons, buzzards and vultures, which soar skywards, then wheel round to swoop towards the mesmerized audience and snatch a lump of raw meat from a gloved hand, apparently in time to the medieval music accompanying these feats. After the show, which children find thrilling, crouching down as the huge wings rustle just above their heads, you can pay a call on a hundred-odd birds of prey in their little wooden huts. Some have wing spans up to 3 metres. Others are extraordinary-looking, like the long-legged secretary bird with its huge doe eyes and sweeping lashes, and what seems to be a feather headdress, or the funny little round white blob of a creature with slitty eyes, a type of owl from northern Scandinavia (Easter to end Oct, pm only; daily May to end Aug, otherwise Tue–Sun).

Key data

Provins	77160
T.O.	**Maison du Visiteur,** Chemin de Villecran, ⓣ 01-64-60-26-26, ⓕ 01-64-60-11-97
Access	Paris 91km, Vaux-le-Vicomte 45km, Disneyland Paris 55km, Fontainebleau 55km; **rail** from Paris-Est, **RER** line A4 to Marne-la-Vallée-Chessy, then **buses**
Sights	**Collégiale Saint-Quiriace** (Romanesque/Gothic church); **Eglise Saint-Ayoul** (one-time pilgrimage church, much rebuilt); **Eglise Sainte-Croix** (Gothic/Renaissance church); **Grange aux Dîmes** (medieval tithe barn, with tableaux re-creating atmosphere of Provins's trade fairs), open year-round; **Musée de Provins et du Provinois** (local history museum in Romanesque building), 4 rue du Palais, ⓣ 01-64-01-40-19, open pm year-round (mornings by appointment), weekends only in term-time; **Ramparts** (medieval walls and fortifications); **Souterrains** (underground passages), open year-round, generally weekends only Nov to Easter; **Tour César** (medieval keep), open year-round
Lunch	Provins
Staying	Provins

On the other side of the Porte Saint-Jean, in the (now dry) moat, *Medieval* **L'Assaut des Remparts**, a noisy, dramatic re-enactment of medieval *warfare* siege warfare, is also staged in the afternoons from Easter to end Oct (weekends and public hols only Apr, May, Sep, otherwise Mon–Fri and Sun). The huge siege engines hurling stone projectiles are mightily impressive and the fierce-looking warriors in medieval dress handling them positively alarming. Great fun – and not a little instruction – is had by all. On Saturday afternoons (from mid-June to end Aug) the same site is the setting for a replay of the fateful tournament that took place in Provins in 1230, when the Count of Champagne challenged the Count of Picardy, at the head of a besieging army, to an equestrian duel that would decide the outcome of the enemy attack. This show, **La Légende de Thibaud**, is again instructive as well as entertaining, since every detail of the ceremony surrounding jousting in the age of chivalry has been carefully researched.

If you are visiting Provins in the rose season, do try to fit in a visit *Rose* to the **Pépinières et Roseraies Vizier** (11 rue des Prés, *garden* ⓣ 01-64-00-02-42) to see the famous 'rose of Provins', *rosa damascena*, and many other varieties of old roses blooming in the delightful rose garden, and maybe buy one or two (they can be sent to your home). You can also buy rose-petal jam made on the premises, as well as little bottles of rosewater (the French swear by it as a cure for insomnia) and rose-scented soaps. To reach it, turn left off the rue Saint-Thibault into the rue des Jacobins, and enjoy a pleasant walk in the surrounding streets at the same time, perhaps continuing to the Cordelières' convent.

Ile de France ~ south & southeast of Paris

The forest surrounding the town of **Fontainebleau**, much visited for its royal palace, is popular with Parisians for the many opportunities it offers for walking, biking, riding and even rock-climbing. Both the forest itself and the little village of **Barbizon** on its western edge have also long attracted painters, as has **Moret-sur-Loing** just beyond its southeastern edge, in a river valley blessed with several attractive villages. River trips can be enjoyed here, continuing into the adjoining Seine Valley, which again has pleasant riverside villages.

Just north of the forest, the magnificent château of **Vaux-le-Vicomte** is one of the most important in the Ile de France. You can walk for hours in its beautifully restored grounds and feel almost that you have the place to yourself, whereas Barbizon and parts of the Fôret de Fontainebleau can feel crowded.

19 Vaux-le-Vicomte

The magnificent 17th-century residence built by superintendent of finance Nicolas Fouquet at **Vaux** offers a classic illustration of the old adage about pride coming before a fall. But a visit there is particularly interesting because the château and its gardens acted as a catalyst for the splendours of Louis XIV's palace at Versailles.

Fouquet was in his mid-twenties and a rapporteur of the Paris *parlement* (judicial assembly) when he bought a small estate east of Paris in 1641. An ambitious and energetic man from a family of lawyers, he turned out to be a highly able financier. He soon caught the eye of Cardinal Mazarin, chief minister to Anne of Austria, who was acting as regent until her son Louis XIV came of age. In 1650 Mazarin appointed him *procureur-général* – a post equivalent to attorney-general. Three years later he was, in modern parlance, finance minister.

Cardinal Mazarin

As part of Mazarin's team, he had seen how the cardinal had amassed a colossal fortune by mixing his own financial affairs with those of the state. So had Jean-Baptise Colbert, also working for Mazarin, and with ambitions of his own. By 1656 Fouquet, copying Mazarin's methods, had increased his own fortune to such an extent that he had been able to add more and more land to his estate at Vaux and was now ready to replace its modest château with a residence in the grand manner.

He had always been a generous patron of the arts and knew exactly

who to turn to. He picked a team of three men about the same age as himself (he was now forty-one): the architect Louis Le Vau, the painter Charles Le Brun, and an up-and-coming landscape gardener called André Le Nôtre. This was Le Nôtre's first major commission, but Le Vau had already designed parts of the Louvre in Paris, and Le Brun had been France's most influential artist for nearly a decade.

Le Vau

Le Nôtre

By 1761, after a mere five years, the three of them, with an army of over 18,000 labourers and craftsmen, and a budget of around 15 million francs, had created a palatial residence made up of a central domed structure flanked by four large corner pavilions. Le Brun's grandiose decorative scheme involved ceilings painted with mythological and other scenes, much gilding and stucco, and tapestries woven to his designs in a workshop he had set up in the village (the nucleus of the future Manufacture des Gobelins in Paris). Le Nôtre had tamed the landscape to create a geometrically organized garden adorned with statues and fountains, ornamental pools and immaculate parterres. And Fouquet's emblem, a squirrel, was woven into tapestries and carved on mantelpieces throughout.

Le Brun

167

Fouquet was delighted. But his triumph was to be short-lived. Mazarin, whose protégé he had always been, had just died. The king, now twenty-two, famously announced that he was going to take the reins of state into his own hands. And he ordered an inquiry into how Mazarin's enormous fortune had been acquired. Colbert, already jealous of Fouquet, realized that once it became obvious that Mazarin had helped himself from the state's coffers, he too would be under suspicion of connivance in embezzlement. So he set out to deflect attention on to Fouquet – and engineer his rival's downfall – by hinting that the superintendent of finance was as venal as Mazarin.

Colbert's treachery

Louis decided to take a long, hard look at Vaux and invited himself along to see it in its just-completed glory. The unsuspecting Fouquet, welcoming the opportunity to show off his fabulous domain, rashly pulled out all the stops and orchestrated a party to end all parties. He gave the dramatist Molière just two weeks to put together a new-style play-cum-ballet. He ordered his steward François Vatel to organize a sumptuous banquet and have it served on solid gold plates – one of several sweet courses was to acquire lasting fame (see box, p. 49). He arranged for all Le Nôtre's fountains to play at once.

Molière

The big day came on 17 August and everything went like clockwork, with Molière's *Les Fâcheux*, a three-acter on a theme drawn from Horace's *Satires*, scoring a big success. But the king was shocked and angry at Fouquet's obvious wealth and extravagance. Less than three weeks later he had him arrested on charges of embezzlement and even *lèse-majesté* – by none other than a captain in the King's Musketeers called the Comte d'Artagnan, the companion of Alexandre Dumas *père*'s 'Three Musketeers'.

Fouquet was not without friends. Among those who begged for clemency was another of his literary protégés, Jean La Fontaine, the future author of the celebrated *Fables*, who wrote a poem calling on the 'nymphs of Vaux' to plead with the king on his behalf. But Colbert was busy supplying the court with forged documents incriminating Fouquet. After three years he was duly found guilty. But the judges refused to bow to royal pressure and imposed neither a death nor a custodial sentence. Instead they ordered him to leave the country for ever. Louis, furious, claimed that as Fouquet was privy to state secrets, banishment was inappropriate. He insisted on his being imprisoned for life, in the same prison as the 'Man in the Iron Mask'

Fouquet's downfall

Key data

CHÂTEAU DE VAUX-LE-VICOMTE 77950 Maincy
℡ 01-64-14-41-90, open Mar to 11 Nov

Access	Paris 55km, Fontainebleau 20km; **rail** to Melun, then taxi or 6km walk
Lunch	Self-service restaurant in château
Staying	Chaumes-en-Brie, Fontenay-Trésigny, Fontainebleau
Also	Fontainebleau

– he may even have been the mystery man himself, according to some – where he died in 1680.

Meanwhile Louis had taken over the triumphant triumvirate of Le Brun, Le Nôtre and Le Vau to create a Vaux on a larger scale – at Versailles. And so Fouquet, though always a loyal servant of the crown in his fashion, had indirectly set in train a process that would, barely a century after his death, lead to the French Revolution and the downfall of the monarchy.

Visiting Vaux

Thanks to the determination of a wealthy industrialist, Alfred Sommier, who saved Vaux from destruction by buying it in the late 19th century and gradually restoring it, you can now see the château and gardens more or less as they were in the days of their splendour. You can admire the proportions of the oval **Grand Salon** beneath the dome (though its decoration was not yet finished when Fouquet was arrested), and the richly decorated **Salon d'Hercule** and **Salon des Muses**, all overlooking the magnificent vista of the gardens sweeping towards the forest; visit the opulent private rooms designed for Fouquet and his second wife. They are full of paintings and tapestries and wonderfully ornate furniture from various periods – the canopied bed and lace-draped dressing table in the **Chambre Louis XV** and the pale-grey panelling in the next-door bedroom are exceptional. To add to the effect, music is played throughout the château, and the sideboards are groaning with fruit and wine.

The wine cellars and kitchens can be visited, too, and the stables now house a **Musée des Equipages** (Carriage Museum). You can spend hours exploring the huge grounds with their neatly trimmed hedges, their statues and grottoes, their lakes and canals ('club cars' for hire if you're feeling tired). And the château also has a pleasant self-service restaurant, appropriately called L'Ecureuil (Squirrel), which is also open on the magical evenings (Saturdays from May to mid-October) when the whole of Vaux, including the gardens, is lit by thousands of candles – a treat worth planning ahead for. Another treat takes place in the afternoon of the second and last Saturday in the month: Le Nôtre's fountains and waterfalls leap into life between 15.00 and 18.00 (April to October).

Carriage Museum

Candlelit evenings

20 Fontainebleau, Barbizon

Château de Fontainebleau

Like many a vast palace or château in France, the **Château de Fontainebleau** started life as a modest hunting lodge, albeit a royal one enlarged by Louis IX in the 13th century to create a turreted feudal manor house. And although it is now fronted by a fairly busy town, it still lies on the edge of an extensive forest that attracts walkers and riders, climbers and cyclists, nature lovers and Parisians in search of a few hours of peace and quiet and lungfuls of fresh air. The palace gardens are popular too, for quiet strolls and lovely forest views.

Tips for visitors

First, a word of warning: visiting the palace can be frustrating. It is huge, divided into separate sections, and run in a somewhat officious way, so that you may be hustled out, or at any rate prevented from lingering, well before the official closing time – for instance, by having the shutters slammed shut just as you are trying to study a fresco or a beautiful piece of painted panelling. As a lunchtime closure operates for most of the year, you will have a job fitting everything in (though the same ticket is valid after lunch). On top of that, some sections or individual rooms are liable to be shut because of staff shortages, and others, especially the private royal and imperial suites, may be open only part of the day (usually in the afternoon). The guided tour to these (extra payment required) is interesting, but liable to overrun, so you may find that it is too late afterwards to return to the main body of the palace.

Having said all that, it is certainly worth making the effort to see as much as possible, as this is one of the most interesting of royal palaces, full of beautiful things and the scene of some key historical events. Most of all, it was the favourite residence of most of France's monarchs and emperors for over seven and a half centuries, not only because of the hunting on offer in the forest, but because they apparently felt at home there. Napoleon famously commented: 'This was the kings' true dwelling place', using the term *demeure* to indicate that it was where they lived, not merely an official residence. This is not strictly true in all cases, as Louis XIV, for one, made Versailles his 'true dwelling place', though he always spent the hunting season at Fontainebleau. But several kings, including Louis's father Louis XIII, Philippe IV, François II and Henri III were born there – and Philippe IV died there too, after a hunting accident. And Louis XIV's private wedding to his long-term mistress Madame de Maintenon took place here, as did Louis XV's to his Polish queen Marie Leszczynska.

A royal favourite

The thing to remember is that from the time of Louis le Gros, 'Fat' Louis VI, who died in 1137, right down to Napoleon III in the mid-19th century, France's rulers spent part of the year at Fontainebleau, with their families as well as their courtiers. And when they moved in, they did what lesser mortals do – they redecorated, restored, rebuilt or added new rooms or wings. The result is a complicated jigsaw puzzle of a building, in an endearing mixture of architectural and decorative styles.

The most significant contributions were made by François Ier, his son Henri II and widowed daughter-in-law Catherine de Médicis, and his ex-son-in-law Henri IV, and then by Louis XV and Napoleon. But virtually every ruler added something. Louis VII built a chapel, the **Chapelle Saint-Saturnin**, that was consecrated by none other than the exiled Thomas à Becket, Archbishop of Canterbury. Charles V, a great patron of writers and translators, endowed it with his priceless collection of manuscripts, which would one day form the nucleus of the Bibliothèque Nationale, France's great state-owned library.

Thomas à Becket

That was in the late 14th century, over a century before François Ier,

Fontainebleau Palace: the celebrated double horseshoe staircase

François Ier

who came to the throne in 1515, decreed the basic plan we see today, by building a full-scale palace on the foundations of the medieval manor house. All that is left of this is the 12th-century keep, right in the centre and earmarked by François for his bedroom. His initial architect was a Frenchman, Gilles Le Breton. But he then imported the Italian artists Sebastiano Serlio, Giovanni Battista Rosso (known as 'Rosso Fiorentino') and Francesco Primaticcio, as well as the sculptor and goldsmith Benvenuto Cellini, to decorate his new palace, ushering in the second, Mannerist, phase of the French Renaissance. With their large teams of painters and stucco artists, these Italians formed what is known as the 'First School of Fontainebleau'. And to furnish the rooms they had so beautifully decorated, François sent them off to Italy to buy the finest of Italian furniture, *objets d'art*, sculpture and paintings, including such masterpieces as Leonardo da Vinci's *Mona Lisa* (transported by Henri IV to the Louvre in Paris, where it still hangs).

First School of Fontaine-bleau

After François's death in 1547, Henri II continued his father's great work of embellishment, aided and abetted by his mistress Diane de Poitiers (see **Anet**). In particular, he commissioned Philibert Delorme, Diane's architect at Anet, to complete the magnificent **Salle de Bal** or **Salle des Fêtes**, originally designed as a loggia without window panes. Henri's widow Catherine de Médicis added new suites or rooms, and gave its name to today's entrance courtyard, the **Cour du Cheval Blanc** ('White Horse Courtyard'), by placing in it a plaster copy of Marcus Aurelius's steed in Rome, originally intended as the basis of a bronze equestrian statue.

Henri II

The former husband of their daughter Marguerite de Valois, Henri IV, enjoyed spending time, and considerable sums of money, at the palace, where his son Louis XIII was born – and christened, along with his sisters, beneath the cupola over the **Porte du Baptistère**,

Henri IV

added for the occasion. Henri also completed the **Chapelle de la Trinité**, straightened out and added to the **Cour Ovale** at the palace's heart, built a large new courtyard beyond it, the **Cour des Offices**, added a two-storey wing housing the **Galerie de Diane** and the **Galerie des Cerfs**, overlooking the **Jardin de Diane**, and, on the other side of the garden, the **Jeu de Paume**, where an early form of tennis was played.

Second School of Fontaine-bleau

The new rooms were decorated by a team of artists, both French and Flemish, known as the 'Second School of Fontainebleau'. Their main medium was not the fresco favoured by their Italian predecessors but oil painting on plaster, wood panel or canvas. A decorative but practical flourish was added by Louis XIII in the shape of the famous double horseshoe of a stone staircase leading up to the main entrance, while Louis XIV had the grounds landscaped by André Le Nôtre.

Louis XV

Louis XV made many changes, not all of them beneficial. He sadly demolished the right-hand wing of the White Horse Courtyard, housing the beautiful **Galerie d'Ulysse**, adorned with Renaissance frescoes depicting highlights from Homer's Odyssey, by Primaticcio and his assistant and successor Niccolò dell'Abbate. It was replaced by a much duller wing of residential quarters, now known by the equally dull name of **Aile Louis XV**. He also converted the sumptuous bedroom-and-bathroom suite designed for François Ier's mistress, the Duchesse d'Etampes, into a staircase – though fortunately this time the Primaticcio and dell' Abbate frescoes were left unscathed. He lowered ceilings to fit in another storey of bedrooms – hardly surprising, as he would turn up at the palace with a retinue of over two thousand people. Louis XVI added a whole new suite of rooms backing on to François Ier's beautiful gallery, and his queen Marie-Antoinette masterminded the decoration of what are now some of the palace's prettiest rooms.

Napoleon

Most of the furniture was auctioned off during the Revolution. Then Napoleon took the place in hand. He pulled down the fourth side of the White Horse Courtyard, replacing it with decorative railings. He turned the King's Bedroom into a majestic Throne Room. And he launched into a whirlwind campaign of fitting out the rooms and suites that had been stripped of virtually everything: six hundred suites were furnished in a mere nineteen days, with some twenty thousand items that he had brought back to Fontainebleau. Josephine was allowed free reign, too, to have several rooms arranged in the latest Egyptian or Roman styles.

Second Empire

A few decades later, the last French king, Louis-Philippe, embarked on a wide-ranging, and often heavy-handed, restoration programme. And his successor, Napoleon III, refurnished and redecorated many rooms in the often pompous and overblown Second Empire style. Much of their work, especially the painting over of delicate frescoes, has gradually been removed, and recent restoration has been much more sensitive.

Visiting the palace

Try to remember this history of constant change as you explore the palace, and as guided tours of the main rooms, called the **Grands**

appartements, are infrequent, keep a firm eye on the plan you will be given. Be prepared too to find yourself from time to time in surprisingly ordinary corridors or unadorned back staircases leading betweeen the grandly furnished rooms. It will add greatly to your enjoyment if you remember that rebuilding and redecoration were not always uppermost in the inhabitants' minds. Great events took place here over the centuries. Louis XIV signed the Revocation of the Edict of Nantes in one of the state rooms in 1685, thus at a stroke depriving the country of a good quarter of a million of its most energetic subjects – the Protestant Huguenots who opted for emigration. Napoleon signed the act of abdication in his private sitting room in 1814. You can sense Josephine's shock when she rushed to join her emperor husband at Fontainebleau five years earlier, after his victory at Wagram, only to find that the doorway between their bedrooms had been walled up on his orders. Within months she was out of the picture, the marriage dissolved, and on April Fool's Day the following year Marie-Louise of Austria became Napoleon's new bride.

Historic events

Other love affairs, legitimate and illegitimate, started and ended here. In 1657, Queen Christina of Sweden, immortalized by Greta Garbo in a 1933 Hollywood movie, had her favourite, the Italian Marchese di Monaldeschi, executed in cold blood in the **Galerie des Cerfs**. A few years later, at a court reception, Louis XIV spotted the shy Louise de La Vallière, who soon became his first 'official' mistress. Gossip had it that he also shocked his mother by dallying in the forest late at night with his sister-in-law, Henriette, Duchesse d'Orléans, the daughter of Charles I of England and Henri IV's daughter Henrietta-Maria.

Sweden's Queen Christina

But the most dramatic event of all took place where your visit begins, in the **Cour du Cheval Blanc**. It concerns Napoleon, who engineered the impressive view of the palace façade by opening up this courtyard, popularly known nowadays as the '**Cour des Adieux**' or 'Farewell Court'. For it was here, on 20 April 1814, that the emperor, forced to abdicate, but still adored by the surviving veterans of his *Grande Armée*, bid them an emotional farewell before embarking on the journey to exile on Elba, over which the Treaty of Fontainebleau had pronounced him sovereign. Try to picture the short, stocky figure emerging to stand at the top of the horseshoe steps, then slowly walking down to embrace the loyal General Petit and with him the flag he was holding, while his Old Guard sobbed in disbelief as their hero leapt into his carriage and shot out of the courtyard. It is interesting that French visitors generally associate the palace more with Napoleon than with any of his predecessors, which no doubt explains why the **Musée Napoléon**, housed in the **Louis XV Wing** to the right of the courtyard, is often more crowded than the state rooms or private apartments. The opposite wing, the **Aile des Ministres**, was built by François Ier in 1528 – you can see his initial 'F' on the chimneys.

Napoleon's farewell

Sadly, you cannot enter via those wonderful stone steps. Instead you must head for the door in the middle of the Louis XV Wing. If you want to take the **Petits Appartements** tour, make sure to check times as soon as you go in, and reserve a place in advance if necessary.

The Grands Appartements

To describe every room would require a book in itself, so I can merely refer to some of the highlights. Visits normally start with the **Galerie des Assiettes**, an oak-panelled room adorned with a collection of Sèvres porcelain plates (see p. 77) depicting France's major châteaux, and made to commemorate the wedding here of one of Louis-Philippe's sons in 1831. This room forms part of the **Appartement des Reines-Mères** (Queen Mothers' Apartments), also known as the **Appartement du Pape**, as it was here that Pope Pius VII lived from 1812 to 1814, a prisoner of Napoleon. But the rest of this set of rooms, occupied at various times by Catherine and Marie de Médicis and by Anne of Austria (all of whom acted as regents for their underage sons), have been closed for restoration for some time and no date has been set for their reopening.

Renaissance gallery

So you continue via a faceless corridor and an antechamber, to be dazzled by the beauty of the **Galerie François Ier**, a light-filled gallery adorned by Rosso and Primaticcio in the 1530s. Before going in, admire to your left the **Chapelle de la Trinité**, where Louis XV married his Polish bride. Its decoration is a fine example of the work of the Second School of Fontainebleau, just as the Gallery is of the First School.

Beyond here, the **royal apartments** overlook the Cour Ovale, the central courtyard round which the original manor house was built. The **Salle des Gardes** has superb painted beams dating from Louis XIII's tenure but is otherwise in a mixture of styles. To the right you come to the **Escalier du Roi**, the 18th-century King's Staircase built into the Duchesse d'Etampes's suite, still with its original frescoes by Primaticcio illustrating the life of Alexander the Great (looking strangely like François Ier) and his elegantly elongated sculptures. Beyond Madame de Maintenon's rooms, the **Salle de Bal** (Ballroom) is almost twice as wide as the Galerie François Ier and much more imposing with its massive fireplace flanked by caryatid-like figures cast from ancient Roman statues. The frescoes are the work of Primaticcio and Niccolò dell'Abbate, many of them depicting the goddess Diana, in deference to Henri II's mistress Diane de Poitiers.

Diane de Poitiers

Retracing your steps, you reach the rooms used by the royal family in François Ier's day. They include the **Salon du Donjon** or **Deuxième Salle Saint-Louis**, in the medieval keep. It was used as a bedroom by Louis VII in the 12th century, then by all his successors down to and including Henri IV, who appears on horseback in a bas-relief over the fireplace, his scarf flying out behind him. Primaticcio's frescoes and stucco work have been replaced by 18th-century panelling.

Galerie de Diane

The impressive **Galerie de Diane**, in the long Henri IV wing, originally led from Marie de Médicis's rooms to the aviary that once delighted the royal family and courtiers. The decoration of scenes featuring the goddess Diana, plus Henri's victories in battle, had been so damaged by Napoleon's day that he had it replaced with incidents from French history. Joan of Arc and Charlemagne both appear. The restoration was completed, in neo-classical style, by Louis XVIII. But then Napoleon III converted it into the library you see today.

The second suite of royal rooms, backing on to the first and overlooking the Jardin de Diane, was added by Catherine de Médicis. It gives some interesting glimpses into the very different tastes of the royal ladies – and those of their age. The **Grand Salon de l'Impératrice**, with its pretty sage-green and pink carpet, was designed as a games room for Marie-Antoinette. The **Chambre de l'Impératrice** has a ceiling painted for Anne of Austria; fireplace, panelling and alcove for Marie Antoinette; and Empire décor for Josephine. But the prettiest room is the intimate **Boudoir de la Reine**, for which Marie Antoinette chose a decorative scheme in silver and gold, with delicate painted scenes in a style inspired by the recent excavations at Pompeii, charming little carved scenes over the doors depicting the Muses at work, and a tiny white marble and gilt fireplace. The roll-top desk and table by the celebrated cabinet-maker Jean-Henri Riesener, made for this room, were tracked down in the United States and brought back to the palace in the 1960s.

Marie Antoinette

The **Salle du Trône**, all white and gilt panelling, is a creation of Napoleon's – hence the gilt eagles and the letter 'N' embroidered in the velvet covering of the throne. Previously the king's bedroom, it has a portrait of Louis XIII by the royal painter Philippe de Champaigne. Beyond the **Salle du Conseil**, with 18th-century paintings in soft pinks and steely blues by François Boucher and Carle van Loo, are Napoleon's private rooms, backing on to the Galerie François Ier. The **Salon de l'Abdication**, decorated in red and gold, witnessed the moment of high drama on 6 April 1814 when Napoleon sat down at the little pedestal table to sign the act of abdication – and allegedly tried to poison himself shortly afterwards.

Napoleon's abdication

The Petits Appartements

More memories of Napoleon await you in the rooms below François Ier's gallery. Here the king once had a suite of baths modelled on those of the Roman emperors – it was in these private rooms that he kept the *Mona Lisa*. Many of the panelled rooms are rather dark and dingy, despite some restoration, but there is much of interest. Most are still as they were in Napoleon's day, which explains the number of clocks – he hated it when people were late. Most have their Louis XV or Louis XVI fireplaces and other architectural features, but the hangings and furniture reflect First Empire taste. Some of the decoration and furniture is in the Egyptian style that was fashionable after Napoleon's victories there, while later pieces are more classical Roman in inspiration. Josephine's **Salon Jaune** is very elegant. The furniture in the **Salon Vert** has been re-upholstered in pale green, but the pale bronze hangings in Napoleon's mother's bedroom were originally purple and the pale grey fabric round Josephine's bed has faded from bright lapis lazuli blue.

First Empire Style

The tour usually ends with the **Galerie des Cerfs**, beneath the Galerie de Diane. It has intricately painted ceiling beams and paintings of France's châteaux, plus the stag's heads that give it its name. This long light room was built by Henri IV in 1600 as a place to hold celebration banquets after a day's successful hunting.

Hunting is also the theme of the **Jardin de Diane**, which you can cross after leaving the Petits Appartements. Its focal point is a bronze of Diana, the goddess of hunting, posing elegantly on a pedestal above a fountain whose water spouts are stags' heads, while four mournful seated hounds gaze into the distance.

The museums

Napoleonic Museum

Before exploring the rest of the gardens, you can visit two museums that are separate from the palace proper, though there is no extra charge. The **Musée Napoléon**, in the Louis XV Wing, is devoted to Napoleon's whole family. Here you can see the emperor's uniforms and his swords, carved with silver eagles, his medals and spurs, even his stockings and gloves, plus such intimate items as nail scissors, shaving bowl – and portable bidet, for use, perhaps not quite on the battlefield, but during his campaigns. The familiar painting in his coronation robes by the studio of Baron Gérard is here, and so is Gérard's portrait of Josephine. A whole room is filled with gifts showered on him, and there is some stunning furniture, like the desk-cum-table made by a Venetian glassmaker. His second wife Marie-Louise features in another room, while the displays on their son, the 'King of Rome', include a Gérard painting of him as a wide-eyed baby.

The lower floor is devoted to Napoleon's powerful mother, Maria-Letizia Ramolino, '*Madame Mère*', and to the male siblings he put on the thrones of Europe – Joseph, King of Spain, Louis, King of Holland, Jerome, King of Westphalia – and his sisters Elisa, Pauline, Princess Borghese, and Caroline, whose husband, Marshal Joachim Murat, was made King of Naples.

Chinese Museum

You can also visit the small **Musée chinois**, opened by Napoleon III's wife Empress Eugénie in 1863. Its exhibits include war booty taken by the French army from the Summer Palace in what was then Peking, and from elsewhere in China. This 'Chinese Museum' is in the pavilion built by Louis XV's architect Jacques-Ange Gabriel at the end of the Louis XV Wing, overlooking the **Cour de la Fontaine** end the **Etang des Carpes** (Carp Pond).

The grounds

Carp pond

This carp pond has given rise to many fanciful legends (see box) and feeding the huge carp that do undoubtedly glide lazily about in it is an old-established pastime. You can go boating here too, from June to October, a romantic way of enjoying the view of the palace and appreciating just how large it is – it looks more like a whole townscape seen from here, or from the **parterre**. This large square garden was originally laid out for François Ier but redesigned for Louis XIV, probably by André Le Nôtre. Beyond the carp pond, the **Jardin anglais** is considerably smaller than it used to be but still centres on the spot where the spring or fountain that gave the place its name – the 'Fontaine Bliaud' – once spurted.

On the other side of the Parterre, beyond the **Route des Cascades**, stretches the **canal** built for Henri IV. There are lovely walks to be had here, but this is also a convenient way of returning to the town rather than walking back through the palace courtyards, whose cobbles are distinctly tiring on the feet. You can leave the grounds on the far side

The Fontainebleau carp

Despite their huge size, the eponymous fish in the **Etang des Carpes** or Carp Pond are definitely not the ones that François I enjoyed feeding four and a half centuries ago. Nor, a persistent legend to the contrary notwithstanding, do they date from Napoleon's day.

Such misinformation was clearly prevalent in the 19th century, too. One governor of the palace, Auguste Luchet, a Republican by inclination and a noted gourmet, was accused by the anti-Republican press of having fried and eaten the 'historic carp that François Ier fed with breadcrumbs, and to which the Duchesse d'Etampes used to throw golden rings'.

The unromantic truth is that the pond has been drained on several occasions, and its inmates eaten. Cossack soldiers feasted on Fontainebleau carp in 1815. Allied soldiers followed their example during the First World War, and the occupying German troops during the Second.

of the parterre and walk round to the **place d'Armes**. A little further on in the **place Napoléon-Bonaparte** are several cafés with tables outside. The main shopping street, the **rue Grande**, has a good bookshop, the Librairie Michel, selling large-scale maps of the forest that will enable you to explore it without getting lost. Before doing so you might like to find out yet more about Napoleon and his military career by visiting the **Musée Napoléonien d'Art et d'Histoire militaire**, which is devoted to just that, and includes a scaled-down reconstruction of the moving farewell scene.

The town

Otherwise the town is pleasant but has nothing much to see, as it is so dominated by the palace. But exploring the forest, on foot, by car or by bike, enables you to see not only some well-known beauty spots and woodland scenes that feature in paintings by many an artist, major and minor, but two attractive villages and a beautiful private château.

The Fôret de Fontainebleau

The **GR1** and **GR11** major hiking trails both pass through the forest, but there are hundreds of other marked paths. Mountain bikes can be hired at the rail station and at various other places in the town, including *La Petite Reine* (14 rue de la Paroisse, ☎ 01-64-22-72-41), which also has less sporty machines. Horse-riding is also available (check with the tourist office).

The forest is famous for its rocky outcrops and boulders and stretches of sandy soil, creating wild-seeming landscapes – the French words used are *désert*, meaning 'wilderness', and *chaos*, the picturesque term for a jumbled mass of boulders such as you can see at places like the **Gorges de Franchard**. Here the novelist George Sand once sat on a limestone boulder in the moonlight to tell her lover Alfred Musset her life story (see **Nohant**), after which he may or may not have had some sort of hallucination during which he saw an apparition. If he did, he was in good company: Henri IV allegedly saw the ghost of a wild and dishevelled huntsman, and this terrifyingly large figure is immortalized in the **Carrefour du Grand Veneur**, near

Gorges

Tinguely's mysterious cyclops

One of the oddest sights in the Ile de France is also one of the strangest pieces, or rather assemblages, of contemporary sculpture to be seen anywhere. In a clearing in the Forêt de Fontainebleau about 1km from Milly-la-Forêt (signposted), stands the monumental, 22.5 metre tall *Cyclop* masterminded by the Swiss sculptor Jean Tinguely, and worked on by a group of fourteen sculptors, including himself and his wife Nikki de Saint-Phalle.

The huge and monstrous face, high up among the tree tops, is covered in little bits of mirror, its single eye mesmerizingly beaming forth a golden light. Saliva gushes out of its gaping mouth, cascading down its lolling tongue, and a crocodile clings to its cheek. The huge flapping ear was carved by another Swiss, Bernhard Luginbühl. You can climb up inside it, slither along footbridges, goggle at a theatre show of sorts, even pay homage to France's Jewish deportees courtesy of sculptor Eva Aeppli.

The whole colossal enterprise took over fifteen years to complete, eventually opening to a bewildered public in 1994. And for the record, it took over 300 tonnes of steel to build it ...

Guided tours only, on Fri, Sat and Sun, from late Apr to late Oct.

To book your place on a tour (compulsory), contact Milly's tourist office (℡ 01-64-98-83-17, Ⓕ 01-64-98-94-80).

the **Chaos d'Apremont**, which offers beautiful views of the **Gorges d'Apremont**.

All these places are well signposted, as are the various recommended itineraries, like the **Circuit du Désert** or the **Circuit des Druides**, but you must have a map to be on the safe side. Both the Apremont and Franchard gorges are much used by keen climbers, since the limestone outcrops give them a chance to practise full-scale rock-climbing, with ropes, so near to Paris. The same is true of the **Massif des Trois-Pignons**, the starting point for a whole host of delightful walks.

Rock-climbing

Barbizon

The Gorges d'Apremont are also easily reached from the 'painters' village' northwest of Fontainebleau that has long been a mecca for tourists. Barbizon's high street, the **rue Grande** (also called **Grande-Rue**), is lined with art galleries, restaurants and hotels. Most of them sprang up in the late 19th or early 20th century to cater for the art-loving foreigners – and French visitors – who flocked to Barbizon to see this tiny village that had become home to a colony of artists from about 1848 to the outbreak of the Franco-Prussian War in 1870.

Most of the original painters were landscape artists, seeking inspiration in the Fôret de Fontainebleau. Among them were Théodore Rousseau, whose house-cum-studio is open to the public. Others, especially Jean-François Millet, himself of peasant stock, preferred to paint scenes of rural life, like his famous *Angélus*, now in the Louvre in Paris. Millet moved to Barbizon, then peopled mainly by woodcutters and their families, in 1849, a few years after Rousseau. The two of them, and their friend the landscape painter 'Diaz', formed the

Barbizon artists

nucleus of what has become known as the Barbizon School of painters. Their work is characterized by accurate depictions of land-scapes and of the rural community at work, painted matter-of-factly, without an eye to the 'picturesque', and invariably *sur le motif*, meaning that they painted on site, rather than in a studio. In this they heralded the work of the Impressionists.

Other well-known artists who painted in the nearby forest are Camille Corot, who was in Barbizon as early as the 1820s, Claude Monet, and Camille Pissarro. Writers came here too, among them Robert Louis Stevenson, who wrote his *Forest Notes* in the village in 1876.

Robert Louis Stevenson

The resident artists liked to congregate at the **Auberge Ganne**, now restored and converted into an interesting museum (see box, p. 181). Its chic modern entrance contrasts with the charmingly old-fashioned **Maison-Atelier de J.-F. Millet**, its walls covered in paint-ings and old photographs of the Barbizon painters. You can buy modern watercolours here, and reproductions of canvases by the original artists. **Rousseau's studio** is now an outpost of the Auberge Ganne.

Today's visitors to Barbizon are mostly well-heeled. Most of the many hotels and restaurants are expensive, and you are unlikely to pick up a bargain among the paintings. Gift and souvenir shops dot the high street. Yet you can still sense something of the old village atmosphere, especially in the evenings, when the day trippers have departed, and this is a good base for exploring the forest. Bike hire is available, or you might like to take it easy by being driven along the forest rides in a horse-drawn *calèche* or barouche.

Milly-la-Forêt, 19km west of Fontainebleau, is also a good starting-point for walks, as it is close to the Massif des Trois-Pignons. It has long been known as a centre for growing med-icinal plants and herbs, known in both French and English as 'simples', a theme taken up in the charming decorations by Jean Cocteau in the **Chapelle Saint-Blaise-des-Simples**. Cocteau, poet, painter, film-maker, playwright, lived in Milly, in a small house close to the château, and is buried in

Frescoes by Jean Cocteau in Milly-la-Forêt

Cocteau's frescoes

the garden surrounding this little 12th-century chapel, once attached to a leper hospital. His paintings are striking in their simplicity, with his familiar strong outlines, especially in the triangular-shaped image of Christ crowned with thorns over the altar. Plants with hairy stems or jagged leaves snake up the whitewashed walls and round the door, a cheeky cat gazes upwards, ears pricked, whiskers bristling. In the garden you can see the real thing – eighty-odd 'simples' have been planted there.

Milly has two other claims to fame. The first is old: the venerable raftered wooden market building, dating from 1479. The second is new:

Key data

FONTAINEBLEAU 77300

T.O. 4 rue Royale, ☏ 01-60-74-99-99

Access Paris 65km; **rail** from Paris-Lyon, then local bus to town centre and château; **rail** from Moret-sur-Loing; **buses** from Provins; **excursions** from Paris

Sights **Château** (royal palace), including **Musée Napoléon** (displays on Napoleon and his family) and **Musée chinois** (Chinese collections), ☏ 01-60-71-50-70, open year-round, closed Tue; **Musée Napoléonien d'Art et d'Histoire militaire** (military collections related to Napoleonic era), 88 rue Saint-Honoré, ☏ 01-64-22-49-80, open Tue–Sat, pm only

Lunch Fontainebleau, Barbizon

Staying Fontainebleau, Barbizon, Flagy, Moret-sur-Loing

Also Barbizon, Moret-sur-Loing, Provins, Vaux-le-Vicomte

BARBIZON 77630

T.O. 55 rue Grande, ☏ 01-60-66-41-87

Access Paris 58km, Fontainebleau 10km; **buses** (infrequent) from Fontainebleau

Sights **Auberge Ganne** (inn decorated by painters, now museum), 92 rue Grande, ☏ 01-60-66-22-27, open year-round, closed Tue; **Maison-Atelier de J.-F. Millet** (Millet's house and studio), 27 rue Grande, ☏ 01-60-66-21-55, open year-round, closed Tue; **Maison-Atelier de Théodore Rousseau** (Rousseau's studio), 55 rue Grande, ☏ 01-60-66-22-38, open year-round, closed Tue

Lunch Barbizon

Staying Barbizon

Also Fontainebleau, Vaux-le-Vicomte

Chapelle Saint-Blaise-des-Simples (chapel decorated by Jean Cocteau) 91496 Milly-la-Forêt, ☏ 01-64-98-84-94, open Easter to end Oct daily except Tue; otherwise weekends and public hols only

Château de Courances
91490 Courances, ☏ 01-64-98-41-18, open Apr to end Oct, pm weekend and public hols only

Cyclop (monumental sculpture by Jean Tinguely), see box, p. 178

Auberge Ganne

Right in the middle of Barbizon's main street, 'Old Man Ganne's Inn' was a popular meeting place in the 19th century for the local artists' colony. During the convivial evenings they spent there, they would cover the walls, wall cupboards and furniture with paintings – maybe in exchange for a litre or two of wine, sometimes just for fun. Most of these have happily survived. They have been carefully restored and can be admired in the old kitchen and dining rooms on the ground floor. The upstairs rooms have some wall paintings, too, along with a collection of canvases, drawings and engravings by artists belonging to the *Ecole de Barbizon* or Barbizon School. They are arranged by theme: one group consists of animal paintings, featuring sheep and cows, chickens and dogs, even monkeys; another of scenes painted in the Fontainebleau Forest; a third of views of the village and its inhabitants.

the peculiar **Cyclops** constructed in the forest by Jean Tinguely and assorted fellow-sculptors (see box, p. 178).

Then 5km north of Milly (11km west of Barbizon) is the lovely *Courances* **Château de Courances**, a handsome brick and stone building in the style known as 'Louis XIII', though it was originally built in the mid-16th century by Gilles Le Breton, François Ier's first architect at Fontainebleau. The grounds are fed by no fewer than seventeen springs, and this enabled André Le Nôtre, or one of his followers, to create a wonderful 'water garden', full of shimmering pools and canals *Water* and little waterfalls. The garden façade is magically reflected in what *garden* the French call a *miroir d'eau*, or 'water mirror', an ornamental lake. The garden is particularly beautiful when the autumn tints of the trees are duplicated in these shining surfaces. And the small Japanese garden complements the formal perfection of the 'embroidered' *jardin à la française*.

The château was built for Henri II's finance supremo Cosme Clausse, then redesigned for another leading servant of the crown. Over the years it has been much altered – it once had frescoes by Primaticcio – but it is still privately owned and lived in, and you can visit some beautifully furnished rooms.

21 Moret-sur-Loing

Long ago a royal defensive town guarding the border between the fledgeling kingdom of France and the lands of its enemies the Dukes of Burgundy and the Counts of Champagne, Moret is now a most attractive little place whose placid river landscapes have appealed to painters for centuries. It makes a good starting-point for exploring the pretty Loing Valley and some quiet towns beside the Seine popular with weekending Parisians.

A 10-minute walk from the station brings you downhill to a medieval gatehouse, the **Porte de Samois**, part of the old fortifications, and the **tourist office** (ask for a street map), then on along the main street, **rue Grande**, with some medieval houses, to a second gatehouse, the **Porte de Bourgogne**, guarding the bridge over the river Loing. The view from either end of the bridge makes it obvious why Moret has long been a haunt of painters.

Alfred Sisley

It is particularly associated with the Franco-British Impressionist Alfred Sisley, who lived here for the last twenty years of his life, dying in 1899 in a house with a north light near the church, now called the **Villa Sisley** (not open to the public), at the age of sixty. Another famous, if occasional, inhabitant was the statesman Georges Clemenceau, twice prime minister, whose daughter-in-law has set up a small **Clemenceau Museum** on the outskirts of Moret, in the riverside house called **La Grange Batelière**, built by his son Michel (a 15-minute walk across the river and to the right along the N6, signposted).

Marie Leszczynska

Also associated briefly with the town was the young Polish princess who so unexpectedly became Queen of France when the fifteen-year-old Louis XV took her as his bride. Marie Leszczynska, the daughter of the exiled (and impoverished) King Stanislaus, was seven years older than her husband-to-be, who came to meet her just outside Moret during a violent storm on 4 September 1725. He had been driven over from Fontainebleau, where they were to be married the following day. The bride spent the night in Moret, in the castle keep where, just over a century earlier, another young king, the bridegroom's great-grandfather and immediate predecessor Louis XIV, had held his extravagant finance supremo Nicolas Fouquet prisoner (see p. 168).

Another illustrious personage who slept in Moret for just one night was Napoleon. That was in 1815 and he was on his way back from his first exile on Elba. But there is no evidence to suggest that François Ier ever slept in the exuberantly decorated Renaissance house that bears his name and now – after a curious history (see box, below) – overlooks the courtyard behind the town hall in rue Grande

An itinerant house

Right in the centre of Moret, just behind the *mairie*, is a fine Renaissance façade fronting what is generally known as 'the François Ier house', though as far as anyone knows it had nothing to do with the king.

When it was first built, the house stood in the Grande-Rue, roughly where numbers 40 and 42 are now. It was bought in the 1820s by an army officer called Colonel de Braque, who had it dismantled and shipped off to Paris. It was reassembled in the Cours-la-Reine, an avenue near the Seine and the Avenue des Champs-Elysées. The colonel was a passionate admirer of the famous Comédie française actress Mlle Mars and the point of uprooting the house was to offer it to her as a present, though she never lived there.

Over a century later, in 1956, it was carted back to Moret and placed where the mayor and his corporation could keep a firm eye on it.

Moret-sur-Loing's riverscapes are popular with painters

(signposted). It does, however, have a medallion with the king's head, easily recognized by the long nose and sardonic expression, and a particularly fierce-looking salamander (his emblem).

Just before the Porte de Bourgogne, the rue de l'Eglise on the right leads to **Notre-Dame church**, an interesting example of the Early Gothic style, with a Late Gothic portal and many other additions. Its finest feature is its elaborately carved Renaissance organ loft. Beyond here are **Sisley's house** (on the corner of the rue Montmartre) and the **castle keep**. If you walk back to the rue Grande via the rue de Grez, you can admire the **Logis du Bon Jacques**, one of several medieval half-timbered houses to have survived in Moret. It was here that the local nuns used to sell the barley sugar that is still made to their recipe today (see p. 185).

A pleasant **riverside walk** leads off the rue de la Pêcherie (to the left off the rue Grande, just before the Porte de Bourgogne), or you might like to hire a canoe or a bike.

Moret stages a spectacular *son-et-lumière*-plus-actors pageant on Saturday evenings from late June to early September (tickets can be booked in advance at the tourist office). Six hundred of the locals take part and the show includes fireworks over the river. A series of monthly concerts takes place in the Eglise Notre-Dame, with guided tours of the town and its riverscapes in the afternoon, and for a week in June, concerts are held all over Moret and the surrounding villages.

Son-et-lumière

Exploring the riverside villages

Sisley also lived briefly in **Veneux-les-Sablons**, just west of Moret. According to the locals, it inspired a large number of his canvases, a claim also made by **Saint-Mammès**, 2.5km northwest of Moret, at the spot where the Loing meets the river Seine. This small village with its

Saint-Mammès

Romanesque church is something of a boating centre. The river bank is lined with moored barges, and on Sunday afternoons you can take a pleasant boat trip to **Samois-sur-Seine** and back. Surprising as it may seem, this sleepy place, with some lovely houses by the river *Jazz* and climbing up the hillside, was for many years the home of the *festival* jazz musician Django Reinhardt, who is buried in the local cemetery and in whose honour an annual jazz festival is staged in June.

Thomery   Between Saint-Mammès and Samois is **Thomery** (6km north of Moret), famous for the delicious (and very expensive) Chasselas grapes that have been grown along the old stone walls since the early 18th century. On Wed and Sat afternoons you can visit the **house and studio of Rosa Bonheur**, once a very popular painter, mainly of animal scenes, who scandalized the local bourgeoisie by dressing in men's clothes, but was nevertheless the first woman ever to be awarded the Légion d'honneur. She died in the same year as Sisley.

West of Moret

Loing If you follow the **Loing Valley** westwards from Moret, you can explore
Valley a series of picturesque, clearly prosperous villages offering delightful river views that still attract painters:

- **Montigny-sur-Loing** (7km from Moret), with a Romanesque church
- **Bourron-Marlotte** (9km from Moret), the home of the landscape

Key data

MORET-SUR-LOING 77250

T.O. 4bis pl. de Samois, ℡ 01-60-70-41-66, Ⓕ 01-60-70-82-52

Access Paris 70km, Fontainebleau 10km; **rail** from Paris-Lyon via Thomery and Fontainebleau (continuing to Montigny-sur-Loing, Bourron-Marlotte/Grez-sur-Loing; and, on another line, Saint-Mammès); **buses** from Fontainebleau, Grez-sur-Loing

Sights **Villa Sisley** (Alfred Sisley's house); **Eglise Notre-Dame** (Early Gothic church); **Maison François Ier** (Renaissance house); **Musée de l'Histoire des Religieuses et du Sucre d'Orge de Moret** (Barley Sugar Museum), 5 rue du Puits-du-Four, ℡ 01-60-70-41-66, open Easter to end Oct, weekends only; **Musée Clemenceau**, La Grange Batelière, ℡ 01-60-70-51-21, open Sun pm

Lunch Moret, Samois-sur-Seine, Thomery

Staying Moret, Montigny-sur-Loing, Fontainebleau

Also Fontainebleau

Atelier de Rosa Bonheur
12 rue Rosa-Bonheur, 77810 Thomery, ℡ 01-60-70-06-19, open Wed and Sat pm; **buses** from Fontainebleau
Musée vivant de l'Apiculture gâtinaise (Beekeeping Museum)
La Cassine, 45220 Châteaurenard, ℡ 02-38-95-35-56, open Mar to end Oct (Wed and weekends only Mar, Apr, Sep, Oct)

The nuns' barley sugar

Moret-sur-Loing has been famous for its barley sugar for over 350 years. The recipe was first invented by Benedictine nuns in the local convent, using cane sugar flavoured with barley, plus a little vinegar. It was originally intended for medicinal purposes and was said to be good for sore throats. By 1638, the mother superior (a cousin of the poet La Fontaine) was making gifts of little sticks of the barley sugar. And *Le sucre d'orge des religieuses de Moret* (barley sugar made by Moret's nuns) soon became a highly prized delicacy at the royal court at nearby Fontainebleau.

A century and a half later, a few years before the French Revolution led to the dissolution of monasteries and convents, the nuns moved away from Moret, taking their secret recipe with them. But one elderly nun who had survived the Terror happily rediscovered it – she was even called Sister Felicity – apparently at the urging of Napoleon, who had heard of the delicacy and wanted to try it. When he eventually did so, it was clearly to his liking, as he plied the old nun with a gold coin for every tin or box she managed to produce.

But when Sister Felicity died, the recipe was again lost. Then another elderly lady enters the story, a local spinster who had remembered the ingredients. Eventually production was started up again in the early 19th century by the Sisters of Charity, who were running a hospice in Moret, on the corner of the rue de Grez. They opened a shop to sell their barley sugar, which again became very popular, sold individually or wrapped or in little round or rectangular tins.

Production continued down to the late 1960s. But the hospice was no longer flourishing and was closed in 1972. Two years earlier one of the nuns handed on the recipe to a family of confectioners in the town, the Rousseaus. Encouraged by the 'Produits et Terroir' association, they relaunched the nuns' barley sugar yet again, still using the traditional packaging. And in 1995 they opened a little museum in one of Moret's oldest houses, displaying early documents and equipment. The little tins of barley sugar make attractive presents.

painter Jean-Baptiste Corot for nearly forty years, housed a lively colony of artists and writers from the mid-19th century to the Second World War, including Auguste Renoir and Camille Pissarro, Emile Zola and Henri Mürger, whose *Scènes de la vie de Bohème* inspired Puccini's opera *La Bohème*. Its elegant 16th-century château was briefly the home of Louis XV's father-in-law Stanislaus Leszczynski.

● **Grez-sur-Loing** (11km from Moret), an ancient village that again has long been popular with artists, has an interesting Romanesque church, a lovely old stone bridge, a ruined tower and a wash house; Robert Louis Stevenson met his future wife here.

All these villages on the southern edge of the Forêt de Fontainebleau are in the region known as **le Gâtinais**, famous for its honey, referred to as *miel du Gâtinais*. If honey's your thing consider travelling south to Châteaurenard, which has a **Museum of Beekeeping**.

Berry ~ north

The far north of the Berry forms part of the **Sologne**, a region of forests and heathland dotted with fish-filled meres, long popular with the huntin'-shootin'-and-fishin' brigade, but nowadays attracting just as many nature lovers and the environmentally conscious, who enjoy rambling and cycling, riding or even driving a horse-drawn caravan along the quiet roads and forest tracks. Opportunities for such pursuits are legion, and the landscapes have a lonely beauty, tinged with melancholy, that is very appealing to the romantically inclined.

The villages here, with their façades in patterned brick and half-timbering and their distinctive church porches, contrast with the stone houses in the **Pays Fort** further east, while the Sologne's marshy terrain gives way to rich, clayey soil and meadows, separated by thick hedges and clumps of trees. These in turn are followed by the vine-clad hills of the **Sancerrois**, culminating in the hilltop town of **Sancerre** itself, high up above the river Loire.

To the south of both regions lies the **Champagne berrichonne**, a rolling plateau of arable land, centring on the Berry's capital, **Bourges**, with a magnificent cathedral, many fine buildings and a clutch of museums in its picturesque old streets.

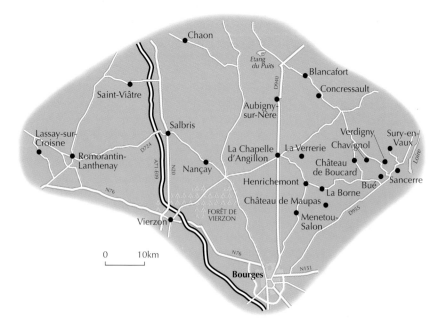

Most of the villages are linked by bus services setting out from Bourges and there are many marked paths for hikers and ramblers in the Sologne and the Sancerrois. Roads are generally quiet, though in the Sancerrois the grape harvest may slow you down.

22 In and around the Sologne

The Sologne villages, often prosperous thanks to an influx of Parisians in the shooting season, are peaceful, secret-seeming places, harbouring cosy inns serving traditional regional cuisine based on game and mushrooms from the forests and freshwater fish from the local rivers and meres. Hidden in the forests are many a private château, whose turrets can occasionally be glimpsed. The young Henri Fournier, later to become 'Alain-Fournier', author of *Le Grand Meaulnes* (see box, p. 233) was born on the edge of the Sologne in **La Chapelle d'Angillon** and spent his summer holidays there and deep in the Sologne at **Nançay**. He was clearly inspired by several local châteaux and manor houses, including **La Verrerie**, southeast of **Aubigny-sur-Nère**, a small town with many half-timbered houses that makes a convenient centre for exploring the area. The two places are connected by their associations with a branch of the Scots Stewarts, and with the 'Auld Alliance' between Scotland and France against the English (see p. 64).

You can learn all about the Aubigny Scots by visiting the **Musée de la Vieille Alliance** (Auld Alliance Museum) in the town's château, which reverted to the French crown in 1672, when that branch of the Stewart line died out. A year later it was presented to Louise de Kéroualle, the long-time mistress of an English king – by the French king for whom she had probably been spying (see box, p. 188). A video presentation in English will fill you in on episodes such as the Battle of the Herrings

La Verrerie: Gothic chapel and loggia

187

Louise de Kéroualle, Duchess of Portsmouth

In 1673, the lovely château of La Verrerie was presented to the Duchess of Portsmouth, the mistress of Charles II of England, by another king, France's Louis XIV.

Born Louise-Renée de Penancoët de Kéroualle in Brittany in 1649, she travelled to England at the age of twenty-one, as lady-in-waiting to Charles's sister Henrietta-Anne, who had married Louis's brother Philippe, Duc d'Orléans. Henrietta was secretly acting as an envoy of the French king when she talked Charles into signing an Anglo-French alliance that became known as the Treaty of Dover. And it seems likely that Louise de Kéroualle's true role was to help to win the English king over.

Charles, who was then nearly forty, was certainly much taken with her pretty, little-girl looks – the diarist John Evelyn refers to her 'childish, simple and baby face' – and after over a year of stubborn resistance (stubbornness is one of several Breton characteristics that Louise seems to have had in full measure), she went through a curious 'ceremony' and became the royal mistress.

After Henrietta's return to France – where she died two weeks later, probably by poisoning – Louise stayed on in England. Three years later she joined the ranks of the English aristocracy when Charles granted her the title of Duchess of Portsmouth, though she was never accepted by the king's subjects, who always thought of her as a foreign adventuress. When her son by the king, Charles Lennox, was three years old, she persuaded Charles to ennoble him too, and he became Duke of Richmond, a title still held by her descendants today. Diana, Princess of Wales was a distant descendant.

During her many years in England, 'Madame Carwell', as she was popularly known – Charles's nickname for her was 'my dearest Fubbs' – was criticized for her extravagance, but was a generous patron to French artists. She had excellent taste and invited painters like Charles Le Brun and Pierre Mignard to work for her in her adopted country.

Shortly after Charles's premature death in 1685, Louise returned to France. By now she was both an English and a French duchess, as she had persuaded Louis XIV, to whom she was distantly related, to revive the duchy of Aubigny the previous year. She spent much of her time on her Aubigny estates in later life, generally living at La Verrerie in the summer. She retained her aristocratic bearing and looks to the end, according to Voltaire, who referred to her 'noble and pleasant face' at seventy.

By a curious coincidence, her death at the age of eighty-five, on 14 November 1734, occurred forty-seven years to the day after that of Nell Gwyn, Charles's better-known mistress.

(1428), in which the familiar name of Sir John Falstaff appears.

The château, built in the early 16th century, partly in local brick, by Robert Stewart, also houses the town hall, and a second museum, devoted to the Berry novelist Marguerite Audoux (1863–1937). Robert Stewart had a major influence on the town we see today: after virtually all its houses had burned down in 1512, he allowed the inhabitants to collect wood from his forests to rebuild it, a magnanimous gesture that resulted in whole streets of most attractive half-timbered houses with decorative carvings. Look out for the **Maison François Ier** opposite the tourist office, the **Maison du Bailli**, in the rue du Bourg-Coutant, where no. 17 is adorned with the salamander that was François Ier's emblem, and, in the rue des Foulons, one of only two houses to survive the fire, the **Maison du Pont-des-Foulons**.

The town has a prosperous feel as you stroll round, with good shops – try to find the local speciality of gingerbread (*pain d'épices*) – and well-kept squares. **Saint-Martin**, a church built in the transitional style as Romanesque gave way to Gothic, again owes much to Robert Stewart, who added six chapels after the fire. Don't miss the soldiers fast asleep in the Entombent in the third chapel on the left or the beautiful wooden Pietà.

Gingerbread

La Verrerie and La Chapelle d'Angillon

The red thistle of the Stewarts can also be seen at the beautiful Renaissance **Château de la Verrerie**, romantically mirrored in a lake against a backcloth of the **Forêt d'Ivoy**. You can stroll beside the lake before admiring the intricately carved Italianate loggia with its frescoes in delicate colours and the little Gothic chapel, with more frescoes, before going inside to tour the elegantly comfortable wing added in the 19th century behind the loggia. Among the interesting furniture and objects on display are four alabaster statuettes of mourning monks from Jean, Duc de Berry's tomb, one of them holding his nose to choke back his tears. You can also see the library of a 19th-century ancestor of the present owners, Eugène-Melchior de Vogüé, whose book on the great Russian novelists launched a vogue for Russian literature.

To take full advantage of the lovely setting, consider spending the night in one of the large and beautifully furnished bedrooms★ or enjoy a leisurely meal in the cottagey restaurant in the grounds, *La Maison d'Hélène.*★

On the far side of the Forêt d'Ivoy, **La Chapelle d'Angillon**, too, has a turreted château overlooking a lake: the **Château de Béthune**, housing an interesting little museum devoted to Alain-Fournier, whose birthplace you can see nearby, in the avenue Alain-Fournier. Also inside the château is a collection of 18th- and 19th-century costumes, books, weapons and other objects connected with Albania's royal family.

Alain-Fournier

Albanian Collection

This château was once a feudal castle built, at least in part, by a Norman knight called Gillon de Seuly (hence the name 'Angillon'). The severe early medieval keep is still standing, flanked by a residential wing that was embellished over the centuries by a whole series of noble families, including the Gascon dynasty to which Henri IV's mother Jeanne d'Albret belonged – the king himself visited the château (as did his grandson Louis XIV, staying in the room now known as the King's Bedroom or *Chambre du Roi*).

By the time it was bought by Henri's great minister Maximilien de Béthune, Duc de Sully, in the 17th century, it was a graceful dwelling

Château de Béthune at La Chapelle Angillon

with staircase turrets in pinkish brick, while on the opposite side of the courtyard an Italianate loggia boasts an equally graceful arcade beneath which the *jeu de paume* (an early version of tennis) was played. Sully added the terrace overlooking the lake, adorned with appealing stone cherubs.

As you admire the view, you can muse on the fact that for nine hundred years, right down to the 18th century, the château and its estate formed part of a miniature principality, poetically called Boisbelle, which included the land on which Sully built the town of Henrichemont (see p. 206).

The atmosphere is particularly pleasant in this château, where you will be offered a glass of local wine in the guardroom after your tour. You can also buy a bottle or two, along with books by and about Alain-Fournier, in the château's own shop, and even attend Sunday mass in the chapel.

Nançay   About 20km west of La Chapelle, deep in the Sologne, is **Nançay**, the home of Alain-Fournier's father. The general shop run by his uncle, the background to a crucial scene in the novel, can still be seen on the village square, opposite the church, though it is now a private house. And in the local château is another little museum full of Alain-Fournier memorabilia. The stables have been converted into an attractive gallery where local artists show and sell their work. Outside the village is a famous radio-astronomy observatory, occasionally open to the public.

Argent-sur-Sauldre and beyond

Local customs   North of Aubigny, Argent has a cosy inn★ and, in the château, a museum on local crafts and customs, with many exhibits connected with witchcraft and sorcery in the Berry (see box, p. 16). The top floor has a superb set of chestnut rafters. An outbuilding houses a collection of work by a Bulgarian potter, Vassil Ivanoff, who worked in La Borne (see pp. 205–6).

If you are interested in pottery and china, a famous centre of glazed earthenware can easily be reached from Argent: the riverside town of **Gien**, where you can visit the **Faïencerie**, with a showroom and a museum illustrating the techniques involved since an Englishman, Thomas Hall, discovered that Gien's clayey, sandy soil was ideal for making the type of earthenware originally produced in the Italian town of Faenza. Hall bought a former monastery in 1821 and set up the faience works in the buildings where it has remained ever since. Some of the designs on display are heavy and elaborate, others, like a wonderful peacock vase, art nouveau in inspiration. You might be able to spot a bargain here, as seconds are often sold off at very reasonable prices, along-side the elegant dinner services and decorative objects for which Gien is well known.

Brinan-sur-Sauldre: 'gossips' church porch

The town also has a museum devoted to a pursuit that has long been enjoyed in this part of the world – *la chasse*, or hunting, shoot-ing and fishing, which will be much in evidence if you explore the Sologne, especially in autumn. Even if you disapprove of such things, you will soon see what an influence they have had on fine and applied art in France by studying the museum's extensive collections of paintings, tapestries and more modest objects. Here too is a collec-tion of knives and crossbows, rifles and nets used by *chasseurs* down the ages. *La chasse*

But to learn more about witchcraft and sorcery, you should head for the entertaining **Musée de la Sorcellerie** at **Concressault**, another one-time Stewart fief southeast of Argent (see box, p. 16). *Sorcery*

Between Argent and Concressault lies **Blancafort**, a village whose church has a characteristic slate-roofed porch-cum-belfry. A pleasant walk beside the canal can precede or follow a visit to the turreted **Château de Blancafort**, built in warm pink brick and surrounded by a lovely formal garden. It dates from about 1450, but was rebuilt a couple of centuries later. The interior, with a rare wooden spiral stair-case, is filled with beautiful 17th- and 18th-century furniture and tapestries. Note the tooled leather on the dining room walls, and the fine oak panelling in the library. *Blancafort*

Another interesting example of Berry church architecture can be seen if you follow the river Sauldre west from Argent to **Brinon-sur-**

Gossips' porch

Sauldre, again with a typical Sologne inn★ offering good cuisine. The church here has a splendid *caquetoire*, the almost-onomatopoeic local word for a long overhanging porch creating a covered area lined with benches where parishioners can linger after mass for a good old gossip (*caqueter* meaning 'to prattle' or, in the case of hens, 'to cackle'— see p. 191). The village has several timber-framed brick houses with complicated herringbone patterns.

Water sports

The landscape round here is dotted with meres. Nearer Argent, the **Etang du Puits** is the Sologne's largest, popular for swimming and a range of watersports.

Saint-Viâtre

To learn more about the economy and ecology of this characteristic Sologne terrain, and the important part that *étangs* play in the life of the Solognots, continue westwards to **Saint-Viâtre**, where the **Maison des Etangs**, a pleasing half-timbered building, has interesting displays on traditional draining, breeding and fishing techniques, as well as a huge range of leaflets on local flora and fauna and on rambling paths. It was set up by an organisation called Sologne Nature Environnement (☏ 02-54-88-79-74), a useful source of information on nature walks.

Romorantin-Lanthenay

For yet more on life in the Sologne, catch up with the river Sauldre again further south at **Romorantin-Lanthenay**, also accessible via a scenic local rail line from **Salbris**. This pleasant old town with a gastronomic reputation (see box, p. 51) and an interesting history – the 'blond giant' François Ier was brought up there – has recently acquired a smart new museum, the **Musée de Sologne**, attractively housed in two converted watermills and in the town's oldest building, the Tour Jacquemart. So the museum sits astride the river, with a series of footbridges (complete with self-service restaurant) linking the different buildings.

Shooting ...and poaching

Well-presented displays illustrate the Sologne's natural habitats, and you can learn much about the popularity of the region with the well-to-do after Emperor Napoleon III had had the land drained and cleared – he and his wife the Empress Eugénie owned three Sologne châteaux. A video of film footage of life in a local château during the shooting season in 1935 is fascinating. Here too you can learn about poaching, an important topic in this part of the world (and one that is also addressed in another new museum, the **Maison du Braconnage** (House of Poaching) in **Chaon** near Brinon-sur-Sauldre). The museum also has a section on the history of Romorantin, once an important cloth-manufacturing centre, nowadays the home of Matra cars (small motor-racing museum on the outskirts).

A locature

Something of the life of the poorest Solognots can also be gleaned in the **Locature de la Straize**, west of Romorantin. This tiny 16th-century farmhouse, the home of agricultural labourers – which is what *locature* means – consists of a single room that would have housed up to ten people, plus their pigs and chickens, down to the 1940s. It is crammed with furniture, farm implements and assorted objects connected with local rural life, customs and crafts, including touching old wedding photographs, and is a good place to take children.

Key data

AUBIGNY-SUR-NERE 18700

T.O. rue des Dames, ⓣ 02-48-58-40-20 (or *Mairie*,
ⓣ 02-48-81-50-00)

Access Paris 180km, Bourges 46km; **buses** from Bourges,
La Chapelle d'Angillon, Argent-sur-Sauldre

Sights **Château des Stuart**, ⓣ 02-48-81-50-00, housing **Musée
Marguerite Audoux** and **Musée de la Vieille Alliance** (on
Auld Alliance between France and Scotland), open year-
round, but Sun only Dec to Easter, and weekends only
Easter to end June and mid-Sep to end Nov; **Eglise Saint
Martin**; **half-timbered houses**

Lunch Aubigny, Argent-sur-Sauldre, Oizon, La Verrerie

Staying Aubigny, Argent-sur-Sauldre, La Verrerie

Also Sancerrois

Château de Béthune
18380 La Chapelle d'Angillon, ⓣ 02-48-73-41-10 (Aubigny 14km),
open year-round

Château de Blancafort
18410 Blancafort, ⓣ 02-48-58-60-56 or 02-48-58-60-11 (Aubigny
9km, Argent 8km), open mid-Mar to end Oct

Château du Moulin
41230 Lassay-sur-Croisne, ⓣ 02-54-83-83-51 (Romorantin 9km),
open Mar to mid-Nov

Château de Valençay
36600 Valençay, ⓣ 02-54-00-10-66 (Romorantin 32km), open Mar
to mid-Nov (gardens open year-round)

Château de la Verrerie
18700 Oizon, ⓣ 02-48-58-06-91 (Aubigny 10km), open Easter to
end Oct (restaurant)

Locature de la Straize
41230 Gy-en-Sologne, ⓣ 02-54-83-82-89 (Romorantin 18km), open
mid-Mar to mid-Nov, weekends and public hols only, or by appointment

Maison du Braconnage
41600 Chaon, ⓣ 02-54-88-68-68 (Brinon-sur-Sauldre 8km), open
Apr to mid-Nov

Maison des Etangs
41210 Saint-Viâtre, ⓣ 02-54-88-93-20 (Brinon-sur-Sauldre 31km),
open mid-June to mid-Sep or by appointment

Musée des Arts et Traditions populaires
Château, 18410 Argent-sur-Sauldre, ⓣ 02-48-73-33-10 (Aubigny
(bus) 10km), open mid-Apr to mid-Oct, pm only

Musée de la Course Automobile
29–30 faubourg d'Orléans, 41200 Romorantin-Lanthenay,
ⓣ 02-54-96-91-28 (Aubigny 58km), open mid-Mar to mid-Nov

Musée de la Faïencerie de Gien
pl. de la Victoire, 45500 Gien, ⓣ 02-38-67-00-05 (Argent (bus)
20km), open year-round (seconds shop closed Sun)

Key data continued

Musée imaginaire du Grand Meaulnes
Château, 18330 Nançay, ☎ 02-48-51-80-22 (La Chapelle d'Angillon 20km), open mid-Mar to mid-Dec, weekends only (otherwise by appointment)

Musée international de la Chasse
Château, 45500 Gien, ☎ 02-38-67-69-69 (Argent (bus) 20km), open mid-Feb to end Dec

Musée de Sologne
Moulin du Chapitre, 41206 Romorantin-Lanthenay Cedex, ☎ 02-54-95-33-66 (Aubigny 58km), open year-round

Musée de la Sorcellerie
La Jonchère, 1840 Concressault, ☎ 02-48-73-86-11, open Easter to end Oct.

Observatoire radio-astronomique
18330 Nançay, ☎ 02-48-51-82-41 (La Chapelle d'Angillon 20km), open second Sat in month, pm only (no charge, but you must request visit in advance)

Château de Moulin

The *locature* is in peaceful countryside west of **Lassay-sur-Croisne**, where you can visit one of the prettiest châteaux in France, the little pink-brick **Château du Moulin**, in a fairytale setting in the middle of a lake where stately swans glide. It dates from the late 15th century and was lived in by the same family for over four hundred years. It is still lived in, and has some beautiful furniture, tapestries and paintings, as well as a collection of early weapons.

Valençay

South of Romorantin, and on the same local rail line from Salbris, the **Château de Valençay** is just in the Berry – in what is known as the **Boischaut du Nord** – but bears little resemblance to the more homely manor houses mostly found there. It is huge and palatial, with extensive gardens in which peacocks strut and graceful deer somewhat oddly cohabit with animals usually seen in zoos, including kangaroos. It is essentially Renaissance, but in the grand manner, with massive domed turrets and tall roofs surmounted by chimneys, while the decoration is classical in spirit. This mixture of styles is partly due to the addition of later wings, but taken as a whole it was clearly a suitably grand place to be used by Napoleon's foreign minister, the wily and cynical statesman Talleyrand, as a setting for the lavish receptions his soon-to-be imperial master wanted him to lay on for foreign dignitaries. Talleyrand bought it in 1803, and lived there on and off until his death in the château in 1838. His descendants owned it right down to 1980. The interior is equally palatial, with mostly Empire furniture and furnishings, and many mementoes of the great

Vintage cars

man. In the grounds is a large collection of vintage cars, the **Musée de la Course Automobile.**

The hiking trail known as the **GR du Pays de Valençay** passes through the village, eventually joining up with the GR46.

23 A walk in Bourges

Bourges, the capital of the Berry, is undeservedly neglected by foreign visitors: magnificent Saint-Etienne de Bourges must be the least known of the great French cathedrals. Yet the town centre has many other interesting buildings, some housing museums; a network of picturesque old streets that have changed little since the town was rebuilt after a devastating fire in 1487; and an unhurried provincial charm combined with excellent shopping that makes staying there a delight. And – a big plus point in France – only its most recent museum makes an entrance charge.

An important centre in the Roman period, when it was known as Avaricum (meaning 'rich in water'), it became a flourishing medieval town housing the court of the munificent Jean, Duc de Berry (of Book of Hours fame), and was briefly the capital of France in the reign of Charles VII, Joan of Arc's 'little Dauphin', who was mockingly nicknamed 'King of Bourges' by the English.

Modern Bourges is rather surprisingly the capital of pop, rock, jazz, folk and popular song: it throbs with life in the spring when the

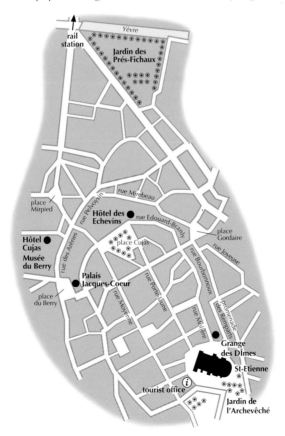

Bourges's Maison de la Culture – a national first

In 1964, General de Gaulle and his energetic arts minister, the writer André Malraux, performed the official opening ceremony for the Maison de la Culture in Bourges, though it had been operating since the previous year. This was the first of a whole series of arts centres designed to bring art and culture to the people, as well as fostering the work of creative artists and bringing it to the notice of a wider audience. The original plan was to build a 'House of Culture' in each of the country's economic regions. In fact only twelve were built, and the operation has been judged to be only a partial success. But Bourges' is certainly one of the most dynamic, not least because of its involvement in the city's hugely successful festival of popular song, Le Printemps de Bourges (see p. 40).

Bourges'
Spring

Printemps de Bourges, one of the world's biggest non-classical music festivals, comes to town (see p. 40).

The **place Mirpied**, a short walk from the station, makes a good starting point for exploring the old centre, which is blessed with many pedestrian streets. Walk along the rue Cambournac to where it meets the **rue Pelvoysin**, admiring the half-timbered medieval houses. The **Hôtel Pelvoysin**, now a bank, was the home of the cathedral architect. Continue along the traffic-free **rue Mirebeau**, some of whose houses still have their medieval gables, to the picturesque **place Gordaine**. Then turn into the most attractive **rue Bourbonnoux**, lined with 15th- and early 16th-century buildings. On the corner with the **rue Joyeuse**, don't miss the **Maison des Trois Flûtes** (now a *pâtisserie*), with flutes carved on a wooden post. Almost opposite, the **Hôtel Lallemant** houses the **Musée des Arts décoratifs** (Applied Arts Museum).

Decorative
arts

The house was built in 1494, shortly after the Great Fire, by a prosperous family of drapers, probably from Nuremberg (*allemand* is French for 'German'). So it is Gothic, with mullioned windows, but the decoration, executed right at the beginning of the 16th century, is among the earliest examples of Renaissance art in France, with characteristic shell motifs and medallions. Inside, the decoration reflects Bourges's reputation as a centre for alchemy (the great Jacques Coeur – see box, p. 200 – may have dabbled in it). You will spot a wealth of alchemical symbols, especially on the coffered ceiling of the little **oratoire** (chapel), where an angel appears to be peeing into a clog.

The pleasing rooms, some with intricately patterned parquet floors, are full of inlaid spinets and ebony cabinets, tapestries and paintings. Keep an eye open, too, for many small decorative carvings, like a jester with asses' ears beneath a spiral staircase, or little monks on the vaulted ceiling, greeting you as go in. Right at the top is a collection of toys and games, some 17th-century.

Ramparts
walk

The narrow **passage Casse-Cou**, off the rue Bourbonnoux to the right, brings you to the **Promenade des Remparts**, overshadowed by the remains of the Gallo-Roman walls, once bristling with watchtowers, now with medieval and later houses built up against them.

This peaceful walkway (pleasant tearoom★ if you're feeling peckish) leads into the **rue des Trois-Maillets**, facing the cathedral. Turn right to admire, on the corner of the rue Molière, the **Grange aux Dîmes**, a large medieval tithe barn. Continue past it to face the superb west front of the Cathédrale Saint-Etienne.

Cathédrale Saint-Etienne

The cathedral, built in two main phases from 1195 to its consecration in 1324, is basically contemporary with Chartres Cathdedral and with Notre-Dame in Paris. Although it differs from them in several important respects, the influence of the great building projects underway further north is clear – not surprisingly, since Bourges's bishop was the brother of his counterpart at Notre-Dame.

Cathedral sculpture

The west front already indicates how unusually wide it is, with five massive portals surrounded by a wonderfully lively 'storybook in stone'. I have no space to describe the sculpture in detail, but must mention my favourites: the sequence of little scenes depicting Noah and his Ark, and the busy Resurrection on the central portal, where the rounded limbs of the dead energetically clambering out of their graves give them a surprisingly youthful look. Above them, the elect glide piously towards Abraham's bosom, while the damned scuttle off to Hell, prodded by smirking devils twice their size. Early evening is a good time to admire the dexterity of the medieval masons, when the Berry limestone takes on a beautiful golden tinge.

Le Nôtre's gardens

Above the portals is a huge rose window, donated by Duke Jean and known as the '*Grand Housteau*', a Berry term meaning 'large opening'. Before going inside to see it, it is instructive to walk round to the **Jardins de l'Archevêché**, pleasant public gardens originally designed by Louis XIV's master gardener André Le Nôtre. From here you can enjoy sweeping views of the double row of flying buttresses, which always remind me of guy ropes holding down a vast tent. This will prepare you for one of the unusual features of the interior: there is no transept. And you can also see how at the triangular-shaped east end, where the ground is some 6 metres lower, the Romanesque chancel with radiating chapels sits on top of a lower church (misleadingly called a crypt), built in what was once the moat flanking the Roman walls.

Master craftspeople

The fine classical building overlooking the gardens, once the archbishop's palace, is now the town hall. Part of the ground floor has recently been turned into the **Musée des Meilleurs Ouvriers de France**, presenting the work of craftspeople who have earned the coveted distinction of being France's 'best workers', plus the history of this laudable scheme, instituted by the government in 1924.

The cathedral interior

A uniform space

You can enter the cathedral by the south portal, which has more interesting sculpture surrounding a Christ in Majesty. Once inside, you are immediately struck by the vast, light-filled space. This impression is partly due to there being no transept: instead of the usual cruciform shape, the interior is a single, unified whole, supported by massive piers – nearly twice as thick as Notre-Dame's –

The Damned: stained glass in St-Etienne, Bourges

Stained glass stretching right down to the far end of the apse. But it is also due to the three sets of windows pouring light in, those in the very tall nave being, most unusually, all in grisaille, apart from a small rose window, while the chancel is a blaze of jewel colours from the stained glass. The biblical stories depicted in these superb windows, where red predominates (rather than blue, as in Chartres), are relatively easy to make out because the cathedral is so light. Do watch out for Salome, in a flaming red dress, dancing on her hands in the John the Baptist window (second chapel on the right). Opposite here, the Jacques Coeur Chapel has a wonderful Annunciation window.

Lower church The 'crypt', too, is unusually light, as it is not below ground level. Here you can see a recumbent effigy of Duke Jean, an old man in shining white marble, with a tame bear cub crouching at his feet, and the newly restored rood screen depicting the twelve apostles. Below this lower church, the crypt proper is a survival of an early Romanesque church.

A saintly shepherdess

Appropriately for a region that grew prosperous on the wool trade and still rears many sheep, the Berry's patron saint was a modest shepherdess. There are conflicting versions of the life story of St Solange, but it seems certain that she was beheaded in 878 by a ferocious feudal baron called Bernard de Gothie. She is much venerated in the region and a pilgrimage is still held on Whit Monday from the village that bears her name, Sainte-Solange, about 10km east of Bourges, with a Romanesque church of the same name. The pilgrims make their way to Bourges Cathedral, where a chapel is dedicated to her.

The Berry novelist George Sand, a passionate advocate of the virtues of the region (see box, p. 209), chose the name Solange for her daughter.

Another statue of the Duc de Berry, smiling this time as he kneels in prayer, appears on one side of the Lady Chapel above, with his wife Jeanne de Bologne, in an elegant high-waisted dress, on the other side. The sacristy was presented by Jacques Coeur, whose son Jean was to be appointed bishop of Bourges. There is much else to see, but if you are feeling fit, do allow enough time to climb up the North Tower for spectacular views over the cathedral roof and the town.

The **rue Porte-Jaune** is the best place for a last look at the sculpture on the west front. Before walking down it, you might like to visit the **tourist office** in the rue Victor Hugo to ask about concerts and other events in Bourges and the Berry. Several cafés nearby make this a good place for a break.

Visiting Coeur, Cujas and Estève

Turn left off the rue Porte-Jaune in the rue Louis-Pauliat and you come to the busy **rue Moyenne**, sporting on the right a flamboyant, Gothicky post office. Continue past it until you come, on the left, to the rue du Docteur-Témoin. Turn right off it into the cobbled rue Alexandre-Dumas and you find yourself in the **place Jacques-Coeur**, facing a genuine Gothic mansion, one of the finest secular medieval buildings to have survived in France, and built by one of the most fascinating men of his (or any) age.

Before going inside the **Palais Jacques-Coeur**, note the romantic 19th-century statue of him in the square. Then admire the highly decorated façade, and the little *trompe-l'oeil* stone figures apparently peering over balconies – a witty detail that is a harbinger of much that is to come as you tour the huge palace built for Jacques Coeur from 1433 to 1450.

Jacques Coeur

Again I have no space to do justice to this most interesting building, designed in the Late or 'Flamboyant' Gothic style, but with a number of features heralding the Renaissance – not surprisingly, as on his visits to the pope, Jacques Coeur had acquired a taste for the deluxe lifestyle of the great Italian patrons of the arts like the Medici. Approving of their liking for comfort and privacy as well as elegance, he insisted on sanitary arrangements that were centuries ahead of their time in France, with inside lavatories and proper ventilation (remember that at Louis XIV's Versailles, valets were still running around the grand rooms with chamber pots); an

Statue of Jacques Coeur

A medieval tycoon

In his book *A Little Tour in France*, Henry James calls Jacques Coeur 'a Vanderbilt or a Rothschild of the fifteenth century' – a suitably exotic label for this extraordinary man who was born in Bourges in about 1400, the elder son of a furrier working for the Duc de Berry's court, and rose, by dint of enormous ambition, energy and a thoroughly modern business flair, to occupy one of the key posts in the kingdom, as *Grand Argentier* (Treasurer) to the royal household. A telling illustration of the rise of the bourgeoisie in late medieval France, he became one of his royal master's wealthiest subjects.

In his early twenties he managed to enter the service of the new king, Charles VII, derided by the English as the 'King of Bourges'. By 1427 he was involved in the lucrative business of, literally, coining money – and pocketing the duties that went with it. Three years later he embarked on a new career in import-export, with his own merchant fleet. His ships sailed from France's near-moribund Mediterranean ports, laden with furs and cloth destined for the Middle and Far East, returning with silks and spices, perfumes and precious gems.

This flourishing business revived the ports. Impressed, the king put Coeur in charge of the Paris Mint, then of the finances of his household. This gave him an opportunity – perfectly legal in those days – to keep the royal family and court supplied with the luxury goods he was already trading in. The great wealth he had amassed even enabled him to lend them substantial sums. Eventually he was financing the final campaigns of the Hundred Years' War.

In 1441 he was ennobled, but remained a businessman at heart, starting up a new venture as a mineowner. His golden touch made him many enemies. They were no doubt behind his sudden arrest for embezzlement in 1451, not to mention the rumours that he had poisoned the royal mistress Agnès Sorel. The king failed to stand up for him, and he was tortured and thrown into prison.

His death seems peculiarly appropriate for such a bold adventurer. He escaped after three years, sought protection from the pope in Rome, and took part in his successor's naval expedition to defend the eastern Mediterranean against the Turks. Wounded in a naval battle, he was taken to the island of Chios, where he died in 1456.

ingenious system of steam baths reached via a separate staircase; and an overall design that meant you did not constantly have to walk through rooms, since each led off a corridor. Other practical innovations included a serving hatch, and the idea of having various parts of the building set aside for specific functions and labelled accordingly. So the courtyard entrance to the kitchens is indicated by a carved scene with a cook apparently scouring a pan and another using a pestle and mortar.

Hearts & scallops

The internal decoration features hearts and scallop shells galore: *coeur* means 'heart', scallops are *coquilles Saint-Jacques*, and both featured on the newly ennobled merchant's coat of arms. But there is so much else besides: crinkly cabbage leaves, snails, monkeys, frogs, winged deer, the royal fleur-de-lys, countless alchemical symbols, and a host of figures busy jousting or playing chess, hunting or spinning, playing a Berry *cornemuse* (see box, p. 15) or steering a galleon. The compulsory guided tour gives you plenty of time to have a good look at these, as well as some beautiful wooden vaulting, and the delicate ceiling paintings in the chapel, probably the work of the greatest French painter of the age, Jehan Fouquet.

A meal in the old-established *Jacques-Coeur*★ opposite will allow you to contemplate the irony that Messire Jacques had little time to enjoy his splendid new home before his downfall. If you prefer to press straight on, head for the steps beside the palace leading down to the **place du Berry**, from where you can see the much sterner rear façade, built on to the remains of the town's Roman walls. Walk past it to the **rue des Arènes**. On the left, the Renaissance **Hôtel Cujas**, bought in 1585 by the legal pundit after whom it is named, is now the **Musée du Berry**.

The first room in this local history and archeology museum is full of delights. An appealing cherub from the Duc de Berry's palace is one. Another is a set of marble and alabaster prophets and mourners from his tomb, some with their faces hidden inside their hoods. The rest of the collections are a mixed bag. Prehistoric and Gallo-Roman artefacts and stelae excavated locally, including ophthalmic instruments and toilet articles like tweezers and make-up mirrors, are displayed on the ground floor. Egyptian archeology is on the first floor, along with Berry craftwork, such as pottery from La Borne (see pp. 205–6) and traditional musical instruments). On the second floor are medieval ceramics.

History & archeology

Turn left out of the museum and continue to the place Planchet, then turn right into the rue du Commerce. Facing you once you reach

Key data

Bourges	18000
T.O.	21 rue Victor-Hugo, ℡ 02-48-24-75-33, ℻ 02-48-65-11-87
Access	Paris 229km, Issoudun 37km, Saint-Amand-Montrond 44km, Châteauroux 69km; **rail** from Paris; **buses** from all over the Berry
Sights	**Cathédrale Saint-Etienne** (Gothic cathedral); **Musée des Arts décoratifs** (applied art), Hôtel Lallemant, 6 rue Bourbon-noux, ℡ 02-48-57-81-17, open year-round; **Musée du Berry** (archeology, local history), Hôtel Cujas, 4–6 rue des Arènes, ℡ 02-48-57-81-15, open year-round; **Musée Estève**, Hôtel des Echevins, 13 rue Edouard-Branly, ℡ 02-48-24-75-38, open year-round; **Musée des Meilleurs Ouvriers de France** (life and work of master craftsmen), Hôtel de Ville, pl.Etienne-Dolet, ℡ 02-48-57-82-45, open pm only, closed Jan; **Palais Jacques-Coeur**, pl. Jacques-Coeur, ℡ 02-48-24-06-87, open year-round
Lunch	Bourges
Staying	Bourges

the **place Cujas** is a Bourges landmark, the **Maison des Forestines**, where a delicious confectionery speciality has been made since 1879 (see box, p. 57).

In the **rue Edouard-Branly**, leading off the square, the **Hôtel des Echevins** is another splendid Gothic/Renaissance mansion. For over three hundred years it was the town hall, housing the municipal magistrates (*échevins*) and the mayor. But since 1987 it has been a museum devoted to the work of the contemporary Berrichon painter Maurice Estève (see box, p. 234).

Maurice Estève

The most striking feature of the exterior is the richly decorated octagonal staircase turret, which contrasts with the circular tower on the 16th-century wing nearer the street. Inside there is more Gothic carving, in the spacious rooms that form a surprisingly successful background to Estève's boldly coloured canvases. The collection is large and offers a good opportunity to follow the development of this self-taught painter whose work, even at its most abstract, was often inspired by his native Berry.

Temporary exhibitions are staged in the Fine Arts Academy almost next door to the museum. Steps down from the street bring you back to the rue Mirebeau. If you feel in need of some greenery, the **Jardin des Prés-Fichaux**, a restful public garden on land that was once marshland, is not far from here. If a meal seems more in order, the rue Bourbonnoux has several restaurants, including my favourite, *Le d'Antan Sancerrois*.★

24 The Sancerrois

The rather sleepy old town of Sancerre is a fine sight, high up on its rounded hill overlooking the river Loire and surrounded by vines. The gently hilly surrounding area, known as the Sancerrois, is famous for its grapey, dry white wines, though fragrant red and rosé Sancerres are also made, the rosés being a distinctive colour that is almost salmon. This is also an area well known for its goat's cheeses, especially the little round *crottins de Chavignol* (see box, p. 204). Buy some of each and you will have the key ingredients for a picnic as you explore the wine villages and the nearby châteaux.

Sancerre

Thanks to its strategic site, Sancerre itself has had an eventful history, but all that is left of its medieval fortifications is a cylindrical keep, the **Tour des Fiefs**. The views from the top (if you happen to be there on a Sunday afternoon), or from the **Esplanade de la Porte César** nearby, are superb, plunging down to the broad sweep of the Loire.

Otherwise there are no real sights, but the tourist office in the middle of the **place Nouvelle**, half hidden beneath a curious 'bunker',

Walking map

can supply a walking map to guide you round the narrow old streets and help you identify some picturesque medieval and Renaissance

Countryside near Sancerre

houses, many with little balustrades at the top and flower-filled courtyards you can peer into. The **rue aux Juifs**, with a good cheese shop
and leading downhill to the **rue Saint-André**, is particularly attractive. The marked itinerary includes the **belfry** beside the **church of
Notre Dame**, and the doorway of the ruined Romanesque **church of
Saint-Père-la-Nonne**, some fragments of which can also be seen
beside the tourist office.

Cheese shop

As you stroll, you will come across craft boutiques and antique
shops (many open only at weekends except in high summer), and,
since this is very much a gourmet area, a good choice of restaurants,
charcuteries and *pâtisseries* selling local specialities. At the *Auberge
Joseph Mellot* in the Place Nouvelle you can taste Sancerre and
Pouilly-fumé wines from a wine-producing family who have been
active in the area since 1513. Visits to their vineyards and cellars can
be arranged by appointment. Ask at the tourist office about other
local producers offering tastings, and about cheese producing farms
where you can taste and buy. Sancerre has a big wine fair duing the
Whitsun weekend, and another at the end of August. Other fairs are
held in the wine villages nearby.

Local wines

At the foot of Sancerre's hill, **Saint-Satur** has a 14th-century church
that was never completed and a golf course, **Le Golf de Sancerre**
(℡ 02-48-54-11-22). The canal running beside the Loire (**Canal
latéral**) is used for boating (boat hire available) and other watersports.
If you follow it north to **Bannay** (10km from Sancerre), you can visit
the **Jardin du Tisserand** (Weaver's Garden), an attractive 'living' museum devoted to silk-making and weaving. You can see silkworms being
reared (from May onwards), learn how the silk is made and woven,
and buy silk articles too. The pleasant local restaurant, *La Buissonnière,*★ offers meal-plus-museum packages.

Bannay

Wine and cheese villages

Chavignol Only 3km from Sancerre, **Chavignol** is a good place to start exploring the wine area, with its deep orange and rich brown soil, its views
across the vines to Sancerre and its attractive villages where opportunities to taste and buy are legion. Chavignol's red-tiled houses and
inns, little square with fountain and winding high street are all charming. You must of course taste the eponymous *crottin*, which is generally
smaller here than the cheeses on sale in Sancerre. Cheese-producers
Bué in nearby **Bué** are allowed to use the *crottin de Chavignol* name too.
But Bué has another claim to fame: its **Foire aux Sorciers** (Witches'
Fair) held on the first Sunday in August. It was originally called *Foire
aux Birettes*, from a Berry term for a mysterious white phenomenon
with no visible head, a cross between a ghost and a witch or sorcerer.
The fair was rather surprisingly started up by the local *curé*, who decided to tackle his parishioners' persistent belief in witchcraft (see box,
p. 16) by, as it were, annexing it to the Church.

Other villages where wine can be tasted and bought include
Amigny, **Verdigny** (with a modest wine museum) and **Sury-en-Vaux**,
clustered close together among the vines.

Crottin de Chavignol: a few tips

The little round goat's cheeses made in or near the wine village of Chavignol near Sancerre have had the AOC (*appellation d'origine contrôlée*) status
since 1976. So as with wines, you will know that if you buy a *crottin* with the
AOC label, it has been made within a specified radius of the village and
adheres to standards laid down by the government body in charge of
quality control of all AOC produce. And as with other cheeses, connoisseurs
like to look for the words *fermier* ('farm-made') or *artisanal* ('made by traditional methods'), to reassure themselves that it has not been produced
on an industrial scale, by industrial methods. The locals refer to five different stages of ripening:

● **mou**: the day after it has been strained
The cheese is still soft and white; it is delicious sprinkled with salt and
freshly milled black pepper, chopped shallots and chopped herbs (especially chives); eat with a spoon
● **coudré**: a week after straining
It is starting to firm up and take on a fuller flavour, but still has the fresh
taste of the very young cheese
● **bleuté**: 10 days after straining
It is blueish on the outside and full of flavour, with a firm yet smooth con-
sistency; it has now reached the true *crottin de Chavignol* stage
● **très sec**: 3 weeks after straining
It is now very dry and crumbles when cut; the taste is strong and ripe – a
cheese for connoisseurs
● **repassé**
Older cheeses shrink in size and may be left to ripen even further, until
they become softer and take on a fairly sharp taste that is not to everyone's
liking

Key data

SANCERRE 18300

T.O. Nouvelle Place, ☏ 02-48-54-08-21

Access Paris 203km, Bourges 46km; **rail** to Cosne-sur-Loire (10km east), then bus; **buses** from Bourges; also buses from Menetou-Salon and Henrichemont

Sights **Tour des Fiefs** (medieval keep, can be climbed only Sun pm); **Beffroi** (bell tower) of Notre-Dame church; **Saint-Père-la-Nonne** (ruined Romanesque church); **medieval streets**

Lunch Sancerre, Bué, Chavignol, Saint-Satur

Staying Sancerre, Saint-Satur

Jardin du Tisserand (Silkmaking Museum)
18300 Bannay, ☏ 02-48-72-32-10, open Easter to end Oct (pm only in Apr, May, Oct)

Château de Boucard
18260 Le Noyer, ☏ 02-48-58-72-81, closed Jan

Musée de la Poterie and **Centre céramique de la Borne**
18250 La Borne, ☏ 02-48-26-70-66/02-48-26-96-21, open Easter to end Oct, weekends only in term time

Galerie du Livre
50 rue des Billets, Boisbelle, 18250 Henrichemont,
☏ 02-48-26-74-44/02-48-58-71-03, open July to end Sep, otherwise by appointment

Château de Menetou-Salon
18510 Menetou-Salon, ☏ 02-48-64-80-54/02-48-64-80-16, open Easter to end Sep

Château de Maupas
18220 Morogues, ☏ 02-48-64-41-71, open Palm Sun to mid-Oct; also Sun only mid-Oct to mid-Nov

Beyond the vines

The **Château de Boucard**, on the Route Jacques-Coeur 15km west of *Boucard* Sancerre, enjoys an idyllic setting amid flowery meadows beside the river Sauldre, which flows round it to feed its wide moat. With its plain walls, cylindrical keep and many watchtowers it appears to be a small-scale medieval fortress from the outside. But once you have crossed the moat and walked into the courtyard, the style is pure Renaissance, with a wealth of stone carving – I particularly like the cherubs' heads – and mullioned windows. The 16th-century parquet floors and panelling are still in place in the main building, which has some interesting furniture and a kitchen still equipped with its 17th-century spit – in full working order, as the guide will demonstrate. Classical concerts are held on July Saturdays in one of the barns.

Boucard has some examples of the pottery made since Roman *La Borne* times in **La Borne**, southwest of the château. This pretty village, typ- *potteries* ical of the Berry, was a major stoneware centre in the late 17th and 18th centuries, and production continued right up to the

The rural Château de Boucard

Second World War. It has recently enjoyed a revival thanks to an influx of potters from all over the world, working in individual studios (some of which can be visited, especially at weekends) and making both one-off pieces and traditional Berry designs. A **Pottery Museum** has been opened in a former chapel, and you can look at the work of current potters in the schoolhouse, before heading for their studios or buying from one of several craft shops. Another attraction here is a delightful tearoom.★

Henrichemont, 4km from La Borne, also has a few potters, but it has recently decided to focus on the traditional techniques involved in book production. An old tannery has been turned into the **Galerie du Livre** (Book Gallery), with displays on hand-made paper, typesetting, printing and binding. The town owes its name (an adaptation of Henrici Mons or 'Henry's Mount') to a plan of Henri IV's minister the Duc de Sully to build a town in honour of his sovereign that would be a place of sanctuary for his fellow-Protestants. It was never finished, but you can see the regular plan of eight streets meeting at a large central square with a fountain.

Menetou-Salon

Two more Route Jacques-Coeur châteaux lie south of here. One, **Menetou-Salon**, actually belonged to Jacques Coeur, but was completely rebuilt in the 19th century in a neo-Gothic style apparently inspired by the Palais Jacques-Coeur in Bourges. Inside it feels rather like a Scottish baronial hall, with its panelling and chandeliers made of horns. One of the outbuildings houses a collection of vintage cars.

Local wines

Menetou-Salon wines (see p. 54) are becoming increasingly popular in both Britain and North America. The village has several cellars where you can taste and buy, as well as a pleasant inn.★

Ceramics

Menetou-Salon wines, made on the estate, can also be bought at the **Château de Maupas**, whose pride is its collection of nearly nine hundred glazed earthenware plates from faïenceries all over France and elsewhere, displayed all the way up the staircase. It also has Gobelins tapestries, and objects connected with the Comte de Chambord (the posthumous son of the last Duc de Berry and a claimant to the French throne), and with his mother, the colourful Duchesse de Berry. In front of the château, a handsome 15th-century building with a tall hexagonal tower on this side and a cylindrical tower on the other, are formal parterres.

Berry ~ west

Western Berry centres on the departmental capital Châteauroux, at the heart of the **Champagne berrichonne** plateau. Further west lies the marshy **Brenne**, a nature reserve where rare species of flora and fauna can be seen, and where hiking, riding and biking are popular, while to the south are the **Creuse Valley**, offering a gentle micro-climate and many opportunities for watersports, and the **Boischaut du Sud**, a peaceful region of rolling meadows and bosky valleys.

Although this is a predominantly quiet, rural area, it has many attractive small châteaux, a few pleasant little towns, and a number of literary associations thanks to Honoré de Balzac's frequent visits to **Issoudun** and George Sand's attachment to her manor house at **Nohant**. The Creuse Valley has long been a haunt of painters, of whom Claude Monet is the best known. Small hotels and rustic inns can be found everywhere, camping is common and *gîtes d'étape* for walkers and cyclists are available.

For long-distance walkers, hiking trail **GR46** includes Château-roux to Sarzay and La Châtre. A side walk known as the **GR des Maître Sonneurs** visits George Sand country, starting from La Châtre and taking in Nohant and Saint-Chartier, while the **GR du Pays des Mille Etangs** crosses the Brenne and takes in Fontgombault Abbey.

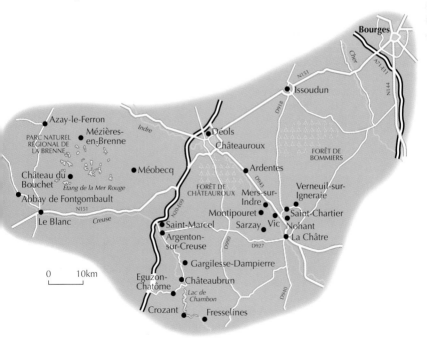

The **GR du Pays de Val de Creuse** starts at the Argentomagus archeological museum and continues southwards along the valley via Gargilesse to Crozant. Leaflets with maps, and showing where bikes, horses and canoes can be rented, are available from tourist offices.

25 La Châtre, Nohant

The small town of La Châtre, perched up on a hill above the river Indre in the Boischaut du Sud, lies at the heart of what has been known for about a century and a half as 'La Vallée Noire', the Black Valley. The phrase was invented by the novelist and journalist George Sand, the pen name of the daughter of a local aristocrat (see box, p. 209), who said of the rolling pastureland dotted with thick hedgerows: 'As you look into the distance, you see that lovely blue that becomes purple and very nearly black on stormy days.' Here she set many of her rural tales, describing buildings and landscapes that can still be seen today.

Both La Châtre and nearby Nohant, her home for much of her life, are served by frequent buses and are well placed for expeditions into the pretty countryside that has changed surprisingly little since her death. The area is crisscrossed by marked footpaths and offers plenty of delightful picnic spots.

La Châtre

La Châtre – the name probably comes from Latin *castrum* – pays homage to the valley's most famous daughter in the **Musée George-Sand et de la Vallée Noire** (George Sand and Black Valley Museum), housed in the massive square keep that is all that has survived of a medieval castle. The ground floor has a well-displayed collection of stuffed birds, some of them very rare, but the upper floors are devoted to George Sand and her circle, and to local history, art and customs.

This is a good place to learn about the novelist and her family and friends before visiting Nohant. You can study family trees, read letters and see photos of the many literary lions of the day who were constant visitors to Nohant. Here too are showcases on other Berry writers, like Maurice Rollinat (see box, p. 216), and paintings of the Black Valley by local artists. The history and crafts section has some beautifully made examples of traditional Berry musical instruments, the *vielle* and the *cornemuse* (see box, p. 15), along with pottery, furniture and lace bonnets. On the floor above, children will enjoy a collection of models of wheeled vehicles of all kinds, made by a retired hairdresser with no pretensions to being an artist, but an urge to hand on knowledge to future generations, as the museum's labelling charmingly puts it.

The hilly streets in the old part of the town are worth exploring and the views from the old stone bridge over the Indre are delightful.

George Sand and the vagaries of fame

The prolific novelist George Sand was born in Paris in 1804. Her real name was Amantine Lucile Aurore Dupin and she was the daughter of a great-grandson of the Polish king Friedrich Augustus II, Elector of Saxony. Her mother, a former milliner called Sophie Delaborde, was the uneducated but beautiful daughter of a birdseller.

After her army officer father's accidental death when she was four, she was brought up at Nohant in the Berry by her paternal grandmother. Grieving for her lost son, this aristocratic lady no doubt wanted her little namesake to take his place and often had her dressed in boy's clothes. She engaged her son's tutor and confidant as tutor to the little girl, and he too encouraged her to wear men's knee breeches and shirts for riding and hunting.

So it seemed only natural, when she left the loutish Berry husband she had married at eighteen, and settled in Paris in 1831 with her two children, to follow the advice of her practical and thrifty mother by wearing male attire. Men's clothes were much more convenient and hard-wearing, said Sophie. And so when Aurore started writing as a means of earning her living, she was often to be seen in greatcoat, trousers and waistcoat, stout boots, a grey felt hat and tie – and sometimes smoking a cigar.

This 'transvestism' scandalized polite society, especially when she compounded her masculine persona by adopting a male pen name. Her publisher chose 'Sand', an abbreviation of the surname of her one-time lover and co-author Jules Sandeau. But she chose 'George' because it meant 'farmer' in Greek, and thus seemed synonymous with 'Berrichon'.

She went on to become a bestselling and famously disciplined author with over a hundred meticulously researched novels, plays and stories to her credit; she was the friend of a host of celebrated men and women in literary, musical and artistic circles; she was interested in radical politics, became a political journalist and wrote pamphlets for the Interior Ministry during the 1848 Revolution.

And yet she is chiefly remembered for wearing male dress and for her colourful love life, particularly her liaisons with men younger than herself, like the poet Alfred de Musset and the composer Frédéric Chopin, who wrote much of his greatest work when he was being cosseted by her at Nohant. Somewhat oddly, she was also accused of being a lesbian.

Given this obsession with her behaviour, it is perhaps not surprising that her books are often dismissed as being less interesting than her life. But this ignores her reputation as a stylist, admired by Flaubert and Proust, and by a bevy of fellow-authors in Britain, including William Thackeray and Charlotte Brontë. Nowadays she is read mostly for her short tales of simple country life in her native Berry, starting with *La Mare au diable* in 1846.

Nohant

To see how George Sand lived in the Berry, you must travel a few miles north. The tiny village of Nohant seems at first more English than French, with its little Romanesque church, fronted by a porch, on one side of what looks for all the world like a 'village green'. There is even a village inn★ opposite the church. But the manor house on the third side of the green is very French: beyond tall

The village church at Nohant, opposite George Sand's manor house

wrought-iron gates a gravel drive shaded by limes leads to a pleasant 18th-century house, unpretentious but comfortable, with pale-blue wooden shutters.

George Sand's house

This was the house where George Sand spent well over half her life. Here she entertained her many friends from the world of arts and letters and her lovers, especially the pianist and composer Frédéric Chopin, who spent the whole of seven summers there.

The house seems sadly run down in places, but the guided tour is full of interest. It starts with the kitchens, filled once again with the gleaming copper pans of George Sand's day, then continues past an elegant portrait of her granddaughter Aurore, and into the dining room, lined with family portraits and the table set for a (purely imaginary) dinner attended by some of Nohant's illustrious house guests, including Prince Jérôme Napoleon, Pauline Viardot and Turgenev, Alexandre Dumas fils and Flaubert. Also on the ground floor are the drawing room and the elegant bedroom used by Marie-Aurore de Saxe, George's much-loved grandmother, and the little boudoir where she wrote her first novel, at a desk built into the wall, and slept in a hammock. At the far end, the little theatre where some of her plays were staged also houses the puppet theatre whose boards were trod by the 137 life-like marionnettes (made by Maurice Sand but dressed by his mother) now displayed in an outhouse.

Upstairs you can visit Chopin's rooms and the pretty blue bedroom where George Sand slept as a teenager, and again at the end of her life. A stroll round the well-kept garden brings you to the little burial ground near the house where you can pay your respects to the family's graves. The church outside is dilapidated but worth a quick look, and lunch or dinner in the rustic restaurant of the village inn★ rounds off a highly atmospheric visit.

The George Sand trail

Within a short distance of Nohant and La Châtre are a dozen or so places connected with George Sand and her novels.

Just north of Nohant, **Vic** has a Romanesque church whose frescoes the novelist was instrumental in saving. Nearby **Saint-Chartier** is the setting for parts of her novel *Les Mâitres Sonneurs* (1852–3). An international festival takes place here during the weekend nearest to 14 July, Le Festival des Mâitres Sonneurs, that attracts players of the traditional musical instruments that feature in this novel (see box, p. 15). East of Saint-Chartier, the Château de Coudray at **Verneuil-sur-Igneraie** (known for its pottery: *mazagrans* have traditionally been made here, see box, p. 54) is where the young Aurore Dudevant met Jules Sandeau, whose name was to inspire her own pen name.

Saint-Chartier

Jules Sandeau

West of Saint-Chartier you can see the 'Devil's Pond' that gave its name to *La Mare au Diable* (1846), in the Bois de Chanteloube near **Mers-sur-Indre**, and imagine Germain and Marie losing their way in the eerie autumn mist.

Montipouret appears in *François le Champi* (1850), but is visited chiefly because nearby you can still see the **Moulin d'Angibault**, the watermill from *Le Meunier d'Angibault* (1845). The same novel largely takes place in the medieval castle of **Sarzay**, rechristened 'Blanchemont'. It, too, is in the process of being restored, though not without a major battle between the owner and the conservation Establishment (see box p. 212).

This highly picturesque castle, with its cylindrical pepperpot towers shooting skywards out of a bed of green meadows, is a delight to visit. As you walk through the gateway you are met by goats and cockerels, guineafowl and Muscovy ducks, carthorses and the odd peacock – a true *basse cour* (farmyard) more or less as would have been found inside the outer walls in the late

The 'farmyard' entrance to Sarzay Castle

Middle Ages, when a fortress had to be self-sufficient in case of invasion and siege. The idea has been to re-create something of the atmosphere of a French rural castle towards the end of the 14th century, when a feudal lord called Mathieu de Barbançois built Sarzay to repel marauding English troops during the Hundred Years War.

As well as the four tall, machicolated corner towers and the fifth staircase turret, another thirty-eight watchtowers were originally spaced out along two sets of surrounding walls, and the moat was crossed by four drawbridges. Children will enjoy hearing about all this, and then you can wander about inside the surviving structure, admiring old stone fireplaces, bread ovens hollowed out in the thickness of the walls, original tiling and the superb wheel-shaped rafters supporting the tower roofs.

You can savour the atmosphere to the full by staying in the *gîte* in the farmhouse, or in one of several B & B guestrooms in an adjoining building.

A late 20th-century hero

A modest Electricity Board employee living in the depths of the Berry unexpectedly became a folk hero and a darling of the media when he came up against the entrenched conservatism – and innate snobbery – of the guardians of France's architectural heritage.

In 1982, Richard Hurbain fell in love with medieval **Sarzay Castle**, a ruin with a proud past and a literary pedigree as the setting for one of George Sand's novels. He promptly bought it, for 790,000 francs – the price of a small house in the Paris suburb where he lived with his wife, a nurse, and three small sons. The place was in a sorry state. It had not been lived in since 1722, and floors had fallen in, walls and towers collapsed. The chapel had been taken over by chickens.

Undeterred, he set to with enthusiasm to restore his castle, expecting to get some help from the State – it was a listed building after all. Eventually, after thirteen years of applying for grants, he was given a derisory 50,000 francs. Meanwhile, he had consulted the local archives, taught himself about medieval military architecture, and rebuilt the walls and towers single-handed, using chunks of masonry he had rooted out all over the area, and faithfully following the original plans. He gradually filled the rooms with old furniture and farming tools. And he even started digging out the moat, which had been filled in over the centuries.

This proved to be the sticking point for the conservation Establishment. Claiming that he was no expert, and could easily have damaged the foundations in excavating the moat, and anyway he shouldn't have done any work without consulting them, they took him to court for infringing rules governing 'historic monuments'. With support from various associations and sympathetic experts, he fought back. He now seems to have avoided the hefty fine – or even prison – with which he was threatened. But the whole sorry story has raised questions in the media about how France looks after its heritage.

Key data

La Chatre 36400
T.O. sq. George-Sand, ☎ 02-54-48-22-64
Access Paris 299km, Argenton-sur-Creuse 39km, Châteauroux 36km, Issoudun 44km, Saint-Amand-Montrond 52km; **buses** from Châteauroux, Nohant, Châteaumeillant, Culan
Sights **Musée George Sand et de la Vallée Noire**, 71 rue Venôse, ☎ 02-54-48-36-79, closed Jan
Lunch La Châtre, Nohant, Saint-Chartier
Staying La Châtre, Nohant, Saint-Chartier
Also Châteaumeillant

Nohant-Vic 36400
T.O. 'Escapade en Berry', pl. de Nohant, ☎ 02-54-31-07-37
Access La Châtre 5km, Châteauroux 30km; **buses** from La Châtre, Châteauroux, Châteaumeillant, Culan
Sights **Maison de George Sand**, ☎ 02-54-31-06-04, open year-round
Lunch Nohant, Montipouret
Staying Nohant, Saint-Chartier, La Châtre, Ardentes

Château de Sarzay (medieval castle)
36230 Sarzay, ☎ 02-54-31-32-25 (La Châtre 7km, Nohant 6km), open year-round

26 The Creuse Valley

Argenton-sur-Creuse

The river Creuse winds picturesquely through the attractive little town of Argenton-sur-Creuse, which makes a good centre for exploring the river valley. From the 17th-century bridge, **Le Vieux Pont**, you can enjoy delightful views of the old houses, some with overhanging verandahs or carved wooden balustrades, tumbling down the hillside to the river. As you climb up the narrow streets to the pilgrimage chapel of **Notre-Dame des Bancs**, topped by a glittering statue of the Virgin Mary (more lovely views from the terrace), you will spot many a Renaissance doorway or old stone turret. On the other side of the river, the busy traffic-free **Grande Rue** is full of tempting *charcuteries* and confectioners.

Argenton was long a cloth-making town and has recently celebrated the fact by opening the **Musée de la Chemiserie et de l'élé-gance masculine** (Museum of Shirt-making and Male Chic). The well-displayed collections take you through the history of masculine dress, from scratchy medieval tunics woven from hemp, or even nettle fibres, to romantic billowing 19th-century shirts worn with floppy ties

Museum of Male Chic

Houses with overhanging verandahs at Argenton-sur-Creuse

and cravats, and modern soft and silky luxury models still made in the area, for upmarket makes like Pierre Cardin or Christian Dior. Some interesting sociological observations are made on matters such as changing attitudes to cleanliness – for instance, in the 19th century well-off bourgeois families would send their laundry to England.

Living archeology

Just outside the town to the west, at **Saint-Marcel**, is another well-planned modern museum, the **Musée archéologique d'Argentomagus**. This museum is on the site of the Gallo-Roman settlement from which Argenton developed, and is built round the excavations that continued there for many years. The idea was to create a 'living museum', and the emphasis is on teaching children about the early inhabitants of the Berry. Much use is made of video presentations, lighting effects, demonstrations (with audience participation) – of arrow shooting, writing on wax tablets and the like – designed to win over the most recalcitrant museum-haters.

Since the site was never built over, but simply became farmland (mainly used for vine-growing), it is remarkably complete: you can visit the theatre and clamber around streets and temples both outside and beneath the museum. A highlight is the little domestic altar, the only one of its kind from ancient Gaul to have survived.

Southwards from Argenton

Gargilesse-Dampierre

The attractive stretch of the Creuse Valley winding towards the Massif Central, surrounded by pastoral scenery and often lined by steep cliffs, has long been popular with painters. Picturesque **Gargilesse-Dampierre**, 13km from Argenton, still has its artists' colony, and is also on the George Sand trail (see box, p. 209). The novelist first visited the village in 1849 and made regular visits from 1857 onwards, setting several of her novels there. The **Villa Algira** has been turned into a small museum by her grand-daughter Aurore and gives a good idea of how she lived there, roping in the local children to join her butterfly-catching expeditions, writing, entertaining artists and writers.

In one of her books, *Promenades autour d'un village*, she describes Gargilesse and its chief glory, the Romanesque church built into the walls of the ruined medieval castle, which was rebuilt in the 18th century. The lively carved scenes on the capitals are not easy to see but it is worth persevering (binoculars are useful). Here are Samson and Delilah, Daniel in the Lions' Den, a Nativity, a bevy of bulls' heads, and the four-and-twenty elders of the *Book of Revelation*, arranged in groups of threes. Equally lively are the wonderfully preserved frescoes in the crypt, in soft ochres and terracottas. The Three Kings seem to be offering a bowl of fruit rather than frankincense and myrrh, while their groom sits patiently waiting on a rock, clutching the horses' bridles. I particularly like the solid-looking donkey in the Flight into Egypt, and the dead clambering shakily out of their coffins at the Resurrection.

Sculptural detail

Medieval frescoes

In August, the church is the setting for concerts staged as part of Gargilesse's International Harp Festival, started over thirty years ago. Art exhibitions are held in an outbuilding of the château and elsewhere throughout the summer.

Beyond here the valley continues to the ruins of **Châteaubrun Castle**, which feature in two Sand novels, and the **Lac de Chambon**, popular with watersports enthusiasts. **Eguzon-Chantôme** has a small local history and crafts museum, the **Musée de la Vallée de la Creuse**. At the southern end of the lake are the ruins of **Crozant**, a 13th-century fortress.

You next come to **Fresselines**, home of the Berry poet Maurice Rollinat (see box, p. 216). It is much visited by art lovers, as its site, overlooking the confluence of the Creuse with one of its tributaries, so appealed to one of Rollinat's visitors, the painter Claude Monet, that he embarked on a series of canvases here (see box, p. 217).

The River Creuse at Fresselines

Maurice Rollinat

When Claude Monet first visited Fresselines (see box, p. 217), he was accompanied by the poet Maurice Rollinat, who was born at the end of 1846 in Châteauroux.

Rollinat initially earned his living as a civil servant, publishing his first collection of poems, *Dans les Brandes*, when he was in his early thirties. Many of these describe the peaceful Berry countryside, but later his work was influenced by Baudelaire and Edgar Allan Poe, blending realism with an elegaic *Angst* that is well summed up in the title of his best-known collection, *Névroses* or 'Neuroses' (1883).

He was a talented musician, too, setting some of Baudelaire's poems to music, and often singing songs of his own composition at literary bars and cafés in Paris.

But he increasingly became prey to bouts of melancholia and abandoned metropolitan life to settle in the quiet Creuse Valley, where he became a passionate angler. Yet he continued to write and played host to many a writer and painter. His illustrious visitors often referred in their letters to the delicious meals he had cooked, his speciality being spit-roasted fish.

As his illness worsened he made three attempts at suicide and eventually died in a clinic on the outskirts of Paris at the age of fifty-six. The museum in La Châtre (p. 208) has several display cases devoted to his life and work.

Key data

ARGENTON-SUR-CREUSE 36200
T.O. 13 pl. de la République, ☎ 02-54-24-28-13
Access Paris 300km, Châteauroux 31km, La Châtre 39km; **rail** from Paris-Austerlitz, Châteauroux, **buses** from Châteauroux, Le Blanc
Sights **Musée de la Chemiserie et de l'élégance masculine** (history of male dress), rue Charles-Brillaud, ☎ 02-54-24-34-69, open mid-Feb to end Dec; **Notre-Dame des Bancs** (pilgrimage chapel); **Musée archéologique d'Argentomagus** (archeology), Saint-Marcel, ☎ 02-54-24-47-31, open year-round
Lunch Argenton, Tendu
Staying Argenton, Bouësse, Gargilesse
Also La Brenne

CREUSE VALLEY
GARGILESSE-DAMPIERRE 36190
T.O. Le Pigeonnier, ☎ 02-54-47-85-06/02-54-47-83-11
Access Argenton-sur-Creuse 13km
Sights **Eglise Notre-Dame** (Romanesque church); **Villa Algira** (George Sand's house), ☎ 02-54-47-84-14, open Apr to early Nov
Lunch Gargilesse-Dampierre
Staying Gargilesse-Dampierre, Argenton-sur-Creuse

Musée de la Vallée de la Creuse
Rue Athanase-Bassinet, 36270 Eguzon-Chantôme, ☎ 02-54-47-47-75, open June to end Sep, otherwise by appointment.

Monet at Fresselines

The Impressionist painter Claude Monet liked to embark on 'campaigns' to places that had attracted his painter's eye, generally staying there for several weeks at a time and working on the same scenes in different lights. He first visited the Creuse Valley in early 1889, with the writer Gustave Geoffroy. The two of them were shown round by a friend of Geoffroy's, the Berry poet Maurice Rollinat (see box, p. 216), who was then living in Fresselines. When Rollinat took them to a local beauty spot to admire the spectacular views down into the deep gorge carved out by the river, Monet was so enthusiastic that he returned in early March and set about painting a series of canvases that he hoped to exhibit in Paris alongside sculptures by Auguste Rodin.

Despite appalling weather, with bitter winds that forced him to paint in gloves and smear the inside of them with glycerine to soothe his chapped hands, he soldiered on. When beautiful weather at last arrived towards the beginning of May, he was distraught at the changes he found, writing to his wife Alice of his disappointment, after a three-week absence, at being so dazzled by the light reflected off the water that he felt he might be forced to abandon the series. The arrival of spring caused another problem, too. He eventually had to hand over 50 francs – and call on the local priest to intercede for him – for permission to have the leaves stripped off a venerable oak that appeared in five of his canvases, so that he could finish the winter scenes as he had first seen them.

27 La Brenne

The strange stretch of marshy land known as La Brenne lies in the southwest corner of the Berry. Most of this often mysterious, sometimes desolate, nearly always beautiful region of some 1300 reed-fringed meres and wooded hills was officially designated a nature reserve (the **Parc naturel régional de la Brenne**) in 1989. It is particularly rich in wildlife and is popular with nature lovers, especially ornithologists eager to spot the 250-odd species of birds that can be seen here, well over half of the species found in the whole of Europe. Some, like the gadwall, are very rare. Mallards and pochards, bearded tits, black tailed godwits and black-necked grebes, great reed warblers, whiskered terns and marsh harriers, bitterns, purple herons and snipe all haunt the Brenne.

250 bird species

Botanists are in their element too: the meres, originally dug by monks from the local monasteries to provide water for their flocks, are surrounded by meadows where gentians and orchids grow. Then the cistalo or cistude, also known as the European pond tortoise, can be spotted plunging into waters where fish farmers breed carp and tench, roach and pike. And the Brenne also has a deer park, the **Parc animalier de la Haute-Touche**.

European pond tortoises

217

The Etang de la Gabrière

This is also a place to ponder the widespread survival of belief in witchcraft in the Berry. When the mist hovers over the meres and meadows you, too, may well think you can see will-o'-the-wisps and the goblins and ghosts that people the legends of the Berry (see box, p. 16).

Nature-watching is well organized. You can visit specialist reserves (see box) and join nature walks or bird-watching expeditions. The observatories are open free of charge (bring your own binoculars) and most of the well-designed information panels are in English as well as French. The village of **Mézières-en-Brenne** is the best place to start: its tourist office is packed with leaflets on local flora and fauna, brochures about walking tours and riding or biking parties, the staff are particularly helpful, and it also houses the **Maison de la Pisciculture**, an information centre on things aquatic, with aquaria full of local species of fish. An organization called **La Randonnée de la Brenne** (℗ 02-54-38-12-24) offers guided group walks three times a year: a day's outing, complete with meals, in May and October, and a three-day weekend outing in August, with the nights spent in well-equipped tents.

Specialist nature reserves

Etang de Bellebouche
℗ 02-54-38-32-36, open May to Sep, three observatories; also watersports

Parc animalier de la Haute-Touche
Obterre (5km north of Azay-le-Ferron), ℗ 02-54-39-20-82, open Easter to end Oct; deer park plus antelopes, llamas, monkeys, wolves

Réserve naturelle de Chérine
Open end Apr to end Aug; observatory (good place for spotting European pond tortoises); guided tours

Réserve ornithologique de la Gabrière
Birdwatching centre south of Chérine reserve, ℗ 02-54-37-47-47

Mézières is also the starting point of a 35km signposted itinerary called the **Circuit des Etangs de la Brenne** (*étang* being the French term for a mere, large pond or small lake).

Mézières

If you like combining nature study with sightseeing, the Brenne does have some sights too, and a few small villages worth exploring. Mézières itself has an interesting church with a Renaissance chapel, and the remains of its château have been attractively restored: the Maison de la Pisciculture is in one of its turrets. **Méobecq** has an exceptionally tall abbey church with a Romanesque apse, originally consecrated in 1048 and part of an abbey founded some four centuries earlier. Its design is unusual, with tall square-cut piers.

Méobecq

South of Mézières, near Rosnay, the **Château du Bouchet**, a medieval castle, can be visited. It has a collection of stuffed animals and birds from La Brenne, which can be admired before or after a visit to the nearby **Etang de la Mer Rouge**.

On the northwest edge of the Brenne, the **Château d'Azay-le-Ferron** is set in lovely formal gardens. The architecture is mostly Renaissance, though the fortified cylindrical tower is earlier. It has a fine collection of furniture, much of it 19th-century.

Fontgombault Abbey

The pleasant town of Le Blanc can be used as a base for exploring the Brenne, but has little to see apart from the **Ecomusée de la Brenne et du Pays Blancois**. This is a small natural and local history museum

Ecomuseum

Key data

Parc naturel régional de la Brenne
Info   Maison du Parc, Le Bouchet, 36300 Rosnay,
        Ⓣ 02-54-28-12-13
T.O.   Le Moulin, 1 rue du Nord, 36290 Mézières-en-Brenne,
        Ⓣ 02-54-38-12-24, Ⓕ 02-54-38-13-76
Access (to Mézières-en-Brenne) Paris 277km, Le Blanc 27km,
        Châteauroux 41km; **buses** from Châteauroux to Mézières
        and Méobecq, changing in Le Blanc
Sights **Ecomusée de la Brenne**, Château Naillac, Le Blanc,
        Ⓣ 02-54-37-25-20, open May to end Dec; **Maison de la**
        Pisciculture, pl. Jean-Moulin, Mézières-en-Brenne,
        Ⓣ 02-54-38-12-99; **Château d'Azay-le-Ferron**,
        Ⓣ 02-54-39-20-06, closed Jan
Lunch Mézières-en-Brenne, Lingé
Staying Mézières-en-Brenne, Lingé, Le Blanc, Argenton-sur-Creuse,
        Buzançais

Château du Bouchet
36300 Rosnay, Ⓣ 02-54-37-82-89, open year-round
Notre-Dame de Fontgombault
36220 Fontgombault, Ⓣ 02-54-37-12-03, open year-round

Benedictine abbey

with permanent displays on the Brenne and the work of naturalists past and present. But 8km further west along the river Creuse is the very interesting **Notre-Dame de Fontgombault**, a well-restored Benedictine abbey originally founded towards the end of the 11th century.

The first abbot was Pierre de l'Etoile, whose recumbent effigy can be seen inside the abbey church. Its Romanesque chancel with five radiating chapels has survived intact, and the view from outside, with the cluster of chapels surmounted by a tall cupola over the crossing, is magnificent. The nave and many of the abbey buildings were restored in the 19th century by a devoted local priest, after over a century of neglect following its dissolution in 1741 and the usual depredations at the time of the French Revolution. A community of Trappist monks settled there in 1849, but the abbey has now reverted to the Benedictine order and a group of monks from Solesmes Abbey near Le Mans has moved in. Solesmes has long been famous for its beautiful Gregorian chant and you can listen to masses with Gregorian chant at Fontgombault too, usually at 10.00 and 17.00 on Sundays, and at 18.00 the rest of the week (℡ 02-54-37-12-03 to check).

Pottery

The church is much visited for the Romanesque stone statue of the Virgin Mary in the right-hand aisle, alleged to bring succour to those on the point of death. Many visitors also come to buy the attractive glazed pottery made by the monks.

28 Châteauroux, Issoudun

Châteauroux

Home of Gitanes

Châteauroux, the busy capital of the Indre *département*, is an important industrial centre (Gitanes, those archetypal French cigarettes, are made there) but is well endowed with gardens. It has some interesting buildings, too, and as it is on the fast Paris-Toulouse rail line and well served by buses, it could make a convenient jumping-off point for visiting George Sand country (pp. 208–11).

Shopping

The **Forêt de Châteauroux** to the south offers pleasant walks, as well as providing the game that features predominantly on local menus. One regional speciality to look out for is *pâté de judelle*, *judelle* meaning 'coot'. You may well find this in the town's excellent *charcuteries*, as Châteauroux is a good place for shopping, with many confectioners selling Berry treats like *lichouneries*, and a good open-air flea market on the first Sunday of the month from October to June.

Another local *charcuterie* speciality is *andouille de Déols*. **Déols** is now a suburb of Châteauroux, but was once much more important. A major Gallo-Roman town, it became a prosperous centre in the early Middle Ages after the building, in 917, of a large Benedictine abbey. The tall Romanesque bell tower of the abbey church is all that has survived, with some lovely carved capitals at the base. The surrounding monastery buildings (gradually being restored) were so extensive that the feudal lord Raoul de Déols had a new residence built on the other

Napoleon's faithful companion

Henri Gratien, Comte Bertrand, born in Châteauroux in 1771, was Napoleon's aide-de-camp early in his career and became one of his most loyal generals.

He accompanied his hero into exile on Elba, and then a year later, in July 1815, after the Battle of Waterloo and Napoleon's second abdication, insisted on sharing the ex-emperor's banishment to distant St Helena. He remained faithful to the end and was at Napoleon's side when he died in 1821. He presided over his funeral on the island, and nearly twenty years later was among the little expedition that brought his remains back to France and the poignant ceremony at Les Invalides in Paris.

In 1830 he had been appointed to the post of commandant of the élite Ecole Polytechnique in the capital. And he had also written a biography of Napoleon. He retired to his home town, where he died in 1844, in the house that is now a museum devoted, among many other things, to Napoleon's life and times (see below). His own remains were moved to Les Invalides three years later, so that he could be at his emperor's side in death, as he had always been in life.

side of the river Indre. This **Château Raoul** gave birth to a new town that became known, after various distortions, as 'Châteauroux'.

Lord Raoul's castle was badly damaged during a siege by Philippe Auguste in the early 13th century, and was eventually rebuilt some two hundred years later, with an octagonal central tower. It can still be seen at one end of the town, picturesquely reached via the **Porte Saint-Martin**. It was the birthplace of Châteauroux's most famous son, Henri Gatien Bertrand, a Napoleonic general (see box).

General Bertrand's home is now an art and local history museum, the **Musée Bertrand**, with interesting Napoleonic collections. Close by are the 13th-century **Eglise Saint-Martial**, with a later belfry, and the **Couvent des Cordeliers**, also 13th-century, now used for exhibitions and concerts. Behind this building you can enjoy pretty views over the Indre valley and admire a restored **wash-house** in the rue du Gué-aux-Chevaux.

Strolling between this cluster of buildings and the Château Raoul, you come across many half-timbered medieval houses and some fine 17th- and 18th-century mansions. Start in the **rue Grande**, beside Saint-Martial. If you turn off to the right shortly after the museum you come to rue Claude-Pinette, which leads to the **rue des Pavillons**. Turn left to walk along this interesting street as far as the **rue du Grand-Mouton**. At the far end, the **Grande Echelle** brings you to the **rue de l'Indre**, with many attractive houses. Return via the Grande Echelle to the **rue des Notaires**. The rue Descente de Ville to the right leads to the Porte Saint-Martin, but first turn left to explore the streets leading to the **place du Palan**, where part of the fortifications has survived.

Fine old houses

On the banks of the Indre, the **Parc des Loisirs de Belle Isle** has a camp site, an open-air pool and various sports facilities, as well as pretty riverside picnic spots.

Ardentes, 15km southeast via the Indre Valley in attractive wooded countryside, has a Romanesque church, **Saint-Martin**.

A Berry star

It seems rather surprising that the quiet provincial capital of Châteauroux should have produced the larger-than-life star of countless excellent French films, **Gérard Depardieu**.

He was born here in 1948 and came from humble origins. His rough 'street kid' background has fed many a muck-raking article, but thanks to his outstanding acting abilities and his likeable manner he has managed to rise above all that to become probably France's biggest box-office draw.

His first film was Roger Leenhardt's *Le Beatnik et le Minet*. That was in 1965. Since then he has appeared in movies by most of the top French and European directors, including Alain Resnais (*Stavisky*, 1974, and *Mon Oncle d'Amérique*, 1979), Bernardo Bertolucci (*1900*, 1976), François Truffaut (the magical *Le dernier Métro*, 1980) and Andrzej Wajda (*Danton*, 1982). Although he has remained true to the theatre that was his first love, he is associated in most people's minds with the memorable figures he has impersonated on celluloid in recent years: Auguste Rodin (in *Camille Claudel*), Marcel Pagnol's Jean de Florette, Balzac's Colonel Chabert, and – a huge international success – Cyrano de Bergerac.

Issoudun

Pleasant little Issoudun, with its ancient towers, its photogenic stone bridge, its charmingly old-fashioned shops and lively open-air market, seems to have changed little since it was described by Honoré de Balzac in his novel *La Rabouilleuse*.

Honoré de Balzac

Memories of Balzac add interest to your visit: he came here often when he was visiting his friends the Carrauds (see p. 223), frequented the Auberge de la Cognette (see box), and even attempted to make his fortune by promoting the town's best-known product (see p. 224).

But Issoudun has other reasons to detain you. Strategically sited on a hill at the heart of the flat Champagne berrichonne region, at the confluence of several rivers, it was first a Gallo-Roman settlement, then a prosperous royal town in the Middle Ages, with an imposing castle of which the cylindrical keep, the **Tour blanche**, built by Richard the Lionheart in 1202, is still standing, attractively surrounded by a garden. Nearby is the **beffroi** (belfry), in fact one of the massive gateways in the long-vanished castle walls. Also in the town centre, **Saint-Cyr**, a collegiate church possibly founded by Charlemagne, has good medieval stained glass and carved choir stalls.

A modern artwork

Behind the town hall, and surrounded by elegant 17th- and 18th-century mansions, Issoudun has rather surprisingly acquired a very modern 'installation', **La Place des Miroirs**, by German sculptor Marin Kasimir. This complex of eight large mirrored screens is adorned with 'anthropomorphic' letters spelling out the town's name, except for the initial 'I', which is involuntarily added by passers-by as they are reflected in the mirrors.

Another recent innovation is the modern building added in 1995 to the **Hospice Saint-Roch**, attractively set beside the river Théols. This beautiful group of buildings, with a medieval core centring on a charming garden, and two 17th- and 18th-century wings, was once a hospital specializing in treating plague victims (St Roch or St Rock, Italy's San Rocco, allegedly achieved miraculous cures during a plague epidemic). It is now a museum displaying both contemporary and ancient art (and most unusually charges no entrance fee). A modern bronze adorns the garden and the painting collection includes a startling canvas by Alfred Courmes (who died in 1993 at the age of 95) of St Roch in bowler, rolled-up shirt-sleeves and waist-coat, with his trousers dropped round his ankles to show the plague pustules on his upper thigh.

Museum of art

The highlight of the medieval sculpture collection is the double **Tree of Jesse** in the chapel, its interlaced branches – oak on one side, fig on the other – swarming with high relief saints and biblical figures clearly carved from life, as each face is full of character. Do allow plenty of time to enjoy this superb decoration, which reminds me of Indian sculpture in its very three dimensional treatment and its mass of figures. But don't miss the well-displayed pharmacy collection.

Modern Issoudon is known for its leather goods. Another speciality is Reuilly wine, from a village that also produces goat's cheeses.

Balzac's 'angel of friendship'

One of the novelist Honoré de Balzac's most loyal women friends – though never his mistress – was born in Issoudun in 1796. The youngest child of a Republican-minded draper, Zulma Carraud (née Tourangin) became a close friend of Balzac's sister Laure at boarding school.

A short, lively woman with a slight limp, she had, according to a well-known painting by Edmond Viénot, rather masculine features, with a decided chin and a straight mouth. When she was twenty she married a second cousin, an artillery captain fifteen years older, François-Michel Carraud, and two years later moved with him to Saint-Cyr-l'Ecole near Paris, as he had been appointed director of studies at the famous military academy there. Laure Balzac had meanwhile married and was living nearby in Versailles. The two couples became close and Honoré, who often visited his sister, soon met Zulma.

They apparently embarked on what the French call an *amitié amoureuse*, an intimate (but not sexual) friendship, and corresponded until Balzac's death. Zulma became a kind of safety valve, once writing that she acted as a refrigerator 'when you are about to go up in steam'. Balzac often stayed with the Carrauds at Frapesle, outside Issoudun.

Three days after his wedding to Madame Hanska in 1850, he wrote Zulma a grateful letter, referring to Saint-Cyr, Frapesle and Angoulême, where he had 'gathered strength ... assuaged my longings'. A few months later he was dead, but Zulma lived on for another half-century, dying in 1899 at the age of ninety-three – a famous author herself.

The Carrauds had retired to Nohant-en-Graçay in the Berry. In teaching the village children to read and write she discovered her vocation. In 1852 she published a moralizing tale for girls, *La Petite Jeanne, ou Le Devoir*, which became a bestseller and was awarded a prize by the Académie française. A year later came a boys' title, *Maurice, ou Le Travail*, followed by many more. Right to the end of her long life she worked for the poor at Nohant, where two thousand people attended her funeral.

A historic inn

Issoudun's delightful restaurant **La Cognette**★ was once an inn run by Monsieur and Madame Cognet. The landlord had formerly been a groom in an aristocratic household before starting up the inn in the early 19th century, when he was in his mid-fifties. He was blind in one eye, possibly as a result of a riding accident. His wife, about fifteen years younger, was an attractive and energetic woman who soon built up a reputation for her excellent cuisine.

The novelist Honoré de Balzac, a frequent visitor to Issoudun thanks to his friendship with Zulma Carraud (see box, p. 223), was a regular from about 1823 to 1830, speaking of the Cognets warmly in his letters. He also describes the Auberge de la Cognette, as it was then called, in his novel *La Rabouilleuse*, which is largely set in Issoudun.

Key data

CHÂTEAUROUX 36000
T.O.   pl. de la Gare, ℡ 02-54-34-10-74
Access Paris 266km, Issoudun 29km, Argenton-sur-Creuse 31km, Bourges 67km; **rail** from Paris-Austerlitz, Issoudun, Argenton-sur-Creuse; **buses** from Argenton-sur-Creuse, Bourges, Châteaumeillant, La Châtre, Culan, Nohant
Sights **Château Raoul** (medieval castle); **Couvent des Cordeliers** (medieval monastery), open during exhibitions; **Eglise Saint-Martial** (Romanesque church); **Musée Bertrand** (fine and applied art, archeology, local history, Napoleonic rooms), 2 rue Descente-des-Cordeliers, ℡ 02-54-08-33-49, open year-round, closed Mon (pm only mid-Sep to June)
Lunch Châteauroux, Ardentes
Staying Châteauroux, Issoudun, Ardentes
Also Issoudun, Nohant, Argenton-sur-Creuse

ISSOUDUN 36100
T.O.   pl. Saint-Cyr, ℡ 02-54-21-74-57
Access Paris 243km, Châteauroux 29km, Bourges 38km; **rail** from Paris-Austerlitz, Châteauroux; **buses** from Bourges, Châteauroux
Sights **Beffroi** and **Tour blanche** (remains of medieval castle); **Eglise Saint-Cyr** (Gothic church); **Musée de l'Hospice Saint-Roch** (medieval and contemporary art, pharmacy), rue de l'Hospice-Saint-Roch, ℡ 02-54-21-01-76, closed Jan, also Tue from Nov to Apr (pm only winter weekdays), and Mon and Tue from Apr to Oct); **Place des Miroirs** (sculpture installation), pl. de l'Hôtel-de-Ville
Lunch Issoudun, Diou, Saint-Outrille
Staying Issoudun
Also Châteauroux

Berry ~ southeast

The south-east of the Berry is quiet and rural, a green land of gentle hills and rolling meadows dotted with clumps of trees. It is nowadays crossed by the A71 motorway, which continues on south into the Auvergne region. But its roads generally carry little traffic, and despite several important sights, like the beautiful Cistercian **Abbaye de Noirlac**, the châteaux at **Meillant** and **Ainay-le-Vieil**, and impressive **Culan Castle**, it has never become a major tourist area.

This means that you are most unlikely to meet crowds. However, the other side of the coin of being off the beaten track in tourist terms is that getting about without a car is not easy, especially out of termtime. But several sights are only a short taxi ride from the pleasant little town of **Saint-Amand-Montrond**, which is served by trains from Paris. And the quiet roads and gentle hills make this good cycling country. For keen walkers, the **GR41** hiking trail passes through Culan.

29 Around Saint-Amand-Montrond

The small and prosperous-seeming town of **Saint-Amand-Montrond**, with a lively open-air food market on Wednesdays and Saturdays, makes a good base for exploring the châteaux and churches in the surrounding pastoral countryside, dotted with white cows. But it is not without interest itself, not least because it enjoys something of a reputation as the Berry's 'culinary capital'. Its *charcuteries* and confectioners' are good places to buy local specialities (see **Food and drink**), including the goat's cheese known by the town's name.

Saint-Amand-Montrond

Local specialities

The town's name comes from the saint who founded a monastery on the site in the early 7th century, and is honoured in the **Eglise Saint-Amand**, a Romanesque church in an attractive district of old streets in the town centre. The main portal, topped by a row of little heads, is flanked by other doorways, with clusters of columns and decorative rounded arches. The effect is particularly fine at night, when the west front is illuminated, but do also walk round to admire the chancel with its radiating chapels. Inside, the Romanesque sculpture on the capitals is well worth studying in detail.

Romanesque sculpture

A short walk away is the **Musée Saint-Vic**, housed in a Renaissance mansion reached through a pretty garden. It is essentially a local

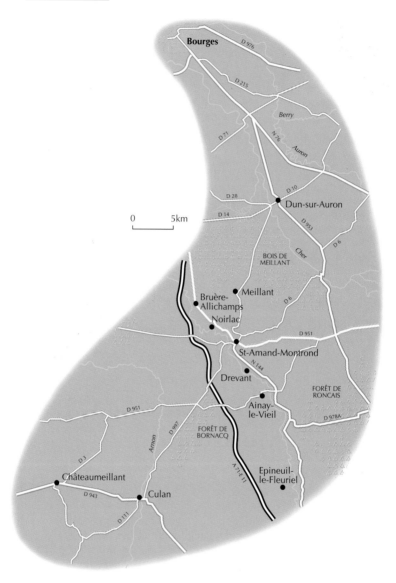

history museum, with a good collection of Gallo-Roman finds.

On the strategic 'round hill' (*mont rond*) that forms the rest of the town's name are the ruins of the **castle**, dating back to the late 10th century, frequently enlarged, and bought in 1605 by Henri IV's minister just before he was created Duc de Sully. At the same time he acquired a number of other Berry estates, including Culan (pp. 234–5). Sixteen years later he sold Saint-Amand on to Henri II de Bourbon-Condé. The Condés turned the medieval castle into a mighty stronghold. But ownership by one of France's leading noble families was not always a blessing, and when they became involved in the Fronde rebellions, the fortress was besieged for a full ten months by the royal troops, in 1651–2, and eventually razed.

The Condés

Noirlac Abbey

In the Cher valley just north-west of Saint-Amand, surrounded by meadows, lies the lovely **Abbaye de Noirlac**, built in pale honey-coloured local stone. Now beautifully restored, it is well known for its summer concert season.

It was founded in the mid-12th century by monks from Clairvaux and is a particularly pure example of the austere early architectural style adopted by the Cistercians, though the graceful decorated arches in the **cloisters**, dating from the 13th and 14th centuries, show how the sobriety of the early style was later softened.

The model displayed in the building where you buy your ticket (with a good bookshop and display panels on the Cistercian Order and

Noirlac Abbey: the refectory

the life led by the monks) shows that the abbey and monastery buildings are remarkably complete. The pure lines of the **church**, built on a simple plan with a straight-ended chancel, create a feeling of serenity that is enhanced by the modern stained glass, in soft pink and grey tones. It is strange to think that after the French Revolution, this glorious space was used as a china factory – the purple tinge at the bottom of the columns, caused by the heat from the kilns, is the only clue to this sacrilege.

The nave of the church runs along one side of the cloisters, while the other buildings, as is usual in Cistercian monasteries, are grouped round the other sides. You can visit the **salle capitulaire** (chapter-house), the **scriptorium**, **the monks' dormitory** on the floor above (divided into a series of small panelled cells in the less ascetic 17th century) and, on the south side, the **refectory**. To the west is the large **bâtiment des convers**, part of which has disappeared. Here the lay brothers were in charge of the ground floor *cellier*, used to store food, wine and grain, and slept in the upstairs dormitory.

Explanatory panels in both English and French tell you about the way the various rooms were used and guided tours are also available. To add to your enjoyment, there is a pleasant restaurant right opposite the abbey.★

About 4km northwest of the abbey, a Gallo-Roman milestone at **Bruère-Alli-champs** may, or may not, mark the exact centre of France (see box, p. 63).

Meillant

Renaissance highlight

The **Château de Meillant**, in the little village of the same name just north of Saint-Amand, is a highlight of the Route Jacques-Coeur and one of the loveliest châteaux in central France, set in gardens where peacocks flaunt their plumage.

The site was once a Roman settlement, over which a feudal castle was built, complete with ramparts, moats and seven tall towers. One of its lords, Ebbes de Charenton, restored the castle in 1127, and nine years later founded the Abbaye de Noirlac (see p. 227). A century later Meillant had become, through marriage, a possession of the lords of Sancerre, one of whom built the Gothic **Tour des Cerfs** towards the end of the 13th century. But the château we see today is largely Renaissance, thanks to Charles d'Amboise, governor of Milan, whose family had, once again, acquired it through marriage.

Italian team

When Charles returned from fighting in Italy he brought in his luggage a fine collection of paintings, marble sculptures and much else besides, and in his retinue, a team of Italian architects, sculptors and painters, including Fra Giocondo, who had worked with Michelangelo on St Peter's in Rome. These Italian artists and craftsmen transformed the medieval castle into a grand early Renaissance residence. They created a richly decorative east façade, adding a polygonal staircase tower, the **Tour du Lion**, which offers a good illustration of how the Late (or Flamboyant) Gothic style developed under the influence of Renaissance artists. The delicate, lace-like carving is witty in its exuberance: *trompe l'oeil* figures peer out from behind pillars, bearded 'wild men of the woods' clutch shields, and elaborately fluted columns and pictorial coats of arms are everywhere. The richness of this façade – which includes two elegant dormer windows unlike anything elsewhere in France, described by the sculptor Auguste Rodin as 'as lovely as the headdresses worn by Breton girls' – contrasts interestingly with the sober west façade dating from two centuries earlier and reflected in the old moats. Equally elaborate is the free-standing **chapel**, with a Flemish altarpiece swarming with carved figures depicting Christ's Passion.

Madame de Montespan

The interior is richly decorated too, particularly the **Grand Salon** with its painted ceiling beams, its huge fireplace topped by a musicians' gallery, its tapestries and paintings, including one of Louis XIV's mistress Madame de Montespan, an ancestor of the present owners. The dining room has another monumental fireplace, and a carved and coffered ceiling, while the brightly coloured Gothic vaulting in the **Salle du Lit de Justice** boasts curious little grotesque figures, including crouching jesters in motley. The monks and soldiers carved on the ceiling in the **Galerie des Césars** are equally vigorous, though this room is mainly visited for its classical sculptures collected by Charles d'Amboise, now set in medallions.

Meillant survived the Revolution virtually intact, thanks to the popularity locally of the Duc de Charost, whose family had inherited the lordship. His wife's descendants still live in the château today, giving it the feeling of a stately home rather than a museum. For instance the chairs in the Grand Salon are arranged companionably in groups, as though their occupants had just gone out for a stroll in the grounds.

A medieval garden

Bringing 'forgotten' vegetables back to the dining table is in vogue these days. But at the early 12th-century **priory of Notre-Dame d'Orsan**, south-west of Saint-Amand-Montrond, Patrice Tavarella and Sonia Lesot have gone a stage further and resuscitated a forgotten style of gardening: the intensive horticulture practised in medieval monasteries.

These two architects from Paris, with virtually no previous experience of gardening, started by restoring the abandoned priory, then moved on to planting, training young trees to form screens enclosing secret little 'rooms and cloisters of greenery', as they like to call them. The overall design is based on careful study of medieval manuscripts and drawings, and on the principles of functionalism, symbolism and aesthetics under-lying monastery gardens and orchards up to the Renaissance.

Thus the kitchen garden symbolizes the road to Jerusalem, while the stone fountain in the middle of the gardens, with its square basin, may be functional, yet also denotes the four rivers of paradise. Then the rose gar-den, a profusion of pink and white blooms, represents the Virgin Mary, the symbolism underlined by the use of Madonna lilies at the foot of the old varieties of roses.

The symbolism is explained during the guided tours, conducted by the designers or their gardeners and sometimes continuing on into the wood-land beyond the priory gardens. Other highlights are the medicinal herb gardens, used for growing over fifty different species, and the raised beds surrounded by wattle frames, bursting with splendid specimens of the gourd family, in the kitchen garden. In the *parterre de blé*, twin beds are dug in the shape of large St Andrew's crosses and planted with broad beans and wheat, to indicate the Christian ideals linked to the goal of subsistence that was one of the keys to medieval monastic life. **Prieuré Notre-Dame d'Orsan**, 18170 Maisonnais, ☎ 02-48-56-27-50, open May to end Oct.

History in miniature

I recommend that you do the same before visiting a new attraction in one of the outbuildings, **La Mini'stoire**. This offers an overview of French history in miniature: beautifully made scaled-down models of a medieval village, a Renaissance château, an elegant 18th-century drawing room and a busy 19th-century street scene, accompanied by appropriate noises off, are popular with both children and adults.

Dun-sur-Auron

Both the river Auron and the Canal du Berry flow past what remains of the medieval walls of this tiny town northeast of Meillant, beyond the Forêt de Maulne. Once a fully fortified stronghold guarding the border between the French kings' possessions and the territory of the Dukes of Aquitaine, it is now a sleepy little place that is pleasant for strolling, with its low medieval houses lining the pedestrianized **Grande-Rue**, leading to one of the old gateways in the fortifications, crowned by a tall **belfry**. Go through it and you come to the canal, and to an interesting little museum devoted to the life of the *mariniers* (boatmen) who once plied it in their barges. A lifesize reconstruction of the bargees' living quarters is popular with children.

Barge Museum

Dun-sur-Auron: detail of sculpture

Dun also has a collegiate church, the **Collégiale Saint-Etienne**, built in the transitional style between Late Romanesque and Early Gothic, but seeming more Romanesque with its fantastic creatures carved in stone. Don't miss the pelican, and biblical scenes like Daniel in the Lions' Den. Note too the unusual benches built right into the walls, with wooden divisions. The outside, built in a local reddish-coloured sandstone, is decorated with more carved scenes, moustachioed faces, and even what appear to be cats.

Ainay-le-Vieil

A personal favourite

Ainay-le-Vieil is one of my favourite French châteaux, not least because it has been lived in by the same family for over half a millennium – the descendants of the Seigneurs de Bigny who bought it in 1467, a couple of decades after it had briefly belonged to the 'medieval tycoon' Jacques Coeur (see p. 200). (The nearby Château de Bigny – not open to the public – has been in the family even longer, for over a thousand years.)

Ainay lies in the Cher valley south of Saint-Amand, in a little village of the same name that is virtually a stone's throw from the border with the old province of the Bourbonnais, and now with the modern region of Auvergne. This strategic position meant that it started life as a medieval fortress. Indeed it still appears so from the outside, with its nine sturdy cylindrical towers surmounted by pepperpot roofs, set in thick crenellated walls forming an asymmetrical octagon. But once you have crossed the moat (in fact a narrow tributary of the Cher) and walked through the huge postern gate, you discover Ainay's secret: hidden inside those forbidding walls is a graceful Renaissance residence, its delicately carved doorways, staircase tower and balconies, and its light-filled rooms, a world away from the heavy lines of the fortress lit only by arrow slits.

The guided tour includes the **Grand Salon**, whose decoration was specially designed for Louis XII and his new bride Anne of Brittany. They visited the château in 1500 and their arms and initials feature on the enormous stone fireplace: gilt fleur-de-lys on an appropriately royal-blue ground for the king, Anne's ermines below. Their portraits hang in the **dining room**, which has intricately painted ceiling beams. So does the Grand Salon, several of whose portraits are of members of the Colbert family, ancestors of the current owners. One

Family portraits

of them depicts the statesman Jean-Baptiste Colbert, Louis XIV's chief minister, after whom the **Salon Colbert**, its walls elegantly hung with bright green fabric, is named. Here and elsewhere you can admire precious objects and mementoes connected with Colbert and with other illustrious personages, like a tiny music box that belonged to Queen Marie Antoinette, or a miniature of Empress Josephine and a pair of pistols given by Napoleon to General Auguste Colbert.

The corner tower beyond the Grand Salon houses a little **chapel**, whose brightly coloured 19th-century decoration

Ainay-le-Vieil

has recently been carefully removed, to reveal delicately painted scenes in beautiful soft tones dating from over three centuries earlier. The chapel still has its 16th-century stained glass and coffered ceiling, adorned with coats of arms.

The charming rose garden, fragrant with old roses – at least one variety dates back to the early 15th century – makes a photogenic setting for views of the postern gate. Lovely views of the château and down to the moat can also be enjoyed from the **sentry walk** on top of the walls. *Rose garden*

Roughly 4km north of Ainay, on the pretty road to Saint Amand, is **Drevant**, a village where exacavations have turned up parts of a Gallo-Roman amphitheatre. *Roman ruins*

Key data

Saint-Amand-Montrond 18200
T.O. pl. de la République, ☎ 02-48-96-16-86
Access Paris 286km, Bourges 44km; **rail** from Paris-Austerlitz, Bourges; **buses** from Bourges
Sights **Eglise Saint-Amand** (Romanesque church), **Musée Saint-Vic** (local history, arts and crafts), 10 rue Philibert-Audebrand, ☎ 02-48-96-55-20, open year-round, closed Tue
Lunch Saint-Amand
Staying Saint-Amand, Farges-Allichamps

Dun-sur-Auron 18130
T.O. pl. du Châtelet, ☎ 02-48-59-85-26 (June to end Sept)
Access Saint-Amand 21km, Bourges 27km; **buses** from Saint-Amand, Bourges
Sights **ramparts**, **belfry**, **medieval houses**; **Collégiale Saint-Etienne** (Romanesque and Early Gothic church); **Musée du Canal de Berry** (life of canal boatmen), Le Châtelet, ☎ 02-48-59-50-40, open May-end Sep daily; Apr and Oct pm only, closed Sun and Mon
Lunch Dun-sur-Auron
Staying Dun-sur-Auron

Abbaye de Noirlac
18200 Bruère-Allichamps, ☎ 02-48-96-23-64 (Saint-Amand 5km, Meillant 8km), open year-round, closed Tue from Oct to Feb
Château d'Ainay-le-Vieil
18200 Ainay-le-Vieil, ☎ 02-48-63-50-67 (Saint-Amand 10km), open Feb to end Nov
Château de Meillant
18200 Meillant, ☎ 02-48-63-30-58 (Saint-Amand (bus) 7km), open Feb to mid-Dec

30 Epineuil-le-Fleuriel, Culan, Châteaumeillant

Epineuil-le-Fleuriel

This tiny village is a quiet spot these days, without even a restaurant, but it is a must for anyone interested in French literature. The writer Alain-Fournier (see box, p. 233) lived here from 1 October 1891, a couple of days before his fifth birthday, to 1898, when he was sent to school in Paris, though it was the family home until 1902.

'I like the marvellous,' he wrote to his brother-in-law Jacques Rivière in 1911, 'only when it is firmly rooted in reality.' And here you can glimpse the reality behind the magical childhood world he conjures up in *Le Grand Meaulnes*. Epineuil features as 'Sainte-Agathe', a name borrowed from a hilltop pilgrimage chapel 15km to the west. The *fête étrange* stumbled upon by Meaulnes in a 'domain without a name' was partly inspired by tales the young Fournier had heard of a splendid christening party thrown by the owner of the Château de Cornançay just west of Epineuil.

Although Alain-Fournier blends two very different landscapes some 90km apart – the green and hilly southern Berry with the marshy terrain of heath and meres in the north – the country round Epineuil seems endearingly familiar to readers of the novel, who cannot fail to be moved by the little **schoolhouse** once presided over by his parents. Thanks largely to the devoted efforts of another married couple of teachers posted to Epineuil, Andrée and Henri Lullier, who still live in the village, the school is now, not a museum, but a sort of memorial to the novel, its creator and its main protagonist, called simply **L'Ecole du Grand Meaulnes** (Le Grand Meaulnes's School). It also offers interesting insights into teaching methods at the turn of the century.

Alain-Fournier and Le Grand Meaulnes

The writer Henri Alban Fournier (known by his pseudonym of 'Alain-Fournier') was born on 3 October 1886 in La Chapelle d'Angillon (see p. 187). His father, a teacher, came from a modest Berry family in Nançay, deep in the Sologne west of La Chapelle. His mother came from La Chapelle itself, where the bulk of the summer would be spent after his father was posted in 1891 to Epineuil-le-Fleuriel.

Readers of his only novel, *Le Grand Meaulnes*, published in 1913 just a year before his death in battle, often imagine him as a dreamy introspective young man, happy only amid the beloved landscapes of his native Berry.

But this was only one side of Henri Fournier's complex character. A keen sportsman, he also became something of a young-man-about-town in Paris, frequenting literary circles, and contributing book reviews, art criticism and a column on the literary world to various journals, as well as having poetry and short stories published.

It was in Paris, too, that the key event in his life took place: his brief encounter in 1905 with Yvonne de Quièvrecourt, a beautiful, golden-haired upper-class young woman who, though he only met her again on two occasions, dominated much of his thoughts for the rest of his life and is immortalized in his novel as 'Yvonne de Galais'.

Yet his longing for this unattainable *princesse lointaine* or 'far-away princess' did not prevent him falling in love with other women. It is pleasant to know that he seems to have gone to his death happy in the knowledge that his love for the famous actress 'Madame Simone' was reciprocated.

Le Grand Meaulnes went on to be translated into over thirty languages, and is now an established classic. Its English titles include *The Lost Domain*, *The Wanderer* (also used for the 1967 film version directed by Jean-Gabriel Albicocco), *the Milk of Paradise* (a radio play), and *La Fête étrange* (a ballet).

You can take a guided tour, or a cassette in French or English (ask at the *Bâtiment d'Accueil* just before you reach the school). The classrooms with their old-style sloping-topped desks and inkwells, the kitchen and living room, the parents' bedroom (where the novelist's little sister Isabelle also slept), his own bedroom up in the attics, lit only by a tiny skylight, and the highly atmospheric attic rooms beyond, looking as if the family had only just left, have all been reconstructed as they are described in the book Isabelle wrote about their childhood. The whole effect is almost creepy, as you feel that you really have gone back in time.

Culan

Right in the south of the Berry, standing guard over the old border with Aquitaine on a hilltop overlooking the narrow valley of the river Arnon, the **Château de Culan** is for once not merely an aristocratic dwelling, but a full-scale castle or fortress, complete with three massive conical towers. The wooden siege hoardings below the pepperpot roofs of the towers are still in place and are included in the guided tour.

The castle was besieged by King Philippe-Auguste for three months before eventually yielding, and children will relish the gory details of

A self-taught painter

Maurice Estève, whose vibrantly coloured canvases fit so well – so unexpectedly well – into the Hôtel des Echevins in Bourges (see p. 202), was born in Culan in 1904, into a modest family. And although Paris was his home from the age of eight, he was a frequent visitor to his birthplace, and after his father's death turned one of the rooms in the family house into a studio, where he still paints today.

He gradually built up a considerable reputation abroad, especially in Scandinavia, but was relatively little known in France until he was in his eighties, when a major retrospective exhibition of his work was staged at the Grand Palais in Paris in 1986.

Entirely self-taught, Estève exhibited in various group shows in the 1930s and 1940s, attracting the attention of painters of the calibre of Georges Braque, Henri Matisse and Robert Delaunay, who commissioned some murals from him for the Exposition Universelle held in Paris in 1937. Yet he has never moved in artistic circles and when, in the 1920s and 1930s, he experimented with different styles, including surrealism, pointillism, cubism and expressionism, he was influenced by his visits to museums and exhibitions rather than by direct contact with other painters.

From about the mid-forties – when he was able to start earning his living by his brush – his work became increasingly abstract. He paints directly on to the canvas, without preparatory drawings, creating solid blocks of colour that interlock with each other, almost like a jigsaw or a stained-glass window. A good example of this is the first painting in the Estève Museum, *Skibet* (1979), used as a design for a postage stamp in 1986 to celebrate his retrospective. This title is the name of a Viking ship, but many of his titles are references to his native Berry: the names of villages and hamlets near his birthplace, or dialect words, like *Charasson* (1981), meaning 'scarecrow'.

how medieval siege warfare was conducted (though they may be disappointed to learn that boiling water was poured through the arrow slits rather than the legendary oil, which was far too precious a commodity). They can also clamber about to their hearts' content in the soaring Gothic timber framework of the roof above the guardroom, peer into grisly dungeons scattered with skulls and bones, and shiver at the nails driven into the halberds to prevent the halbedier's hand slithering about in his enemy's slowly congealing blood.

Culan Castle overlooking the River Arnon

The castle was rebuilt after the siege, then completely redesigned in the 15th century. It came under attack again at the end of the Fronde uprising in 1652. A diorama recreates this key moment in the castle's history, while other highlights are enacted in tableaux with lifesize figures in rooms inside the castle, many of them still with their medieval fireplaces. One depicts Joan of Arc, who visited Culan during her stay in Bourges in the winter of 1429–30, after the victorious siege of Orléans, when the Amiral de Culan had been one of her doughty lieutenants.

The Salon Rouge features the letter-writer *par excellence* Madame de Sévigné, with her host at Culan in the 1680s, that dashing soldier – better known as 'le Grand Condé'. Also here in effigy is the novelist George Sand (see box, p. 209), to whom a separate room is devoted.

An archive room is also open to the public. But do leave time to walk round the castle. The **Notre-Dame Garden** lies between the castle and what was once its chapel (now the parish church) – don't miss the little figure on the wall blowing a horn. The sloping castle garden has been planted to show how a medieval garden would have looked, with everything trained espalier-fashion.

Medieval garden

It is pleasant, too, to walk down by the bridge over the Arnon, and in the village, which was the birthplace of the painter Maurice Estève (see box, p. 234).

Châteaumeillant

Once a Gallo-Roman centre and garrison town called Mediolanum, Châteaumeillant is now a small town in the heart of the fertile Boischaut region, well known for its wines. A good collection of artefacts found during local excavations, including several hundred amphorae, can be seen in the **Musée Emile Chenon**, in a medieval manor house.

Key data

CHATEAUMEILLANT 18370
T.O. rue de la Victoire, ⓣ 02-48-61-39-89
Access Paris 340km, La Châtre 19km, Châteauroux 53km, Argen-
ton-sur-Creuse 58km; **buses** from Châteauroux, Nohant, La
Châtre, Culan
Sights **Eglise Saint-Genès** (Romanesque church); **Musée Emile-
Chenon** (Gallo-Roman artefacts, medieval displays), rue de
la Victoire, ⓣ see T.O.
Lunch Châteaumeillant
Staying Châteaumeillant, Culan, La Châtre

Château de Culan
18270 Culan, ⓣ 02-48-56-64-18 (Châteaumeillant (bus) 12km),
Saint-Amand (bus) 23km), open mid-Feb to Nov
Ecole du Grand Meaulnes (background to Alain-Fournier's novel)
18360 Epineuil-le-Fleuriel, ⓣ 02-48-63-04-82 (Ainay-le-Vieil 14km,
Culan 20km), open Feb to mid-Nov, closed Mon

The town's 16th-century **château** is now the gendarmerie and the
part-Romanesque **Eglise du Chapitre** has been turned into the town
hall. But the **Eglise Saint-Genès** is still a place of worship. This
Romanesque church, completed in 1150 on a basically Benedictine
plan, has a fine west front, with a beautiful doorway and a series of
blind arches with narrow columns. It is built in veined pink and grey
sandstone from Saulzais-le-Potier, south of Saint-Amand-Montrond
(local tourist offices can produce leaflets describing the *Route du
Grès rose* or 'Pink Sandstone Circuit').

The pure lines of the lofty interior are very beautiful. The unusual
design offers an example of what is known as the *passage berrichon*:
the broad chancel is ringed round by six apsidioles or apsidal
chapels arranged in pairs with communicating passages. As you walk
round, you feel rather as if you are in a cloister. The carved capitals
repay close study, with their little scenes depicting the Creation, the
Temptation of Adam and Eve, followed by them being driven out of
paradise, Cain murdering Abel, and a wealth of stylized plant motifs,
animals and people, including a couple of peasants embracing.

Hotels and Restaurants

For general advice about hotels and restaurants, see **Practical Information**. The **Food and drink** chapter gives you an idea about what sort of cuisine you can expect to find.

I have no space to provide comprehensive lists of hotels and restaurants, but have aimed to suggest the sort of places that are appropriate for anyone exploring the areas described in this guide. The majority of the hotels listed are traditional French establishments, many of them family run, comfortable but not luxurious, though I have made a few suggestions for château hotels in the countryside or 'grand hotels' in towns for that special occasion, especially when they offer special deals at weekends or certain times of year. I have also included a few more modest hotels, mainly in towns. Whenever possible, I have chosen quiet hotels. Those in towns are mostly well placed for sightseeing and/or for the station.

In selecting restaurants I have again thought in terms of places that are convenient for sightseeing, or for exploring the countryside. The majority have at least one moderately priced fixed-price meal, but may well offer a special 'gourmet menu'. Whenever possible, I have preferred restaurants offering some regional dishes. In the countryside I have chosen mostly inns and village restaurants frequented by locals or tourists, rather than those used for business entertaining, though it is not always easy to separate the two (and a *menu affaires* or 'business lunch' is often a bargain).

As always in France, prices may vary considerably within one establishment. Most restaurants offer a range of *menus*, the term used for fixed-price meals. The more expensive ones may be available only on Sundays, and conversely the least expensive ones are often not served on Sundays or public holidays. An increasing number of restaurants, though obviously not the top gourmet places, offer good-value children's meals (*repas d'enfants*).

A rough price guide is indicated by the following symbols:

F   up to 120 francs
FF   125 to 195 francs
FFF 200 to 300 francs
FFFF over 300 francs

These prices are for a two- or three-course meal without wine or coffee (though some menus do include one or both of these).

Price variations also occur in hotels. The charm of traditional hotels, as opposed to the chain variety, is their lack of uniformity. So they may have a few more modest (perhaps as yet unmodernized) rooms alongside more comfortable ones. Again I have given a rough guide to prices per head:

F   up to 200 francs
FF   225 to 300 francs
FFF over 300 francs

These prices apply to two people sharing a double room, without break-fast. Alas, those travelling alone are liable to have to pay more. However, many hotels will only make a small extra charge for adding a child's bed; some will even agree to three adults sharing a room for the same price. The letters LF indicate a Logis de France hotel (see pp. 30–1).

When writing to any of the places listed here, use the postcode given after the name. Put this before the place name (e.g. 18200 Ainay-le-Vieil). Fax numbers are given for hotels, as you can normally confirm a booking with a fax indicating your credit card number. Telephone and fax numbers given here all include the initial 0 that must be used within France. If you are calling from abroad, omit the 0 after the country code. Restaurant entries with no telephone number indicate that advance booking is not appropriate.

Although information on price banding and closures was accurate at the time of going to press, it is always wise to check.

AINAY-LE-VIEIL 18200
Crémaillière (F–FF), pl. de l'Eglise, ⓣ 02-48-63-50-14, cl. Nov to Easter. Traditional village inn with red-checked tablecloths and filling country dishes, very close to château.

ANET 28260
Dousseine, route de Sorel, ⓣ 02-37-41-49-93. Just outside village, small, quiet and well-run, with garden, but no restaurant.
Restaurants
Auberge de la Rose (F–FF), 6 rue Charles-Lechevrel, ⓣ 02-37-41-90-64, cl. Sun for dinner, Mon. Attractive beamed dining room right in village; also 7 modest rooms ⓕ.
Manoir d'Anet (FF–FFF), 3 pl. du Château, ⓣ 02-37-41-91-05, cl. Tue for dinner, Wed, Thur for dinner. Opposite château; friendly service and reliable cuisine.
Trou Normand (F–FF), 31 rue Diane-de-Poitiers, ⓣ 02-37-41-90-48, cl. Tue. Good-value home cooking with Norman flavour, few minutes' walk from château.

ANGERVILLE 91670
France (FF), pl. du Marché, ⓣ 01-69-95-11-30, ⓕ 01-64-95-39-59. Old-established family-run coaching inn, well modernized but full of character, with comfortable, spacious beamed bedrooms; old courtyard cleverly converted to make spacious entrance plus cobbled patio for sum-mer meals. Friendly service and excellent cuisine (FF) based on beauti-fully fresh local ingredients, including Méréville watercress (see p. 48).

ARDENTES 36210
Chêne Vert (F–FFFF), 22 av. de Verdun, ⓣ 02-54-36-22-40, cl. Sun for dinner, Mon, most of Jan, first half Aug. Good, rather elegant restaurant not far from Châteauroux; wide range of *menus*; also 7 rooms (F–FF).
Gare (F–FF), rue de la Gare, ⓣ 02-54-36-20-24. Good-value local cuisine, carefully cooked and served.

ARGENTEUIL 95100
Moulin d'Orgemont (FFF–FFFF), rue du Clos-des-Moines, ⓣ 01-34-10-21-47, cl. Sun for dinner, Mon. Converted watermill with large garden, popular with local families for Sun lunch and for 1890s merry-go-round; mainly classical cuisine, good choice of fish.

ARGENTON-SUR-CREUSE 36200
Manoir de Boisvillers (F–FF), 11 rue du Moulin-de-Bord, ⓣ 02-54-24-13-88, ⓕ 02-54-24-27-83. Creeper-covered 18th-century manor house a few min-utes' walk from river and centre makes peaceful hotel with garden and open-air pool but no restaurant; helpful service, cosy rooms, river views.
Restaurants
Cheval Noir (F–FFF), 27 rue Auclert-Descottes, ⓣ 02-54-24-00-06. Old-established family-run LF in centre, once coaching inn, has large and popu-lar dining room; also 20 rooms (F).

8km north at **Tendu** (36200):
Moulin des Eaux-Vives (FF–FFF),
Ⓣ 02-54-24-12-25, cl. Mon for dinner,
Tue (but open daily July and Aug).
Delightful cottagey restaurant in 18th-
century watermill, with flower-filled
terrace beside river. Interesting cuisine
based on modern versions of traditional Berry recipes.

ARGENT-SUR-SAULDRE 18410
Relais de la Poste (F), 3 rue Nationale,
Ⓣ 02-48-73-60-25, Ⓕ 02-48-73-30-62.
Typical *relais de chasseur* (inn used by
those on Sologne shooting sorties); big
fireplace in attractive dining room,
pretty beamed bedrooms, and good
regional cuisine (F–FFFF, cl. Mon from
Sep to end June).

AUBIGNY-SUR-NERE 18700
Auberge de la Fontaine (F), 2 av.
Général-Leclerc, Ⓣ 02-48-58-02-59,
Ⓕ 02-48-58-36-80. Close to château
in heart of small market town on edge
of Sologne, with restaurant (FF, cl. Sun
for dinner, Mar).
Restaurant
Chaumière (F–FF), 1 pl. Paul-Lasnier,
Ⓣ 02-48-58-04-01, cl. Sun, but daily
July and Aug. Good-value meals in
traditional hotel close to château; 10
modest rooms (F).

AUVERS-SUR-OISE 95430
Auberge Ravoux (FF), pl. de la Mairie,
Ⓣ 01-34-48-05-47, cl. Sun for dinner,
Mon. Modest inn where Vincent van
Gogh spent last months of life (see
p. 126) has been restored to create
traditional bistro with 19th-century
ambience; home-style dishes in
generous portions.
Hostellerie du Nord (FF–FFF), 6 av. du
Général-de-Gaulle, Ⓣ 01-30-36-70-74,
cl. Sun for dinner, Mon, most of Aug.
Popular restaurant with garden near
church, specializing in regional and
fish dishes.
Roses Ecossaises (F), 3 rue de Paris.
Useful tearoom near church for light
lunch (closed evenings).

BANNAY 18300
Buissonnière (F–FFF), 58 route du
Canal, Ⓣ 02-48-72-42-07,

Ⓕ 02-48-72-35-90. Pleasantly sited
beside canal north of Sancerre and
close to Silk Museum (meal-and-
museum deals available); good regional
cuisine, wild mushrooms a speciality;
wide range of *menus*. Also 12 rooms
(F) overlooking canal.

BANNEGON 18210
Auberge du Moulin de Chameron,
Ⓣ 02-48-61-83-80, Ⓕ 02-48-61-84-92,
open Mar to mid-Nov; cl. Tue (except
July and Aug). 18th-century watermill
(some parts medieval) is now welcoming restaurant serving delicious cuisine
in pretty dining room plus informal
museum displaying old mill machinery;
pretty garden and terrace overlooking
millpond for summer meals. Also 13
bedrooms (FF) in adjoining building:
less character but quiet.

BARBIZON 77630
Charmettes (F–FF), 40 rue Grande,
Ⓣ 01-60-66-4-21, Ⓕ 01-60-66-49-74.
Pleasant small family hotel (LF); most
rooms overlook garden or courtyard;
attractive dining room with hunting
décor, interesting cuisine (FF–FFF).
Hostellerie du Bas-Bréau (FFF),
22 rue Grande, Ⓣ 01-60-66-40-05,
Ⓕ 01-60-69-22-89. Historic hunting
lodge on edge of forest is luxury
hotel with attractive bedrooms,
garden, pool; courtyard for outdoor
meals; good but very expensive
cuisine (FFFF).
Hostellerie Clé d'Or (FF), 73 rue
Grande, Ⓣ 01-60-66-40-96,
Ⓕ 01-60-66-42-71. Attractive former
coaching inn, now comfortable hotel
with pretty garden for lazy afternoon
or summer breakfast; some rooms
lead straight out to garden. Rather chic
restaurant (FF, cl. Sun for dinner from
mid-Oct to Easter).
Pléiades, 21 rue Grande,
Ⓣ 01-60-66-40-25, Ⓕ 01-60-66-41-68.
Comfortable, quiet hotel with garden
and very pleasant service; large dining
room (FF–FFF).
Restaurants
Angélus (FF–FFF), 31 rue Grande,
Ⓣ 01-60-66-40-30. Rather grand
dining room, with tables outside in
summer.

Bistro du Musée (F), ⓣ 01-60-66-41-71, 86 rue Grande. Just by restored Auberge Ganne (see p. 181); good for quick lunch or early supper.

Flambée (F), 26 rue Grande, ⓣ 01-60-66-40-78, cl. Mon for dinner, Tue. Specializes in meat cooked over open fire.

BEAUVAIS 60000

Cygne (F), 24 rue Carnot, ⓣ 03-44-48-68-40, ⓕ 03-44-45-16-76. Modest family hotel near cathedral.

Restaurant

Côtelette (FF–FFF), 8 rue des Jacobins, ⓣ 03-44-45-04-42, cl. mid-July to mid-Aug, Sun for dinner, Mon. Near cathedral, small and stylish, inventive variants on traditional repertoire.

LE BLANC 36300

Domaine de l'Etape (F–FF), route de Bélâbre, ⓣ 02-54-37-18-02, ⓕ 02-54-37-75-59. Peaceful 19th-century chateau in large grounds 6km southeast; some rooms in converted farmhouse on estate; angling, rowing, riding in grounds; good restaurant (FF–FFF). Convenient base for exploring Brenne nature reserves.

LA BORNE 18250

Jodi (F), ⓣ 02-48-26-90-80. Charming tearoom combined with grocer's/general store/gift shop in Berry potters' village; good for light lunch.

BOUESSE 36570

Chateau de la Bouesse (FF), ⓣ 02-54-25-12-20, ⓕ 02-54-25-12-30. Turreted medieval château run by Frenchwoman and British husband, 11km east of Argenton-sur-Creuse. Attractively modernized rooms, pretty dining room serving good cuisine based on local produce (F–FFF).

BOUGIVAL 78380

Forest Hill (FF), 10–12 rue Ivan-Tourguenieff, ⓣ 01-39-18-17-16, ⓕ 01-39-18-15-80. Large modern hotel overlooking river Seine, convenient for Turgenev's dacha (see p. 110) and Impressionist sites, has open-air pool and popular Sunday lunch buffet (F).

BOURGES 18000

Angleterre (FF), 1 pl. des Quatre-Piliers, ⓣ 02-48-24-68-51, ⓕ 02-48-65-21-41. Central (right by Jacques Coeur's palace) and old-fashioned in best sense: excellent service, period furnishings, comfortable rooms; pleasant restaurant, too (FF).

Bourbon (FF), blvd de la République, ⓣ 02-48-70-70-00, ⓕ 02-48-70-21-22. Bourges's top hotel, converted from 16th-century abbey; modern rooms, smiling service and outstanding restaurant Saint-Ambroix (see below).

Restaurants

Abbaye de Saint-Ambroix (FF–FFFF), in Hôtel de Bourbon. Quite apart from excellent, subtly flavoured cuisine with regional touches and very reasonable *menus*, setting is exceptional: medieval chapel with lofty pillars, clerestory windows, medieval-style chandeliers and hangings.

Cake & Thé (F), Promenade des Remparts, ⓣ 02-48-24-94-60, cl. Mon, Tue. Charming little tearoom in vaulted room on ramparts walk; good for afternoon teas or early supper.

D'Antan Sancerrois (FF), 50 rue Bourbonnoux, ⓣ 02-48-65-96-26. Lively restaurant with wine bar ambience in medieval building near cathedral, popular with locals for good-value traditional dishes of day plus Berry specialities, chalked up on slate; huge range of wines available by glass. Cl. Mon, for lunch Tue, first half Aug.

Jacques Coeur (FF–FFF), pl. Jacques-Coeur, ⓣ 02-48-70-12-72. Cl. Sat, Sun for dinner, Aug. Bourges institution opposite eponymous palace nowadays serves regional rather than classical cuisine; good service, rather elegant.

BRINON-SUR-SAULDRE 18410

Auberge Solognote (F–FF), ⓣ 02-48-58-50-29, ⓕ 02-48-58-56-00. Typical Sologne inn from outside, rather elegant (yet still cosy) inside, catering to chic clientele on shooting weekends. Cuisine (FF–FFF, cl. Tue, Wed from Oct to mid-Apr, Tue and for lunch Wed from mid-Apr to end June;

also cl. Feb to mid-Mar, and second half Sep), is definitely not rustic, but fashionably flavoursome, served in beamed dining room. Some bedrooms in main building, others in modern building in grounds, all with period furniture.

BUE 18300

Caveau des Vignerons (F–FF), pl. de l'Eglise, ⓣ 02-48-54-22-08, cl. Thur. Cheerful place 4km from Sancerre for tasting carefully cooked local dishes and Sancerre wines; rustic décor.

BUZANCAIS 36500

L'Hermitage (F), Route d'Argy, ⓣ 02-54-84-03-90, ⓕ 02-54-02-13-19. Creeper-covered mansion with conservatory leading off dining room makes comfortable LF, well-run by whole family. Nicest rooms in main building overlook garden; some in separate annexe. Reliable classical cuisine (F–FFF, cl. Sun for dinner, Mon from Sep to end June).

CHABRIS 36210

Plage (FF–FFF), 42 rue du Pont, ⓣ 02-54-40-02-24. Peaceful LF in Sologne, on edge of Berry, close to Cher (canoes for hire). Good-value mainly regional cuisine served in garden in summer. Also 8 rooms (F).

CHANTILLY 60500

Lion d'Or (F), 44 rue du Connétable, ⓣ 03-44-57-03-19. Modest hotel (no private bathrooms) but friendly and convenient for château; restaurant serves range of *menus*, plus pancakes, ices and snacks; garden.
Parc (FF), 36 av. Maréchal-Joffre, ⓣ 03-44-58-20-00, ⓕ 03-44-57-31-10. On fairly busy avenue close to racecourse and station; garden but no restaurant.
7km south at **Lys-Chantilly** (60260).
Hostellerie du Lys (FF), ⓣ 03-44-21-26-19, ⓕ 03-44-21-28-19. Quiet and comfortable, with large garden, on edge of forest; restaurant (F–FF).
5km southeast at **Montgrésin** (60560).
Relais d'Aumale (FF), 37 pl. des Fêtes, ⓣ 03-44-54-61-31, ⓕ 03-44-54-69-15. Spacious hotel

beside village green in former hunting lodge in forest near Etangs de Commelles; cosy bars and lounges, modern, comfortable rooms, nicest overlooking garden, where classical cuisine (FFF) served beneath elegant awning; tennis court.
7km north at **Creil** (60100):
Ferme de Vaux (F), route de Vaux, ⓣ 03-44-64-77-00, ⓕ 03-44-26-81-50. LF converted from farmhouse; disappointingly urban setting, but food is good and imaginative, dining room elegant with old stone walls and pleated silk ceiling (FF–FFF, cl. Sun for dinner, Aug), and staff very friendly; modern bedrooms.

Restaurants

Capitainerie du Château (F), in château kitchens, cl. Tue, Jan, first half Feb. Handy for lunch (no dinners) as buffet service saves valuable sightseeing time.
Château (F–FF), 22 rue du Connétable, ⓣ 03-44-57-27-74, cl. Tue. Good-value meals, with some tables outside, near château stables.
Goutillon (F–FF), 61 rue du Connétable, ⓣ 03-44-58-01-00. Cheerful, lively place presided over by larger-than-life *patron*; racecourse paraphernalia and atmosphere – jockeys and stable lads eat here – and straightforward home-style dishes at modest prices.
Tipperary (F–FF), 6 av. Maréchal-Joffre, ⓣ 03-44-57-00-48, cl. Sun for dinner, Mon, part of Feb, part of Aug. Long-standing brasserie-type restaurant in centre, opposite town hall, decorated with horsey sketches and prints. Reliable traditional cuisine.

CHARTRES 28000

Châtelet (F–FF), 6/8 av. Jehan-de-Beauce, ⓣ 02-37-21-78-00, ⓕ 02-37-36-23-00. Close to station and cathedral; comfortable, traditional rooms (some with cathedral view); no restaurant.
Grand Monarque (FF), 22 pl. des Epars, ⓣ 02-37-21-00-72, ⓕ 02-37-36-34-18. Chartres's 'grand hotel', once a coaching inn: traditional with well-furnished rooms and good restaurant offering range of *menus*, with some local specialities.

Poste (F), 3 rue du Général-Koenig,
℡ 02-37-21-04-27, ℱ 02-37-36-42-17.
Well-modernized hotel in town centre.
Restaurants
Buisson ardent (F–FFF), 10 rue au Lait,
℡ 02-37-34-04-66, cl. Sun for dinner.
Delightful place very near cathedral;
carefully cooked meals in restful and
elegant surroundings, excellent value.
Café Serpente (F), 2 rue du Cloître-
Notre-Dame, ℡ 02-37-21-68-81. Conveniently open all day every day for
brasserie-type dishes and good-value
menus; right opposite cathedral.
Reine de Saba (F). Modest tearoom
opposite cathedral.
Truie qui file (FF–FFFF), pl. de la
Poissonnerie, ℡ 02-37-21-53-90,
cl. Sun for dinner, Mon, Aug. Attractive
old building very close to cathedral, by
covered market. Excellent cuisine with
particularly good fish dishes; more
modest meals served in old cellars.
Vieille Maison (FF–FFFF), 5 rue
au Lait, ℡ 02-37-34-10-67,
ℱ 02-37-91-12-41. Long-standing
restaurant in, as name suggests,
medieval house; very near cathedral.
Classical cuisine, subtly flavoured.
Cl. Sun for dinner, Mon, part of Aug.

CHATEAUMEILLANT 18370
Piet à Terre (F–FFF), pl. de la
Gendarmerie, ℡ 02-48-61-41-74,
cl. Sun for dinner, Mon, mid-Jan to mid-
Mar. Attractive and welcoming; good
inventive cuisine. Also 7 pretty
rooms (F).

CHATEAUROUX 36000
Elysée (F), 2 rue de la République,
℡ 02-54-22-33-66, ℱ 02-54-07-34-34.
Small, central family-style hotel.
Manoir du Colombier (FF), 232 rue
de Châtellerault, ℡ 02-54-29-30-01,
ℱ 02-54-27-70-90. Attractive
shuttered and creeper-covered 18th-
century manor house with garden
beside river Indre, on outskirts; well-
modernized bedrooms, good restaurant (FF–FFF, cl. Sun for dinner, Mon).
Restaurants
Ciboulette (F–FF), 42 rue Grande,
℡ 02-54-27-66-28, cl. Sun, Mon, Jan,
Aug. Right by Musée Bertrand in network of old streets; attractive and good

value, with some regional dishes;
good choice of wines by glass.
CHATILLON-SUR-INDRE 36700
Auberge de la Tour (F–FFF), 2 route du
Blanc, ℡ 02-54-38-72-17, cl. Mon
from Oct to end June. Good regional
cuisine served in cheerful dining room
in 18th-century house; wide range of
menus; also 10 rooms (F).

CHATOU 78470
Maison Fournaise (FF), Ile des
Impressionistes, ℡ 01-30-71-41-91.
Beautifully restored *guinguette*-style
restaurant once frequented by
Impressionist painters (see p. 108);
cheerful ambience, popular with
locals for family lunches at weekends. Good traditional dishes.

LA CHATRE 36400
Lion d'Argent (F), 2 av. du Lion
d'Argent, ℡ 02-54-48-11-69
ℱ 02-54-06-02-24. Friendly LF with
small modern bedrooms, some in
annexe with pool and garden; good
Berry cuisine (F–FF).
Notre Dame (F), 4 pl. Notre-Dame,
℡ 02-54-48-01-14, ℱ 02-54-48-31-14.
Small, quiet and central hotel in
attractive medieval building, well-
modernized inside; no restaurant, but
tables outside for drinks.
Restaurants
Auberge du Moulin Bureau (F–FF),
53 rue du Faubourg-Saint-Abdon,
℡ 02-54-48-04-20. Picturesque creep-
er-draped watermill with 17th-century
millwheel still in place, 1km from centre, houses good restaurant, open only
Feb to mid-Nov, cl. Sun for dinner,
Mon (except July and Aug).
Jardin de la Poste (F–FF), 10 rue
Basse-du-Mouhet, ℡ 02-54-48-05-62,
cl. Sun for dinner, Mon, second half
Sep. In pedestrian street leading off
market square, welcoming ambience,
mainly Berry cuisine.

CHAUMES-EN-BRIE 77390
Chaum'Yerres (F–FF), Pont de l'Yerres,
℡ 01-64-06-03-42, cl. Sun for dinner,
Mon (but no closure July and Aug).
Punning title (*chaumière* means
'cottage' and Yerres is local river) for
peaceful LF in heart of Brie country,

near Vaux-le-Vicomte, specializing in classical cuisine using local ingredients like Meaux mustards and, of course, cheese; also 10 rooms (F–FF).

CHAVIGNOL 18300
Côte des Monts Damnés (F–FFF), ⊤ 02-48-54-01-72, cl. Sun for dinner, Mon, Feb. Good local wines (including one that gives this elegant inn its name) accompany interesting menu of beautifully cooked dishes, some with regional flavour; good cheese board, naturally, in this famous cheese-and-wine village near Sancerre.
Fin Chavignol (F–FF), ⊤ 02-48-54-20-63, cl. Mon for dinner, Tue in summer, otherwise Tue and Wed. Traditional, unpretentious wine-village restaurant with red-checked tablecloths, beamed ceiling and grape and vine motifs throughout.

CHERENCE 95510
Hostellerie Saint-Denis (F), 1 rue des Cabarets, ⊤ 01-34-78-15-02. Very friendly small hotel in quiet village above Seine Valley, near La Roche-Guyon and convenient for Giverny. Small but pleasant rooms, family-style cuisine (FF–FFF) and atmosphere; garden for sitting or dining.

CHEVREUSE 78460
Auberge du Moulin (F–FF), 56 rue de la Porte-de-Paris, ⊤ 01-30-52-16-45, cl. Mon for dinner, Tue. Attractive little place with garden and reliable home-style cooking.
Normand (F–FF), 31 rue de Rambouillet, ⊤ 01-30-52-09-93, cl. Sun for dinner, Mon. Cheerful, friendly, typically village restaurant; home-style cooking, several *menus*, mainly local clientele; convenient for river walk.

COULOMMIERS 77120
Clos du Theil (F–FF), 42 rue du Theil, ⊤ 01-64-65-11-63, cl. Mon for dinner, Tue, second half Feb, second half Aug. In heart of cheese country east of Paris; good-value cuisine.

COURANCES 91490
Auberge Arc-en-Ciel (F), 6 pl. de la République, ⊤ 01-64-98-41-66, cl.

Tue for dinner, Wed. Cheerful village inn, convenient when visiting château.

CULAN 18270
Poste (F), Grande Rue, ⊤ 02-48-56-66-57, Ⓕ 02-48-56-66-80. Modest LF in village, close to castle; generous portions in restaurant (F–FF, cl. Mon). Cl. end Dec to mid-Feb.

DAMPIERRE-EN-YVELINES 78720
Auberge du Château (FF), 1 Grande Rue, ⊤ 01-30-47-56-56, Ⓕ 01-30-47-51-75. Spacious modernized inn right opposite château; comfortable rooms, some with forest views; good restaurant called **Table des Blot** (FF–FFF, cl. Sun for dinner, Mon).
Restaurants
Eau à la Bouche (F–FF), 32 Grande Rue, ⊤ 01-30-52-53-82, cl. Wed. Small family-style, in village high street close to château.
Ecuries du Château (FF–FFFF), ⊤ 01-30-52-52-99, cl. Tue; otherwise lunch daily, but dinner only Fri, Sat, Sun; also teas. Elegant restaurant in former saddle room of château's stables.

DIOU 36260
Aubergeade (F–FFF), 321 route d'Issoudun, ⊤ 02-54-49-22-28, cl. Wed for dinner, Sun for dinner. Pleasant and rather elegant inn with large garden, not far from Issoudun, serves good traditional cuisine at reasonable prices.

DISNEYLAND 77777
For all hotels, ⊤ 01-60-30-60-30. All rooms are designed for a family of four, with either two double beds or a double bed plus bunk beds. Prices vary considerably according to season and French half-term and other holidays. Mid-week rates are generally lower, but a wide variety of packages are on offer, including park entrance fee. The *New York* and *Newport Bay Club* have their own conference centres and often stage large-scale events that can dilute the family atmosphere. The more modest Cheyenne and Santa Fe, and Davy Crockett's Ranch, are very

family-oriented, and *Sequoia Lodge* is also mainly a holiday hotel.

In descending order of price:

Disneyland (FF–FFF). Right at entrance to park, 'grand hotel' in frothy Victorian colonial style, complete with turrets and surrounded by lawns and fountains. Indoor pool, air-conditioning, *California Grill* (FFF) and *Innovations* (FFF) restaurant; breakfast with Mickey Mouse and co at weekends (advance booking essential).

New York (F–FFF) A few minutes' walk from Disney Village, overlooking Disney Lake; art deco design and 1920s Manhattan ambience; air-conditioning; open-air skating rink in winter; *Parkside Diner* (F–FFF) and *Manhattan Club* (FF–FFF, with jazz ambience) restaurants; large conference centre. Elegant high-rise architecture in peaches and greens.

Newport Bay Club (F–FFF) Rather elegant and spacious turn-of-the-century New England yachting atmosphere, with creams and blues both inside and out; window awnings, balconies, verandah overlooking lake, and pleasant pool, opening on to well-manicured lawns in summer. Quietly situated at far end of Disney Lake. Restaurants *Cape Cod* (F–FF) and *Yacht Club* (FFF), specializing in seafood. Air-conditioning.

Sequoia Lodge (F–FFF) Strongly themed hotel beside Disney Lake, designed to re-create atmosphere of national parks in American West. Main building and smaller 'lodges', all in wood and surrounded by tall trees, can seem a bit gloomy from outside, but inside is cosy, with patchwork wall hangings, huge stone fireplaces, wooden floors, mountain chalet-style bedrooms and staff dressed in forest ranger gear. *Hunter's Grill* (F–FFF) for spit-roasts and country music and more basic *Beaver Creek Tavern* (F). Air-conditioning.

Cheyenne (F) Streets of brightly coloured buildings with white-painted fences form Far West village straight out of the movies, peopled with covered wagons and swaggering cowboys. Pony rides, lasso displays, live country music in *Red Garter Saloon*, barbecued meat in *Chuckwagon Café* (F). Cheerful family atmosphere.

Santa Fe (F) Mexican village made up of 40-odd *pueblos* surrounded by cacti-studded desert and reconstructed Indian village. Face-painting, live music in *Rio Grande Bar*, Tex-Mex buffet in *La Cantina* (F). Family-oriented.

Davy Crockett Ranch (F) 'Trappers' village' of self-catering log cabins, each with own barbecue, for 4 or 6 people, in forest setting 15 minutes' drive from theme park (car essential); also camp site. Pool, tennis courts, pony and bike rides, menagerie, farm, general store and self-service *Crockett's Tavern* (F).

Restaurants

Auberge de Cendrillon (FF–FFF), Fantasyland ☎ 01-64-74-24-02. Attractive and cosy restaurant with some tables outside, in shadow of Sleeping Beauty's Castle and overlooked by Cinderella's pumpkin/glass coach; genuine French cuisine.

Blue Lagoon (FF–FFF), Adventureland. Caribbean cuisine and ambience.

Cowboy Cookout Barbecue (F), Frontierland. Basic barbecue grills in large barn; waiters kitted out as cowboys.

Fuente del Oro (F), Frontierland. Tex-Mex specialities in generous portions.

Key West Seafood (FF), Disney Village. Spacious dining room and terrace overlooking Disney Lake; mainly seafood menu.

Silver Spur Steakhouse (F–FF), Frontierland, ☎ 01-64-74-24-56. Charcoal-grilled meat, Western saloon décor.

Walt's: an American restaurant (FF–FFF), Main Street, ☎ 01-64-74-24-08. Strategic site for watching parades, surrounded by photos of Walt Disney himself; American and 'international' cuisine.

DOUAINS 27120

Château de Brécourt (FF–FFF), ☎ 02-32-52-40-50, 🖷 02-32-52-69-65. Large and elegant medieval château, complete with moat, pepperpot turrets and huge stone fireplaces, set in wooded grounds. This '*hôtel particulier*' (see p. 28) offers special weekend deals, indoor pool, tennis court and excellent, mainly classical cuisine (FFF–FFFF).

DOURDAN 91410
Auberge de l'Angélus (F–FFF), 4 pl. du Chariot, ⊤ 01-64-59-83-72, cl. Tue for dinner, Wed, second half Aug. One-time coaching inn with flower-filled courtyard and inventive cuisine, 14km from Rambouillet.

DUN-SUR-AURON 18130
Beffroy (F–FF), 13 pl. Jacques-Chartier, ⊤ 02-48-59-50-72, cl. Sun for dinner, Mon. Good no-frills restaurant in small LF (10 rooms).
Prieuré (F), 10 pl. Bourbon, ⊤ 02-48-59-52-45. Not a hotel or a restaurant, but turreted 15th-century priory where owners offer meals on advance request in convivial atmosphere right in village; also a few rooms.

ERMENONVILLE 60950
Château d'Ermenonville (FF–FFF), ⊤ 03-44-54-00-26, ⑮ 03-44-54-01-00. Historic château overlooking lake, where Jean-Jacques Rousseau lived (and died); grand and very comfortable bedrooms, elegant lounges, good restaurant *Table du Poète* (FF–FFFF); special weekend deals.
Croix d'Or (F–FF), 2 rue Prince-Radziwill, ⊤ 03-44-54-00-04, cl. Sun for dinner, Mon. Small LF with popular restaurant – very light dining room overlooking courtyard-garden, tables outside in fine weather; also 8 rooms (F).

FARGES-ALLICHAMPS 18200
Château de la Commanderie: see 'Staying in a private château' (p. 31).

FLAGY 77940
Hostellerie du Moulin (F–FF), 2 rue du Moulin, ⊤ 01-60-96-67-89, ⑮ 01-60-96-69-51, cl. Jan, second half Sep. Half-timbered building dating back to 1260 was working watermill up to 1950; cosy beamed bedrooms, pretty garden, and interesting cuisine in restaurant (FF–FFF) overlooking mill race; quiet and full of atmosphere.

FONTAINEBLEAU 77300
Aigle d'Or (FFF), 27 pl. Napoléon-Bonaparte, ⊤ 01-60-74-60-00, ⑮ 01-60-74-60-01. Elegant, old-established hotel opposite palace now has pool, fitness room, sauna; very comfortable rooms; good, rather grand restaurant (*Beauharnais*, FFF–FFFF).
Chancellerie (F), 1 rue de la Chancellerie, ⊤ 01-64-22-21-70, ⑮ 01-64-22-64-43. Small, modest and friendly hotel very close to palace; rooms all overlook street but are double-glazed; several can sleep 3 or 4; no restaurant.
Legris et Parc (FF), 36 rue Paul-Seramy, ⊤ 01-64-22-24-24, ⑮ 01-64-22-22-05. Quiet, comfortable hotel in historic mansion near entrance to palace grounds; some rooms lead on to terrace overlooking pretty courtyard; restaurant (F–FFF, cl. Sun for dinner, Mon, Jan).
Londres (FF–FFF), 1 pl. du Général-de-Gaulle, ⊤ 01-64-22-20-21, ⑮ 01-60-72-39-16. Well sited close to palace entrance and bus stop for Barbizon. Comfortable rooms in period style, friendly service. No restaurant.
Napoléon (FF–FFF), 9 rue Grande, ⊤ 01-60-39-50-50, ⑮ 01-64-22-20-87. Near château, stylish and comfortable, with leafy courtyard and good restaurant (*Table des Maréchaux*, FF–FFF).
Richelieu (F), 4 rue Richelieu, ⊤ 01-64-22-26-46, ⑮ 01-64-22-14-61. Modest LF, close to château.
Restaurants
Carpe d'Or (F), 21 rue du Parc. Modest place frequented by ramblers, near entrance to château grounds.
Caveau des Ducs (FF–FFF), 24 rue de Ferrare, ⊤ 01-64-22-05-05. Classical cuisine with particularly good fish dishes, served in atmospheric vaulted 17th-century cellars.

FONTAINE-CHAALIS 60300
Auberge de Fontaine (F), 22 Grande-Rue, ⊤ 03-44-54-20-22, ⑮ 03-44-60-25-38. Cosy inn in sleepy village on edge of Forêt d'Ermenonville, not far from Senlis, has cottagey bedrooms (some on two levels), dining room like country parlour, cobbled courtyard for

summer meals leading to garden, relaxed and friendly service; restaurant serves tasty, mainly Provençal cuisine (F–FFF, closed Tue from Nov to Mar).

FONTENAY-TRESIGNY 77610
Manoir (FFF), route de Coulommiers, ⓣ 01-64-25-91-17, ⓕ 01-64-25-95-49. In Brie country and convenient for Vaux-le-Vicomte, half-timbered 19th-century manor house built for shooting parties; now very comfortable hotel in large grounds, with heated outdoor pool, tennis courts, practice golf course; spacious luxury bedrooms and suites; very grand restaurant serving classical cuisine (FFF–FFFF, cl. Tue in winter).

FOURGES 27630
Moulin de Fourges (FF–FFFF), 38 rue du Moulin, ⓣ 02-32-52-12-12, cl. Sun for dinner, Mon (except July and Aug), Jan. Not far from Giverny, watermill in romantic setting on bank of river Epte, once favourite haunt of Impressionists; delicious Norman cuisine, good range of *menus*.

GARGILESSE 36190
Artistes (F), ⓣ 02-54-47-84-05, ⓕ 02-54-47-72-41, cl. Fri for dinner, and Sun for dinner in winter. Small LF full of somewhat bohemian atmosphere, in attractive village; cottagey dining rooms with paintings by contemporary artists, cheerful service and good-value unpretentious meals. Also 10 modest rooms (F).

GIEN 45500
Rivage (FF–FFFF), 1 quai de Nice, ⓣ 02-38-37-79-00, cl. Mon for lunch, mid-Feb to mid-Mar. Long popular for beautiful terrace right over river; equally beautiful contemporary cuisine. Also hotel (F–FFF).

GIVERNY 27620
Jardins de Giverny (FF–FFF), chemin du Roy, ⓣ 02-32-21-60-80, open for lunch daily except Mon, dinner on Sat only; cl. Feb. Attractive typically Norman building with garden; good classical cuisine with regional touches.
Nymphéas (F), rue Claude-Monet,

ⓣ 02-32-21-20-31, cl. Mon and Nov to Apr. Modest place for light meals geared to visitors to Monet's house and garden; often crowded.

GRESSY-EN-FRANCE 77410
Manoir de Gressy (FFF), ⓣ 01-60-26-68-00, ⓕ 01-60-26-45-46. Very comfortable hotel on site of 17th-century manor house near Roissy-CDG airport, built to re-create manorial atmosphere, round garden with open-air pool; attractively decorated rooms, spacious public areas, good restaurant serving traditional cuisine; special weekend deals; free shuttle bus from airport or RER station.

GUERMANTES 77400
Relais de Guermantes (FF), ⓣ 01-64-30-13-03. Friendly inn near Château de Guermantes for straightforward meals. Cl. Tue for dinner, Wed.

HENRICHEMONT 18250
Soleil levant (F–FF), 15 rue de Bourgogne, ⓣ 02-48-26-71-38. Popular restaurant in LF hotel in heart of village.

HEUGNES 36180
Auberge d'Heugnes (F–FF), ⓣ 02-54-39-06-43, cl. Sun for dinner, Mon, Feb. Archetypal Berry inn beside village church; good cooking at generously low prices.

ILLIERS-COMBRAY 28120
Florent (F–FFF), 13 pl. du Marché, ⓣ 02-37-24-10-43, cl. Sun for dinner, Mon. In heart of village. Devout Proustians will choose menu made up of dishes referred to in *Remembrance of Things Past*, but there are other choices too. Pleasant atmosphere and interesting local dishes.

L'ISLE-ADAM 95290
Cabouillet (FF–FFFF), 5 quai de l'Oise, ⓣ 01-34-69-00-90, cl. Sun for dinner, Mon. Very popular at turn of century and still good; overlooking river; mainly classical cuisine; also 6 rooms (F).
Gai Rivage (FF–FFF), 11 rue Conti ⓣ 01-34-69-01-09, cl. Sun for dinner, Mon. Again overlooking river, inventive cuisine.

ISSOUDUN 36100
Cognette (FF–FFF), 26 rue des Minimes, ⓣ 02-54-21-21-83, ⓕ 02-54-03-13-03. Owners of delightful restaurant of same name (see below) have converted row of nearby almshouses into charming bedrooms, some on two levels, with their own little gardens.
Restaurants
Cognette (FF–FFFF), 2 blvd de Stalingrad, ⓣ 02-54-21-21-83, cl. Sun for dinner, Mon, Jan. Inn frequented by Honoré de Balzac (see box, p. 224), turned by friendly family into several elegant dining rooms; delicious cuisine based on Berry repertoire, stylish but warm atmosphere. A really special place.
Pile ou face (F–FFF), rue Danielle-Casanova, ⓣ 02-54-03-14-91, cl. Sun for dinner, Mon. Several *menus* with regional dishes, friendly service, inner courtyard for outdoor dining.

LASSAY-SUR-CROISNE 41230
Auberge du Prieuré (F). Handy for light meal before or after visiting Château du Moulin.

LEVROUX 36110
Relais Saint-Jean (F–FFF), 34 rue Nationale, ⓣ 02-54-35-81-56, cl. Sun for dinner, Wed for dinner. Former coaching inn makes charming restaurant with views of fine collegiate church from outdoor tables; good-value cuisine with Berry flavour.

LINGE 36220
Auberge de la Gabrière (F), ⓣ 02-54-37-80-97, ⓕ 02-54-37-70-66. Modest LF beside Etang de la Gabrière in Brenne nature park; lovely views from dining room; regional cuisine.

LOUVECIENNES 78430
Auberge Les Tilleuls (FF), 2 quai Conti, ⓣ 01-39-69-00-97. Long verandah beside Seine makes delightful setting for summer meals in this large inn with faithful local clientele; pleasant year-round, and well-placed for visiting Bougival, Marly and Saint-Germain-en-Laye; traditional cuisine, good service.

Aux Chandelles (FF–FFF), 12 pl. de l'Eglise, ⓣ 01-39-69-08-40, cl. Wed, Sat for lunch, second half Aug. Small restaurant with garden in village square, uphill from river; subtle, inventive cuisine.

LUZARCHES 95270
Château de Chaumontel (F–FFF), ⓣ 01-34-71-00-30, ⓕ 01-34-71-26-97. Princes de Condé's hunting lodge is now pleasant hotel set in large grounds, with riding and angling on offer; good restaurant (FF–FFFF).

MAINTENON 28130
Saint-Denis (FF), 5 pl. Aristide-Briand, ⓣ 02-37-23-00-76, cl. Thur. Opposite château, with terrace overlooking river; also a few rooms (F).

MAISONNAIS 18170
Jardins du Prieuré (FF–FFF), Prieuré de Notre-Dame d'Orsan, ⓣ 02-48-56-27-50. Newly restored priory gardens (see p. 229) have most attractive restaurant serving cuisine based on vegetables and herbs grown in garden. Open only May to end Oct.

MARLY-LE-ROI 78160
Fou du Roi (FF–FFF), 6bis Grande-Rue, ⓣ 01-39-58-80-20, cl. Sat for lunch, Sun, Aug. Reasonable prices for this expensive part of the world; inventive cuisine and smiling service; in village up above Seine.

MENETOU-SALON 18510
Auberge Cheu L'Zib (FF–FFF), ⓣ 02-48-64-81-20. Typical Berry inn specializing in regional dishes. cl. Wed, part of Feb, part of July.

MEZIERES-EN-BRENNE 36290
Boeuf Couronné (F–FF), pl. Charles-de-Gaulle, ⓣ 02-54-38-04-39. Friendly LF coaching inn dating from 17th century is good place to try freshwater fish from Brenne after visiting village's aquarium; or as base for exploring nature reserves (8 rooms, F); attractive beamed dining room, good, mainly regional cuisine.

MILLY-LA-FORET 91490
Colombier (F), 26 av. de Ganay. Modest place in centre for quick meal.

MONTIGNY-SUR-LOING 77690
Vanne Rouge (F), rue de l'Abreuvoir, ⊤ 01-64-45-82-10, cl. Sun for dinner, Mon. Pleasant riverside hotel offers good-value meals (F–FF).

MONTIPOURET 36230
Relais d'Angibault (F). Modest café-restaurant frequented by locals for filling meals at budget prices before visiting Moulin d'Angibault (p. 211)

MORET-SUR-LOING 77250
Auberge de la Terrasse (F–FF), 40 rue Pêcherie, ⊤ 01-60-70-51-03, Ⓕ 01-60-70-51-69. Half-timbered LF riverside inn; friendly ambience, cosy rooms; restaurant (F–FF, cl. Sun for dinner, Mon).
Restaurants
Ecu de France (F), 63 rue Grande. Modest, friendly little restaurant beside Porte de Bourgogne, convenient for light lunch. Cl. Sun for dinner, Mon.
Porte de Bourgogne (F–FF), 66 rue Grande, ⊤ 01-60-70-51-35, cl. Tue, Wed. Again, right by Porte de Bourgogne; popular with locals for good home-style cooking, with some Burgundian dishes.

NEAUPHLE-LE-CHATEAU 78640
Domaine du Verbois (FF), 38 av. de la République, ⊤ 01-34-89-11-78, Ⓕ 01-34-89-57-33. Spacious 19th-century mansion midway between Versailles and Thoiry offers quiet and comfortable rooms in period style, elegant public areas and restaurant that feels like private dining room; good cuisine based on local produce (FF–FFF, cl. Sun for dinner).

NOHANT 36400
Auberge de la Petite Fadette (F–FF), ⊤ 02-54-31-01-48, Ⓕ 02-54-31-10-19. On village green, with terrace overlooking Romanesque church and George Sand's manor house, this LF, run by same family for generations, is named after one of the novelist's most popular books; modernized, pretty

bedrooms; welcoming dining room with big fireplace, good place to try Berry dishes like *poulet en barbouille* (see p. 50).

NOIRLAC 18200
Auberge de l'Abbaye de Noirlac (F–FFF), ⊤ 02-48-96-22-58, cl. Wed, Jan and Feb. Former chapel opposite Cistercian abbey has small front room and bar for sandwiches and light lunches, and small dining room serving interesting country-style dishes.

OIZON 18700
Château de la Verrerie (FFF), see 'Staying in a private château' (p. 31).
Restaurants
Bien-aller (F–FF), ⊤ 02-48-58-03-92. Picturesque village house (once a grocer's) with garden near Château de la Verrerie offers stylish variants on regional dishes; relaxed atmosphere, excellent value. Cl. Wed.
Maison d'Hélène (F–FFF), in grounds of Château de la Verrerie, ⊤ 02-48-58-58-06-91, cl. Tue and for lunch Wed. Cosy cottage serves good meals in lovely setting from Easter to mid-Nov.

ORGEVAL 78630
Moulin d'Orgeval (FF–FFF), ⊤ 01-39-75-85-74, Ⓕ 01-39-75-48-52. Peaceful traditional hotel with stream flowing through grounds, 8km from Saint-Germain-en-Laye. Dining room, with tall windows overlooking river, serves good classical cuisine (FF–FFFF); bedrooms have views over garden.

OSNY 95520
Moulin de la Renardière (FF), rue du Grand-Moulin, ⊤ 01-30-30-21-13. Converted watermill near Pontoise; pretty garden and riverside terrace; interesting dishes on single good-value *menu*. Cl. Sun for dinner, Mon.

PORT MARLY 78560
Auberge du Relais Breton (FF–FFF), 27 rue de Paris, ⊤ 01-39-58-64-33. Dishes from traditional French repertoire in generous portions; by Seine, not far from Alexandre Dumas's château. Cl. Sun for dinner, Mon, Aug.

PORT-VILLEZ 78270

Le Gueulardière (FF), 1 route Nationale, Ⓣ 01-34-76-22-12, cl. Sun for dinner, Mon. Delightful inn close to Monet's house at Giverny, but on opposite bank of Seine; good classical cuisine served in countrified dining room gleaming with copper pans; very pleasant atmosphere and service.

PROVINS 77160

Vieux Remparts (FF), 3 rue Couverte, Ⓣ 01-64-08-94-00, Ⓕ 01-60-67-77-22. Family-run hotel in heart of Old Town, with modern bedrooms and spacious beamed dining room; leafy garden/courtyard for summer meals. Interesting cuisine (FF–FFF) and very courteous service.

Restaurants

Auberge de la Grange (F–FF), 3 rue Saint-Jean, Ⓣ 01-64-08-96-77, cl. Tue for dinner, Wed. In medieval building in Old Town, opposite Grange aux Dîmes. Cheerful service in two small and cosy dining rooms with open fire, plus tiny courtyard. Good-value *menus*.

Boudinière des Marais (F–FF), 17 rue Hugues-Le-Grand, Ⓣ 01-60-67-64-89, cl. Sun for dinner, Mon. In lower town, understandably popular with locals for good-value traditional cuisine, served in generous portions.

Petit Ecu (F), 9 pl. du Châtel, Ⓣ 01-60-67-62-22. Good-value regional dishes in medieval building overlooking Old Town's main square; under same management as *Vieux Remparts*. cl. Jan and Feb.

RAMBOUILLET 78120

Bisson (F–FFF), 1 pl. du Château, Ⓣ 01-34-83-23-82. Right opposite palace; popular garden-terrace for summer meals; traditional cuisine.

Cheval Rouge (FF), 78 rue Général-de-Gaulle, Ⓣ 01-30-88-80-61, cl. Sun for dinner, Tue, first half Aug. Small restaurant near palace, first opened in mid-18th century; good classical cuisine; garden, heated terrace.

RARAY 60810

Château de Raray (FFF), Ⓣ 03-44-54-70-61, Ⓕ 03-44-54-74-97. Elegant 17th-century château 10km

from Senlis, with painted beams, and walls and gateways topped with frieze of lifelike sculptures of hounds, stag and wild boar; a must for film buffs, as it was setting for Jean Cocteau's *La Belle et la Bête* (see box p. 7), the name used for elegant restaurant serving classical cuisine (FF–FFFF). 10 large and stylishly sober bedrooms, 2 tennis courts, golf course and club-house (special weekend deals include green fees).

LA ROCHE-GUYON 95780

Bords de Seine (F–FF), 21 rue du Docteur-Duval, Ⓣ 01-30-98-32-52, Ⓕ 01-30-98-32-42. Lovely riverside setting, attractively modernized bedrooms, and good-value meals in restaurant overlooking the Seine, plus peaceful terrace (F–FF).

Au Vieux Donjon (F–FF), 2 rue du Général-Leclerc, Ⓣ 01-34-79-70-06. Friendly, family-style restaurant opposite château; traditional dishes.

ROMORANTIN-LANTHENAY 41200

Grand Hôtel du Lion d'Or (FFF), 69 rue Georges-Clemenceau, Ⓣ 02-54-94-15-15, Ⓕ 02-54-88-24-87. Luxury hotel in late-Renaissance mansion in heart of attractive capital of Sologne (coaching inn from 1774). Very expensive, but just right for a special occasion, with elegant atmosphere, beautifully furnished bedrooms and air-conditioned suites, delightful inner patio/courtyard, excellent service, and exceptional cuisine (FFFF, cl. mid-Feb to mid-Mar).

Orléans (F), 2 pl. du Général-de-Gaulle, Ⓣ 02-54-76-01-65. Small hotel right in centre has popular restaurant (F–FF) and 10 modest rooms, quietest overlooking rear courtyard.

Restaurants

Auberge du Lanthenay (F–FFF), pl. de l'Eglise, Ⓣ 02-54-76-09-19, cl. Sun for dinner, Mon. Peaceful inn just outside town, with garden, serves excellent cuisine at reasonable prices. Also 10 rooms (F).

Colombier (F–FF), 18 pl. du Vieux-Marché, Ⓣ 02-54-76-12-76. Old coaching inn in centre for good regional dishes; also 10 rooms (F).

249

Vénitiens (F), 5 rue des Poulies, ⓣ 02-54-96-02-05. Friendly, near museum, good value; some Portuguese dishes.

SAINT-AMAND-MONTROND 18200
Poste (F), 9 rue du Docteur-Vallet, ⓣ 02-48-96-27-14, ⓕ 02-48-96-97-74. 16th-century coaching inn, central and full of character: you can almost hear coaches clanking into huge courtyard and horses whinnying as you settle into your cosy bedroom after excellent dinner in welcoming dining room (F–FFF, cl. Sun for dinner, also Mon in winter).

Restaurants
Croix d'Or (F–FFF), 28 rue du 14-juillet, ⓣ 02-48-96-09-41, cl. Fri for dinner from Nov to Mar. Welcoming brothers offer good cuisine (some regional dishes) in spacious dining room in pleasant LF hotel with 11 rooms (F).

Saint-Jean (F–FFF), 1 rue de l'Hôtel-Dieu, ⓣ 02-48-96-39-82, cl. Sun for dinner, Mon, part of Sep. Attractive restaurant near interesting Romanesque church looks like private house with burgundy awnings and shutters; good-value cuisine, lively atmosphere, summer meals in courtyard.

SAINT-CHARTIER 36400
Château de la Vallée bleue (FF), route de Verneuil, ⓣ 02-54-31-01-91, ⓕ 02-54-31-04-48. Cl. mid-Nov to Mar. Dr Pestel lived in this 19th-century chateau near Nohant, where the novelist George Sand was his patient; now comfortable hotel surrounded by large garden with open-air pool and practice course for golf freaks; restaurant overlooking rose garden offers imaginative variants on traditional Berry dishes (FF–FFF).

SAINT-GERMAIN-EN-LAYE 78100
Cazaudehore La Forestière (FFF), 1 av. Président-Kennedy, ⓣ 01-30-61-64-64, ⓕ 01-39-73-73-88. Spacious and peaceful Relais et Châteaux member in Forêt de Saint-Germain, run by Cazaudehore family for generations; elegant modern rooms in lovely garden setting, chic restaurant in separate build-ing for mainly classical cuisine, beautifully served (FF–FFFF, cl. Mon); excellent service, fashionable ambience.

Ermitage des Loges (FF–FFF), 11 av. des Loges, ⓣ 01-39-21-50-90, ⓕ 01-39-21-50-91. Well-modernized rooms on edge of forest, not far from château; summer meals, often with Mediterranean flavour (F–FF), served on attractive terrace.

Pavillon Henri IV (F–FFF), 19–21 rue Thiers, ⓣ 01-39-10-15-15, ⓕ 01-39-73-93-73. Louis XIV didn't just sleep here, he was born here (see box, p. 113). Elegant hotel with lovely views over Seine valley offers grand, beautifully furnished rooms and appropriately regal classical cuisine (FFF–FFFF).

Restaurants
Auberge Le Grison (F), 28 rue au Pain. Modest little place in main shopping street, beside tourist office and Debussy Museum; good for light meals.

Brasserie du Théâtre (FF–FFF), pl. du Château, ⓣ 01-30-61-28-00. Lively 1930s-style brasserie right by château and RER station.

SAINT-JEAN-DE-BEAUREGARD 91940
Auberge de Beauregard (FF), ⓣ 01-60-12-00-08, cl. Sat for lunch, Sun. Pleasant restaurant with garden close to château with its interesting garden.

SAINT-OUTRILLE 18310
Grange aux Dîmes (F–FFF), pl. de l'Eglise, ⓣ 02-48-51-12-13, cl. Wed and part of Feb. Tithe barn (which is what name means) in village midway between Issoudun and Romorantin, converted into restaurant serving excellent local produce; lower-priced *menus* are good value.

SAINT-REMY-LES-CHEVREUSE 78470
Cressonnière (FFF–FFFF), 46 route de Port-Royal, ⓣ 01-30-52-00-41, cl. Tue, Wed, part of Aug. Pricey, but worth it for delicious cuisine and attractive creeper-covered building with garden; wide range of *menus*.

SAINT-SYMPHORIEN-LE-CHATEAU
28700
Château d'Esclimont (FFF),
Ⓣ 02-37-31-15-15, Ⓕ 02-37-31-57-91.
If you feel like a spot of château living,
this turreted, moated Renaissance
château in spacious grounds, close to
Rambouillet and Maintenon and also
convenient for Chartres, and offering
tennis courts, open-air pool and
angling, is a good bet: elegant rooms,
some in separate buildings, including
watchtower, all in grand style; four
dining rooms, one adorned with hunting trophies, another with Spanish
leather wall hangings.

SAINT-VIATRE 41210
Auberge de la Chichone (F–FFF),
pl. de l'Eglise, Ⓣ 02-54-88-91-33,
cl. Tue for dinner (but not in July, Aug),
Wed, Mar. Typical Sologne inn with
pretty courtyard, frequented by
hunting/shooting/fishing fraternity;
good cuisine based on local produce,
especially game in season; 7 small,
rather dark but cosy rooms (F).

SAMOIS-SUR-SEINE 77920
Hostellerie Country Club (F), 11 quai
Franklin-Roosevelt, Ⓣ 01-64-24-60-34,
Ⓕ 01-60-24-80-76. Good position
beside river makes up for unattractive
exterior: modern rooms have balconies
offering river views; garden, tennis
court; restaurant (F–FFF, cl. Sun for
dinner, Mon.)

SANCERRE 18300
Panoramic Ⓕ, rempart des Augustins,
Ⓣ 02-48-54-22-44, Ⓕ 02-48-54-39-55.
Quiet rooms in modern building,
some in period style, some modern,
with big picture windows offering
views over vineyards suggested by
name; open-air pool; restaurant (*Tasse
d'Argent*, F–FFF, cl. Wed in winter) has
separate entrance next door.
Saint-Martin (F), rue Saint-Martin,
Ⓣ 02-48-54-21-11, Ⓕ 02-48-54-39-55.
Well-modernized turn-of-century
hotel, with restaurant (F), but open
only Easter to end Oct.
Restaurants
Auberge de la Pomme d'Or (F–FFF),
pl. de la Mairie, Ⓣ 02-48-54-13-30, cl.

Mon, and Wed for dinner. Pretty dining
room in small one-time coaching inn
feels like private house; friendly atmosphere, often inventive cuisine based
on regional recipes, good wine list.
Moussière F, 13 Nouvelle Place,
Ⓣ 02-48-54-15-01. Useful place on
main square for inexpensive meals
and for trying out local wines.
Tour (F–FFF), 31 Nouvelle Place,
Ⓣ 02-48-54-00-81. Medieval building
close to Sancerre's Tour des Fiefs with
elegant downstairs dining room boast-
ing fine fireplace, plus upstairs dining
room with views over vines; excellent
classical cuisine with many regional
dishes and delicious Sancerre wines.
3km north at **Saint-Satur** (18300):
Laurier (F–FF), 29 rue du Commerce,
Ⓣ 02-48-54-17-20. Creeper-covered
LF, attractively furnished with country
antiques, serves tasty regional cuisine;
also 8 rooms (F). Cl. Sun for dinner,
Mon, Nov.

SAVIGNIES 60650
Auberge de la Poterie (FF–FFF), 14 rue
de Beauvais, Ⓣ 03-44-82-27-72, cl.
Mon and Tue for dinner, Wed. Half-
timbered building in potters' village
near Beauvais; interesting cuisine with
regional flavour.

SENLIS 60300
Hostellerie de la Porte Bellon (F–FF),
51 rue Bellon, Ⓣ 03-44-53-03-05,
Ⓕ 03-44-53-29-94. Fine old coaching
inn, complete with turret and vaulted
cellars, overlooking leafy square on
edge of Old Town and right by bus
stop from Chantilly; cosy dining room
for traditional, mainly regional dishes
(F–FFF), and garden for summer
meals; oak-panelled bar; some of
18 bedrooms have old beams.
Restaurants
Gril des Barbares (F), 19 rue du
Châtel, Ⓣ 03-44-53-12-00, cl. Sun for
dinner, Mon. Spit-roasted meat in
atmospheric medieval cellars near
cathedral; cheerful atmosphere, live
music Thur, Fri and Sat evenings.
Scaramouche (FF–FFFF), 4 pl. Notre-
Dame, Ⓣ 03-44-53-01-26, cl. Wed,
part of Aug. Right by cathedral; small,
elegant dining room, good service and

delicious cuisine with occasional regional touches; tables outside on cathedral square in summer.
7km north, at **Fleurines** (60700):
Vieux Logis (FF–FFFF), 105 rue du Général-de-Gaulle, ⓣ 03-44-54-10-13, cl. Sat for lunch, Sun for dinner, Mon. Excellent cuisine in elegant beamed dining room (or in garden) in forest clearing.

SENLISSE 78720
Auberge du Gros Marronnier (F), 3 pl. de l'Eglise, ⓣ 01-30-52-51-69. Cosy rooms in attractive building in heart of village, with garden and terrace for summer meals beneath the chestnut tree that gives it its name; well placed for exploring Vallée de Chevreuse.

THOIRY 78770
Etoile (F–FFF), 38 rue de la Porte Saint-Martin, ⓣ 01-34-87-40-21, ⓕ 01-34-87-49-57. Small traditional hotel near château; some rooms modest, others grander and quite pricey; garden; wide range of *menus* in restaurant (F–FFF, cl. Sun for dinner, Mon).

THOMERY 77810
Vieux Logis (FF–FFF), 5 rue Sidi-Carnot, ⓣ 01-60-96-44-77. Good restaurant in 18th-century mansion in village near Moret-sur-Loing and Fontainebleau, with open-air pool and garden; also 14 small but attractive rooms (FF).

TOUCHAY 18160
Auberge des Sept Soeurs (F–FF), ⓣ 02-48-60-06-77, cl. Sun for dinner, Mon. Charming village inn not far from Jardins du Prieuré (see p. 229); remarkable-value meals, carefully cooked.

VAILLY-SUR-SAULDRE 18260
Auberge du Lièvre gourmand (F–FFF), ⓣ 02-48-73-80-23; cl. Sun for dinner, Mon (except July and Aug), mid-Jan to mid-Feb. One of *Tables gourmandes du Berry* (see p. 32); good-value regional cuisine in attractive old inn well placed for visiting La Verrerie château and sights near Aubigny-sur-Nère; also quite near Sancerrois vineyards.

VALENCAY 36600
Espagne (FF–FFF), 9 rue du Château, ⓣ 02-54-00-00-02, ⓕ 02-54-00-12-63, cl. Jan and Feb. Courtyard-garden is ideal for enjoying classical cuisine (some regional dishes) in old-established Relais et Châteaux member; elegant and comfortable; restaurant (FF–FFFF, cl. Mon, Tue for lunch.

VATAN 36150
France (F), 16 pl. de la République, ⓣ 02-54-49-74-11. Friendly little hotel northeast of Issoudun, with plain but adequate rooms and restaurant (F–FF, cl. Tue for dinner, Wed, Feb).

VAUX-DE-CERNAY 78720
Abbaye des Vaux-de-Cernay (FF–FFF), ⓣ 01-34-85-23-00, ⓕ 01-34-85-11-60. Very comfortable hotel (once Rothschild residence) with feeling of Scottish baronial hall: blazing fires, dark panelling, comfortable armchairs; grounds include ruins of medieval abbey, lake (meals beside it in summer); rather grand restaurant (FF–FFFF), plus popular Sunday brunches; concerts; special weekend and one-night ('arrêt d'un soir') deals on offer.
Haras (FF), ⓣ 01-34-85-23-00. In grounds of abbey (see above). Small rooms overlooking pool or courtyard, décor on horsey theme, no separate restaurant, but good way of enjoying grounds, lake and main building (where breakfast served) at lower cost.

VERNON 27200
Evreux (F), 11 pl. d'Evreux, ⓣ 02-32-21-16-12, ⓕ 02-32-21-32-73. Cosy half-timbered building with garden in town centre; 15 modest but comfortable rooms; good, mainly Norman cuisine, at reasonable prices, in *Relais normand* restaurant (FF–FFF, cl. Sun for dinner).

VERSAILLES 78000
Home Saint-Louis (F), 28 rue Saint-Louis, ⓣ 01-39-50-23-55, ⓕ 01-30-21-62-45. Friendly family

hotel in quiet street near Carrés Saint-Louis and royal kitchen garden; only short walk from palace.

Paris (F), 14 av. de Paris, ℡ 01-39-50-56-00, ℻ 01-39-50-21-83. Small and well sited close to palace and Rive Gauche station; pretty frontage, pleasant service; recently renovated rooms (some triples).

Richaud (F–FF), 16 rue Richaud, ℡ 01-39-50-10-42, ℻ 01-39-53-43-36. In town centre near Rive Droite station; traditional; most rooms recently modernized.

Trianon Palace (FFF), blvd de la Reine, ℡ 01-30-84-38-00, ℻ 01-39-49-00-77. Luxury hotel few minutes' walk from palace; magnificent bedrooms, pool, tennis court, fitness centre, excellent *Trois Marches* restaurant (see below), plus brasserie in grounds.

Versailles (FF), 7 rue Sainte-Anne, ℡ 01-39-50-64-65, ℻ 01-39-02-37-85. In small street close to palace; breakfast outside in summer.

Restaurants

Athos (F), 5 rue du Marché-Neuf, ℡ 01-39-50-04-53, cl. Sun. Tiny place in heart of Carrés Saint-Louis, good for quick but properly cooked lunch or supper.

Baladin Saint-Louis (FF), 2 rue de l'Occident, ℡ 01-39-50-06-57. Again, in heart of Carrés Saint-Louis, elegant yet cosy, on two floors, with tables outside in summer; inventive, good-value cuisine, lively and friendly ambience. Cl. Sun.

Cuisine bourgeoise (FF–FFFF), 10 blvd du Roi, ℡ 01-39-53-11-38, cl. Sat for lunch, Sun, most of Aug. Traditional bistro near Musée Lambinet serves fashionable cuisine in modern idiom, based on very fresh ingredients and subtle flavours.

Londres (F–FFF), 7 rue Colbert, ℡ 01-39-50-05-79. Cheerful brasserie right beside palace with popular open-air terrace; crowded for much of year.

Pascal Le Falher (FF–FFF), 22 rue de Satory, ℡ 01-39-50-57-43, cl. Sat for lunch, Sun. *Pot-au-feu* with meat or fish is speciality in this small place near palace and royal kitchen garden. Décor gloomy, but service cheerful.

Potager du Roy (FF), 1 rue Maréchal-Joffre, ℡ 01-39-50-35-34, cl. Sun for dinner, Mon. Deliciously fresh cuisine in small dining room hung with pictures; right by royal kitchen garden and close to palace; very pleasant service.

de la Reine (F–FFF), 8 rue de la Chan-cellerie, ℡ 01-39-50-07-82. Old favourite very close to château; small, with pretty china and pleasant service; interesting cuisine at reasonable prices. Cl. Sun for dinner, Mon, Aug.

Trois Marches (FFF–FFFF), 1 blvd de la Reine, ℡ 01-39-50-13-21, cl. Aug. If you decide to round off visit to royal apartments with right royal feast, this is one of France's top restaurants, in luxurious *Trianon Palace* hotel (see above). Prices are appropriately regal, but you can still eat well if you go for the lunchtime 'business menu'.

VOVES 28150

Quai fleuri (F–FF), route Auneau, ℡ 02-37-99-15-15, ℻ 02-37-99-11-20. Peaceful LF 24km from Chartres. Good regional cuisine in cosy dining room with blazing fire in winter, tables in pretty garden in summer (F–FFF, cl. Sun for dinner, also Fri for dinner in winter).

Acknowledgements

Marie-France de Peyronnet, an energetic promoter of the Route Jacques Coeur and the Abbaye de Noirlac, first introduced me to the Berry many years ago and has been enormously helpful at all times. Sylvie Lahuna and her team at the Comité régional du Tourisme de l'Ile de France provided efficient and friendly help whenever I called on them.

Particular thanks to both of them, but also to Vanessa Arbuthnott, Jane Dorner and Jean Richardson, who accompanied me on various fact-finding trips and whose stimulating company made the whole strenuous exercise far more interesting; to Danièle Denis, who took me to Port-Royal, and Marie-Henriette Tims, who visited the Château de Monte-Cristo with me; to Sylvia Fromentaud of the CDT de Loir-et Cher; Marc Doria, former director of Bourges's tourist office, and Elisabeth Bertin, and Pascale Delgrange at the CDT du Cher; Claire Joyes in Giverny; Henri-François de Breteuil at the Château de Breteuil, head of La Demeure Historique; Claude Combet and Thierry Lefèvre, authors of *Le tour de France des bonbons* (Robert Laffont, 1995), for their willingness to share their extensive knowledge of regional confectionery specialities; and to Jean-Yves Montagu, who told me about the Berry's Scots connections; Dominique-Charles Janssens at the Auberge Ravoux in Auvers-sur-Oise; François Vieillard, formerly at the tourist office in Provins, and his successor Stéphanie Danis.

Many thanks too to Gemma Davies for her patience, and to Susan McIntyre.

Index